"*Varieties of Feminism* is both a magisterial history of the German women's movement and a provocative rethinking of feminism in its different national and global incarnations. Challenging the theoretical dominance of the U.S. model of feminism, Ferree brilliantly argues that developments in Germany provide a better guide to the future trajectory of women's struggles around the world."

—*Leila J. Rupp, University of California, Santa Barbara*

"In telling the story of the institutionalization of gender politics in Germany over the past half century, Ferree provides rich theoretical insights for understanding the specific ways in which gender intersects with other inequalities."

—*William Gamson, Boston College*

"The history of the German women's movement is compelling in itself, but it is also an important demonstration of the errors of imagining feminism everywhere on the model of a dominant U.S. liberalism. National trajectories are varied, and gender issues woven in different ways into political, cultural, and personal histories. Though focused on the past, Ferree's work helps us see the openness of the future."

—*Craig Calhoun, New York University*

"Ferree's work is a brilliant comparative and historical analysis. Her empirically rich and theoretically sophisticated account illuminates the diverse dilemmas and opportunities facing proponents of different varieties of feminism. The book offers an innovative approach to gender and politics that other scholars are sure to find compelling."

—*Ann Shola Orloff, Northwestern University*

"Myra Ferree's important study of German feminism emphasizes complexity, intersectionality, inconsistencies, and strategic concerns. Because of the many vantage points from which she views the German feminist project, Ferree serves the study of feminism across the globe by offering a model for understanding its differences."

—*Bonnie Smith, Rutgers, The State University of New Jersey*

"*Varieties of Feminism* is a tour de force of social science and feminist theory. Ferree provides the theoretical tools for analyzing the 'relational realism' of systems of gender as well as a vision of what feminist political struggle might look like in the future."

—*Lynne Haney, New York University*

VARIETIES OF FEMINISM

VARIETIES OF FEMINISM

German Gender Politics

in Global Perspective

Myra Marx Ferree

Stanford University Press
Stanford, California

Stanford University Press
Stanford, California

Printed in the United States of America

Library of Congress Cataloging-in-Publication Data

Ferree, Myra Marx, author.
 Varieties of feminism : German gender politics in global perspective / Myra
Marx Ferree.
     pages cm
 Includes bibliographical references and index.
 ISBN 978-0-8047-5759-1 (cloth : alk. paper)--ISBN 978-0-8047-5760-7 (pbk.
)
 1. Feminism--Germany--History. I. Title.
 HQ1623.F47 2012
 305.420943--dc23   2011040194

Typeset by Bruce Lundquist in 10.5/15 Adobe Garamond

CONTENTS

PREFACE AND ACKNOWLEDGMENTS

This book has been a long time in the making. The research on which it rests was spread out over almost thirty years, and many of the specific cases mentioned in various chapters were analyzed in their particulars in journal articles and book chapters written at various points in these years. But my ambition remained to write a book that could fill in the background for those who are not experts on Europe in general, or Germany in particular, and to explain why and how understanding this case would contribute to understanding conflicts and dilemmas feminists face around the world. I hope this book finally meets that goal.

I remain as convinced as I was in 1985, when I first began to engage these issues, that it is important academically and politically to not confuse liberal feminism, especially in its American incarnation, with feminism in general. I also strongly believe that it is equally important not to discard the important democratic critique that political liberalism has brought to socialists and moral reformers, both those who identify with feminism and those who do not. There is a tendency to confuse the political claims of liberalism, such as human rights, individual citizenship, and personal freedoms, with the priority given to markets by the capitalist political economics commonly called neoliberalism. In my view, this confusion is both academically unsound and politically regrettable, since it makes it more difficult to see the ways in which deep and effective democracy remains an unattained goal, even in states that pride themselves on being democratic. True democratic inclusion does require eliminating social obstacles to participation, but these are not merely economic and never have been. Women's struggle for full citizenship went well beyond winning the vote, and it still continues today. The story here highlights how changes in family law, in employment rights, and in political representation are part of the democratic claim for personal autonomy and access to decision-making for which in feminists in Germany have successfully fought. Their claim for autonomy rests on liberal notions of individuals, rights, and representation and was radical in their context.

Because the German struggle is more often about women's autonomy and collective representation and less often about gender equality than American feminism is, the comparison between the two movements is often used throughout the book to highlight the gaps and weaknesses of both approaches. By exploring how feminists in Germany—East and West—deal with the problems they considered most fundamental, namely, democratic self-determination and personal autonomy, this book offers an alternative understanding of the positive elements in liberalism. The German case, where liberalism is not as ubiquitous as it is in the United States, suggests that liberalism offers a valid critique of mere social protection, and a distinctive set of benefits that can be realized, even if to reach that goal will demand that certain socialist principles of equality be more institutionalized than they ever have been in the United States. In their participatory liberal challenges to the communitarian but patriarchal forms of Christian conservatism and democratic socialism, German feminists demonstrate the great value of being able to assume their government's commitment to equality as a value and to build deeper democracy from that base, while Americans cannot. This difference in what levels of protection and freedom are secured matters for the development of both feminist movements and for the societal changes each accomplished over time.

While the book itself has taken a long time to be written, it has also grown with the passage of time from a story about a few organizations and issues in Germany at a particular moment to a longer narrative about how these organizations and issues have changed and changed their society. I have thus given the book a structure that highlights key events and their effects on the longer-term developments that make deep social change realizable without claiming that a strong form of causal relationship exists among these outcomes. Along with historical shifts in opportunity, which actors themselves help to make, there are still strategic choices to be made that are not predetermined in their courses.

Because the American version of liberal politics and neoliberal economics is still an outlier globally, this book also argues that German feminism provides a more realistic model for what the trajectory of feminist struggles looks like in most parts of the world. There, also, the strategic choices of feminist actors confront long-developing structures of constraint and opportunity shaped by national contexts in which socialist politics have mattered more than in the United States. Hopefully, this case will highlight these choices in ways that feminists in other countries also find helpful. With this in mind, I have also tried to diagnose the tensions among class and gender, race and nationality in Germany and the United States in their own distinctive forms, not because they generalize in their specific paths, but because each national context calls for a similarly close analysis. This interplay of historically institutionalized inequalities with dynamic and contested discourses, strategies, and resources shapes feminist politics everywhere.

The research process that underlies this book, and my engagement in German feminist politics more generally, can be traced back to encounters I had in the early 1980s with specific feminist researchers working on the theoretically important sociological question of the relationship between gender and class in Germany, a question with which I was already concerned in my US work. Gradually, our conversations led me to explore and try to explain how our vantage points converged and where we saw things differently. For innumerable discussions, occasional formal interviews, and incredible and enduring personal hospitality during the following thirty-plus years, I thank Regina Becker-Schmidt, Christel Eckart, Ute Gerhard, Carol Hagemann-White, Gudrun-Axeli Knapp, and Margit Mayer most especially. Their willingness to provide vital introductions and institutional resources leaves me forever in their debt. Over the years they improved my German, my networks, my library, and my ability to think theoretically and historically more than I can ever say. They do not bear any responsibility for the errors that surely remain in this book, despite their generous efforts to correct me, but if this work offers insights, they certainly should share full credit for them. Carol McClurg Mueller also deserves special thanks for encouraging me to write my first comparative article on German feminism in 1985, when I was temporarily holding a chair position in women's studies at the J.-W.-Goethe University in Frankfurt. She also encouraged me to bring the unification process itself into my story in 1990, when I was supposedly in Berlin to study just the emerging institutionalization process for Western feminists.

This book also would not have been possible without a great deal of support of many kinds from other sources. The German Academic Exchange Service, the German Marshall Fund of the United States, the American Academy in Berlin, the Center for Research on Women and Gender at the University of Wisconsin-Madison, and the Marie Jahoda International Fellowship of the Ruhr University, Bochum, have all been essential in providing me with semesters of support for research and writing time. Even with their generous financial support, it has been a challenge to keep the book project rolling when there were also always studies of specific events or individual issues to be written up.

One study that both added depth and breadth but subtracted available time from this book project involved examining abortion as a political issue that developed very differently in the United States and Germany. The US side of this collaborative research project was funded by the National Science Foundation (Grant SBR9301617) and the TransCoop program of the Alexander von Humboldt Foundation and was hosted in Germany by the Berlin Science Center (WZB). Through the generous sponsorship of its then-president Friedhelm Neidhardt, the WZB provided me with a home away from home on multiple occasions during the course of this multiyear project, which was conducted collaboratively with William A. Gamson, Dieter Rucht, and Jürgen Gerhards. I appreciate not only my coauthors' contributions to our common research but also our debates about fundamental interpretations, usually across country lines, which highlighted national assumptions about gender and politics that might otherwise have remained invisible.

Other studies of particular issues—women and labor unions, the women's childcare strike of 1993, the unification of Germany and its impact on gender policy, and the headscarf controversies—were conducted with Silke Roth, Eva Maleck-Lewy, and Susan Rottmann. Especially with Silke and Eva, I found our discussions of the broad political issues in these and many other events and controversies for feminists in Germany and the United States over the years were not only pleasurable but hugely important for me in shaping an understanding of intersectional differences within Germany. In addition, Susan Rottmann and Ilse Lenz added depth and nuance to my understanding of majority-minority relations within Germany in different periods. I also thank Kathrin Zippel, Silke Roth, Eva Maleck-Lewy and Bernhard Maleck, Ilse Lenz, Aili Mari Tripp, and Lisa D. Brush for their long-standing encouragement and inspiration. I know I would never have been able to persist in this book project without their belief in its value; it would have been a much weaker book without their probing questions.

I am also deeply grateful to the many individual German feminist activists and researchers who were willing to be interviewed, some of them in great depth and on multiple occasions. In addition to about sixty formal interviews done in the years immediately following the fall of the Berlin Wall, I sat down and talked feminist politics, went to feminist events, and hung out in feminist organizations (and sometimes wrote up my field notes) with students, colleagues, activists, and friends of friends more times over the years than I can count. Among the many, a few stand out for their willingness to go above and beyond the call of duty in offering feedback, food, and friendship. I would be remiss not to thank Sylvia Kontos, Theresa Wobbe, Claudia Neusüß, Ingrid Miethe, Marianne Weg, Irene Dölling, Sabine Berghahn, Ilona Ostner, Sabine Lang, and Elisabeth Beck-Gernsheim by name here.

Finally, as the book itself gradually began to get written, it benefited enormously from the careful reading and critical suggestions offered by Lisa D. Brush, Silke Roth, Leila Rupp, Sylvia Walby, Jane Collins, Shamus Khan, Donna Harsch, Hae Yeon Choo, Susan Rottmann, Katja Guenther, Kathrin Zippel, Angelika von Wahl, Patricia Yancey Martin, Aili Tripp, Axeli Knapp, Ute Gerhard, Ingrid Miethe, Benita Roth, Alicia VandeVusse, and Nicole Skurich. I was also incredibly fortunate to have Kate Wahl as my editor for Stanford University Press, since she was one of my most constructively critical readers, whose suggestions helped make this a much better book. Coming into the home stretch, I have been blessed with excellent professional editorial assistance from Alison Anderson, a friend for even longer than I have been working in Germany, and consistent and conscientious help from Jess Clayton, who was all that one could wish for in a graduate assistant, and then some. Jess has always been willing to go the extra mile, and her energy helped enormously to carry me to the finish line.

In addition to those who have directly engaged with the substantive issues of the book, there are those whose broader perspectives on German history and European politics or on feminist activism and global transformation have helped me to formulate my ideas over the years. Working in Madison with scholars such as Jonathan Zeitlin, Marc Silberman, and Klaus Berghahn (in the European Studies Alliance) and Aili Mari Tripp, Jane Collins, Christina Ewig, Pamela Oliver, and Gay Seidman (in gender and women's studies and sociology) has been a priceless learning experience. International feminist networks with central nodes around such accomplished scholars as Carol Hagemann-White, Regina Becker-Schmidt and Axeli Knapp, Mieke Verloo, Susan Gal and Gail Kligman, Barbara Hobson, Ilse Lenz, Sylvia Walby, and Ann Orloff have introduced me to many more people and ideas than I could possibly enumerate to thank.

Last and by no means least, I wish to thank my husband Don, who endured the entire process with me and without whose emotional support and creative conflict-solving skills this entire project might have ended years ago. He kept the home fires burning more than once when I was off in Germany for a semester, hosted various visitors to our home, served as an impressively skilled travel agent, helped me get my level of chronic overcommitment to a more manageable level, and took on some of my other workload so that in the final push I had the time I needed to finish. The best reward I can offer him is finally to say, it's done, and thanks.

ABBREVIATIONS

ABM   Arbeitsbeschäftigungsmaßnahmen (special make-work programs)

AK   *Arbeitskreis* (a working group)

APO   Außerparlamentarische Opposition (extra-parliamentary opposition)

AsF   Arbeitsgemeinschaft socialdemocratischer Frauen (Social Democratic Party women's association)

BDF   Bund deutscher Frauenverein (coalition of women's associations)

BfM   Bund für Mütterschutz und Sexualreform (League for the Protection of Mothers and Sexual Reform)

BIG   Berliner Interventionsprojekt gegen häusliche Gewalt (Berlin Intervention Project Against Domestic Violence)

CDU   Christlich Demokratische Union Deutschlands (Christian-Democratic Union, major conservative party)

CSU   Christlich-Soziale Union in Bayern (Christian Socialist Union, Bavarian sister party to the CDU)

DFD   Demokratischer Frauenbund Deutschlands (German
               Women's Council)
DFR   Deutscher Frauenrat (National Women's Council)
DGB   Deutscher Gewerkschaftsbund (main trade union
               confederation)
ECJ   European Court of Justice
EEOC   Equal Employment Opportunities Commission (US)
ERA   Equal Rights Amendment (US)
EU   European Union
EWL   European Women's Lobby
FAM   Frauenakademie München (women's project in Munich)
FDP   Freie Demokratische Partei (Free Democratic Party)
FINNRAGE   Feminist Network of International Resistance to the New
               Reproductive Technologies and Genetic Engineering
FRG   Federal Republic of Germany (called West Germany)
GDR   German Democratic Republic (called East Germany)
GSS   *Gleichstellungsstelle* (gender-equality office)
NGO   Non-governmental Organization
ÖTV   Gewerkschaft Öffentliche Dienste, Transport und Verkehr
               (municipal employees' union)
PfA   Platform for Action approved by world governments in
               Beijing (UN Conference of 1995)
RAF   Rote Armee Fraktion (Red Army Group)
SED   Sozialistische Einheitspartei Deutschlands (Socialist Unity
               Party, governing party of the GDR)
SDS   Sozialistischer Deutscher Studentenbund (West German
               Socialist Student Association)
SPD   Sozialdemokratische Partei Deutschlands (Social
               Democratic Party)
TAN   Transnational advocacy network
UFV   Unabhängiger Frauenverein (Independent Women's
               Association, East German women's organization)
WAVE   Women Against Violence in Europe

VARIETIES OF FEMINISM

CHAPTER 1

PRACTICAL THEORY
AND THE POLITICS
OF GENDER

O N JANUARY 21, 2005, the German parliament (the Bundestag) began discussing a bill to outlaw discrimination in employment, housing, and forms of private contracts. The law would cover discrimination based on gender, skin color, ethnic origin, disability, age, and religion, and it set up a national office to receive complaints and manage statistical information.

But what does it mean to target discrimination in 2005? One might compare the bill to the 1964 Civil Rights Act in the United States and wonder why it took more than forty years for Germany to get to this point. Another might see it as a response to the European Union (EU), for without Europe-level guidelines prohibiting discrimination and demanding member-state action, would Germany even then be considering such a bill? Yet another might observe that, although lacking antidiscrimination laws, German policy long included a strong constitutional mandate for gender equality. The constitution not only asserts that women and men have equal rights (something the US constitution still lacks) but also mandates the state take steps to realize this equality in practice.[1]

German women are certainly visible as political actors. The government in 2005 was headed by Angela Merkel, the first female chancellor. The proportion of women in the Bundestag has steadily risen since the 1970s; in 2005, before Merkel became chancellor, it stood at 32 percent (twice the US figures: 16 percent in the House and 14 percent in the Senate).[2] German federal states, counties, and municipalities have more than a thousand women's affairs offices charged with advancing women's rights. Gender mainstreaming—scrutiny of public policies for disparate effects on women and men—is institutionalized by federal law.

Among European countries, however, Germany's commitment to gender equality hardly stands out. West Germany had been especially slow in taking measures to enable women to enter the paid labor force, combat stereotypes of women and men or reform family law and social services to be gender neutral. When Sweden and Finland joined the European Union, they succeeded in shifting this more conservative transnational body toward affirming gender equality, mandating "women-friendly" state actions. The EU's resulting directives, along with the incorporation of the different political culture of East Germany, challenged the state to change its approach to women's welfare.[3]

So is Germany a reluctant latecomer to combating discrimination against women, an exemplary case of feminist political leadership, or a middle-of-the-pack European welfare state? I argue that it is all three, and the variation reflects the different ways women understand and pursue their political interests. The diversity of feminist aims and strategies is easiest to recognize when countries face different problems because of the considerable gap in their standard of living, as between the United States and China. Although highly industrialized countries like Germany, other members of the EU, and the United States face similar challenges and have comparable resources to meet them, their gender arrangements and women's movement mobilizations are also quite various—not simply more or less good for women, but good for different women and in different ways. Like the varieties of capitalism that Hall and Soskice identified, the varieties of ways that feminism works in different countries matter.[4]

As this book will show, Germany's feminism is premised on political assumptions that stress social justice, family values, and state responsibility for the common good. Over generations, compromises between conservatives and social democrats have institutionalized a different set of premises from those of the US and UK women's movements. The latter privilege liberal individualism and equal rights, and they are often presented as if their politics exemplified feminism overall. Comparing German feminism to this more familiar equal rights model, this book explores how the politics of gender and intersections among social justice movements take distinctive forms that reflect core assumptions about the state, gendered citizenship, and individual rights.

Although the archetypical US case forms a sometimes explicit point of theoretical comparison, the empirical basis of this study is the nonliberal German case. Because most states are not liberal, the frequent equation of feminism with the distinctive shape liberalism gives it may limit appreciation of the challenges and opportunities women's rights struggles face around the world. In other nonliberal contexts, feminists dealing with their own national priorities and institutional opportunities may find parallels to the story of how the German women's movement has developed and changed in interaction with its society and state. The German case is also interesting in itself. Following one case over time offers unparalleled opportunities to see historical legacies, path-dependencies, and strategic choices interacting and transforming movement results.

Like the United States and many other countries, Germany had a highly active and visible feminist movement in the 1970s. Yet when I said I was writing a book that would carry the movement's story to the present, many Germans asked, "But is there any women's movement today?" This is a question many Americans might also ask. Where have these women's movements gone, what have they accomplished, and where might we look for them in the present and future? Have different paths really led to the same outcomes?

The changes I trace will help, I hope, to answer these questions and also broader conceptual ones. First, how are material resources and discursive opportunities connected? Do shifts in political discourse effect material social change? Showing how the class-gender-race intersection works differently in Europe and the United States may help shed light on the consequences the institutionalization of class politics has for gender mobilizations and for equality-difference debates among feminists. Second, what happens to movements when some demands are so mainstreamed into politics that they hardly appear as change, but other demands remain too radical to consider? Comparing how in Germany a strong antidiscrimination policy still seems radical and in the United States paid leaves for mothers are deemed utopian and out of touch with real-world politics invites the question of what makes any political claim radical.

This book reconsiders the conventional notion of radicalism in politics—which associates it with violence and physical disruption—and in feminism—

which associates it with hostility (often to men), anger (rather than hope), and (exclusively) unconventional forms of politics. I argue that radicalism is relational, a specific type of challenge to the politics of a particular time and place. That which is radical stands at the margins, conflicts with institutionalized patterns of power, and in the long or short term undermines the pattern itself. When radical change happens, underlying political relationships change: women become citizens, states take responsibility for popular welfare, and family formation becomes a matter of individual choice rather than kin advantage. Whether abruptly or incrementally, a fundamental transformation occurs— and becomes invisible. The new world that seemed alien and disturbing now appears to be the ordinary, natural arrangement of things.

Because systems of power differ, so do these transformative challenges. This book looks at how arrangements of political power are naturalized, exploring the close connection between feminist movements and national politics. Material legacies of movement mobilizations in the form of institutional resources matter, but so do the discursive legacies that define the questions politics should answer, making some seem common sense and others absurdly radical. To the extent Germany has a less-told story of feminist change, it provides fewer taken-for-granted expectations and more opportunities to see alternative paths, taken or not.

Although focused on the development of the women's movement in Germany, this book offers moments of comparative reflection on alternatives in other contexts to highlight the effects of strategic choice and institutional embedding. The division of Germany into East and West after World War II offers one such contrast. The selective appropriation of ideas and strategies that flow transnationally among movements is another indication of how feminisms respond to their contexts. Contrasts with the United States provide American readers with an opportunity to reflect on their own assumptions, while offering Germans and others skeptical of liberalism a different lens on how its claims may be radically transformative.

The book focuses on what is and is not recognizable, achievable, and actually won by and for feminist politics in Germany, but my aim is to illuminate more general processes of feminist transformation. The differences among systems as to which claims are radical and realizable emphasize politics as a struggle rooted in historically developed material and cultural conditions.

WHY GERMANY?

The German case is distinctive in several ways. Most importantly for my argument, Germany is not a liberal state. Many of the ideas Americans find obvious, such as the central role of individual rights and equal economic opportunity in allowing women full participation in all the goods society offers, owe their prominence to the dominance of liberal political philosophy. Liberalism has not played as important a role in Germany as in the United States or even Britain. German politics has drawn on both conservative views of patriarchal authority and social democratic ideals of justice to forge a social welfare state that prioritizes family support and the social reproduction of the nation. This difference in the material and cultural meanings of the nation-state shapes the work cut out for feminists. Thinking about a nonliberal political context offers a way to theorize the differences in the struggles faced by women's movements around the world.

Germany is not a dominantly social democratic state like Sweden, nor an insistently secular one like France. After World War II, West Germany called itself a "social market economy," but the principles guiding its development owed more to Christian conservatism than to social democracy, and East Germany was created as a communist state. German social democrats have been more organized and influential than classical free-market liberals, but they have more often than not been in the political opposition; explicitly Christian parties led the government in the West, and authoritarian socialism dominated in the East. Policies that encouraged women's paid work and reduced the gender wage gap were much more difficult to realize in West Germany than in its Nordic neighbors, and East German policies that embraced gender-equality goals were discredited by their association with repressive government. The German struggle over a balance between religiously based conservatism and social democracy provides a model for thinking about feminism in many parts of the world. Where social democrats are presumed to be an ally, many of the priorities and struggles in women's movement politics will be affected in ways that are unfamiliar, and hence neglected, in American theorizing about political mobilizations.[5]

Germany is also a federal state. Its central government is limited in many ways, and its states have different traditions. In particular the states that were part of the formerly communist German Democratic Republic (GDR) are more secular and ambivalent about socialist legacies. They are now subordinate to a larger, more prosperous, powerful Western section that kept the name, nearly all the laws, and the self-concept of the Federal Republic (FRG). The West invested massively in transforming the East, but the Eastern states are still facing more poverty, losing population, and struggling over political identity more than two decades after unification in 1991. Unification has been a vast natural experiment in the effects of political culture and institutions over time.

No less important is the religious difference between north and south. Germany, like the Netherlands, has not committed itself to being a secular state, so both Catholic and Protestant churches have institutional influence. Catholics dominate in the south and the Rhineland, and Protestants in the center and north, but most people, especially in the East, rarely darken church doors. Germany, like many other European countries, struggles with assimilation of immigrants and accommodation of religious and cultural differences. Rethinking what it means to be a full citizen of the German state is complicated by its regional and immigrant diversity, interpreted through the lens of its history of dictatorships, division, and war.

Like twenty-six other European states, Germany also is part of the European Union, indeed its largest and richest member. The EU is less than a state but more than an international organization. As a transnational body, it has been steadily widening and deepening membership since its origins in the postwar economic recovery of the 1950s. Its rules about gender equality and interpretations of what its members can and must do to be gender-fair have a large and growing impact. Both member-states like Germany and the global networks in which German and European feminists participate are ever more influenced by EU-level gender politics. German variation among its federal states and its membership in a "female-friendly" EU gender regime provide important resources for thinking about the interaction among the many levels of political choice, from local to transnational, that define feminist agendas.

Thus no one would call Germany typical, but its policy paths and feminist struggles are also familiar. Equality and difference, autonomy and exclusion, participation and representation challenge women's movements around the world. Liberal political pressures at the transnational level, social democratic parties with influence in government, and cross-cutting interests by religion, ethnicity, and regional and individual economic position are hardly unique to

Germany. Readers familiar with women's movements in other countries will surely see conditions and choices in this story that echo those found elsewhere. Although this book does not claim to be a comparative study, each chapter explicitly engages with examples of such parallels and differences.

Moreover, Germany is certainly not isolated from the rest of the world, and transnational flows of ideas and individuals are highly relevant, as later chapters will discuss. But looking closely at one specific case offers opportunities to see how the prism of local history bends nonlocal influences into particular patterns that vary over place and time. American influences may loom large at times, but their Americanness is more visible to Germans than to Americans, whether as part of their appeal or as a reason for rejection. The shifting global balance of power, in which liberal institutions are growing but American-style feminism is no longer the trendsetter, is both cause and consequence of changes in what German and other national women's movements embrace.

Because this is a story of change, it is not a finished story. The struggles depicted here produce institutional and discursive outcomes that will be used again as tools for later struggles. The chapters approach the story semichronologically, with thematic stresses showing how developments influence those that follow. I argue that social justice movements are forms of politics best understood as *emergent*—tipped and turned by choices and strategies that continue to interact—and *intersectional*—drawing gender, race, class, ethno-national, and other justice struggles into relationship.

RELATIONAL REALISM
AS A PRACTICAL THEORY OF FEMINISM

I detour here to present the concepts that inform this analysis. This overview also locates the emergence and intersectionality of social movements in a broader perspective on gender that I call *relational realism*, a way of approaching gender relations as part of a complex, multilevel system.[6]

Relational realism as a perspective combines attention to the objective conditions of a historically material world with the creative capacity of human imagination to socially construct and communicate understandings of it that have material consequences. Relational realism therefore emphasizes an unending struggle to fit the material world to human perceptions of what it is and can be, a struggle waged among people and groups with different social locations, conflicting material interests and varying power to realize their objectives. In other words, both utopian visions and pragmatic constraints define the substance of politics, producing practices that arise in actual relationships among actors over time. Politics is about choices, and the options do not merely map onto culture, ideology, or material position.

Because relational realism begins from the recognition of human diversity and struggle, it cannot be a theory only about gender. It privileges a complex understanding of intersectionality in which race, class, and gender are social forces that continually define each other through institutional interactions. As Evelyn Nakano Glenn elegantly described race, class, and gender: "They are *relational* concepts whose construction involves both *representational and social structural processes* in which *power* is a constitutive element."[7]

Relational realism gives equal theoretical weight to discourses (through which representations of reality are socially constructed and made politically effective) and material conditions (through which structural arrangements are institutionalized, resources distributed, and opportunities for action created and constrained). It rejects methodological individualism, emphasizing instead the connections among concepts, persons, and institutions, relations shaped by power in historically emergent interactions. The contingent outcomes of the meeting of diverse human purposes in particular struggles are the foundations for future social arrangements. A practical theory is a redescription of this process in a form useful for guiding human decisions.

A practical theory of feminist politics, therefore, is one that offers heuristics for empowering women in their political choices, such as with whom to ally or what goals to prioritize. Maxine Molyneux's distinction between "practical" and "strategic" gender interests is a classic example of practical theory, and if this book is successful it will improve on such existing feminist theories of politics. Unlike Molyneux's model, for example, the relational realist perspective does not privilege nonlocal actors or see a single theory of feminism as attuning women's choices to some universally knowable strategic interest.[8] This book thus takes issue with not only the historical materialism Molyneux employed to classify certain interests as strategic, but also the social constructionism that ignores material constraints and makes achieving social change seem a matter of movements wanting particular changes badly enough to just make them happen.

THEORETICAL TOOLS FOR
RELATIONAL REALIST POLITICAL ANALYSIS

The theoretical elements for understanding the story that follows fall into three broad categories: the *system of gender relations* as part of a social order characterized by intersectional relations of power; the *role of political institutions* in the process by which social justice movements are shaped by and shape their societies; and the *significance of political discourse* as an element of both structure and agency in making change. Each element offers part of the overall explanation of how gender politics get done.

Gender Relations

Raewyn Connell advanced several useful ideas for approaching feminist political struggles in a multilevel, emergent and intersectional way. First, Connell distinguished the concept of a gender *regime*—the organization of gender relations in a particular institution like the corporation, family, or state—from the gender *order*—the totality of the gender regimes operating in a particular time and place.[9] For example, the gender regime of industrial capitalism may be broadly similar across countries, but the industrial phase of capitalism is not uniform, static, or uncontested, and how it is intertwined with other regimes within and across institutions will produce very different local gender orders, with a variety that is evident even from one shop floor to the next.[10] The social order encompasses a gender order along with all other organized relationships—age, nation, sexuality, ethnicity—intersecting in particular local manifestations.[11]

Keeping gender regime as a concept tied to specific institutions makes it easier to see how these regimes conflict as well as reinforce or echo each other across institutions to make certain feminist changes radically transformative in one setting but perhaps not in another. For example, the distinctively modern regimes in the institutions of paid work and family care create time conflicts, yet they depend on each other economically. "Reconciliation of work and family," affirmed as a not particularly radical political goal by the EU, can mean different things depending on which institutions are expected to change and whose time and money will be reallocated to achieve a new balance.

The multiplicity of levels at which change is felt, the conflicts among institutions, and the recurring rebalancing among them are evident across other regimes of inequality as well. These tensions—the "contradictions" in capitalism between innovation and predictability, individual economic advantage and essential common goods; the "American dilemma" of racism interwoven with valuing equal rights, democracy, and independence; the "paradox" of affirming both gender equality and difference—identify inconsistencies in institutional regimes and their expression in concrete inequalities.[12]

A second conceptual contribution Connell offers is an emphasis on *gender projects* rather than gender identities as the root of politics. Projects are forward-looking, goal-directed sets of actions. A gender project expresses a conscious or unconscious commitment to particular organizations of gender relations.[13] Gender projects that are political are about changing or preserving a specific gender order or regime, and gender projects that include a conscious aim to empower women collectively are those I define as *feminist*. Gender projects, like all political projects, are inherently intersectional. Movements build alliances using identities that result from the intersections of multiple political projects.

Thus gender relations can change as an effect of projects with other aims. Collective gender projects also inevitably have consequences for other social relations of inequality.[14] An early feminist project was simply to name "a group called women."[15] Women of color in the United States who were mobilized by this project were also productively critical of its limits. The feedback they provided, a recognition that social justice movements were operating as if "all the women are White, all the Blacks are men," first elicited their own political claim to be recognized as women of color with a distinctive perspective and then led to a broader theoretical approach called *intersectionality*.[16]

Intersectional analysis assumes that feminist political projects can be pursued by movements and organizations that are not exclusively feminist in orientation, and that women's movements (organized collective action by women, addressing women as a specific constituency) are not always feminist. Women's movements can be vehicles for racist or antiracist politics, serve economic justice or exploitation, even argue for women's subordination. Feminist projects themselves vary in content and inclusiveness depending on context, but they are political projects with women's empowerment as an objective. Their effects need to be evaluated in connection with the other political projects with which they are inevitably entangled.[17]

The version of intersectional analysis advanced here follows Glenn in arguing that race, class, and gender are relational social forces through which power operates materially and discursively. Race, class, and gender are important political relations and consistently give rise to political struggles, but they are not the only such relations (consider sexuality, nationality, and age, for example), nor are they uniformly significant across different institutions.[18] A fundamental goal of this book is to trace how race, class, and gender intersections differ in significant ways in the United States and Germany and why this difference matters. Chapter 2 sets out some of the parameters of these intersections.

Political Institutions and Social Change

Relational realism does not make a strong distinction between agency and structure, since what is done by social actors today may, as a direct result of their action, become an institutionalized aspect of the social order (a social structure) tomorrow.[19] However, scholars interested in social change have found it analytically useful to distinguish between an opportunity structure and active mobilizations for and against change taking place within the limits and possibilities given by that structure.[20] *Opportunity structures* are the political institutions that constrain and enable choices and shape outcomes. Policy scholars as well as social movement researchers have focused on the "windows of opportunity" for change produced by specific institutional arrangements of parties, political elites, and other organizations, resources, and leaders, as well as by institutionalized discourses.

Although policy is a steady stream of output of government decision making, most policy researchers tend to imagine an opportunity structure as a closed and stable system in which "windows" occasionally open. This picture is largely accurate in that politics tends to become institutionalized, actors consolidate power over material and cultural resources that advance their agendas, and most changes are modest. Few outputs of a policy system transform agendas, shift power relations, or redistribute resources in a major way. Policy actors may or may not realize which changes will turn out to be transformative ("radical") because the relationships among elements are complex, contingent, and emergent.[21]

For example, it is unlikely that the US Supreme Court, in affirming the principles of family privacy and limiting state intervention into individual women's decision making, expected that *Roe v. Wade* would transform American political conflicts for decades to come. Although carefully framed within the discursive limits of US liberalism, as a "reform" should be, the decision also

articulated the recognition of women as full citizens that was emerging transnationally and that opened a particular window of opportunity for feminism.
This broader transformation of women's citizenship remains deeply contested
in the United States.

The expansion of abortion rights in West Germany in the 1970s could be
said to have come through that same "window," yet the "wall" of discourse in
which the window opened was significantly different.[22] This wall—the limit on
what is thinkable by political change agents and on what states are seen as properly doing—is what I call a *discursive opportunity structure*. It is institutionalized
in authoritative texts like constitutions, laws, and court decisions. The German
discursive opportunity structure in which this window opened differed from the
US one. Where the US court affirmed privacy and individual choice, the German court saw a constitutional obligation to protect life and directed the state
to take more effective action than criminalization to shape women's decisions,
but acknowledged that women inevitably held the final decision in their hands.
Because of the different structure of the national discourses in which the transnational opening took place, the material and discursive results for women who
want to terminate a pregnancy are quite different in Germany and the United
States. But as we will see in Chapter 3, it is difficult to call them uniformly better (or worse) for women.

Institutions also form material opportunity structures: arrangements of
power and resources become routine and taken for granted over time, *institutionalized*. The specific institutional structure of a place and time is what Raka
Ray called the "political field" in which movement agendas are formed and political strategies considered. She described the development of women's movements in two Indian cities as channeled in different ways by the dominance of
a single political party (homogeneous political field) in one and the competition among parties (heterogeneous field) in the other. She presented, as I do, a
study of movements as parts of a political field with an institutional character
and history that is structurally important. Chapters 4 and 5 respectively consider
the "radical" countercultural projects and "mainstream" projects for inclusion
in political parties and systems West German feminists took up in response to
the distinctive field of opportunities their state presented. The two strategies
are related, and the chapters trace the transformations they together brought to
German systems of representation of women and women's concerns.

The intersection of nationally based social movements, which was the taken-for-granted institutional form of political projects in the twentieth century, with the emergent institutionalization of transnational advocacy networks at the regional and global level at the end of the millennium, is also part of the transformational story of feminism that the German case illuminates. The German process of feminist institutionalization in and through the state discussed in Chapters 6 and 7 is unlike the American one in that it involves the reconstitution of state sovereignty internally (in the unification of East and West Germany) and externally (globalization in relation to EU authority). This analysis highlights the debates over getting closer to the state, and what the state can and should do to change gender relations, which resemble debates in other countries that also have developed extensive gender policy agencies and frameworks for women's input into decision making.[23]

Discursive Politics and Framing Work

Relational realism brings *discourse* centrally into the understandings of what politics is about and how it is done. Building from Nancy Fraser's argument that need definition is the first stage of politics and Michel Foucault's notion of genealogy as a historical analysis of the power that words and categories acquire, the practical theory of relational realism uses a critical analysis of the institutional frameworks of concepts and the framing strategies of specific actors to reveal the workings of political discourse about feminism and gender.[24] For feminists, the specific meanings of motherhood and citizenship, equality and autonomy, group-based difference and collective power are at the center of this part of the story. *Framing* is the term used for this discursive work.

I define *framing* as an *interaction in which actors with agendas meet discursive opportunities as structured in institutionally authoritative texts.* This opportunity structure may be taken for granted in accounts of movements' framing struggles, yet authoritative texts—constitutions, administrative regulations, laws, court decisions—are crucial to shaping outcomes. Such texts are usually considered policy documents, but they are also institutionalized results of past interventions to frame issues. As such, they reflect the state's projects, the alliances among movements, and the discursive "walls" in which windows of opportunity open. I distinguish between *active framing* efforts and the institutionalized *discursive opportunity structures* given by frames already in authoritative positions. Frames institutionally anchored in political texts, such as laws, court decisions, and administrative regulations, have power to include and exclude issues and choices from the realm of politics. These texts are not a single master frame, but rather a network of meaning, a framework, shaping and shaped by the active framing done by actors with agendas.[25]

Thus the transnational campaign to insist that "women's rights are human rights" did not simply "bridge" a claim about women's rights to an existing master frame about rights or even human rights; the campaign changed the practical meaning of "rights" and extended the sense in which women's experience was validated as human, and did so in a transnational context in which denying women full citizenship in the human community had become increasingly problematic over the previous century.[26] As feminists recognized in creating new words for long-existing oppressions (sexual harassment as a term was coined in 1974), absence of discursive resources in the framework of political meanings supports the status quo. One of the most radical actions a movement can take is to transform the language of politics.[27]

This book is an effort to demonstrate how acting politically in a certain framework means that the projects actors embrace—their *agendas*—are created through the interaction of institutional discursive opportunity structures with the whole selves actors bring to these settings. They think strategically, but with different experiences and goals in mind. Some actors in a social justice movement try to frame a change as modest, practical, yet important, thus a feasible *reform* within the current system; others frame their claims as transformative, sweeping, and perhaps unachievable in the current political institutions. Because these latter, *radical* frames do not resonate with the available discursive opportunity structure, they may not be efficacious. Whether an idea resonates may not matter to radical framers—their desire to be effective may be less powerful than their desire to be visionary, theoretically coherent, or morally pure. However radical in intent, the actual impact of claims-making may be more or less transformative in practice than anyone anticipates.

Reformers and radicals may differ more in the local opportunity structures they confront than in their personal dispositions or political intuitions. Mary Katzenstein demonstrated this in her comparative study of feminists in the US Roman Catholic Church and the US military. Both groups were raised in the same political culture and confronted hierarchical and male-dominated bureaucracies. But in the church, radical discursive politics challenging the premises of the system took hold, while in the military, reformist approaches to inclusion dominated. The military feminists had resources in existing law (discursive opportunities) for being effective that those in the church did not, and each organizational polity shaped the agendas of the activists within it.

Scholars have suggested that a tension between the radical and reform wings of a movement can be productive (a so-called radical flank effect) and reflect a self-conscious division of labor between organizations.[28] For example, Amy Mazur and Dorothy McBride have led a decade-long project of European analysis on the effect of what they call "state feminism"—the expansion of policy machineries dedicated to women's empowerment—on achieving feminist policy goals. They contend that the most successful strategy combines insiders and outsiders: advancing electoral representation of women, placing feminists in the administrative policy machinery of the state and mobilizing women's movement activists.[29] I attempt to complement their organizational analysis with a discursive one, and I consider what is radical in or outside the context of the state and when and how the relations among radical and reform ideas may be practically productive of change.

The process of change traced in this book reveals feminist actors with radical and reform agendas in Germany. They come together in cooperation and conflict in ways that reflect historically and locally specific struggle, successfully institutionalize only some of the organizations and discourses they produce, and reevaluate their agendas based on their experiences of success and failure.

CONTEXTUALIZING THE GERMAN FEMINIST MOVEMENT

Although this book is a story of changes in feminism, its purpose is not to evaluate what "real" feminism should be or whether the German women's movement has become more or less feminist, more or less radical, or more or less powerful. It attempts to assess instead what feminism, radicalism, and movement strength have come to mean in Germany. I use comparisons across time and context to highlight what is included and excluded in these terms. But I will have failed if readers take the comparisons as evidence that the German women's movement is better or worse, stronger or weaker in the abstract than some other movement.

In fact, assuming that there is only one dimension, called strength or effectiveness, along which movement successes differ leaves us unable to answer questions such as: Why do American women not demand paid parental leave as Germans have? Why are Western German women more skeptical of state child care than those in the eastern part of the country? Why do virtually all American feminists value the right to serve in the military when most German feminists deplore it? Why are German feminists so deeply divided over laws prohibiting Muslim women from wearing a headscarf, when Americans find this unproblematic? Why have some feminists in Germany welcomed gender mainstreaming as a strategy from the Beijing Platform for Action, while others see it as co-optation? Such internal debates and national differences can be understood only by disentangling the many threads that run through history and institutions to form local configurations. In that sense, the German case stands as one test of a set of hypotheses about how national politics still set a framework for gendered inclusions and exclusions despite globalization.

This case may also be a contribution to the practical feminist theories being developed in many different contexts. Around the world, women's movements are sharing information about what has and has not worked for them. Relational realism highlights systematic variation to suggest appropriate generalizations about situated feminist experiences of intersectional politics.

German Feminism in a Global Context

Several kinds of variation in gender orders and political institutions facilitate comparing the German case to others. First is the relative centrality of the state and its *capacity* to act to realize its political agenda.[30] The German state is less active in civic affairs than in some countries, but far more so than the US state is. In Germany, state funding is a primary resource for social movements, and the state helps individuals across the income spectrum reconcile work and family needs by providing direct support from taxes for child rearing, health care, and education from preschool through graduate training. Many social actors deride cutbacks in state involvement in securing the welfare of all its citizens as *neoliberalism*—giving absolute priority to the merits of the market, privatization, and competition. Pro-state actors frame neoliberalism as the most dangerous export America offers because it threatens the state's capacity to realize social justice. This book highlights the tension in feminism between classical liberalism as political claim about self-determination and individuality and neoliberalism (or market-liberalism) as an ideology about the superiority of market-led decision making.

Second, states vary in the nature and extent of their welfare provisioning. Modern nation-states all consider themselves responsible for the welfare of their populations. How they interpret and carry out this responsibility varies dramatically, from the minimalist free-market approach of the United States to the strongly state-led interventions of Scandinavia. Identified particularly with the work of Gøsta Esping-Anderson, models of *welfare-state regimes* distinguish three basic types of institutionalized policy traditions for responding to class inequalities: the social democratic model of which Sweden is the exemplary case; the conservative corporatist model Germany represents, and the liberal market-based model of which the United States is the purest form. This typology makes economic power and social redistribution the key aspects of difference among states' welfare policies, putting the primary emphasis on the political aspect of a political economy.[31]

A third model of difference among states is the historical one advanced by T. H. Marshall, who distinguished among the types of rights that states extended to citizens. He saw full *citizenship* as encompassing civil, political, and social rights and argued that there was a typical trajectory through which states and groups of citizens passed. Civil rights such as access to education and free association led to political rights such as voting and collective representation in political parties, which led to social rights such as a minimum income and decent housing and transportation systems.[32] Although feminist scholars have shown that this sequential model does not fit the realities of women's citizenship (they may well have had protective legislation securing their social rights before having the right to vote or hold office), the recognition that states vary in the kinds of rights they offer and when and to whom they offer them is useful in placing the German case in a global perspective. German citizens have been under fascist, state socialist, and democratic governments, and they have had political, social, and economic rights extended and curtailed at different times.

A fourth dimension of state variation is in the gender order itself. Feminist theorists have identified the *male breadwinner model* as a form of family politics states adopted in the era of industrialization, often through male workers' collective organizing to demand a family wage but also through corporate decisions to use gender to manage men's and women's performance at work.[33] This arrangement ("traditional" not in a historical, but in an ideological sense) divides wage-earning work for men from unpaid family-care work for women, and to a greater or lesser degree confers citizenship rights on earners and caregivers unequally. States vary in how they treat motherhood and caregiving: from a strongly institutionalized male breadwinner system (such as Germany) through a marketized care and dual-earner model (such as the United States) and a state-supported dual care-and-earnings approach for women and men (emerging in Scandinavia).

Another part of the gender order of specific states is how they limit women's *autonomy*, which O'Connor, Orloff, and Shaver define as women's ability to form economically viable households and make reproductive decisions independent of male control. Without equal participation in political decision making, women's autonomy in forming private households remains under men's public control. As Lisa Brush points out, to focus narrowly on women's well-being through the lens of motherhood and the well-being of unmarried mothers overlooks other aspects of institutionalized male power and control, from violence on the streets, in dating, and in the home, to domination of formal organizations such as governments, unions, and corporations.[34] States divide the power to regulate women's choices into that exercised in "private" households and that made part of "public" policy for women's citizenship, solvency, and safety. As Germany shows, autonomy, variously understood, is just as central to understanding feminist movements as the equality claims that focus on gender differences in political, civil, or social rights.

These dimensions of variation in states—their capacity to act, willingness to use redistributive means to curb class inequalities, types of citizenship rights they guarantee, and role in organizing interpersonal care and individual autonomy in a gender order across institutional regimes—form the political context for which a practical theory of feminist politics must account. These dimensions guide my analysis of when and how German developments reflect processes similar to those in other countries.

Contextual Comparison for American Readers

Because of the hegemonic US position in the world system, American readers may need a special reminder not to see their movement as the norm. US feminists today are more aware of global women's mobilizations than they were during the cold war, but they may still assume that women's movements follow the same lines as theirs. Even non-US feminists often treat American feminism as the standard case from which their own follows or diverges, assuming, for example, that the "waves" of feminism the United States experienced are found across the globe.[35]

This situation partly reflects the important role US feminists played in the 1960s and 1970s reemergence of active feminist organizing in many Western countries.[36] In this period, the United States saw broad protest against women's subordination, innovative policy tools to fight sex discrimination, and radical ideas, such as naming sexual harassment. American feminist scholars began studying the women's movement in the United States almost as soon as it began and offered practical theory for feminist activism based on their own experiences, but their assumptions may not hold very well outside the United States.

First, treating "feminism" and "women's movement" as synonyms can be misleading in contexts in which women are organized politically in gender-specific groups around their identities as mothers, sisters, or wives but not around a goal of empowering women collectively. In the early 1970s, most US women's organizations (like the League of Women Voters or Girl Scouts) quickly embraced women's empowerment and specific feminist goals such as adding an Equal Rights Amendment to the Constitution, as did a number of mixed-gender groups. So for US activists, there was little reason to stress whether the organizational form feminism took was a social movement or an institutionalized women's group, mobilized as women or mixed in gender, or affiliated with political parties or not. When organizations on the political Right (like Concerned Women for America and the Independent Women's Forum) then mobilized as movements on an antifeminist agenda, the term "women's movement" in the United States already implied "feminist," making them difficult to categorize or understand. In other parts of the world, the distinction is clear: *women's movements* include conservative organizations mobilizing politically around members' gender identity, and *feminist* describes people, groups, policies, and activities that aim to enhance women's autonomy and power (their negative and positive freedoms).[37] Since feminists may or may not rely on women's movements (rather than political parties, mixed-gender social justice movements, or individual efforts), I use this linguistic distinction to help explain why women's movements only sometimes are preferred as a strategy by feminist activists.

Second, the classic distinction among *radical, liberal,* and *socialist* types of
feminism is a practical theory about specific objectives associated with frames
based in Anglo-American experience. The label *radical* appeared especially fitting
in relation to the dominant stream of liberalism that informed these national
political traditions, with which its gender difference claims had little resonance.[38]
It is less useful in Germany, as what was labeled radical in the United States
was often mainstream there. In the usage of this book—and most political sociology—*liberal* is not a synonym for "progressive," as it often appears to be
in ordinary American political discourse. Rather, liberal refers to a historically
developed political orientation in which individual rights are central, the state
is limited, and public and private are sharply divided. Private enterprise and
the rights of owners are protected, individual freedom and choice are held up
as core values, and government is seen as having limited responsibility in making such options actually accessible.

In a global context, the US commitment to liberalism as the organizing
culture of the political system is exceptionally strong. This means that a domestic gender politics that resonates with expressed American values is also "liberal," making "liberal feminism" appear to be a synonym either for moderate,
pragmatic positions or for accepting all the depredations of global capitalism
as normal or even desirable. If the United States is used as the model, political
liberalism as a democratic position on empowered citizenship becomes conflated
with a neoliberal orientation to the economic order. This is misleading, especially when applied to nonliberal contexts, where liberalism can be a force for
democratic critique of authoritarianism, even in its patriarchal protective forms.

Germany has not been primarily liberal in either the classic democratic
or neoliberal market-fundamentalist sense, but it has had a feminist women's
movement, beginning around the same time (1848) as in the United States,
and waxing and waning on a schedule that only partly matches that of the
United States, as Chapter 2 will show. To reject liberalism in Germany (and in
many other parts of the world) is mainstream. It is certainly not radical, as this
position is in the United States. The label *socialist* also cannot capture the important differences in culture and political allegiances between supporting the
state socialist regime in East Germany, being a passionate social democrat, and
belonging to fringe communist groups (*K-Gruppen*) in the West. The category
"socialist feminist" is thus relatively useless analytically in Germany.

Today, Germany is moving in different directions than the United States in how it is changing gender relations in different institutional domains and discursive frameworks. This is part of what makes it such an interesting and important case, especially for Americans. In a previous book, Beth Hess and I told the US feminist story—from the history of the movement to its working out of new feminist politics in an era of globalization and generational change.[39] Chapter 2 will present a comparative prehistory of the United States and Germany to highlight how race and class, liberalism and socialism have intersected with gender politics; the remainder of the book focuses on the structures, ideas, and effects of the German women's movement itself, using comparisons to suggest why these developments took the course they did and why these paths remain consequential.

THE PLAN OF ANALYSIS

The following chapters deal with selected, concrete challenges facing feminism in Germany, attempting to capture the opportunity structures that German feminists faced and the mobilizations that responded to—and sometimes changed—them. The story of each period has consequences for the next and builds on the frameworks bequeathed by prior struggles, yet each chapter is also an account of a distinctive set of political choices that put in motion certain forces and inhibited others.

Chapter 2 develops the history of feminism in Germany by means of contrast with the United States in the nature and explicitness of its class and race struggles and its institutionalized liberal, Christian, and socialist politics. The structures and practices of the state and the consciousness of the movement in the long century from 1848 to 1968 show the different frameworks in which the feminism in the 1960s emerged. I compare and contrast the East and West German institutionalization of gender and family to some extent, but leave the deeper exploration of the effects of these political frameworks for Chapter 6 when unification makes them painfully apparent.

Chapter 3 takes up the story proper, describing the postwar reemergence of feminism in the late 1960s and early 1970s and the early development of this movement in West Germany. Beginning in the student movement, as women's liberation did in many countries, this West German version of autonomous feminism faced its own set of problems and formed its own agenda, even when it adopted ideas and strategies from the transnational remobilization of feminism. The central feminist self-definition as "autonomous" critiqued the public gender order of the male breadwinner family in the West and the power of the Communist Party in the East. The discourse of autonomy also captured other concerns of West German activists that crossed the public-private divide, including self-determination in sexual and reproductive matters and the recognition of mother-work as significant social labor. The struggle over abortion rights revived a controversy from the 1920s and became the key political struggle that defined the movement's goals.

Chapter 4 examines the strategies adopted in the 1970s and early 1980s in West Germany as the "autonomous women's movement" tried to create a better society for women. Autonomous feminists organized against domestic violence, sexual assault, and sexual harassment through an emergent form of women-only direct action, the feminist "project." Rapid multiplication of such autonomous social change projects in the 1970s and early 1980s in West Germany defined this period as the "project feminist" phase of the movement. Nonviolence as a principle of feminism also emerged in a path-dependent way from the legacy of World War II, the cold war rearmament on both sides of Germany, the open struggle between the West German state and those it defined as "terrorists," and women's budding resistance against militarism in the East. New alliances with peace, antinuclear, and environmental activists emerged as possibilities just as the institutionalization of feminist projects in the West sharpened debate over the appropriate relation of feminists to the state and to partisan politics.

Chapter 5 takes up the growing engagement with the state and the issue of feminist institutionalization through, rather than against, party politics. The emergence of the Green party in the 1980s changed the opportunity structure by offering a way of doing electoral politics not so tied to the classic Left-Right division. In particular, the Green strategy of establishing women's offices in government and the "zipper list" alternating women and men's names as candidates for office opened a window for innovations in representing women as citizens and extending women's rights. The discourse of voice and the strategy of autonomous women's organizing now entered formal political institutions.

Chapter 6 examines the crises that German unification provoked for feminists in East and West, particularly with regard to defining the needs of women as a group. Diversity among women became the most contentious issue for feminism in this period. System competition between the German states had been a lever for creating benefits for women as mothers in both countries, but the gender order institutionalized in East and West produced different discourses about needs and patterned the lives of women along different lines. West German feminists' initial hope that East German women would be easy recruits to "their" movement died shortly after the wall fell. Residents of the East found themselves "immigrants in their own country." Faced with unfamiliar laws and procedures, frequently unemployed but facing different opportunities from those they had known in state socialism, these new citizens of the Federal Republic struggled to adapt, and sometimes they succeeded. But the different priorities they brought to feminism initiated a turn, or *Wende*, for the whole movement whose effects are still visible twenty years later.

In Chapter 7, differences among women are still the focus, but the level shifts to consider the new issues of feminist politics posed by the agendas arising in the growing transnationalization of German politics. Poststructural feminist theories unsettled a long-standing framing of gender as a material structure like class, while transnational feminist actors put new political strategies like gender mainstreaming on the table. Postunification Germany was a more assertive and self-aware international actor, and the gender politics of the EU and United Nations (UN) became more influential. The interface between national and EU level policymaking provided a new set of levers for feminists to use to shift national policy machineries around gender and women's rights, but also transformed the discourse of feminism in significant ways.

Chapter 8 is a type of conclusion, but one that raises questions for the future. It returns to the issues of autonomy, state authority, and discursive transformation but now places these in the context of directions taken in past decades. By highlighting the particular changes of recent German gender politics, from the election of Angela Merkel as the first woman chancellor to the reconstruction of the gender order in family-policy reforms, it asks what opportunities are opening and closing in this millennium. With the debates over what makes a good family as the fulcrum, the chapter returns to consider the initial formulation of race, class, and gender as differently institutionalized in the United States and Germany, asking what the extreme income inequality in the United States and heightened concerns about cultural differences in

Europe imply for the future of feminist agendas. It concludes with questions about the present and future challenges of gender projects.

Those who think radical transformation of the present social order is necessary may nonetheless see in this account of forty years of German feminism the possibilities of incremental changes over a generation to realize radical goals. There are many alternative paths for modernizing gender relations and strategic uncertainties in any unfinished struggle. Yet, as a matter of praxis, attending to the historically constructed frameworks of discourse and the ongoing framing that activists do may offer relationally realistic understandings of feminist struggles and strategies around the world.

CHAPTER 2

CREATING
WOMEN CITIZENS
National Frameworks for Gender Equality
and Self-determination, 1848–1968

"I AM RECRUITING women citizens for the empire of freedom," wrote Louise Otto-Peters (1819–95) in 1848. All across Europe, women and men were rising up against the power of the aristocracy. In this general ferment, German bourgeois revolutionaries like Otto-Peters were trying to create a modern liberal nation-state out of the patchwork of principalities and dukedoms.

From the beginning, the debate about German nationhood included women's rights as citizens and their participation in the full spectrum of work, education, and civic life in the new era of industrialization and urbanization. Otto-Peters typifies the intertwining of the "woman question" with the overall cause of a unified, liberal German nation-state.

Unfortunately, the liberal revolution of 1848 failed. Germany unified in 1871 as an empire built on monarchy, militarism, social hierarchy, and repression of the Left rather than democratic citizenship and political freedom. The struggle for women to be citizens had to be carried forward in a social system in which the fundamental principles of modern citizenship—democratic rights and political freedoms—were not secured. The battle over the kind of nation-state Germany would be remained unresolved for a century and a half, and the story of feminism continues to be intertwined with this struggle in complex and contested ways.

The liberal institutional and discursive frameworks of the American nation-building process are far from the German experience. The liberal revolution that failed in Germany in 1848 succeeded in the United States in 1776. American national identity was forged through racially specific modes of inclusion. In Germany, as this chapter shows, class inequality as the epitome of social injustice and political organization along class lines formed the institutional framework for gender politics. Class politics failed to gain traction on US soil. Conversely, race is a useless analogy for women's status in Germany for good historical reasons: connecting gender inequality with national or religious differences is problematic for a country still struggling with the legacy of Nazi rule. This chapter traces how events and people in German history constructed the distinctive framework on which its new feminist movement in 1968 began to build.

RACE AND CLASS IN THE FRAMEWORKS FOR GENDER POLITICS

Race and class struggles for social justice do not precede controversies over gender relations; all three are part of what nation-building is about. But they developed differently in the institutions of nation-states in the eighteenth and nineteenth centuries. The relative centrality of race or class lent a distinctive character to gender struggles. This intersectionality played a role in how gender, race, and class politics shaped one another in the turbulent 1960s, as gender politics in Germany and the United States continue to reflect.

Race-first Liberalism as Institutionalized in the United States

The United States developed a politics based on political liberalism and the concomitant view of individual rights and freedoms as central to citizenship. But despite the language of "liberty and freedom for all," rights-bearing individual citizenship was extended only to White men. Slavery for forcibly imported Africans and their offspring and territorial dispossession of Native Americans were legitimated in the discourse of "natural" physical and moral inequality between "races." Founding documents reflected the ideas that slaves were less than full persons and that they and Native Americans needed the tutelage of the White racial authority institutionalized in the state. The dependent, child-like character attributed to the subordinated group was understood also to in-here in each member of the group. Differences among groups constructed as "races" were understood as just as "natural" and "God-given" as those White Americans enjoyed.[1]

Neither the Civil War nor Emancipation ended this regime. The Manifest Destiny of territorial expansion drew on the ideology of White racial superior-ity to make subjugation of former Spanish colonies a moral mission to civilize "our little brown brothers," and, especially in the Southwest, to racialize Span-ish speakers as "Latino." Immigrant workers and their families were included in the American melting pot based on perceived relative "whiteness": political citizenship (immigration quotas, voting rights) and civic citizenship (marriage, housing, education, credit) were explicitly regulated by ethnicity and skin color for Asians and for Europeans of Mediterranean ancestry. Practical inequality in civil and political rights and discourses of racial "natural" differences were institutionalized as defining individuals and the nation.[2]

This racial character of nation-building meant that the state was constructed on subordination of persons based on "difference." Unlike European states that imaged themselves as ethnically unitary—the German *Volk*, for example—the United States defined itself as ethnically mixed but hierarchically organized. In Germany race was a basis for being seen as outside the nation; in the United States it was a basis for incorporation but in complex relations of oppression, exploitation, and devaluation.[3]

From the beginning, this dynamic of race offered American feminists a lens for seeing how women also were devalued and exploited in family, community, and nation. From the earliest antislavery and pro-women's rights lectures of the 1830s, American women found that a critical attitude toward racial hierarchy helped develop awareness of gender subordination, for themselves and their audiences.[4] Feminists compared women to slaves, and when Sojourner Truth asked, "Ain't I a woman?" she challenged the invisibility of African American women's specific experiences in this analogy. This touched a nerve that continues to resonate strongly for US feminists. Useful as the analogy to race has been, it created distortions and blind spots for White feminists, particularly the ten-dency to imagine "all the women are white, all the blacks are men" and to lose

sight entirely of women of color, their issues and organizations.[5] White women
think of themselves (and are thought of) as if they had no race; only women of
color are seen as having conflicts of interest between race and gender politics.[6]

Nonetheless, the alliances between groups working on feminist causes and
racial justice have been long and strong. For many Americans, not only women
of color, these are not two distinct causes but one coherent struggle for realizing
the liberal ideals of American independence. Despite conflicts about inclusion
and priorities, the discursive and institutional mandate for mutual support is
strong enough to make a gender-race alliance of justice interests seem natural
to many. When women of color led in theorizing such intersectionality, they
spoke to many feminists who saw a need to contextualize gender in relation
to race and other systems of inequality. A politics that includes rights for *all*
women in a context of continuing racialized inequality depends crucially on
racially inclusive feminist organizations. Few, however, noted that the way intersectionality developed in the United States tended to privilege the connections among race and gender and leave class relatively unanalyzed.[7]

Because racism has never been uncontested in American history, the struggles
against it have left institutional legacies too. American structures of opportunity
include civil rights legislation and its implementing decisions and regulations.
Electoral maps and partisan alignments follow historical cleavages drawn and
redrawn through racial contestation. The Civil War, Reconstruction, Jim Crow,
the Alien Exclusion Acts, Japanese internment, the Civil Rights Act, the Voting
Rights Act, the Philadelphia Plan (for affirmative action in hiring and contracting), the *Bakke* decision (on "reverse discrimination" in professional education),
the Civil Rights Restoration Act, *Loving v. Virginia* (ending antimiscegenation
law), and many other milestones lie along this path.[8]

The "American dilemma" Swedish sociologist Gunnar Myrdal identified
between individual rights and racial subordination remains key to how Americans imagine social justice. The characteristic terms of the struggle are ensuring equal civil and political rights ("creating equal opportunity"), overturning
group stereotypes about differences ("ending prejudice"), desegregating institutions ("fighting discrimination"), and preserving individual choice ("supporting freedom and democracy").[9] These concepts, rooted in the tension between
liberalism and White privilege, provide the language for speaking about feminism, too. Americans find it hard to imagine a feminist discourse that does not

equate equal opportunity with women's rights, emphasize gender desegregation of institutions, value women's antistereotypical behavior, and defend individual choice. This framework is institutionalized in authoritative American texts, not merely in the attitudes of individual Americans, and provides the cultural tools for various discursive struggles.[10]

This commitment to liberal language of equality makes "sameness/difference" debates about gender in the United States politically meaningful. Race and gender may be depoliticized by being conceptualized as mere differences, and the "diversity" of individuals framed as innocuous or even as an asset from which the nation and its businesses profit.[11] Yet any difference attributed to biology holds implicit meaning as legitimating inequality, so debates over science (especially genetics and developmental and evolutionary psychology) have a prominent role in saying what differences are and how they matter. Because the hierarchical relations of race and gender rest on a historically institutionalized politics of imputed biological difference, not merely on abstract liberalism, the ability to claim difference as a positive justification for state action is limited; entitlement to social justice as a citizen of the United States rests on being or becoming an individual "like everyone else."

Race has not offered a useful comparison to gender for German feminists, and even today the idea that gender and race are naturally similar does not resonate for German women, even if the notion is familiar from US feminist discourse. Some would point out how new racial difference and immigration stresses are to Europe; I argue below that similar tensions have been very much part of German and European nation-building processes. But unlike the US settler society, European states imagined community and constructed national identities by drawing distinctions between people inside and outside the nation-state. Crucial debates included whether Germany should be "large" (all territories in which there were German populations) or "small" (only territories inhabited virtually exclusively by Germans) and whether citizenship should be limited by religion (not only what rights Jews should have, but how Catholics in Protestant areas should be treated and vice versa).

To speak of race in regard to Germany, furthermore, is inevitably to evoke the searing image of the Holocaust. Jewish immigration from Russia and Eastern Europe into Germany, seen as relatively urban and tolerant, was endemic in the nineteenth century. The new migration of the so-called *Ostjuden* provoked tensions and crises across Europe when these "backward" rural migrants joined the more assimilated Jews who had been "outsiders within" for generations. Racialization of religion—the definition of Jewishness as overriding diverse national origins, and as a heritable trait rather than a set of beliefs, personal practices, and community loyalties—led to previously unimaginable levels of atrocity by the Nazis. But this process was by no means unique to Germany, nor was complicity in the genocide of Jews restricted to Germans.

When Nazi anti-Semitism radically racialized the state, it began by denying Jews their citizenship and ended by denying their humanity and destroying their lives. The horrors perpetrated by National Socialism and its allies across Europe made race into a taboo subject after World War II and created a feeling of shame about their national past among many postwar Germans. It is challenging to Europeans to think about race as a historically changing political relation, or about the racialization of religion as a continuing problem. Nonetheless, there are objective similarities (as well as differences) in the stresses introduced by the immigration of Muslim, often rural, populations into European cities today and the stresses felt in a previous century. Even for discussing these issues of ethnicity/religion/nationality, the language of race is too heavily freighted to be useful.

The usability of race as a political discourse about inequality is also shaped by colonialism. The German Empire had fewer colonies than the British, Spanish, Portuguese, or Dutch, but it was not an insignificant actor in Africa in the late nineteenth and early twentieth centuries.[12] Like the colonial projects of the larger empires, German domination was combined with an ideology that made subjects "not us." Race is imagined as about another "nation"—as immigrants challenging the borders, as colonies far away, even as the genocide of the Jewish people—rather than as an ongoing struggle over power and subordination within a community of which racialized others are part. Claims for rights, freedom, independence, and citizenship are made for the excluded racial others in terms that offer little conceptual leverage for women trying to increase their standing within the German national community.

Class-based Politics as the German Norm

Class, not race, was the defining conflict in struggles for justice in Germany. Conflict between a clerical-military-landowner alliance (the Right) and a socialist-democratic-liberal alliance (the Left) took different forms as European nation-states emerged, but the fight was waged with particularly high intensity in Germany. The size and power of the socialist party in the German Empire, the political battles of the Weimar era that both brought socialists to power and made them the targets of fascist and nationalist attack, the interweaving of socialist, pacifist, and feminist politics and the repression directed at them as antipatriotic forces, and the polarization of the two German states during the cold war all contributed to making class relations and politics the main axis around which German claims for social justice revolved. This story will be the substance of the next section of this chapter, as I show how feminist organizations and discourse were formed in these battles and left legacies for the 1960s generation. First, however, I briefly note the contrast given by the US experience.

What is called *American exceptionalism* largely consists in the weak influence of class politics and socialist organization in the United States. The United States has never had a majority socialist party beyond local government.[13] US partisan alignments are better predicted by race and region than by class interests. In Europe, the classic "Christian" parties have typically represented traditionalists (defending religious, patriarchal, nationalist authorities, whose values they call "traditional"). The European liberal parties—more or less strong in different countries—make economic arguments for individual autonomy in family and community matters, business-supporting economic policy, and minimal engagement by the state.[14] In the 1960s, US Democrats and Republicans were both liberal parties in this sense; Democrats over time embraced more social democratic commitment to use the state actively for social justice, and Republicans have moved toward the traditionalist-nationalist conservative positions associated with religious parties.

Class conflict is therefore not something US politics directly addresses. Even speaking of class is, to a large extent, taboo in political discourse: there can be discussion about "the poor" and "the rich," but the assumption of both elites and citizens is that nearly everyone is "middle class."[15] These income groups are also not depicted as engaged in a conflict in which they have diverging interests, as "workers" and "capitalists/employers" would be. Consequently, rather being useful to mediate such a conflict, government is expected to do as little as possible. A government active in economic matters is pejoratively labeled "socialist."

Around the world, the political significance of class has led to the peaceful emergence of social democratic welfare states that mediate class conflicts, but also to violent communist and fascist dictatorships that attempt to repress it. Germany, unlike the United States, has experienced all three outcomes. Regardless of the specific form of government, the institutional framework for political issues in Germany has revolved around class. Even as regimes changed repeatedly over time, the German states affirmed, first, that class is a *social relation* of production that is part of the underlying structure of society and is not going to disappear, and second, that the state therefore has an obligation to make class relations an *object of politics*. The state has an affirmative responsibility to make a livable political community by policies that manage and mitigate the problems class inequality produces. Which groups the state favors, and how, are the proper objects of political struggle.

When gender is understood as "like class" in Germany, it is being constructed as a *social relation* of exploitation among groups and an appropriate *political object* of state intervention. This analogy continues to be fruitful for German feminists. It is not a resonant argument in the United States, and feminists rarely find institutional leverage in class-based alliances. There are American "socialist feminists" who are strongly committed to bringing the two models of social justice together, but practical social justice feminism in US politics has largely focused on racial injustice and has lacked a resonant frame to engage class and gender politically.[16]

This fact has kept US conflicts over the relations between socialism and feminism limited to small academic milieus in which abstract theory is debated. There, framing that uses this analogy gained some currency—thinking of gender as about "social relations of reproduction" rather than of production, looking at women as a group defined by their position in the relations of reproduction (as workers are in the relationships of production), and appealing to the state as having an active responsibility to mitigate the consequences of inequalities. While it appeals to academic feminists to offer Sweden as a model of an interventionist, woman-friendly state, few of them have considered how unappealing becoming more like Europe is in the wider US political culture, and how unlike the United States and European countries are in the constellation of parties, legal developments, and political discourses that offer tools to realize their vision of justice.[17] Particularly as European states embrace more woman-friendly policies, it is important to be realistic about the lessons their experiences can and cannot offer American feminists and women's movement activists around the world. The particularity of this national story of feminist politics can help clarify such general comparative issues.

To understand the character of the German women's movement as it has emerged and developed since 1968, the famous year of political transformation across Europe, demands a closer look at its history before that moment. Conflicts over class loyalties, struggles with an authoritarian state, and definitions of what a welfare state should do for women are the three important threads to follow through this necessarily brief account of the development of the opportunity structure for German feminist mobilizations.

THE GERMAN "FIRST-WAVE" WOMEN'S MOVEMENT

As in the earlier movements in the United States and France, the first feminists in Germany were liberal revolutionaries. Like their male comrades on the barricades, they were part of the 1848 struggle to form a united democratic state from multiple German-speaking princedoms. The feminist newspaper published by Louise Otto-Peters made her the most visible advocate of the position that a state founded on principles of liberty and equality demanded full citizenship rights for women. Her claim was phrased in terms of "women's right to political and economic self-determination" (*Recht der Mündigkeit und Selbstständigkeit im Staat*), and these broad principles included the right to education, economic independence, access to any profession or occupation, and individual political self-expression.

Such issues of self-determination became the core of the conflict between the "proletarian" and the "bourgeois" women's movements, characterizations that were used polemically at the time and have been adopted by historians as labels.[18] Two closely related debates characterized this conflict: over women seeking economic justice in their own right (*Selbstständigkeit*), rather than protection in male-headed households; over political self-representation (*Mündigkeit*), rather than deferring to any male-led political party to decide what would be good for women. In a climate dominated by struggle over socialism, the answers feminists gave to these questions determined their political alliances and shaped what overall success could look like.

Advocacy for women's economic self-determination cut across class in the early years. Otto-Peters was as strong an advocate for better wages for women factory workers as for women's right to education and a profession. The General Association of German Women (ADF) she founded in 1869 pushed both for women's education (eventually establishing precollege education for girls) and for all-woman trade unions.[19]

Women's own self-representation, their voice as citizens, was the central issue for social, political, and economic rights in feminists' view, but it was not immediately obvious what the new "scientific socialism" emerging in the 1860s and 1870s would make of women's rights, since the male leaders were themselves divided. Ferdinand Lasalle's 1863 position against women's rights was endorsed by the first German trade unions, founded in the 1860s, which did not accept women members before the 1890s.[20] They decried women's employment as "one of the most scandalous abuses of our times" and attacked Otto-Peters for supporting it.[21] But August Bebel, a friend of Otto-Peters, argued that women's employment contributed to their emancipation and that women's status was a marker of national progress. His tremendously influential 1878 book, *Women and Socialism,* made the case for seeing women and the working class as the two most oppressed groups, joining their struggles politically and defining women's employment as a necessary stage of political and social development.

Class Polarization and Feminist Mobilization

Although Otto-Peters believed that claims that "the position of women can only be improved through the position of men flew in the face of all civilization and humanity," Bebel did not agree.[22] His view, which became the official position of the Social Democratic Party (SPD) in 1891, was that women should support the socialist struggle, since only through its victory could they achieve their own. Women's cause was to support socialism since socialists had made women's cause their own by endorsing universal suffrage. The German SPD soon became the largest and most influential socialist party in Europe, but feminists who insisted on women representing themselves were not happy.

The practical conflict focused on SPD opposition to women's unions and liberal women's skepticism about when and how socialists would help women workers. As the later women's rights campaigner, Hedwig Dohm (1831–1919), pointed out, the strategy of seeking a "family wage" for men and "protective" limitations on women's employment at night or in certain occupations did not keep women out of the worst jobs; instead, men's objections to women's employment "began as soon as women began to earn more than a pittance." She argued that women's *own* political organizing was the best means to combat *women's* poverty.[23]

But the SPD increasingly defined a male breadwinner and a female housewife role as what men (and women) really wanted, though working-class women and women socialist leaders like Clara Zetkin (1857–1933) protested. In 1889 Zetkin was still arguing that women "demand no more protection than labor as a whole demands against capital," but the SPD favored state protection and helping women with "their" family responsibilities over women's rights to economic independence and self-determination.[24]

In the 1890s, Zetkin accepted the need for socialist party leadership and a unified struggle of the working class, so gender and class politics split apart. Now liberal feminists appeared not as potential allies but as rivals for support of working-class women. She was vehement that "left-liberal" feminism was dangerous for proletarian unity," and that socialists should refuse to participate in any organization "that limits itself to the problems of feminism."[25] In the party newspaper for women she edited from 1891 to 1916, *Die Gleichheit* (Equality), Zetkin attacked liberal feminists as *Frauenrechtlerinnen*, "women's righters," a term that carried increasing opprobrium.

These "women's righters" were similarly engaged in polarizing feminism on class lines. The main women's umbrella organization, the Bund deutscher Frauenvereine (BDF), formed in 1894 at the impetus of the international women's movement, excluded socialist women and was conservative by international standards. They did not even endorse a demand for women's suffrage until 1902, when Germany's ban on women's political groups was relaxed.[26] Although advocacy for social justice across class lines runs through the writings of left-liberal feminists (Hedwig Dohm, Lily Braun, Minna Cauer, Lida Heymann, and Alice Salomon among the best known), they were not only spurned by socialists but often treated as traitors to their class by other "bourgeois" feminists.[27]

By the outbreak of World War I, two mutually hostile German women's movements were mobilizing, fighting each other in class-defined terms and developing class-based constituencies among women. Middle-class women used higher education and careers as alternatives to marriage, and working-class women struggled under long hours of paid work, child care under brutal conditions, and the needs of husbands who expected service and deference at home. Yet the heart of the "woman question" was always about more than conditions of work. Left-liberals such as Cauer, Heymann, and Braun emphasized this when advocating women's political self-determination. Were women individuals and citizens, or just dependents of men?

It was important for the later development of German feminism that the SPD answered the "woman question" in the latter terms, fostering social protection over self-representation. The socialist party agreed in principle with Christian and nationalist conservatives on a distinct place for women in the family where individual male authority was paramount; it differed in wanting this kind of family for working-class men too. Although it consistently supported women's right to vote, the party—and the trade unions allied with it—disparaged and undermined women's independent self-organization as a threat to the common good of the (patriarchal) family. Neither Left nor Right supported women's self-determination.

"Father-State" and His Daughters

The authoritarian nature of Imperial Germany also shaped the way class and gender intersected.[28] Women were placed outside of politics and subservient to the German state. Socialists were repressed around the world, and women could not vote anywhere, but their capacity for political action was exceptionally limited after the military suppression of the 1848 revolution. Liberal tenets such as universal male suffrage and free speech were not institutionalized in Imperial Germany, and even men's demands for democratic rights faced entrenched opposition.

Class divisions among feminists were exacerbated by the Exceptional Law against Social Democracy, which from 1878 to 1890 made the SPD illegal, producing in socialists a sense of outsidership and in liberals a suspicion that this movement supported "dangerous revolutionaries."[29] Because women were forbidden collective political organization until the Law of Association was relaxed in 1902, they were liabilities rather than assets for liberal political organizers, who feared sharing their exclusion.

Regardless of their class and gender views, all women were political outsiders and dependents of a literally male state, in which the dominant political classes were the military, the agricultural aristocracy in the east (*Junkertum*) and the administrative elites of the state bureaucracy. The German state at the turn of the century was not only socially hierarchical (*Standesstaat*) and politically repressive (*Obrigkeitsstaat*). It was also relatively generous with social benefits. Generally viewed as the originator of the modern welfare state, the conservative Chancellor Otto von Bismarck saw the best interests of the German Empire as served by damping down the conflict between capital and labor. To reduce the oppression fueling socialist enthusiasm, Bismarck's social policy initiated such protections for workers as unemployment insurance, health care benefits, and workplace safety measures.

Would the state also mitigate gender oppression by reforming family law? Change in family authority relations took place in this Empire, but not as feminists hoped. Imperial Germany's 1900 Civil Code (Bürgerliches Gesetzbuch) took a step backward from the rights women had enjoyed in many individual German states. It proclaimed the family as the "*Keimzelle* [the organic basis or fundamental germ cell] of state and society," legally constructing women only as wives and mothers.[30] Although England and the United States had already passed laws ensuring married women control over their own property, the new Civil Code gave husbands the right to forbid wives' employment, to control all income from their property, and to have final say over what was in the best interests of children or marriage.[31] The SPD accepted the change, and middle-class feminists mobilized protests, but in vain.

Family law, broadly understood, became the heart of the self-determination issue for left-liberal feminists. Notable among these groups (excluded as too radical by the BDF) was the Bund für Mütterschutz und Sexualreform (BfM, League for the Protection of Mothers and for Sexual Reform, founded in 1904), led by Helene Stöcker (1869–1943).[32] In the 1910s these "radicals were drawing the consequences of their liberal individualism and applying them to personal life" by pressing for legal equality in marriage, easier divorce, an end to police interference in breaking up free unions, and equal rights for children born of nonmarital relationships.[33] No similarly wide-ranging assault on bourgeois prudery and its consequences for women took place in the United States until the 1960s.

Taking up women's legal self-determination also meant pressing for de-stigmatization of unwed motherhood and decriminalization of abortion. Women should, the BfM argued, be free economically as well as socially to make their own decisions about bearing children. "Father-state" (*Vaterstaat*) was seen as actively supporting male interests by denying women choice over their own lives, both inside marriage (granting men the legal right to make familial decisions) and outside marriage (taking over legal guardianship of children born out of wedlock). Self-determination became crucially linked not to marriage alone, but to motherhood and the state's role in regulating it.

For women's rights and for feminism, Imperial Germany left several important legacies. The significance of class conflict for state politics is most central, since it institutionalized the division between working- and middle-class feminists. Explicit repression by the state, division in a Left-Right partisan struggle, and exclusion from the early development of the welfare state combined to make women quintessential political outsiders. The male-breadwinner family was defined as a social good for all social classes. Father-state was both authoritarian and generous to "his" children, but the maleness of state power was undisguised. Women's self-determination was the defining act of resistance to "his" control, and motherhood emerged as a key arena of struggle, as feminists focused their challenges on the illegality of abortion and legal subordination of unwed mothers.

The "woman question" posed by the modernization of society was therefore an important part of German state formation, even though women were not allowed a political voice in which to give their own answer. As a result, women's desire for autonomy and self-determination was set at cross-purposes with the male-led reconstruction of gender relations in this rapidly industrializing, imperial state. Feminist struggle became a characteristic of the highly politicized Weimar Republic in the 1920s.

SEXUALITY AND NATIONHOOD IN
WEIMAR AND NAZI GERMANY

The German Empire ended with a revolution. In the closing days of World War I, soldiers and sailors rose up against their commanders, and cities were taken over and run by revolutionary workers councils. The provisional, socialist-led government concluded a peace treaty and began to organize a new national state. Gender relations remained a contested element of this new state's authority.

The constitutional assembly that met in Weimar conferred on women the right to vote but explicitly limited women's equality to the public sphere (*staatsbürgerliche Rechte*), rejecting efforts to reform the Civil Code and empower women within the family. Against continuing calls for reform from liberal feminists, the Center Party, the political representative of Catholicism, argued that women's subordination in the family was natural and "prepolitical." There was no broad coalition in Parliament to challenge this view, although some liberal lawyers and socialists called for reform.[34]

Women's claims to self-determining motherhood remained explicitly contested. The openness with which the state intervened to regulate women was matched by women's overt political resistance to state control and demands for state support for their civil rights. This struggle is most clearly seen over the issue of legal abortion.

Abortion Rights as an Unfinished Agenda

Even before the war, the BfM had pressed for the total elimination of Paragraph 218 of the Criminal Code, the law that punished women for procuring an abortion by sending them to prison for five years. The League advocated complete legalization of abortion in the name of self-determination, connected abortion rights to financial and moral support for unwed mothers as equally essential to women's free choice of maternity and control over the conditions of their existence.[35] Its position paper for elimination of §218 argued in 1908, "as a free person, the woman must be allowed to be the mistress [*Herrin*] of her own body. She therefore sees it as an unjust attack on her right to self-determination if she is to be punished because she has destroyed a cell that is at this point only an inseparable component of her own body."[36]

Abortion and women's citizenship were linked in the public mind. The League made legalization of abortion part of public debate before the war, defined from the outset as women's self-determination. Even the conservative BDF challenged §218 as a "shameful paragraph," calling for an end to punishment in cases where there were medical, eugenic, or ethical grounds for abortion. Camilla Jellinek, a member of the BDF's legal commission, wrote passionately, "For me there is no doubt: if men had to bear children, no male §218 would ever have been created!" She demanded complete elimination of the law "in the name of the right to self-determination, in the name of the free personhood of the woman."[37]

German women's limited status as citizens did not deter them from demanding the right to abortion. Control over motherhood was framed as a fundamental civil right. Thus this liberal women's movement was by 1908 emphasizing women's right to self-determined motherhood, when American feminists were barely able to raise the issue of legalizing information about contraception (in the face of national anxiety about the tide of immigration and White "race suicide").

Despite the high level of engagement women brought to legalization of abortion in Germany, even after the revolution that brought a socialist government to power, the criminal law remained virtually unchanged. Socialists kept a focus on class rather than women and did not adopt the feminist self-determination frame. They condemned §218 as a "class paragraph" that was not enforced against middle-class women and focused on working-class women's deaths from botched abortions (estimated at twenty-five thousand annually) and on the "reserve army of labor" produced for capitalists by coercing poor women to bear children.[38] Only the far-Left parties, the USPD and KPD, pushed for repeal, while the main body of the SPD came along "lamely, with hesitation and resistance," Zetkin complained.[39]

The competition among these socialist parties in the Weimar legislature also made it difficult to produce a bill that could pass.[40] Throughout the 1920s, ending the criminalization of abortion grew as a political issue on the streets (leading to more than eight hundred local protest groups and fifteen hundred mass demonstrations against §218 by 1929–30), but parliamentary reformers were only able to slightly widen the exceptions under which abortion might be legal.[41] Efforts to strike the law completely came to naught as the Nazis took power in 1933.

At that point, the abortion issue became inextricably interwoven with the abusive and racist reproductive politics of the Nazi period. In addition to the genocide directed against Jews, other "less worthy" ethnic groups such as Roma (Gypsies) and Slavs (such as Poles) were attacked less systematically, with the Nazis claiming a need to protect and make space for the German people (*Volk*) of the Aryan race. In the name of eugenics, improving this "race" of Germans, the mentally and physically disabled were the first targets for elimination, as "life unworthy of life." Aryan women were to be severely punished for abortion, even as abortions were to be forced on others. In 1935, the Nazis introduced a "eugenic justification" for abortion into the criminal code, and in 1945 they supplemented §218 with a clause demanding the death penalty for abortion "in cases where the vitality of the German people is threatened."[42]

Political and Social Rights

Abortion epitomized the concentration on civil self-determination that characterized the German women's movement. The civil dimension was not, however, their only concern. Political and economic rights were also part of their agendas.[43]

Political citizenship in the form of women's suffrage was conferred by the socialist revolution in 1919, with relatively little popular mobilization. Although suffrage was supported by both the socialist and left-liberal women's movement, it did not bring forth the emotionally and politically intense identification that suffrage campaigns elicited in the United States and Great Britain (or abortion rights did in Germany). The German Women's Suffrage Association (Deutscher Verband für Frauenstimmrecht) was founded relatively late (in 1902, at an international women's suffrage meeting in Washington, DC), and the mobilization remained relatively small on an international scale. For example, Schenk compares the thirteen thousand members in Swedish women's suffrage associations (in a population of about three million) in 1918 to the ten thousand members of the German groups (in a population of thirty-three million) that year.[44]

Women's social citizenship was also not strongly contentious, in the sense that the Imperial definition of women's welfare as secured through the partnership of the state and the male head of the family was continued in both the Weimar Republic and the Nazi dictatorship. Although left-liberal feminists objected, both the socialist and conservative-nationalist parties agreed that the goal was protecting women from (better) paid work and protecting the (male-headed) family by keeping women in the home.[45] In the 1920s, the declining birthrate, the economic crises of inflation and worldwide depression, and more relaxed sexual morality of the urban centers combined to label "the family" threatened. Measures to support childbearing, especially among the middle class, were proposed but few actually enacted in the party gridlock of Weimar. But the National Socialist regime took up the popular demand to support families as part of its agenda, and once coming to power, it passed measures to provide loans to newlyweds to help them establish a family (partially forgiven for each child born), to financially and symbolically reward mothers of large families, to provide summer camps and after-school activities for boys and girls, and to subsidize infant nutrition (all, of course, limited to the "racially pure").[46]

The priority of struggles for civil rights over political or socioeconomic rights of citizenship, that is, the relative emphasis on abortion rights over suffrage and family benefits as the causes for mobilization, was unusual among first-wave women's movements. This feminist agenda created a sense of unfinished business for the German women's movement in two ways. First, while women's suffrage after World War I (in Germany in 1919 and the United States in 1920) could be seen as closing a particular chapter of feminist mobilization in many countries where this had been the movement's priority, the failure to eliminate the abortion law remained a continuing grievance for German women and a claim with which to remobilize in the 1970s. Second, rather than dissipating into a variety of mixed-gender political organizations, as the postsuffrage generation did in many other countries, the first wave of feminism in Germany was brought to an abrupt halt by resurgent nationalism and the Nazi seizure of power. Exclusion from the state deprived the German movement of the "feminists in the woodwork" that provided young Americans with allies among the older New Deal activists and resources from postsuffrage women's organizations.[47]

Militarism and Nationalism

As an authoritarian national state (*Obrigkeitsstaat*) the Prussian-led German Empire placed a high value on hierarchy and obedience and celebrated the role of the military. Both the mobilization of national identity in the years leading up to World War I and the recriminations around the defeat and collapse of the state after the war made feminists even more marginal and maligned.

Facing the demands of war, nationalist sentiment was particularly heightened across Europe and the United States. Helene Lange, one of the BDF leaders, was not unusual in writing in 1915, "The wish to help the state, to be the last modest piece of national strength, sprang up in a single hour in millions of German women."[48] During the war, German state repression—censorship and imprisonment—was unusually powerful for those women who disagreed.[49] After World War I, the turmoil of revolution was also used by the right to attack pacifists, socialists, and feminists.[50] When the Nazis came to power in 1933, the BDF refused to be incorporated into the party machine and dissolved itself, but it had already shrunk into insignificance. Gertrude Bäumer, one of its last presidents, was co-opted into the Nazi mobilization and allowed to publish her magazine *Die Frau* throughout the war.[51] Alice Salomon and other Jewish feminists were forced into exile, along with pacifists and socialists such as Heymann.[52]

Only those feminists attacked in the Weimar and Nazi periods for pacifism or socialism were not seen later as discredited by their association with war and fascism. Their principled rejection of collaborating with the state in World War I appeared in the light of post-World War II experience as a shining example that the country had, to its loss, failed to follow. Unlike the feminist reformers of the postsuffrage period in the United States who chose to work through the political parties, whose efforts were enhanced by the New Deal, and whose legacy could be celebrated as progressive, only feminists who had resisted the state were applauded as worthy foremothers.[53] The lack of a credible reform tradition and relative exclusion from state-led welfare programs before the war defined German women's activism as wholly outside the state, while US feminists were heartened by the New Deal and less skeptical of being involved in state projects.[54]

The Nazi regime further affirmed the self-pronounced maleness of the Imperial German state epitomized in its bureaucracy, its universities, and its military, so women's political outsiderness was unchallenged. This encouraged feminists at first to define women as inherently victims of National Socialism, not recognizing their roles as participants and beneficiaries. How to tell the story of the Nazi dictatorship became a crucial problem for a new generation in the 1960s, as part of a broad West German effort to "cope with its history" (*Vergangenheitsbewältigung*).[55] But, like all German politics after World War II, this challenge was placed in a newly bifurcated nation.

THE COLD WAR AND "SYSTEM COMPETITION"

The four-zone occupation of Germany after World War II began the division of the country into two competing social and political systems, confronting each other with hostility and offering sharply contrasting images of women's roles in society. As the cold war drew a sharp dividing line through Germany, the Red Army, the Soviet government, and Russian-sponsored German socialist leaders determined the shape of post-Nazi politics in the Eastern zone under their command, while the American, British, and French forces created shared institutions in the three Western zones. The face-off over the future of Germany was played out in two major East-West confrontations: the Soviet blockade and airlift of supplies to Berlin in 1948–49, and the building of the Berlin Wall in 1961.

These battles of the cold war exemplify the extent to which the hot front of communist-capitalist confrontation ran through German politics. The gender dimension of nation-building carried forward political legacies and reworked them, now in the context of two hostile states.[56] In 1949 the Soviet zone of occupation in the East became officially a new socialist state, the German Democratic Republic (GDR), led by a single-party government created by the forced merger of the Social Democratic and Communist parties in a Socialist Unity party (SED). The Federal Republic of Germany (FRG) created in the West was structured by the Basic Law (Grundgesetz) that set out constitutional principles under the leadership of Christian-Conservative parties (CDU and CSU). Both new countries had to demonstrate loyalty to the guiding principles of their occupiers and distinguish themselves from each other. For both East and West, shaping an appropriate German state to embody their interests and express their values was done in part though gender and family politics, in part by the gendered politics of militarization and peace.

The definition of the West German state (FRG) as offering a clearly better alternative to the East German state (GDR), and vice versa, helped make gender and family relations central. Since whatever the GDR was for, the FRG was against, the East's rhetorical embrace of antimilitarist and profeminist politics became a reason to discredit pacifism and feminism as "communist" in West Germany. The cold war inspired a similar turn to Christian nationalist principles in the United States in this period (putting "In God we trust" on coins and adding "under God" to the Pledge of Allegiance). System-competition, US-style, defined the United States against "Godless Russia" and its "antifamily" policies, hunted communist sympathizers, demonized the Left, closed wartime child-care centers, and pushed women out of the labor force. West German politics defined itself against the GDR, whose family politics encouraged women's labor force participation and offered particular support for women raising children on their own.

Moreover, the German women's organizations that formed in the few years between the end of the war and the division into two antagonistic states were put in the position of having to choose sides. The polarized positions of the bourgeois and proletarian women's movements were reproduced in the exclusions and suspicions of the cold war, including conflict between liberal and Left groups. On the one side, socialist and pacifist groups merged into the

Demokratische Frauenbund Deutschlands (DFD), which was originally active in all zones. The DFD came under the party domination of the SED in the East, and by 1957 it was officially banned as an "anticonstitutional" group in the West. On the other side was the main umbrella organization in the West zones, the Women's Council, Deutscher Frauenrat (DFR), formed from the 1969 merger of the Deutscher Frauenring, founded in the British zone, and the Information Service for Women (Informationsdienst für die Frau), originally financed by the American High Command to "bring democracy to the Fräuleins." The organizations for women in West and East emerged from and still faced conflicting national projects.

Constructing Gendered Nationhood in the West

The women's civic groups that came together in the DFR understood their umbrella group to be the successor to the pre-Nazi women's organization, the BDF.[57] Like the BDF, it was to be middle-class, nonpartisan, and a lobby rather than a social movement, and like the BDF, it leaned in a conservative direction. Its first president, Theanolte Bähnisch, defined it as moving "far from any suffragette style" and toward a "bread and potato politics" that would help to manage public affairs "like a household."[58] This family-oriented notion of women's politics was embraced in the West as restoring stability and order to the state. The family as *Keimzelle* (nucleus) of the state was to be directly secured through active state policy that would bring back the male-headed family, endangered by the surplus of women created by the war.

Although—or perhaps because—the war left women the majority of the population, created a large number of single mothers, and encouraged reliance on women workers to begin the process of economic reconstruction, the Christian-conservative parties (CDU and CSU) that dominated postwar West German government specifically pushed for the restoration of men's economic and political leadership, with women's role complementary and domestic. This restoration of the "Christian ideal of the family" was explicitly promoted as a bulwark against "godless communism" in the East.[59] Supported by the majority of the SPD no less than by conservatives, the West's social legislation revived the provisions of the Civic Code that gave fathers a position of authority in the family, delegated to this male-headed family responsibilities for economic support of women and children, and reinstated the criminalization of abortion of the Weimar era.[60]

The DFR, like the BDF before World War I, saw women's pacifist and so-cialist groups as antipatriotic and dangerous, saying that "the word peace has become an alias for communism."[61] Even the Women's International League for Peace and Freedom was expelled from under its umbrella. By 1950, chapters of the socialist Deutscher Frauenbund Deutschland (DFD) were excluded from "general" women's congresses in the West. The West German Women's Peace Movement (Westdeutscher Frauenfriendensbewegung) was formed to chal-lenge German rearmament but lost its battle to have the SPD join in resisting this national turn away from repentant antimilitarism. The DFR refused this women's peace group membership in its organization because it saw peace as a suspiciously leftist claim.[62]

Under the mentoring of the British and American occupation forces, and with their active funding, women's groups in the West were guided toward the single goal of civic education. All "real politics" were to be left to the parties, whose policy prescriptions were to reconstruct the German family, military, and state. Such male-defined politics prompted resistance from women activists. Elisabeth Selbert, an SPD representative to the constitutional assembly draft-ing the new state's Basic Law in 1949, was the most effective campaigner. She choreographed an outpouring of indignation and enthusiasm from women's groups all over the country to insure that Article 2 Section 3 of the new Basic Law would affirm, without qualification, that "women and men have equal rights."[63]

Incorporation of this equal rights clause in the constitution was not triv-ial or merely symbolic politics—it had to be fought for, and in principle the wording could have been read as extending not only political but social and civic equality of citizenship to women. But both the legacy of hostility among socialist women to liberal "women's righters" and the institutionalization of gendered state policy (men's family wage and women's protection at work) meant that only a few scattered liberals campaigned for real equality in civic, political, or socioeconomic rights. Accepting equal rights as part of the con-stitutional text, the Constitutional Court also affirmed the "functional dif-ferentiation" between women and men institutionalized since the 1900 Civic Code. Its practical decisions affirming difference reinstitutionalized the politics created to privilege the male-breadwinner family. This support was reimagined constitutionally as support for "the family" as such and took precedence over women's own rights.[64]

Maintaining the male-breadwinner family, including valuing and supporting the complementary role of the housewife, explicitly became part of the "social market economy" intended to make West Germany an effective bulwark against communism. So when the increasing prosperity of the economic miracle of the 1950s brought labor shortages in West Germany in the 1960s, the policy response was to import male labor from other countries, rather than facilitate women's employment, the path taken by other countries such as Sweden. Core to the national values West Germany was defending in the cold war was its breadwinner-housewife family.

Constructing Gendered Nationhood in the East

On the other side, the East German state was also making gender and family relations symbolize its commitment to the socialist claim to emancipate women. It argued that gender relations were indicative of the national development of the state, as Bebel's *Woman and Socialism* had claimed. As the GDR engaged in competition with the West, its boast was in how independent and free its women were, and how well the state supported them in their work both in and outside the family. The GDR also faced a steeper climb back from the war's devastation than the FRG, in part because of the contrasting approaches the occupation took in the East and West.

Unlike the Western Powers' Marshall Plan of economic aid to foster German reindustrialization and democratization, the Soviet occupation dismantled much of the industrial infrastructure of the GDR and shipped it to Russia, and maintained a large number of prisoners of war in captivity for many years (increasing GDR reliance on female-headed families). It also imposed its own version of party unity and one-party government (including placing all civic associations "under the leadership" of the forcibly merged SPD and Communist Party, now known as the Socialist Unity Party, SED). The slide from a postwar, postfascist democratic interlude to a communist (SED) dictatorship meant that all grassroots organizations had to become (again) political echoes of the ruling party or disappear. Existing local women's groups were turned into chapters of the Democratischer Frauenbund Deutschlands (DFD), which took its direction from the SED leadership (and was symbolically led by the party leader's wife, Margot Honecker). All substantive political action, including family policy, came from a small group of male leaders in the Politburo.

Their vision of what was good for women, institutionalized in East German policy, was the opposite of the housewife model of the FRG. In the face of ongoing labor shortages, the GDR claimed to provide emancipation to women through inclusion in the labor force. From 1949 to 1972, it gradually implemented policies to encourage women to "rise" to the ideal of a male "productive worker": first, a legal right to employment and pressure to take a full-time job, then specific affirmative action programs for higher-level qualifications and nontraditional occupations; finally, an effort to expand kindergartens and other child care to facilitate the lifetime, full-time paid employment that was the male norm.[65]

The state also supported women's reproductive labor through direct subsidy of the major costs of living. Rent, basic foodstuffs, and public transportation were kept cheap, but the resulting shortages required huge investments of time, informal bargaining, and party connections to meet the needs of daily life. In the early years, many women took these hardships in stride, as part of the costs of building socialism in their country.

What women's "emancipation" actually meant in the GDR was unclear, even though it was not yet open to question. On the one hand, even though women's wages and access to better jobs were well below those of men, women's need to depend on a male wage to raise children was greatly diminished. In the 1950s and early 1960s women were more likely to be addressed as workers and comrades than as wives and mothers. On the other hand, women's struggle to do the work still defined as "theirs" at home was often overwhelming. Their formal equality as workers was undermined by the reality of their double day. Their ability to organize and articulate their own interests was also severely limited by the dominance of the DFD as the only legitimate "women's movement organization" and the repression of all other points of view.

Thus by the time the Berlin Wall went up in 1961, women in East and West were embedded in contrasting gender and family regimes driven by cold war politics.[66] In the West, de-Nazification and demilitarization were blocked by the occupying powers' decision to prioritize developing West Germany as the front line of anticommunism. A reformed but reinvigorated military, a vigorous social market economy, and a male-dominated, male-breadwinner family were developed as complementary state objectives. In the East, the GDR was to be a showplace for the achievements of socialism, with women's emancipation, as one of its leading accomplishments, displayed to the rest of the world.

Political diversity was subordinated to the forced unity of the SED, and the party leadership—a male reification rather than representation of the working class—exercised the real power of the state.

Once again, women's polarization along lines of class politics was institutionalized. The proletarian women's movement was represented by the passively bureaucratic, co-opted DFD in the "workers' and farmers' state" of the GDR; the bourgeois women's movement was revived in the nonpartisan civic educators of DFR, who—like their predecessors in the BFD—excluded pacifists and leftists. In both cases, the formal organizations available for women's politics were hierarchical, outside the main channels of political influence, uninterested in the unruly and emotional politics associated with social movements, and mobilized to advance their own state's vision of what gender relations should look like. Neither organization challenged the gender institutionalization promoted by male-led parties, making both conservative, though in diametrically opposite ways.

Moreover, divergent opportunity structures were not merely organizational but discursive. Both states endorsed women's rights as principles, but both channeled the meaning of women's emancipation through a filter of family politics shaped by their position in the global conflict over socialism. This structure was available to resonate with transnational calls for women's emancipation as they began to arise in the 1960s, but the particular claims that would be effective in mobilizing German women were distinctly different from those that brought women in the United States and UK out on the streets.

CONCLUSION: LIBERALISM AND FEMINISM

Although a class division between liberal and socialist visions of women's political interests was common in all first-wave feminist movements in industrial societies, Germany was distinctive in the relative weakness of the liberal view, the strength of the socialist one, and the vehemence of the conflict between them. While American feminist organizing was affected by the racial order of the state and the relative exclusion of socialist perspectives from politics, the repeated marginalization of left-liberal feminist discourse had powerful effects in Germany. Understanding this path dependency as both discursive and institutional directs attention to aspects of this history that were influential in the choices German feminists made in the 1960s and beyond.

First, the class-first framework of intersectionality was not so strong a discursive resource in Germany as in countries like Sweden or Finland in the 1960s because of the level of polarization among German feminists. Moreover, suppression of the Left in the West and the diversity-smothering "leadership" of state socialism in the East tended to reduce the political space for women's autonomous mobilization to represent their own interests. When conservative and nationalist parties won, women lost; when socialists won, women's gains were modest at best. Civil liberties such as free association, free speech, and free choices in private matters, the essence of political liberalism, were restricted in all Germany through 1945, and continued to be so in the East. Even in the West, the civil rights claims middle-class feminists had raised in the 1920s were unfulfilled, as family law trumped women's own choices about their private lives. This language of self-determination was a radical discourse with resonance among all German feminists. It had few institutional anchors, but well-known implications for women's freedom to organize politically, act collectively, and make individual decisions about motherhood, work, and sexuality.

Second, the conflict among women on class lines made claims about solidarity problematic in all eras, but also highlighted the importance of solidarity for accomplishing feminist aims. The socialist demand for class-based solidarity had been politically effective, bringing the party to power in Weimar and the GDR. Women's solidarity could be an important political resource, and it could be (at least in theory) created by the choice to subordinate other interests to the common objective of emancipation. Not by ignoring their differences but by deciding that they would not be divisive, women might be able to construct an identity that worked for them as class had for (equally diverse) "workers." Rather than appearing as an appeal to a supposed biological essence—as in the United States—claims to speak "for women" in the German context were more directly political.

Third, the history of authoritarian politics in Germany led women to question what collective political power would be good for. Unlike the liberal ideal of individual interests and pluralist debate, the historical trajectory of German state-building embraced elite decision making and social and political exclusion. Thus women's exclusion from state and politics had become naturalized as an inherent inconsistency between women's nature and the nature of the state. Of course, many other countries had a view of womanhood as peaceful, domestic, child-centered, and cooperative, but German state formation also institutionalized militarism, hierarchy, conflict, and maleness as characterizing the state. Women were more aggressively excluded and suppressed politically, and social welfare-state development after World War II followed patriarchal lines despite the efforts of Weimar women to set a different example.[67] Both domineering and benevolent images of fatherhood were institutionalized in the *Vaterstaat,* so German women could easily debate whether becoming free from this father would be good for them, but they could hardly imagine themselves as the state.

Finally, the agreement between conservative nationalists and socialists that the male-headed family was the nucleus (*Keimzelle*) of the social order and needed the active defense and economic support of the state created material interests for women as well as men in the continuance of patriarchy. West German women's life course was set by family politics that held them out of the labor force but offered them support as mothers and as dependents of men. Dependents' allowances for male workers and a panoply of social welfare benefits, steadily expanded from Bismarck's day, made all family members (correctly) perceive that their welfare depended on that of the male head of household. Liberal states such as the United States and Great Britain had gradually whittled out more and more rights for married women and left women's economic welfare largely in their individual hands, tied though they might be by discrimination against women. The East German regime had certainly not ended discrimination, but it did build on the legacy of single mothers created by war and imprisonment to institutionalize a family support system in which men's breadwinning was no longer central.

But all German regimes focused on family welfare and left women under male authority—their husband's, if married; the state's, if not. East German state socialism bragged about emancipating women but in practice subjected both women and men to the male political elite. In neither state were family politics, whether as welfare or rights, ever "private" matters as liberals would see them, a separate sphere set apart from the public domain. Because reproduction (and thus control over births and children) was always a matter for state concern, the public interest already extended, visibly and powerfully, into the workings of families through the actions of the state.[68] By contrast, the US racial order led to a decentralized family politics, differently conceived and executed across state and even local regimes, depending on the exigencies of segregation and subordination.

Feminists in the United States and other nation-states with traditions of liberal citizenship have been able to make powerful political claims to "equality"—the right to share equally in the rights of citizenship.[69] The distinctive weakness of liberalism as a resource for German feminism makes the "equal rights" approach problematic. Seeing how German feminists had to struggle to be heard lays the groundwork for recognizing the benefits as well as the costs the discourse of liberalism offers. Women would need to find their voices in a historical framework in which feminist claims had centered on autonomy, self-determination, gender solidarity, and resistance to the state. The more liberal elements in these claims remained radical, and articulating them would be a struggle of a different—but not greater or lesser—nature from that facing US feminists. It is to this specifically German struggle the next chapter turns.

CHAPTER 3

WOMEN THEMSELVES WILL DECIDE

Autonomous Feminist Mobilization, 1968–1978

I T B E G A N right after lunch on September 13, 1968. The national assembly of the German Socialist Student Association (Sozialistischer Deutscher Studentenbund, SDS) reconvened and took up its next order of business without discussing the feminist critique Helke Sander had offered just before the break.[1] Sigrid Damm-Rüger, one of the best-known women in SDS leadership, was more than a little annoyed that the meeting was moving on without responding to the points raised by Sander on behalf of the new Action Group for the Liberation of Women in Berlin. So she stood up and let fly—tossing tomatoes at the young man chairing the meeting. Ines Lehman, another leading woman SDS activist, jumped up to protect him, and the meeting erupted in chaos.[2]

What was it all about? One part was unmistakable. Just as tomatoes and eggs were flying regularly from the hands of SDS activists against public targets like buildings and politicians, this demonstration was meant to express collective disapproval. The leadership stood accused of silencing women in their supposedly democratic student politics. Activists and press understood immediately. Widespread coverage of the tomato incident made gender relations in the student movement a matter of public discussion.

Another part remains controversial. What kind of power and freedom did women need and want? Were women in SDS subordinated "brides of the revolution" or coleaders in revolutionary struggle, capable of representing their own interests, with speeches, tomatoes, or both? Were these women declaring themselves in opposition to SDS or expecting this act to bring their concerns into the movement, as part of a fight for common goals? Was the student movement splitting along gender lines, as the tomato-tossing gesture seemed to demonstrate, but the defensive gesture to deny?

The tomatoes brought women's politics new visibility, and initiated a new phase of West German feminist mobilization. The 1968 SDS national congress was an ideal location to make a public stand, since delegates came from all over the country. The women returned home with new ideas, diffusing them nation-wide. The time was as ripe as the tomatoes: the year 1968 has since come to represent an entire period of student mobilization and political unrest, when a "new" Left emerged in Western Europe and the United States, more participatory and movement-like than the "old" Left institutionalized in unions and political parties. This New Left was marked by its nonhierarchical style and public confrontations against state violence. In the United States, demonstrations condemned the bloody involvement in Vietnam and the shooting of student protesters at Kent State. In West Germany, protests focused on American imperialism in Vietnam, the CIA coup that installed the Shah in Iran, and police violence against student protesters in Berlin.[3]

The year was marked by intense conflict but also by revolutionary euphoria among the protesters. The idea that deep social change might actually be possible in the near future was in the air around the world. Women were stepping forward globally to ask just how deeply society must change to include them as full citizens and to determine where women fit in "the revolution." These were not new questions in Germany. Now they reemerged, intertwined with national and global rethinking of democracy and social justice.

Germany's polarization by class among women's groups, its historically justified concern with authoritarianism, its institutionalized state interventions supporting the patriarchal family, and its limitations on women's civil rights, including the continuing grievance about abortion law, shaped the way the transnational revitalization of feminism played out in West Germany. Competition between East and West and the heavy hand of state socialism provided top-down benefits to GDR women but limited the space in which feminist voices could be raised in the East.

In the West, the opportunity structure favored movement mobilization. Student activists in the streets, calling themselves APO (Extra-Parliamentary Opposition), demonstrated against the government. This government was led by a Grand Coalition between the Social Democrats (SPD) and the conservative Union parties (CDU and CSU), creating a supermajority with no meaningful parliamentary opposition (it controlled 90 percent of the votes).[4] When the government fell in 1969, it was replaced by a new coalition between the SPD and the small, liberal FDP (market-oriented and individualist), the first time the SPD had been able to appoint a chancellor since World War II. Chancellor Willy Brandt took as his slogan, "Dare more democracy." His government introduced a number of important changes, for example, giving workers the right to democratic participation in the management of their companies and beginning to open relations with the GDR. The window of opportunity for women to resolve the unfinished business of full citizenship had apparently opened, too. Decriminalizing abortion was back on the table, a change the FDP supported even more than the SPD did.

In the East, the Socialist Unity Party did not allow autonomous movements to blossom. East German women had a narrower window of opportunity and few conventional political tools, but they created a self-expressive space in fiction that they could not exercise in fact. GDR women's writing developed a counternarrative to the socialist claim to have emancipated them, offering a critique of the double day that was heard around the world.

In the West, the tomato toss signaled that women in the student movement saw new options for political action. The word that came to define this new feminist mobilization was *autonomy*. Autonomy meant many things for West German feminists, among them political independence, self-determination, gender solidarity, and resistance to the state. Little of this feminist politics looked like politics as men had defined it. Women strove to construct a culture that would both affirm gender solidarity among women and make them visible in the public arena.

The sections that follow first take up the explicitly political issues that became significant as a window of opportunity opened in 1968 in West Germany. The story begins in the student movement, where Sander's SDS speech provides clues as to why and how motherhood became so politically relevant. It then becomes national, as the feminist agenda of the 1920s returns in the form of renewed public debate over the legal status of abortion. As the movement found its identity, gender solidarity came to the fore, as feminists employed strategies for building awareness of women as a group, both among themselves and in the wider public. The discursive work needed, and the particular choices of how to frame this identity and agenda, drew on transnational sources in nationally specific ways. West German feminists used more overtly political strategies and the East more indirect ones, but language was central for both. Both historical legacies and strategic choices explain why autonomy became the defining concept for this new feminism. The differences in thinking about paid work for women in the class-centered German model of feminism and the race-centered American model help also to explain what made autonomy so important for the movement's future as well.

CONTROLING THE MEANS OF REPRODUCTION: REFRAMING THE POLITICS OF MOTHERHOOD

A four year old in blue jeans and a white shirt with a lace collar runs cheerfully through a large collective household—boy or girl? As a visitor, I have yet to be introduced, and as I watch the youngster, I pick up no gender cue besides the lace collar, which I decide means girl. The child turns out to be a boy, son of one of the five adults sharing the huge Bremen apartment in 1981—a *Wohngemeinschaft* (WG), or housing collective, a rational solution to low incomes and vast old, high-ceilinged apartments. As an American, I am familiar with many mothers' reluctance to put dresses on their daughters. Gender-free child rearing in the United States might include dolls for boys, but rarely lace or ruffles for either boys or girls.

The WGs, no less than the lace-collared boy, are part of the feminist politics that developed around family life in the 1970s in West Germany. This politics both problematized the situation of women as mothers and affirmed the meaning of motherhood in women's lives. Feminists sought to redefine maternity as the source of women's power rather than a justification for subordination, but the concrete problems of child rearing remained. Reconciliation between the time-consuming work of raising children and self-actualization as persons was to be achieved by restructuring gender and family relations based on changing the balance of power—women rather than men would be the decision-makers. Women would insist that the men with whom they worked and lived give up their male prerogatives and try to raise nonauthoritarian, less conventionally masculine boys. To reclaim motherhood from their mothers' version of it, women needed to change, too, to find their collective power to make the world mother-friendly.

Helke Sander's speech was more than a trigger for a tomato toss. It became a movement classic, capturing the claim for control over the power of reproduction that propelled the new movement forward.[5] Sander spoke as representative of the Action Group for the Liberation of Women, which had come together around a kitchen table in West Berlin to talk about their work as mothers.[6] A key issue was how child-care responsibilities blocked them from participating more fully in the student movement. The men were not willing to take on child care, allow children at their events, or even recognize the resultant marginalization of women as a problem. Sigrid Damm-Rüger, formerly a movement leader, was no longer among those at the podium—she had a two year old and was nine months pregnant when she threw her tomatoes.

This West Berlin group saw the practical problems they faced as characteristic of all mothers, and the transformation of mothers' lives as key to the transformation of society. The state had institutionalized a housewife-breadwinner relationship as essential to society's health, so women were locked into domesticity. Public child care was minimal, overcrowded, and oriented to authoritarian discipline of the children of single mothers and the poor. What mother wanted to see her child literally tied up when the teachers could think of no other way to manage their overflowing classrooms?[7] What kind of society raised its children in such a way? Moreover, the student leftists were beginning to ask their parents questions about fascism and criticize the "authoritarian personality" seen as contributing to Hitler's rise, making it easy to recognize that raising children to question authority could be both personally and politically important.[8]

There were empty storefronts all over West Berlin (a newly walled-in and economically struggling city), so these mothers resolved to take advantage of the cheap rents and form child-care collectives. The first five opened in 1968. They came to be known as *Kinderläden* (children's shops) and were emulated throughout West Germany. The storefront collectives were designed to offer antiauthoritarian child rearing and share the work of doing it. Women saw this as giving them time away from their children to do politics, or simply be themselves.[9]

The men in the movement were all for the *Kinderläden* in principle, but they did not share the work in practice. As Sander charged at the SDS congress, "The problem of authoritarian public child care became extended into antiauthoritarian dogma. . . . Naturally enough this did not lead to easier work and more time for mothers—which was the original point of the whole thing—but to still more work."[10] Women experienced the conflict between theory (the commitment they shared with men to a new, less authoritarian society) and practice (the responsibilities men did not share for realizing this new order) most directly in what socialist theory called *reproductive labor*: physical and social production of people.

Reorganizing reproductive labor was also the goal of the housing collectives. In theory, a WG would allow women more time not isolated at home with just their own children, more shared space to develop close friendships with other mothers, and more opportunities to leave their children in the care of someone whose politics of discipline was congenial while being politically active themselves. In practice, the alternative life seemed all too familiar: "unwashed dishes, dirty towels, chaotic kitchens, empty refrigerators, and pee on the toilet seat, because the gentlemen would just not sit down to piss."[11] But now they were not confronting this domestic labor alone; instead, they had a space in which to discuss it. In effect, the WGs created a context for doing politics inside the home. Literally meeting around a kitchen table, women defined child rearing and division of household labor as about power and justice—political issues.

Sander told her male colleagues that women already saw the personal as political. This was an insight women activists wanted to contribute to the whole movement, a lever to move all of West German society forward. Women with children not only formed the basis of society but were so caught in its contradictions that they would be "easily politicized," so men should "follow the women and help them carry out their politics" of addressing women's discontent.[12] To the Action Group women, this seemed one more way for the New Left to rethink socialist theory. Sander later called her confidence that men would follow women's analysis naive.

Sander's reframing of socialist theory struck a responsive chord among women at the conference. They carried its message to many other cities, where women began to develop their own "Women's Revolutionary Councils"

(*Weiberräte*).[13] Their analysis identified women's bodies as "the means of reproduction," essential to society, and thus a potential source of collective strength.
But, because women's power to bear children was actually controlled by men
and the state, it was converted into seeming to be a deficiency and used as a
justification for subordination, as if subordination were a result rather than a
cause of women's weakness.[14]

Class analysis still provided the lens feminists used to analyze gender relations. The subjection of women was not (as conventional socialist theory
claimed) a secondary contradiction added to the primary contradiction of class
relations, but a primary contradiction in its own right. It had to be addressed
by changing the relations of reproduction directly, now that "women were no
longer willing to define their ability to give birth as a naturally ordained social
negative."[15] The "ever-present concern among the Left with the question of
class . . . was no longer seen as the only determining one," since the question
now was "what a society would look like . . . where women with children were
not automatically thrown into a condition of dependence and unfreedom."[16]

After the infamous SDS meeting, the Action Group decided women alone
would have to determine what such a society should look like. By withdraw-
ing from men "in order to put ourselves in the position of finding our own
self-understanding, without compromises or other concerns," they made self-
determination salient.[17] Beginning in 1970, the Frankfurt *Weiberrat* began to
organize "women's forums" for discussing whatever issues women thought
mattered, both to develop a theory grounded in experience, beginning their
consciousness-raising type of organizing, and to create a new public space where
all women would be welcome, men not. That women had "power analogous
to the power of the proletariat" suggested revolutionary change was possible.[18]
This power might be expressed violently—an early and controversial Frankfurt
Weiberrat flyer included a picture of a woman with an ax and a set of penises
(of New Left men) mounted like trophies on the wall.[19] Others saw matri-
archy, as it appeared in socialist theory, as a historical reality of cooperative
nonviolence overthrown by male power. If the "world-historical conquest" of
women preceded the power capitalism exercised over other forms of labor, the
subordination of women was the primal form of exploitation.[20] These roman-
tics celebrated motherhood as peaceful and productive, where maternal power
would make for a harmonious new world.[21]

The essay on "Feminist Tendencies" in the *Women's Yearbook* (*Frauenjahr-buch '76*), published by the new Frauenoffensive press in Munich and edited by a work group of the Munich Women's Center, gives a good sense of early 1970s feminism. Describing their overview as a "kaleidoscope of what is presently 'in movement' and what self-conceptions the movement has," the editors sharply separated feminism from the Left and the Left's claim to represent the general social conflict, but also from being any mere "continuation of the suffragist struggle for the right to vote."[22]

In distinguishing themselves from the Left, the editors emphasized rejecting the leadership role assumed by the party and the primacy of class oppression; in separating themselves from the suffragist struggle, they turned away from claims to inclusion in the existing system of political decision-making. Their *Yearbook* essay on behalf of the autonomous feminist movement argued for patriarchy as the oldest, most fundamental relationship of exploitation. Hence the necessity of feminists' separating from men's organizations on the Left, since they would just use women's efforts to support their own goals, in which women's liberation did not count.[23] They also rejected engagement in policy reform as tokenism. This claim—common in many women's movements worldwide at this time—was framed in terms of specifically German policy developments. The new SPD government had given workers a right to codetermination (*Mitbestimmung*) of company policy by having representatives on corporate boards; the *Yearbook* editors echo the student movement's criticism of codetermination as co-optation.[24]

The editors of *Frauenjahrbuch '76* also explicitly distanced themselves from the language of liberalism, arguing that "equal rights define women's oppression as women's disadvantage." They explicitly labeled the equal rights version of feminism as wanting to be like men, vehemently rejecting claims that "women should enter all the male-dominated areas of society. More women in politics! More women in the sciences, etc. . . . Women should be able to do everything that men do." Their position—and that of the autonomous feminists represented in this 1976 yearbook—instead was that:

This principle that "we want that too" or "we can do it too" measures emancipation against men and again defines what we want in relationship to men. Its content is conformity to men. . . . Because in this society male characteristics fundamentally have more prestige, recognition and above all more power, we easily fall into the trap of rejecting and devaluing all that is female and admiring and emulating all that is considered male. . . . The battle against the female role must not become the battle for the male role. . . . The feminist demand, which transcends the claim for equal rights, is the claim for self-determination.[25]

Their claim for collective self-determination reconfigured socialist theory to remove "productive labor" (in the form of paid employment) from its central position. Rather than "becoming like men" by entering modern capitalist relations, women should return to the roots of their own power. As mothers, women should bring the men with whom they had children (and the boys they were raising) to respect and emulate the feminine as an alternative principle of power. That meant not only lace collars for their boys but demanding that men conform to women's norms rather than the other way around. Reflecting the complaints about men creating housework for women, the WGs operationalized their demand for men to defer to women's authority by developing a rule that men should not stand to pee, a prohibition that became institutionalized with the widespread use of stickers affixed to toilet seat lids, as depicted in Figure 1.[26]

As Marxist theory claimed for the proletariat, women in the *Weiberräte* wanted what "was most their own but also most taken away,"[27] to appropriate for themselves the power that had unjustly been taken from them. The theory put the "means of reproduction," women's ability to give birth, in the position classic theory gave to the "means of production," industrial labor in capitalist social relations. This gave a new frame to the unresolved question of the

FIGURE 1   This widely used sticker, intended to be affixed to a West German toilet lid, was a declaration that women had the power to set the rules for men, and that men could be expected to conform to women's norms rather than the reverse.

legal status of abortion. The women in the relatively small student milieu now worked with this new framing of a familiar issue to bring their demand for self-determination into the wider political arena.

KINDER ODER KEINE: HAVING CHILDREN
MUST BE OUR DECISION ALONE!

Conditions were ripe for a return to the abortion question.[28] The conservative postwar government had resisted legal reform—even rejecting exceptions in the case of rape, a widespread concern in the years of military occupation. In practice the number of convictions for illegal abortions steadily declined, from 1,033 in 1955 to 276 in 1969.[29] Although the law allowed women to be sent to prison for up to five years, the few who were prosecuted received light sentences. Lawyers and civic associations with a liberal philosophy, notably the Humanistische Union (HU), began to call for a reform of §218 to end the hypocrisy of selective prosecution, recognize advances in prenatal testing by providing eugenic exceptions, and finally make an exception for rape. When the SPD took charge of government under Brandt, it announced it would take up the problem.

In fact, the SPD only set up a commission of law professors that returned with a divided recommendation in 1973—a majority for legal abortion in the first trimester with counseling required beforehand (the *Fristenlösung*, or trimester rule), a minority for a wider set of permissible justifications for abortion, but leaving the decision in the hands of a medical authority (*Indikationslösung*, or justification rule). Institutionalized women's groups such as the Association of Women Lawyers (Juristinnenbund), the German Women's Council (Deutscher Frauenrat/DFR), and the women's committee of the SPD (Bundesfrauenausschuss) supported legalization in the first trimester, as did the junior partner party in government, the classically liberal FDP. But the autonomous women's groups that had formed since 1968, such as Frauenaktion '70 in Frankfurt, took to the streets, returning to the demand for complete elimination of §218 that had energized the movement in the 1920s.

Public interest was stirred by a creative protest action, the "self-incrimination" campaign. Drawing on the example of a protest in Paris the previous month, Alice Schwarzer, a feminist and journalist, organized women celebrities publicly to confess to a crime—that they had had abortions. In the June 6, 1971, issue of the popular magazine *Stern*, 374 women acknowledged their own abortions and called for total abolition of §218, not "charity from lawmakers . . . and piecemeal reforms." They also called for sex education, free access to contraceptives, and abortion coverage by health insurance. The campaign laid the women open to both moral disapproval and legal prosecution.[30] Investigations followed, but no prosecutions resulted, and six weeks later there were more than 86,000 similar written acknowledgments from less famous women. Following the feminist lead, 973 men admitted to having been "accomplices" in illegal abortions.[31] This self-incrimination campaign highlighted the hypocrisy of selective prosecution and women's actual need to resort to abortion, even when illegal.

This high-visibility strategy was the first salvo in a feminist campaign about women's self-determination. A national public call for eliminating §218, led by autonomous feminist groups and action committees on the local level, produced widespread mobilization. Nearly every city and town had an "anti-218 group" composed of women, claiming "my womb belongs to me" and "having children or not is our decision alone." Demonstrations targeted churches, government, and organized medicine. They included marches to city hall to formally renounce registration as a member of a church (since churches in Germany are tax-supported, the government tallies members from whom taxes will be collected), imaginative street theater (for example, wearing ball-and-chain and curlers), and "invading" hearing rooms where parliamentary committees were debating reform with no women present (as they did in May 1972 in Cologne). As protests mounted, movement activists began to be tapped as speakers for public hearings.

Protests also targeted doctors, who as a group were largely unsupportive of even modest reforms. Unlike in the United States, German abortion reform was never framed as privacy in medical decision-making, which would give doctors the right to exercise professional discretion, but as part of the overall struggle between women and the medical profession for control over women's health and bodies.[32] On the whole, German doctors were framed as opponents of women's self-determination.[33] The anti-218 groups staged street tribunals in which doctors were "brought up on charges" of hostility toward women and use of dangerous drugs.[34]

Feminist groups also took the lead in researching the technique of vacuum aspiration practiced in the United States and other countries (the more painful D&C was the norm in Germany). Schwarzer convinced the television program *Panorama* to show such an abortion, live. At the last moment, the show was censored by the station and not shown, giving rise to protests on the streets and clandestine showings of the film at feminist events. Both the self-incrimination campaign and the blank screen during the *Panorama* show highlighted the relationship between women and state repression and focused debate on the exercise of state power over women, not on the fetus.

The SPD, as the governing party, had to decide on a course of action. The leadership favored the more limited justification rule, but the party congress voted to endorse legalization in the first trimester. In April 1974, the law passed with a bare majority. It was immediately challenged by the Christian-nationalist parties (CDU and CSU), and in February 1975 it was overturned by the constitutional court, with reference to the clause in the post-Nazi constitution that binds the state above all else to "protect life."

The justices held that it was "not debated" that life began at conception, also unlike the US Supreme Court, which explicitly acknowledged religious diversity of opinion. But they also found that the state had a legitimate interest in protecting the life and health of women, not just the fetus. The state could not expect a woman to bear a child in situations where the burden on her would be too great (*unzumutbar*). The court thus explicitly opened the door to a justification-based law in which doctors and judges could decide what burden was "too great." The Bundestag then adopted a law permitting abortions when a doctor certified that eugenic considerations, situations of rape, risk to the mother's health, or an unspecified condition of social necessity existed. This last reflected the court's explicit discussion of class inequality and poor women, a theme that socialists had made central in Weimar debates. The West German court did not mention the liberal principles of privacy or the separation of church and state.[35]

Feminists were furious. The principle they had affirmed since the 1920s, that women were responsible for their own moral decisions about their own bodies, had been overridden. The law did open a backdoor for getting a safe and legal abortion by finding a doctor who would certify social necessity. In the period when this law was in effect (1976–90), approximately 90 percent of all legal abortions were approved on this social-need justification. The interpretation varied greatly by region, and women continued to protest the narrow and insensitive definition of social necessity applied in some places. But for many women it made safe and legal abortions available in practice.

This opening released some of the public outrage that fueled the broad mobilization of women, but feminists continued to protest the insult to their moral autonomy as decision-makers implied by the state's demand for approval by a doctor. Anti-218 groups publicly ran illegal bus tours to the neighboring Netherlands (where first trimester abortions were legal), so that women could get an abortion without having the humiliation of having to ask for permission. And regular demonstrations against abortion law remained a mainstay of local feminist organizing.[36]

Many other countries were liberalizing abortion laws in this period, and East German politicians were surely aware of this trend as well as of the feminist mobilization across the border. Without fanfare, in 1972 the East German government legalized all abortions in the first trimester.[37] Abortions needed to be done in a hospital, but there was no mandatory counseling, nor questioning women's reasons for her choice.[38] There was no open discussion of the reform at all, although it appears that letters to the party leadership and local representatives played a role behind the scenes. Women (and their husbands) argued that abortion was needed (usually for reasons of illness or more children than they could support), and the decision-makers apparently concluded that the reform was needed, given how difficult economic conditions still were.[39] Comparison with this less restrictive rule in the East now became a continuing source of discontent in the West as well as a point of pride for East Germans. When the West pointed to prosperity to validate its politics, women's greater emancipation was claimed as East Germany's accomplishment and reproductive rights became one potent symbol of this.

For feminists, then, collective independence from the male-led student movement meant autonomy, a term intertwined with both a public political demand for reproductive rights and a personal politics of *Kinderläden* and WGs.[40] Individual resistance to male norms of conduct and men's authority in the family became expressed in organizing apart from the Left and from men as a group. Autonomy meant decision-making in matters of reproduction, not political compromises centered on party strategy or charity from sympathetic judges, doctors, or the state. Becoming autonomous was a process of creating time and space for individual self-development, a claim that from the start had been the part of women's justification for *Kinderläden*. The concept did not lose its meaning of political self-determination, but in the course of the struggle it began to imply more about building up women's personal strengths and collective identity. Investments in self-development for women became a growing focus.

WOMEN'S SOLIDARITY: A GENDER NAMES ITSELF

In the early 1970s, at the local level, women's groups in West Germany not only campaigned against §218, they began to develop a sense of themselves as collectively making politics on behalf of a group called women. Being for women and their interests, as defined by themselves, had been a founding principle of Sander's Action Group in 1968. The notion of a gender "for itself" borrowed and transformed the Marxist distinction between a class with common experiences ("in itself") and one that asserted those interests politically ("for itself"). The related but not identical principle of beginning from one's own experience, rather than from socialist, Freudian, or any other doctrines, defined the early US consciousness-raising agenda too. As feminist activists in West Germany struggled to be "for women," they challenged "male theory" in the New Left and turned their attention to women's political claims in the United States and elsewhere. Building explicitly on the American model, they brought "consciousness-raising" and other US practices into their local groups. *Selbsterfahrung* (self-exploration) groups sprang up virtually everywhere in the West in the early 1970s.[41]

In the East, the blockage of international channels of communication and repression of local organizing not sanctioned by the party prevented this transformative process from gaining a foothold in such explicitly collective ways. One exception was found among women theologians, who were allowed to participate in some international congresses where feminism was in the air, and they laid the groundwork for East German church dissidence in later years.

But in West Germany, as in the United States, the challenges of naming women's experiences with oppression gave rise to diverse discursive resources. Women's centers, women's presses, women's bookstores, and women's bars and cafés blossomed everywhere. The first feminist newsletter appeared in

1973, under the title *Frauen gemeinsam sind stark*—literally, women together are strong, meaning, of course, sisterhood is powerful, the translated title of Robin Morgan's 1971 collection of essays from the US women's movement. Women around the country felt that taking society's discourse about women into women's own hands was a personal and political necessity.[42]

In these groups, women's relationship to the Left was a significant practical and theoretical issue. Within the broad culture of New Left politics, the new feminist movement differentiated itself from the male-led local groups that called themselves "the autonomous movement" (*die Autonomen*). *Die Autonomen* rejected hierarchical organizations and moved politically in the direction of anarchism, without a resonant issue like reproductive rights to reach and mobilize the mainstream. In feminist and leftist organizations, debates raged over how long the women of the *Weiberräte* should struggle to change "their" men's priorities and get issues of gender on the Left agenda, when they saw so few signs of success.[43] As the next illustration suggests, German feminists—in this case a West Berlin small group of socialist women—did not all break with the "male Left" but did appropriate the imagery of socialist revolution to express the fervor of their cause and connect their struggle with that of proletarian women of the past (see Figure 2).

But much feminist politics was being done at the private level of constructing a sense of being a woman "for women." Here the issue was how to relate to individual men. This was not just about the work of reproduction—the housework and child care men were disregarding in both theory and practice—but about sharing the pleasure of sex. In the early 1970s, many small-group discussions and local struggles revolved around the "battlefield of the mattress,"[44] as women tried to make their sexual relationships with men more equal and more rewarding.

This experience became broadly shared with the publication of Verena Stefan's *Shedding* (*Häutungen*) in 1975. As Ingrid Strobl recounts, "The enthusiastic reaction of recognition among hundreds of thousands of women readers was 'that's me' and 'that's just what happened to me.'" She describes it as the story of a woman

who was active in the Left. Unhappy with her body. Sexually unsatisfied. Step by step recognizing her comprehensive exploitation and devaluation, joining the women's movement, developing a new body consciousness, discovering her love for women

FIGURE 2 This poster's imagery draws on early twentieth-century socialist art. Its caption reads: "Forward! Women together are strong [that is, sisterhood is powerful]. International Women's Day. Come to the demonstration on Saturday, March 6, 1971, 2 pm, at Sophie Charlotte Place. Socialist Women's Group of West Berlin."

and "coming to her senses." A perfectly paradigmatic story of development—that's how it really was experienced by a whole lot of women.[45]

Shedding is written evocatively, almost like verse, and was an immediate best-seller, putting its brand-new feminist publisher, Frauenoffensive, solidly in the black. It not only inspired emulation but financially opened the way for a stream of successors, as hundreds of women picked up their pens, trying to put their own autobiographies of sexual awakening on paper.[46]

Shedding exemplified how the meaning of autonomy expanded to merge the call for personal sexual emancipation with justification for an organizational split with the male Left.[47] To embrace self-determination was not only to endorse a collective political goal, recognition of women's right to control their own reproductive power and use it as they chose, but to reevaluate how one's own life was organized. Dozens if not hundreds of *Selbsterfahrung* groups talked about power, and the topic that revealed power experientially was sex. Self-determination in sexual matters required knowledge, so women's centers and women's health centers were established in many cities. Like the "c-r" model itself, the centers drew inspiration from US feminists. They took up physical self-examination with a mirror and speculum, which had been pioneered in California and was already widespread in the United States.[48]

Autonomous feminists saw sexual self-determination as including lesbianism as a possibly empowering and satisfying choice. Because German autonomous feminists were not allies with, or potentially confused with, the Deutsche Frauenrat (as US collectivist feminist groups were with the National Organization for Women, which was trying to be mainstream enough to win cases and pass laws), the idea of recognizing lesbianism was not so explosive as it became in the United States.[49] While some German autonomous feminists resisted consideration of lesbianism as a form of politics, their hostility did not fracture the movement. By the mid-1970s, lesbians organized openly as part of the movement, and it was not a point of concern. Each Pentecost (a three-day weekend holiday in West Germany) there was a lesbian festival, and the rock band Flying Lesbians, founded in 1974, was playing sold-out concerts around the country.[50]

Much was similar in American and German debates about sexuality and self-assertion, including tensions between heterosexual and lesbian women, but the national context made the debate resonate very differently for the movement. Autonomous feminists were simply feminists in Germany. In the United States, "radical feminism" presented a comparable emphasis on self-determination—one that excluded men from the groups engaging in processes of self-examination, sought new words and forms of communication in a vast new wave of independent writing and publishing, and put sexuality in a central position in thinking about power and freedom. Even though American feminist scholar Catherine MacKinnon argued it was really "feminism unmodified," the "radical" label stuck for good reason. Its claims were inconsistent with both the dominant discourse of liberalism and the mainstream feminist groups whose agenda featured equal rights and social inclusion. Autonomous feminism in West Germany was not "radical" in this sense: it was the mainstream of mobilization, led the charge on abortion rights, which was feminism's most visible engagement with party politics, and resisted inclusion (whether in science or sport) as the opposite of real self-determination.

One particularly telling illustration of the difference between the US goal of equal rights and the West German goal of autonomy can be seen in the strategic ways the two movements pursued the ostensibly similar aim of transforming language. There were differences in the movements' own practices. For example, using "women's" as silent synonym for lesbian culture and lesbian identification became common in US feminism by the late 1970s, while lesbian groups themselves chose "womyn" and "dyke" as labels to make their politics visible.[51] "Women's" never meant lesbian in West Germany, as "feminist" or "autonomous" might. It became typical for autonomous German women, especially in the universities, to establish a "*Frauen- und Lesbenrat.*" Such use of "women and lesbians" together to describe feminist literature, meetings, or organizations was common. In the United States such a usage might imply that lesbians were not women or women not lesbians; in Germany it was an accepted strategy "to make lesbians visible."[52]

Overall, the direction of language change feminists sought in the FRG was not inclusion but visibility. The linguistic separation of women and men was a major goal. Critiques targeted how the German language hid women in supposedly inclusive but linguistically masculine terms.[53] As a grammatically gendered language, German demands occupational titles and collective nouns have gender (although neuter is a gender, too). Adding even one man to a group of ninety-nine women singers converted them all into masculine-gendered

Sänger rather than feminine-gendered *Sängerinnen*. Feminists, especially the trenchantly witty Luise Putsch, pointed out the destructive consequences for women's public visibility of such grammatical rules.[54] Declaring that gendered language patterns were social conventions open to change, not natural features of human cognition and communication, autonomous feminists set out determinedly to change them. Women should be made as visible as men, by say, advertising a "*Lehrer/Lehrerin*" teaching job to widen the image of the person that one was looking for, and any self-respecting woman should resist being forced to use an ostensibly gender-neutral but masculine form to describe herself. The supposedly impersonal form "*man sagt*" (one says) even developed an assertively feminist form: "*frau sagt*," expressing resistance to being absorbed grammatically into the "male form."[55]

This separation strategy contrasted with the American inclusive one of inventing new gender-neutral terms (letter carrier or flight attendant) to replace pseudo-generic forms (mailman or stewardess). This strategy paralleled US feminist attacks on segregation and discrimination, for example, suing to end newspapers' practice of separating job notices into "help wanted male" and "help wanted female." West German feminists pursued their dual-gender linguistic strategy energetically. In 1981 Lower Saxony became the first state to use the official title *Professorin*; in 1985 a female student in Hamburg was first granted a *Magistra Artium* rather than a *Magister* for her MA thesis. By 1989, the "feminized inclusive" plural (for example, *SängerInnen*) appeared even in nonfeminist sources.[56] This hard-fought victory made the issue of language particularly fraught as the unification process began in 1990; East German feminists proudly embraced their male-form titles in the male-typical jobs they held and did not understand why West German feminists would accuse them of undermining their own progress.

Yet the gender solidarity being constructed in linguistic struggle was an important part of the meaning of autonomy. A politics that affirmed women's collective power was reinforced by practices supporting an intensified sense of collective identity for the individual, and self-identifying speech is an important daily practice. Women needed to *experience* gender solidarity to feel that they had the ability to stand up and claim a place of their own on their own terms.

In sum, transnational connections with US radical feminist groups were important for developing organizational models and techniques that personalized the political. But unlike the United States, where allies or potential allies criticized such "radical" cultural strategies as apolitical, and mainstream feminists sought civil rights and social inclusion, in West Germany the creation of separate cultural space in which to build gender solidarity was the mainstream strategy for feminists and supported the struggle for public visibility.[57]

East German women did not have this much access to public space, but they also developed a strategy for making private politics visible, despite state censorship. The route they took was through literature, encouraging indirect actions and letters to authorities to make the state more aware of—and responsive to—the incompatibility of the demands it was placing on women collectively. The East German state (unlike many other countries in the Soviet bloc) emphasized women's emancipation as a goal, but initially pursued it only by including women in the "male model" of "productive" work, that is, not merely paid labor, but preferentially industry or agriculture that produced goods rather than supplied services. The state officially expected women to be committed workers but also mothers, wives, and active party members.[58] The gap between state definitions of women's needs and women's self-determination of what was good for them began to be explored in an emerging genre of "women's literature" that targeted the "superwoman" who could do it all and whom the state lauded.

Beginning with Irmtraud Morgner's *The Life and Experiences of the Troubadour Beatrice* (published in the GDR in 1974 and in the West in 1977) and continuing with Maxie Wander's *Guten Morgen, du Schöne* (1977) and Christa Wolf's *Kein Ort, Nirgends* (1979), the new women's literature of the East portrayed the grueling reality behind the superwoman myth.[59] But these works of fiction also offered images of self-confident women for whom both a job and a child were simply part of normal life. This normality was institutionally secured for GDR women in a way it was not for West German women. East German social policy facilitated women's employment by making employers provide on-site child care and cafeterias, as well as a full school day and hot lunches.

East German women eagerly took advantage of the educational and employment opportunities the state offered. Already in the 1970s this created the contradictions of the double day. They entered male-dominated occupations and pursued university degrees to a much greater extent than women in West Germany did. But they did not have the political opportunity to collectively reflect on the limits they faced on the job or the ability to challenge the terms of their inclusion in employment. Because there was less institutional blockage for women in the East than in the West, women in the East had less need to develop a language to challenge employment-centered values.[60] They became professors, carpenters, and accountants rather than fighting for feminine versions of the degrees or occupational titles that would make their presence or absence visible.

The absence of a radical language of feminist difference in the East was therefore due not only to state repression of consciousness-raising groups and political tracts, but also to the difference in opportunity structures that channeled women's interests in personal achievement and social change in different directions. The concrete benefits offered by the East German state, however, came not from engagement with the state but as patriarchally bestowed gifts. The GDR responded to system competition between East and West, its reading of women's literature, and its own interests in increasing labor productivity and population growth by offering new supports for women's reproductive labor.

Abortion was legalized for the first trimester in 1972, but women were also offered an increasing number of incentives to have children. The so-called baby year of paid maternity leave was introduced in 1976, and a paid "housework day" off each month gave married women time to take care of shopping and cleaning.[61] The "mommy politics" the state embraced in the 1970s marked the end of its commitment to bring women into the labor force on the same basis as men, but it did not end discrimination against women, permit women to organize outside the party, or create opportunities for political debates about gender and socialism. The DFD, the women's organization subordinated to the governing SED party, shifted in the 1970s away from being a voice for women on the factory floor and toward affirmations of women's labor at home. Despite the organization's tendency to become a "knitting club," some local groups found space there for more critical discussion.[62]

Given the repression of overt political opposition that characterized the GDR, women's discontent could only bubble up in coded form in literature. This literature so trenchantly named the problems of the double day that feminists in other parts of the world, including the United States, seized on it as capturing their own reality. Western feminists (not only in West Germany) sometimes looked East with envy at the benefits extended to women "over there" (*drüben*), but they also recognized East German women's literature as a deeply resonant critique of patriarchal inclusion.[63] In West Germany, this literature served to justify why seeking to succeed on male terms in the workforce was a foolish goal. In East Germany, concrete gains in the workplace and in economic and civil rights gave women a sense of progress. But the literature that captured the travails of ordinary women and articulated their longings gave the lie to claims that feminism was not stirring in the GDR.

RESISTING "FATHER-STATE":
CHALLENGES TO THE WORK-FAMILY STATUS QUO

Both German states institutionalized what father-state (*Vaterstaat*) should do to support the family and make family relations express state values. Both imagined themselves as generous protectors of women, but made different assumptions about women's needs. Despite its "equal rights" constitutional clause, the FRG institutionalized a strong breadwinner system in which men's roles as earners and women's as dependents were anchored in laws that secured men's privileges as heads of household (even the right to forbid their wives to work for pay), and in court decisions legitimating this power on the basis of "functional differences" between women and men.[64] The GDR framed the state itself as political and economic "head" of the nation, understood as an extended family for which the party made decisions. The state offered substantial economic benefits to families regardless of whether there was a husband present, and it drew women into the labor force, even when they were married.

Unlike the liberal understanding of separation between public and private and a thin, residual role for the state that characterized the United States, both German regimes actively constructed the state as an important actor in employment and family relations. The East repressed labor actions and popular protest, but in the West, the material position of women in the labor market began to be tentatively challenged.

Challenging Functional Gender Roles

Along with *Shedding*, the other 1975 feminist best-seller was Alice Schwarzer's *The Little Difference and its Big Consequences*. This book attacked the "functional differences" argument that the German high court accepted as a legal justification for treating women and men unequally. Schwarzer took the position that there was no gender difference that would be properly important politically, and many autonomous feminists scorned her emphasis on "sameness" as denying reproduction as an important gender difference and maternal power as a politically realizable goal. But women who felt stifled by being defined by their reproductive capacity, many of whom had no direct contact with autonomous feminist activism, found Schwarzer appealing.

Schwarzer's image of the emancipated woman was one who resisted being held down by marriage and motherhood, and who strode forward to make her own way in the world. For this, as well as the powerful personal stamp she put on all her projects, she was often critiqued in the movement as an *Einzelgängerin*, a woman who goes her own way and does not work for the collective good. The tension was between a liberal individual version of an emancipated woman (familiar in the United States as the superwoman) and the more dominant West German framing of emancipation as a collective transformation of power relations. Because Schwarzer did not campaign for the empowerment of motherhood as a social relation, many criticized her as being only interested in freedom for women who were not "typical" women, who were not mothers, carrying the burden of family labor and conventional socialization. But she was even more sharply attacked by those outside the movement as an *Emanze*, the emancipated woman who seems happiest in men's clothes and roles, like the nineteenth-century Luise Aston or George Sand.

Both criticisms strike wide of their mark. On the one hand, Schwarzer shared the conviction with many US feminists that the kind of work and life she was claiming for women was not male but human. As a professional journalist, she used her celebrity to offer herself as an image of liberal feminism that would reconcile achievement and femininity, not unlike Gloria Steinem. As a political activist, she targeted restrictive laws that limited women's self-determination as workers and restricted their reproductive autonomy. These work-restricting laws were often seen by social democrats, Christian conservatives, women themselves as "protective." Resisting such protection, as left-liberal feminists such as Otto-Peters had done, in favor of self-determination was still a radical act in the West German context, though it soon became mainstream in the United States.[65]

On the other hand, Schwarzer was deeply involved in feminist sexual politics, from the self-incrimination campaign for abortion rights she initiated to antiprostitution and antipornography campaigns in the feminist magazine she founded, *EMMA*.[66] Named for socialist Emma Goldman and aiming to be a newsstand rather than movement magazine, *EMMA* published its first issue in February 1977. *EMMA* gave Schwarzer continuing visibility as a feminist voice on political and social issues and, over time, gave voice to other feminist concerns, including sexual harassment. *EMMA* was comfortable with lesbianism and featured art and cultural events that highlighted lesbian presence in and identification with the feminist movement. The cover picture illustrated in Figure 3, for example, would have been shocking in the United States. Schwarzer would be difficult to classify in US terms as a liberal or radical; in West German eyes, she represented feminism.

Both *The Little Difference* and *EMMA* brought Schwarzer's personal vision of women's autonomy to the general public and associated it with the feminist movement as a whole. Yet her views fit uneasily with the autonomous feminist framing of women's issues, not only because she did not embrace a motherhood-as-power frame, but because she felt that women's autonomy depended critically on their economic contributions, political organization, and the freedom they could win in the arenas of law and politics. More a classic political liberal than a market-liberal, she challenged the economic status quo constellation of "social partners"—state, corporations, and unions—that represented men's interests at women's cost, but unlike many of her feminist critics, she thought women's autonomy required economic achievement.

Women Workers and the West German Movement

The idea that feminism implied a warrant for women to stream into the paid labor force as a means of securing individual autonomy via increased financial independence did not become popular in West Germany as it did in the United States. Changes in women's labor force participation in West Germany in the wake of feminist mobilization were trivial, from 48.5 percent in 1966 to 50.3 percent in 1986. By contrast, the American version of women's liberation encouraged many women to take jobs, knocked down institutional barriers of discrimination, and undermined cultural disapproval of mothers' employment. US women's labor force participation rates rose dramatically, from 45.5 to 64.9 percent in the same twenty-year period, whether as cause or consequence of US feminism.[67]

FIGURE 3 This cheerful and sexy *EMMA* cartoon of a lesbian couple, by staff
cartoonist Franziska Becker, indicates how both Alice Schwarzer and her magazine might
be considered radical in US feminist terms. Used with permission of Franziska Becker.

Paid work did not become a crucial issue for West German autonomous feminists for several reasons. First, there was little material infrastructure to support women who sought to increase their economic autonomy. Schools and shops kept short, erratic hours, child care was still scarce and unappealing, and part-time work was rarely available. In 1975, for example, stores typically opened at 9 or even 10 am, closed at 6 pm, were closed for an hour or more at midday and many Wednesday afternoons, and only opened one Saturday afternoon on each month and never on Sunday. Schools rarely offered lunch and often sent children home between 11 am and 1 pm (unpredictably from day to day and week to week).[68] There were fewer than twenty-five thousand early child-care places in the entire FRG.[69] Creating labor-force opportunities for women would have demanded a campaign to build the infrastructure to replace rather than reward the labor this system demanded.

Second, West German women who wanted more economic opportunities in the labor force had few political allies. Unions were dead-set against expanding shopping or school hours or offering more opportunity for part-time work. Longer opening times would be "antisocial" for the (male) workers, who wanted to go home to their families; adding part-time workers was seen as expanding a lower-wage, exploitable, nonorganizable labor force, as women were still seen. The unwillingness of male-dominated unions to listen to any critique on these points, even by their women members, and the willingness of many women members to defer to the union's definition of what was good for women, was taken by autonomous feminists as "proletarian antifeminism."[70] Social Democrats—now in government in the 1970s—were just as likely as Christian conservatives to favor protective legislation that barred women from entire branches of work, forbade them to work at night (except in specified, female-sex-typed jobs like nurse or waitress), and limited physical demands in their jobs (when such demands were a significant source of wage benefits in union contracts), all of which kept women at a pronounced disadvantage in the labor market.[71]

On the job itself, unions were allies, even if sometimes reluctant ones. In Neuss, in the industrial Ruhr, a large women's strike targeted the low-wage grades that were explicitly designated for women and, with the support of the union, managed to get these wage groups eliminated. But a new classification of "light" work recaptured most of that gender distinction (and pay differential). Under pressure from women members, the unions slowly began to redesign pay agreements not to explicitly define women's work as less valuable. Feminist mobilization aimed to convince the constitutional court that it could agree. Both *EMMA* and *Courage* actively publicized the first successful equal pay for equal work case brought in 1979 by workers at Photo Heinze, but unions were not enthusiastic.[72]

A third reason for the marginal significance of paid work as an issue was that autonomous feminists themselves were not enamored of a capitalist economy and instead embraced a politics of "pay for housework" as their strategy for creating financial autonomy for women. This fit well into their claims for positively valuing reproductive labor and reworked the Marxist economic model, in which labor created value that was expropriated by capitalists, to present housework as economically valuable work from which employers and husbands both benefited, but for which neither paid.[73] Since women's labor was productive but created wealth that women did not control, women needed to withhold their labor and force a fair wage for it, whether from their husbands, husbands' employers, or the state on their behalf.[74]

This pay-for-housework theory circulated internationally among socialist feminist groups, but was especially warmly embraced by autonomous feminists in West Germany (and rejected in the United States, even among socialist feminists).[75] The new national feminist magazine *Courage*, named for Bertold Brecht's character, Mother Courage, endorsed it enthusiastically and regularly offered articles in support.[76] Local groups in a number of cities even formed to campaign for pay for housework, in structures similar to those they had organized to fight for abortion rights.

Pay-for-housework was a resonant claim for many West German feminists who were young mothers, students, or both, doing domestic chores they experienced as oppressive. Getting paid sounded appealing and not unrealistic, given how West German state already treated women. Indeed, paying for housework had been partly realized in the FRG in the 1950s through union wage contracts that offered a different wage for the same work by attaching "dependents' allowances" for wives and children to a male worker's paycheck. The state found such unequal pay consistent with the "functional differences" between women and men rather than a violation of the constitution's equal rights clause.[77]

Legal approval for the housewife-marriage as the ideal family was formally removed from the civil code in 1976, but privileging the male breadwinner remained the policy of the Social Democratic and Christian conservative parties. No party objected to bolstering men's wages with dependents' allowances or classifying women's jobs as "light" work in union-management agreements. Arguments for equal treatment of men and women in the workplace were countered by presenting the possibility that an unmarried woman might be hired in preference to "family man" with children to support as obviously unfair.[78] Even most feminists remained sure that protective legislation was better for women than treating women and men the same would be. One leading woman unionist in the main trade union confederation (DGB) confided in 1981 that she had personal doubts about protective measures really being good for women but found no other woman in the central office who even wanted to talk about this issue.[79]

In sum, there was virtually no legal protection in the 1970s against hiring or pay discrimination in West Germany. Few could imagine challenging the mutually supportive institutionalized structures of preference for men as workers and heads of households. The discursive opportunity structure favored a fight about women's self-determination in which reproduction, sexuality, and housework took central position; feminists lacked the discursive and material resources, the allies and windows of opportunity through which a serious critique of women's role in the paid economy could be offered.

CONCLUSION: FEMINIST ORGANIZING IN THE SPACE BETWEEN LEFT AND RIGHT

Autonomy as the central claim for the West German movement meant naming women as a group whose solidarity had a theoretical justification in their reproductive power and a practical implication in their collective self-determination. But autonomy as self-determination extended beyond personal-political decisions about having children, sex, or a paid job. Autonomy also meant a political place that was no longer in thrall to a socialist party and allowed women to determine their own needs apart for the state's paternalistic care—whether from the Right or Left on the political spectrum, or in the form institutionalized in either the East or the West.

Such a struggle to win an autonomous space was not nearly as difficult in states with more liberal frameworks for politics, like the United States, where contesting party dominance was not as serious an issue. The historical paths that gender politics took in Germany before the war, and in East and West Germany afterward, built legacies that shaped the types of needs women defined as important, their discursive and organizational resources, the allies and opponents in their political field, and the changes that seemed feasible. These frameworks for contestation were shaped by class-centered theory, welfare state practice, and a national history in which authoritarianism remained a visible problem to be resolved in every sphere from child care to party and movement decision making.

The transnational borrowing of concepts and organizational forms was therefore strategically selective. Faced with intransigent unions and parties, West German feminists did not see the state as an ally or the law as a tool. This blockage is quite unlike the US experience in the early and mid-1970s, where the Civil Rights Act and the Equal Employment Opportunities Commission laid the groundwork in the 1960s on which the movement began to build. At this early stage, the passage of an Equal Rights Amendment to the US constitution seemed all but assured, as it sailed through the House and Senate to begin the process of ratification by the states. In this one sense, the US opportunity structure was more like the East than the West German one because the state was an ally in opening up opportunities for women in higher education, professions, and trades, and feminists saw this as an expression of women's increasingly full citizenship.

Some US feminists insisted on the significance of the "battle of the mattress" and the need to build solidarity through language, consciousness-raising, and autonomous organizations, but inclusion and advancement—on still largely male terms—found more general resonance, and the more cultural strategies remained "radical." The apparently easy 1973 victory of *Roe v. Wade* in granting legal access to abortion and the absence of any long tradition of state-supported maternity benefits combined to sideline the reproductive issues so central to the West German movement. For West Germans, not only were local autonomous groups the leaders of widespread mobilization of women in the abortion struggle, but their claims also became the core of what "feminism" meant.

Both the history of abortion rights struggles and the antiauthoritarian critique that animated the New Left in West Germany gave autonomous feminists a political vocabulary with which to assert autonomy as a goal and a strategy. Self-determination was understood both collectively and individually. Autonomy—rather than a claim of equal rights—shaped organizational practice, since disdain for the hierarchical organizations of both proletarian and bourgeois women's movements, the DFD and DFR, defined the movement's identity. Local self-exploration groups, anti-218 activist councils, and pay-for-housework groups expressed autonomous feminist politics organizationally. Like so-called radical feminist groups in the United States, German feminists strongly rejected the idea of hierarchy, elections, or formal leaders and were committed to remaining purely collective, grassroots, local organizations. Any formal or national organization structure was a negative role model. They borrowed "c-r" terminology and practices from US models, but rejected NOW's umbrella model of a national organization linking local groups.[80]

Autonomous feminists also concluded that organizational subordination by the Left was inevitable if one chose to work with the Left at all. Louise Otto-Peters's famous words that "the history of all times, and today most especially, teaches that those people will be forgotten who forget to think of themselves" was the lesson autonomous feminists rediscovered in the early 1970s.[81] If women did not represent themselves politically, women would not be heard. Any group that adopted a formal leadership structure and the politics of representation that went with it sold out the women at the base whom it claimed to represent. Something new was needed to give organizational expression to the discursive claim to autonomy, to support the cultural politics of language and individual self-discovery, and to fight for specific institutional political freedoms, such as reproductive rights, about which the organized Left did not seem to care.

These issues of organization became central to the practice of feminism in West Germany in the 1980s. Building on the early 1970s successes in creating a sense of entitlement to self-determination as women—organizationally, interpersonally, and politically—feminists sought to reach out to empower women collectively. But how could small groups of politically aware women help women in general achieve the autonomy they needed and deserved? The answer was found in the form of local projects.

CHAPTER 4

WOMEN HELP WOMEN
The Women's Project Movement, 1975–1985

T HE LITTLE BELL RINGS, indicating that someone has opened the door. Like other customers in the
Frankfurt bookstore, I look up to see who has come in. I'm a bit surprised
to see a young man in a striped scarf and rimless glasses. A typical student, I
think, but what is he looking for in a women's bookstore? The staffer at the
register reacts more forcefully, walking briskly over to him. In a loud voice
and somewhat annoyed tone, she asks what he wants and doesn't he know this
is a women's bookstore. He mumbles something and turns back toward the
door, which the staffer quickly opens for him. He hasn't exactly been thrown
out, but it is clear his business isn't wanted. Although this doesn't seem to me
the best way to make the bookstore profitable, it is consistent with what I've
seen at other women's projects in Germany. They are not only for women,
they are definitely not for men.

This chapter explores the variety of women's projects that blossomed in the
late 1970s and early 1980s in West Germany, the principles on which the projects operated, and the implications of these ideas for their work. Along with
bookstores, shelters for battered women, health centers, and student centers
multiplied like rabbits.[1] These feminist projects were more decisively separatist

than all but the most radical local groups in the United States, where men as customers, students, and antiviolence counselors for men were usually welcome. Autonomous feminists defined themselves as "for women," but what did this commitment imply for their organizational practices?

Differences in opportunity structure made West German projects surprisingly unlike those of even superficially similar US organizations. Mainstream US feminists followed the African American model of demanding equal rights and political, social, and economic opportunity, so their strategies stressed challenging stereotypes and dismantling legal segregation.[2] Relatively few Black and women's groups followed a cultural nationalist strategy that led to separatist organizing. Such radical US feminists gravitated to issues the mainstream neglected, like violence against women and pornography, but the mainstream quickly followed. By the 1980s, US feminists were working together, despite frictions based on their theoretical origins and commitments ("radical," socialist, liberal, career).[3]

By contrast, West German feminists remained adamant in embracing women's political outsider role. They stressed their negative experiences with the state, the Left parties, and other social movements, and they made reproductive power, individual and collective self-determination, and gender solidarity the positive values that defined their movement. They sought political practices that would uncompromisingly express these principles. They rejected women's associations like the Frauenrat, which accepted the modest reforms of abortion law, as taking state "charity" and thus "not feminist." Willingness to fight for self-determination as a principle defined all real feminism, they said. Compromises to create alliances with other non-party-affiliated associations did not appeal to feminists since other nonparty groups also had little political influence.[4] Autonomous, not merely gender-separatist, West German feminists chose to stand apart from organizations of the women's movement no less than from parties and other male-led groups.

The core issue was self-emancipation: how women acting on their own could help other women realize their autonomy. The great majority of West Germans who self-identified as feminist chose to construct new organizations to realize being wholly "for women" as a political practice.[5] "Women help women" became the movement's slogan; its practices ran from bookstores and cafes to research organizations outside universities to safe spaces for battered women to rebuild their lives.

These organizations were uniformly called *projects*, so the decade beginning in 1975 came to be called "women's project movement."[6] As services proliferated, so eventually did the tendency to institutionalize them with state funds. By the end of the decade, the feminists who had launched the projects with such high hopes viewed the strategy largely as a failure, even though their projects had become ubiquitous.

Translating autonomy as a goal into actual practice drew also from the transnational current of participatory democratic development in the highly industrial countries. West German feminists used their history of exclusion to justify their strong, strategic commitment to such nonhierarchical, local groups. Autonomy as a political objective had both a negative sense of rejecting social and political dependence and a positive sense of self-representation and capability-building. Only a certain type of organization, the local project, was seen as able to realize both.

These grassroots projects had strengths but also generated practical contradictions. They produced discursive resources for the movement by developing a wider constituency, a politically active and effective *women's public*. Nonetheless, the commitment to autonomy produced tensions within projects as it came to mean taking women's side and speaking from experience, principles that often conflicted. These tension are clearly seen in the projects for battered women that spread in the 1980s.

Projects for battered women were strongly identified with feminism in the popular imagination and were central to the movement's self-understanding in two ways. First, they challenged the West German state's support for male authority in the family by drawing attention to men's violence against women in the very institution the state authorized to protect and care for women. Second, they were a social laboratory where feminist principles of autonomy were tested in practice. Rather than experiencing an early and gradual transition to social services, as in the United States, West German projects for battered women engaged in a long and mutually transformative struggle with the state.[7]

This organizational response to violence against women already places the issue of autonomy into the broader political context of gendered citizenship. The debates around militarism and nonviolence that also arose at this time further drew attention to women's relation to the state. A historically well-grounded fear of authoritarianism led the women's public in a pacifist direction, a viewpoint feminists shared with many women and the rest of the student movement. Feminist antimilitarism spilled over to revitalize such events as International Women's Day and reopened doors to alliances with other women's groups, male leftists, and antiwar protesters of both genders. This trajectory differed from that in the United States, where the end of the Vietnam War demobilized student protestors and mainstream feminism embraced military service as offering women full citizenship, economic opportunity and counterstereotypical forms of action.

Showing how autonomy as a principle affected feminist practice reveals how organizational development in movements goes beyond mobilizing resources for initial actions, as the expansion of projects sowed the contradictions that eventually ended their dominance as a feminist strategy. The ways that feminist projects grew to fit within West German discursive and material opportunity structures made them vulnerable to internal tensions and external shifts in opportunity. In the end, the frameworks in which these project groups operated both enabled them to grow and constrained their ability to change.

EMBRACING AUTONOMY

Feminist autonomous organizing was not specific to West Germany in this period. Women's movements sprang up worldwide, and in Europe a variety of what were called New Social Movements (NSMs) emerged in the mid-1970s. In Germany, opposition to remilitarization (as part of NATO in the West and the Warsaw Pact in the East) was in sympathy with the anticolonial movements of the global South. The first stirrings of an environmental consciousness could also be seen, often linked with concern about nuclear power plants (and nuclear weapons) and about buildings standing vacant while urban apartments were unaffordable. The strongly hierarchical, disempowering structure of the universities came under attack. These issues diverged from conventional concerns of class-based politics and provided a hothouse in which feminist organizing also flowered. The university student milieu, concentrated in areas of lower-cost housing in major cities, offered fertile soil for many NSMs, in West Germany and across Western Europe.[8]

The NSM culture had echoes in the American New Left of the 1970s, but did not share the concerns of the civil rights movement that polarized US politics.[9] Drawing on a constituency of "postmaterialists," young, well-educated, and estranged from the economic survival politics of their parents' generation, European student-centered movements embraced both individual freedom and social responsibility. For Germans, being antiauthoritarian was especially important. They sought a personally rewarding form of political activism, one that was *basisdemokratisch* (grass roots, local, informally structured).

For feminists, autonomy demanded all this and more. Local organizations doing outreach to a wider community were not characteristic of the rest of the NSM scene; "women helping women" with social services offered challenges and possibilities student-centered organizing did not. Women's control over their own work with and for women was central to the West German feminist definition of autonomy. Feminists in the late 1970s to mid-1980s defined all women as their constituency for nonhierarchical, politically mobilizing work and wanted their organizations to be controlled by women alone.

Writing their own, women-centered rules made the projects separatist, not only by keeping individual men out but as a normative claim to stay apart from the state and capitalism and operate according to distinctive "women's values." Both discursively, in naming their issues for themselves, and organizationally, in remaining independent local groups, autonomous feminists sought to institutionalize women's self-determination. *Autarky* (a wholly independent political-economic system) appealed to them as a strategy.

Most self-identified feminists kept their distance organizationally and discursively from other women's groups, not only from men and mixed-gender associations. They acknowledged the Frauenrat and its member associations as part of "the women's movement" but not as "feminist," terms that remained quite distinct. A woman who chose to work for women's rights in hierarchical women's or mixed-gender organizations was by definition uncommitted to women's self-determination and so not feminist. Politics that addressed gender inequality had to embrace a goal of self-determination and so be done differently from politics as usual. Each local project group had to be collectively self-determining, and each member had a right to self-determination. *Basisdemokratische* action, strongly participatory democracy, was reframed as an inherently feminist style of organization.

Creating a feminist project worthy of the name therefore included rejecting "male-defined" principles and practices, such as hierarchy, power, and the state. Most West German feminists agreed with the editors of the 1976 *Women's Yearbook* that a strategy built on "entering into and mixing in male institutions will not break the thousand year old power of men, will not be able to challenge the values that inhere in every fiber of these institutions."[10]

The story opening this chapter illustrates how such autarky was to be achieved in practice: in local organizations run by and for women alone. The projects, these "islands of utopia," were to actualize a vision of what women's collective self-determination could become and build each woman's personal capabilities for a self-determined life.[11] By means of their political work in the projects, feminists sought to expand the web of meaning around citizenship by removing it from the institutionalized maleness and top-down protectiveness of state politics.

Defining Autonomous Practice Through Projects

Drawing from the energy of the 1972–75 abortion-rights campaign, feminists constructed many different projects. Not merely spaces for feminists to gather and work politically, as the anti-218 groups had been, they had the goal of turning women from a conceptual abstraction into a recognizable social actor. The social construction of "women and lesbian" as this new actor made clear that lesbians were a significant part of this feminist public. It also made lesbians distinct from the many straight women (*Heteras*) engaged in these projects. Paradoxically, lesbians were thus more visible but less dominant than in US radical feminist projects, since US use of "women's" ambiguously to mean feminist and/or lesbian obscured the intersection of gender and sexuality as distinct factors. West German projects were also less easy to frame in US terms as apolitically cultural "radical feminism," since their antiviolence organizing and festivals employed much socialist-inspired political discourse and imagery.[12]

The institutionalization of feminist spaces as movement projects could be said to begin in 1975, when Lillemors, the first women's bookstore, and Frauenoffensive, the first women's press, were founded in Munich. At least five other women's bookstores opened later that year. Between 1975 and 1985, dozens of bookstores and thirty women's archives and libraries were established. They were autonomous in the sense of autarky—founded by independent local groups, self-funded, and initially run entirely on women's volunteer labor. By the end of 1977, there were a dozen local feminist magazines; by 1987 there were fifty.

The 1987 *Women's Yearbook* listed more than fifty women's centers, a dozen coffeehouses and bars, a handful of vacation resorts, and a hotel. The *Yearbook* itself, begun in 1975 and continuing through this decade, offered a collectively authored orientation to the ideas of the movement, with essays by local groups and issue networks (abortion rights, pay for housework, and women's history were prominent). Issue networks summed up what happened, what was expected to happen, and what it all meant, discursively organizing local groups without giving formal directions.

This feminist knowledge economy had the explicit purpose of increasing the circulation of feminist ideas outward as well as being a place—like the smaller scale WGs, *Kinderläden*, and c-r groups—that would draw women into the movement, counter their isolation in the home, provide opportunities to share experiences, and politicize themselves. Local newsletters, cafes, and centers provided sites where agendas could be constructed; the *Yearbook*, Women's Calendar, magazines like *EMMA* and *Courage*, and feminist best-sellers like *Shedding* connected local groups into a discursively organized national movement.[13] These interconnected projects provided "free spaces" in which feminists could find each other,[14] feel at home, and get on with the practical work of the movement: women helping women free themselves.

Beyond the Project Spaces: Building a Women's Public

These projects developed the discourse of feminism, producing new words to name its emergent realities and shifting the webs of meaning for women, politics, and autonomy.[15] *Frauenöffentlichkeit* ("women's public") named a new sense of women as a "gender for itself," a political community with interests and a way to express them. The term was adapted from Jürgen Habermas's notions of a "public" (*Öffentlichkeit*) as a field of discourse, a civil society dominated by institutionalized economic and political interests, and a "counterpublic" (*Gegenöffentlichkeit*) that might form to contest this power. In the latter, the voice-of-experience (life-world) plays a crucial role.[16] Unlike a women's *community*, which could be apolitical and inward-directed, a women's *public* existed to challenge "male" institutions from the perspective of women's experience, their "life-world."

Frauenöffentlichkeit, the counterpublic through which the feminist movement operated, proved efficacious. One example can be seen in the protests about abortion organized by Frankfurt Women's Health Center, one of the earliest and largest movement projects. On July 1, 1975, the Frankfurt police confiscated the center's records and accused fifteen women who had organized bus trips to the Netherlands for legal first-trimester abortions of being part of an "illegal conspiracy." The center used these arrests to publicize its strategy of civil disobedience and raised such a public outcry that the prosecutions were dropped. The bus trips continued without police interference.

This victory was politically significant in two respects. First, it showed that the idea of women's self-determination resonated with women outside the project. The protests provided a concrete expression of the center's power to act "for women" because the *women's public* supported its rejection of police action as illegitimate. Second, while the state did not change the law, it did back off from enforcing it, deferring to women's collective power. The feminist claim to speak for women was thus affirmed by both women and the state.

The women's public was distinct from the projects, like the Frankfurt Women's Health Center, that called it into existence. It responded to feminists and acted for feminist goals, but it was not limited to those who identified as feminists. "Feminist" meant being part of one or more autonomous projects and was discursively distinguished both from participating in the women's movement, the formally organized women's groups, and from being a *frauen-bewegte Frau* (woman-moved-woman), a woman in movement, put in motion by feminism.[17] Local projects were the source of feminist "movement"; the women's public was all those "moved" to act as women, for women, regardless of their institutional location.

Feminists addressed this women's public as potentially powerful but threatened, using an image of a witch as a symbol. Local projects might get together for a general meeting across the city, called a *Hexenfrühstück* ("witches' breakfast"). This image evoked women as both dangerous to men and historical victims of male violence.[18] Feminist demonstrations protesting violence against women drew on this symbol, beginning in 1977 with the first *Walpurgisnacht* (April 30) demonstrations to "take back the night."[19] The take-back-the-night theme was borrowed from the American women's movement but the choice of Walpurgis Night, the historical gathering time of Goddess worshippers, invoked not only women's potential power but also the European history of gendered political repression by church and state. This framing emphasized church and state as a powerful and dangerous alliance, one still opposed to feminist mobilization.

Within Project Spaces: Constructing Principles for Daily Practice

Project feminists developed a set of guiding rules to realize the positive goals of individual and collective self-determination for women. The two most central principles were *Parteilichkeit*, taking sides, and *Betroffenheit*, privileging the voice of personal experience. The theory proved problematic in practice, but the concepts offered crucial standards for evaluating political choices in and across projects.[20]

Parteilichkeit expressed the projects' demand that women "choose sides" in the conflict between men's and women's interests. Gender solidarity did not assume that all women thought alike, or had the same experiences or values, but said only those women who *chose* women's political interests over all other claims to their loyalty deserved to be called feminists. Building alternative political spaces in the projects was a concrete way to choose women's side, outside formal and movement politics. Keeping men out of these spaces was essential to prevent women from being distracted or dominated by men's agenda. Not just orienting your services to women but rejecting men as customers (or as students to your class) was consistent with *Parteilichkeit*, which stressed developing women into a counterpublic that could acquire political muscle.

Betroffenheit further distinguished the projects from politics as usual. "Speaking from direct experience" was framed as the opposite of representative democracy, in which a small number of individuals are chosen to speak for the larger group. Projects claimed that the unmediated participation of those affected by a problem was the feminist way of making decisions. Women who spoke from experience were thereby being set on a path toward individual self-determination, growing in political capacities and claiming their power to make decisions for themselves, becoming a real counterpublic.

The antihierarchical collective organizational structure in the projects was supposed to ensure that all those directly affected would have a chance to speak their own minds, without reference to any division of labor, decision-making rules, or formal educational or training criteria. Hierarchy became defined as male, and rules were seen as infringing on the personal autonomy of women, each of whom knew best what they needed. Discursively, representative democracy was placed in a web of meaning closely tied to maleness, hierarchy, and the state, and it contrasted with self-expression and self-determination, both gendered female.

Although these organizational priorities were not sustainable over the long run, feminists clung longer and more strongly to collectivist structures in West Germany than in the United States. This outsider viewpoint was a rare, more radical position in US feminist projects, most of which valued entrepreneurship, counterstereotypical behavior, and mutual accountability of citizens and state. Autarky offered far more resonant meanings for West German feminists.

CONFRONTING A SYSTEM: CAPITALISM, PATRIARCHY, AND THE STATE

The appeal of autarky as a principle, and the project form for realizing it, reflected the way politics was done in West Germany. The West German system is *corporatist*: political decisions are characteristically brokered among key representative groups. Unions, corporations, and government itself are acknowledged as "social partners" who legitimately direct state policy; political parties lead government. Women were excluded from collective representation by these political institutions, since the institutional influence of the social partners and churches was directed at making family support a higher good than women's rights.[21] Countering these priorities required mobilizing women as a political constituency with a collective voice. Building a women's public and staffing the projects that called it into existence were the means to create that voice.[22]

This framework affected what frames resonated for feminists. Rather than seeing the status quo as violating principles of fairness or individual merit, as liberalism would, West German feminists saw the system itself as *organized against* women's interests. Expressed as *Ganzheitlichkeit* (unity of the system), capitalism, the technocratic rationality of the state, and patriarchal domination in the family were closely interconnected and produced women's oppression. All three institutions were "male" in two senses: structurally, they worked through networks and organizations that placed men as a group in positions of power over women; discursively, they conferred greater institutional value on men and capacities and preferences associated with men.

Project work was imagined as being on the female side of this dualistic system: women's reproductive labor, humane social values, and noncompetitive individual personalities were opposed by men's political hierarchy, economic competition, and technocratic control.[23] The state's technocratic rationality—expressed in bookkeeping practices, rigidly tiered status systems, and structures of age and formal qualification—infringed on the entire life-world for which women were responsible. The projects thus sought to work apart from the state and against the political economy as a whole, to free women from the interlocked oppressions of capitalism and the state and to demonstrate what an alternative, woman-centered political economy would be like.

Political resistance to the system-as-a-whole demanded cultivating different values. Doing work in the projects was framed as resistance to the competitive demands of the market (*Leistungsprinzip*), so selling more books need not be a feminist bookstore priority, making it easier to turn away a potential customer who was a man. The competitive social order or "elbow society" (*Ellenbogengesellschaft*) that privileged those "with elbows" to push others out of their way was to be resisted in project work and defined assertiveness as making women "like men." By affirming women's nonwaged work as valuable, important, and potentially emancipating if done in the right conditions, the West German feminist movement also framed caregiving and social reproduction as something from which women needed no liberation. Autarky should offer conditions in which women could do the female-style labor women were said to value and that society did not (yet).[24]

This dualistic analysis of a male system and a female alternative shaped many projects' norms. For some, women's distance from capitalist modes of production was refigured as moral superiority, which led to project work as a way to protect their undervalued "feminine labor capacity" as a virtue.[25] For others, socially cultivated feminine weaknesses were to be addressed through a project work process in which women together would learn to manage interpersonal separation, combine self-and-other care, and develop a fully balanced personality.[26] While it is possible that the male-breadwinner family structure institutionalized in West Germany actually produced women with personalities less competitive or achievement oriented than men's (or than women's in the United States), it seems certain that the political economy shaped the discursive opportunity structure in which feminists constructed these projects. Women were a constituency feminists addressed in terms of their intrinsic outsiderness to the corporatist system. Maintaining an outsider value system was framed as important to women, both individually and collectively.

Oppositional Solidarity as an Organizing Challenge

Autonomous feminist practice was to be oppositional in two senses: the women's public presented women's solidarity as the entering wedge of political critique by and for women, and the projects developed organizational practices to express values alternative to those institutionalized in the system. In both discursive work and project practices, feminists defined their autonomy by affirming positive principles of association with women and rejecting values identified with institutions of male power, especially capitalism and the state.

Yet these norms of oppositional solidarity among women began to generate contradictions in practice. At the most general level, feminist activists still needed to eat and pay rent, so projects shifted in the early 1980s from purely volunteer labor to trying to pay a wage. Conflict over funds—and the control over other people's labor that wages embodied—grew.[27] One participant asked plaintively, "Every woman made her own compromise between feminist utopia and social necessity, and not everyone is satisfied with each other's solutions. Opening the store twenty minutes late in the morning—is that self-determination at work or socially irresponsible laziness?"[28] The demand that the project provide space for each individual's own development—at her own speed and in her own way—and the demand for collective standards of responsibility for the project's survival structurally conflicted.[29]

To illustrate how complex and contradictory feminist practices were becoming there is no better example than the projects working with battered and abused women. Emblematic of feminism for both activists and the wider women's public, these projects were framed as a unifying challenge to the state role in all women's subordination, not merely a form of escape from a dangerous situation for specific individuals.

Fighting Back: Resisting Violence Against Women

Feminist projects supporting women victims of domestic violence developed internationally in the 1970s. The first German shelter for battered women opened in West Berlin in 1976, inspired by the British example of Chiswick Women's Aid, recounted in Erin Pizzey's 1974 book, *Scream Quietly, or the Neighbors Will Hear.* Many women involved in setting up the project were also sensitized to issues of violence against women through participation in the International Tribunal on Crimes against Women in Brussels that year.[30] Although the idea of creating a place for women to escape their batterers was international, the feminist framework of autonomy turned it into a distinctive form of practice in West Germany.[31]

The term chosen for this Berlin house and subsequent projects in West Germany was simply *Frauenhaus* (women's house), stressing the commonality of helpers and helped, rather than the "shelter" (US) or "refuge" (UK) language preferred in liberal political contexts. The *Frauenhaus* was framed as "part of the struggle against [women's] oppression, not an attempted solution for a circumscribed social problem."[32] It was understood not as a resource filling a gap in state services, but as a site in which *all* participants would be collectively empowered.

To the founders, the very opposite of project work was "social work"—help to needy others—and it was important to make a *Frauenhaus* a place for women's self-transformation. Without a distinction between helper and helped, it was thought that all participants would realize that women who were battered were no different from other women. Women were structurally alike in facing and fearing male violence, even if their specific experiences were different. Carol Hagemann-White, involved in organizing shelter projects in West Berlin and an astute evaluator of their practices, suggested, "The feminist postulate of commonality among women created the frame for these experiences, but was also confirmed by them, since violence in marriage and abuse by men evoked participants' own life-long experiences of fearing male violence and rape."[33] Naming the extent and ubiquity of male violence against women became a fundamental principle of gender solidarity. It connected women's sense of identification with other women at a personal, experiential level with the political project of forming women's identity as a collective actor.

The *Frauenhaus* was also defined as a site for developing individual self-determination. Each woman would make choices for herself, again in explicit contrast to patriarchal-protective state social work. This placed enormous demands on the organizers. Hagemann-White explains, "The autonomous *Frauenhäuser* (autonomy as a form of organization is an unconditional precondition for *Frauenhaus* work) intend to offer an alternative. They want to demonstrate the possibility for a new type of life."[34] *Frauenhaus* women needed to share in this "new type of life" and thus develop a self-directed perspective for the future, not just have somewhere safe to go while finding a new apartment or job. The social-psychological vision of autonomy as a self-determined life took precedence over the material resources that most liberal US or UK feminists saw their shelters/refuges as providing.

As a site for experiencing this alternative way of life, it was crucial that the *Frauenhaus* be organized and run on the principle of autonomy, which included staying "as long as it takes until they again feel themselves in the position to lead an independent life," accepting overcrowding, while US shelters kept strict time limits in order to open scarce spaces for new women.[35] The *Frauenhaus* excluded men, based on their symbolic association with power and authority as police, doctors, and state authorities, not merely their actual or potential violence as individuals, while women's shelters in the United States tended to use "gentle men" to teach children nonviolent conflict resolution.

Autonomy was translated particularly as "self-administration," women making their own rules. Feminists insisted that they run the house by and for themselves, even though they drew their budgets from the state (the first Berlin *Frauenhaus* was supported 80 percent by federal and 20 percent by city funds). By 1979 there were fourteen houses established on feminist guidelines for self-determination (all women who came were admitted, there were no rules other than those chosen by the group, all participants were involved in all decision making); by 1985 there were one hundred, though with variable and unreliable levels of funding.[36] This level of support was a victory for feminist negotiators—in Berlin, the first *Frauenhaus* budget was almost half a million DM per year for three years. It was even more remarkable that they won support on their own terms, since the projects' principles were very unlike those of state bureaucracy. Feminists insisted on doing their own hiring and on nonhierarchical pay criteria for the women who worked there, rather than state pay scales, and they refused to keep records of who used their services lest it lead to stigmatizing them.

Without time limits on stays, the houses were severely overcrowded and offered difficult living conditions. This was rationalized as a collective good, since overcrowding was seen as demonstrating the inadequacy of state provision. It also aroused indignation in the women's public and so strengthened the activists' hand in negotiations with the state. But winning widespread recognition of domestic abuse was a mixed blessing; the state responded by expanding shelters that were not feminist. Competing for state funds with these nonfeminist shelters weakened the projects' ability to insist on strict interpretation of their rules, even though their model remained normatively dominant. Relative to the United States, West German *Frauenhäuser* retained a great deal of administrative control over their internal structure and process.[37] US feminists relatively quickly accepted extensive professionalization, state-defined rules of eligibility and pay, and formal divisions of labor as being the price of funding, and they lost both credit for and control over their shelters.

The gradual modifications in West German practice were not only imposed from outside but also emerged from the contradictions feminists came to see between their principles of taking women's side and speaking from experience. It was hard to take women's side when some women were violent or abusive to their children or other women in the house. Shared decision making and self-determination were hard to apply to women who were abusing drugs or alcohol or allowing children to act out violently. With little or no privacy and no training or experience, self-help discussion circles could become intrusive and abusive. While not rejecting *Parteilichkeit* or *Betroffenheit* completely, each house reevaluated how it put these values into practice.

In this, the *Frauenhäuser* were very similar to other autonomous projects. State funding exacerbated the difficulty of both choosing women's side and allowing women to speak for themselves. First, state support encouraged distinctions between helpers and helped, legitimated a new career path in human services, and strengthened the discourse of motherliness. Second, the projects began to turn their helping toward the women whom the state defined as needy, particularly immigrant women and girls. These inequalities surfaced in the debates over taking funding, "the state's dough."

Ferment in the State's Dough

The lure and problems of state funding both became acute in the mid-1980s, as feminist projects sprang up to address a profusion of needs and clienteles.[38] State financing spread to women's centers, supporting health and education projects that the German welfare state interpreted as fulfilling its mandate to help and protect women. Feminists complained about insufficient financial support, yet emphasized how much their dependency on the state's dough (*Staatsknete*) threatened the autonomy of their movement.[39]

The competition for funding exacerbated structural tensions rooted in seeing women as a group whose interests were diametrically opposite to those of the state. At a basic level, the idea that projects were by and for the women who needed them was contradictory: women in acute need were often in no position to run a project, and it was hard to get funds for projects that served women who were less acutely needy. In the *Frauenhäuser*, the more women fleeing their abusers were recognized as damaged and uncertain about their futures, the more appealing it became to offer them structure, counseling, and experienced staff. State willingness to help projects on their own terms also made being "on the other side" an inadequate definition of feminism. Project feminists needed a new strategic vision for where their work was leading them.

Betroffenheit and *Parteilichkeit* proved more irreconcilable than had been imagined. Speaking from experience (*Betroffenheit*) might capture the women's immediate needs, but taking women's side (*Parteilichkeit*) demanded a larger theory of politics. Which of individual women's actual interests would be in the collective interest of women's autonomy, and in a nonhierarchical structure, who got to make that decision?

In the absence of shared guidelines for transforming, rather than merely opposing, the state, the very fact of being a woman, a general, easy-to-measure experience, often became enough to qualify women-run intervention as a feminist project. Moreover, higher education offered professional skills in listening, counseling, and political organizing that combined well with feminist theory. Women students in the social sciences, psychology, and education were drawn in significant numbers to this work. Project work began to take on the shape of a poorly paid but politically praiseworthy career for women-moved-women.[40]

That feminist projects could pay wages at all was due to activists writing grants to city or state funders, which required identifying a group of women with recognizable needs. State-funded feminist projects, not only the *Frauenhäuser*, were increasingly composed of academically trained women with grant-writing skills and experience, less qualified women working to gain social service experience, and the women being helped, usually women already defined as a problem group by the welfare state: migrants, unemployed women, victims of abuse, prostitutes. Both the division of labor in the project team and the split between client and provider groups gradually became institutionalized. As the need for funding moved projects toward serving "high need" women who were "other" than those who wrote the grants, the difference in accountability between those who put a project together and got it funded and those who came to it for help and support made it impossible to sustain a myth of shared decision making.[41]

As projects became absorbed into the welfare state, their frames shifted from resisting male values to celebrating female ones, especially caregiving and nurturance. Feminist projects became more "motherly" in helping "the needy," rather than offering a site for self-help among adult women defined as equals. Project feminists struggled against women's self-definitions they saw as dangerous, such as returning to a battering relationship, or inappropriate, such as migrant women wanting a German husband to stabilize their residency and obtain work permits.[42] The ethic of care collided with the principle of autonomous choice, and conflicts within the projects over what was in women's best interests became common.[43]

Long-engaged feminists deplored what they saw as an emergent subculture embracing gender stereotypes: "A women's project seemed particularly open to the expectation that it would provide a large motherly presence that could take care of all worries and problems."[44] The positive valuation of motherliness and distinctively feminine labor capacity that feminists had emphasized theoretically was now redeployed to legitimate educated women's position as helpers of needy women, weakening the distinction between project work and social work. As the gap between staff and clients grew, so did the value feminists placed on authority, no longer seeing it as exclusively male. But few feminists exercised governmental authority, leaving them perennial supplicants for funds, a contradiction increasingly galling to feminists who had accrued experience with authority by acting for women through the women's public and in feminist projects.

A Group Called Women: Inequalities and Solidarities

The theoretical claim that women and the system as a whole were on two conflicting sides was further challenged as racial/ethnic women began to point to the ways project feminists were not on *their* side. Spurred in part by transnational discourses from women of color, minority group women in West Germany offered critiques of project practices as inconsistent with feminist claims to give all women an autonomous voice.

Some migrant women drew their ideas from the writings of US and UK Black feminists, especially Audre Lorde who visited Berlin for a writing workshop. German women of color, by raising arguments about being treated as objects of dominant women's charity and discipline, explicitly brought race into the debate for the first time. May Ayim, a poet of Afro-German heritage, was a primary voice in articulating this emergent consciousness of race in West Germany, particularly for women of color themselves.[45] In the United States, race offered a long-established category for understanding inequality, but immigrant German women of color had to struggle to make sense of their experiences of subordinated inclusion.

Recognizing the construct of race as relevant to the situation of immigrant women in West Germany was slow, but it brought a new dimension of complexity to self-help and advocacy principles.[46] Migrant women began their own projects, and their self-organization continued to grow. Confrontations in the mid-1980s (for example, the Congress of German and Immigrant Women in March 1984) meant that the projects for migrant women had in fact been transformative, but not in the sense their founders anticipated. "German women were astonished to see how their 'apprentices' had changed," one migrant woman reported, meaning that the majority were shocked to discover that non-German women now "denigrated their well-meaning work as social work."[47]

Used to thinking of themselves as powerless, feminists of German nationality were slow to acknowledge that they now were seen as representing women in the political system, and that the differences of viewpoint revealed in the projects were anchored in real structures of power both in and outside the projects. For example, migrant women criticized West German women for treating them as an "assignment," acting like social workers, and pushing aside the migrants' own definitions of their problems.[48] Yet seeing a parallel between sexism and racism, showing how the projects institutionalized rather than transcended inequalities among women was not a resonant idea for most West German feminist activists. Non-German-origin women remained represented as "backward, isolated and needy" in West German feminist discourse of the 1970s and 1980s.[49]

As projects institutionalized both a division of labor within the project team and a split between client and provider constituencies, they were forced to reconsider the opposition between women's side and the state. Taking state money was how they were now increasingly able to work "for women," and academically qualified ethnically German women now were exercising authority over other women with state support. But their newly won authority underlined ethnic German women's own self-conception as benevolent mothers. Seeing no parallel between gender and race, they could not understand why they were increasingly criticized by those whom they helped. Even as feminists adopted much of the mission of the welfare state, they remained ambivalent about state power and women's role in exercising it.

West German feminists found it harder to think of women as part of the state, exercising power over others, than either East German or American women did. This was evident as the women's public debated military service. Feminists in West Germany not only were more critical of women's role in the state, but more suspicious of arming it.

"SAND RATHER THAN OIL"
IN THE MACHINERY OF THE STATE

Project women were drawn into direct relationships with the state, receiving recognition and funding as political actors in ways that surprised them. In liberal states forming feminist interest groups was not a radical step, but the emergence of the women's public as a collective actor was disruptive to the West German consensus that politics was a matter of organized interests of the Left and the Right. Feminist voices challenged the centrality of worker-capitalist conflict on the Left and patriarchal family support on the Right.

Engagement with the state in Germany, whether the GDR or the FRG, included consideration not only of welfare and family systems but also state authoritarianism and political violence, concerns sharpened by history. Feminists urged women not to facilitate the state's ability to control and oppress its citizens, by being "oil" in its machinery, but to reduce its power by putting "sand" in its works through protest and resistance.[50]

Given the ravages of German history, it is understandable that state power was distrusted and women's distance from the state applauded. In the 1960s, dealing with the shame of their nation's past (*Vergangenheitsbewältigung*) had already become a major concern. Younger Germans questioned their parents' roles in the Nazi genocide and sought to make more responsible political choices, especially in postcolonial conflicts (such as Vietnam) and Palestinian claims for self-determination (especially as it threatened the existence of Israel). Thinking about the past is always a way of thinking about the present, and how the past was made into a political lesson varied considerably, even among feminists.[51]

Women's relationships with the state and state wrongdoing in the 1930s and 1940s became a subject of conflict among women historians that resonated widely in the West German women's public in the early 1980s. The sides differed as to whether women were simply victims of the Nazi state or whether Christian German women should be held responsible as perpetrators of genocide, even if relatively distant from the central levers of power. This so-called victim-perpetrator (*Opfer-Täter*) debate drew in many feminist historians who examined the roles women played and benefits they obtained under the Nazis.[52] To emphasize women as perpetrators, however minor, was controversial to those who studied women's deaths and exploitation (including sexual) in the camps, the feminists sent into exile, and state manipulation of maternity.[53]

This debate was never just about history. On the victim side, women were seen as sharing collective oppression across boundaries of time and nation. Such feminists were not troubled by Europe's relationship of power with postcolonial nations and women of these cultures. Christina Thürmer-Rohr was an influential exponent of the universality of sisterhood and exclusion from power as a defining feature of all women's lives. On the perpetrator side, women were asked to share responsibility for what the state had done and to acknowledge that they could not stand innocently outside its foreign or domestic policies. Maria Mies, a researcher who studied international development politics, drew feminist attention to women's complicity in global chains of exploitation.[54]

This debate complicated anti- and pro-state postures by highlighting the ambiguous status of women's citizenship. In claiming that women were solely victims, feminists were free to challenge the state in any regard, but they were not challenged to consider how their interests and actions were informed by the benefits and power their citizenship conferred on them. In claiming women were perpetrators, or at least complicit, women could not simply take their oppositional role for granted, but had to decide under what circumstances they had an obligation as citizens to resist the state. As citizens, women needed to confront the issues raised by the exercise of state power. Violence was a fulcrum for this debate.

The Maleness of Violence and the Citizenship of Women

The centrality of the *Frauenhaus* to the women's public was one expression of the movement's concern with the relation between violence and the state. Feminist mobilization against male violence in the home drew attention to the state's tacit support for men's abuse of women. The state claimed a monopoly over the legitimate use of physical force as an expression of the rule of law, but failed to treat men who battered their wives or girlfriends as the criminals they were. The lesson from the antibattering mobilization extended well beyond domestic violence, with the potential for seeing violence itself as a male attribute and the state as sharing this proclivity.

The maleness of violence was debated in relation to revolutionary tactics that turned capitalists and the state into targets. In the mid-1970s, a violent splinter group of the Left, the Red Army Fraction (RAF), led by Andreas Baader and Ulrike Meinhof, allied itself with revolutionary movements in Palestine and Vietnam and carried out high-profile kidnappings and assassinations. Baader, Meinhof, and other leading RAF figures were captured and convicted, but died under mysterious circumstances in prison. Anxious about terrorism, the state stepped up surveillance of the Left in general, instituted loyalty oaths, and curtailed civil liberties in ways evocative of the United States after 9/11.

As violence and the fear of terrorism escalated in West Germany throughout the 1970s, the once obvious association of maleness with violence began to be questioned.[55] By 1977 two-thirds of those on the police's most-wanted list were women, and Meinhof herself became "the icon of these debates, negatively and positively idealized."[56] Her supposed feminism (she had first made her name as a journalist covering the famous tomato toss and was a friend of Alice Schwarzer) made it easy to convert her into a figure whose actions stood for women's emancipation, for better and worse. On the Right, newspapers like *Bild* suggested that women's liberation would "release" them to be just as violent as men.[57] On the Left, student movements glamorized women engaged in revolutionary violence in Vietnam and other anticolonial struggles.[58]

Autonomous feminists agreed with neither Right nor Left. The cadres and marching orders conventionally imagined as part of a revolution were seen as precisely what feminist autonomous organizations were determined to prevent.[59] Feminists deplored revolutionary violence as the false pursuit of equality with men, claiming that RAF women and others sold out their own needs and perspectives to embrace a "masculine" taste for destruction. As a speaker at a 1976 Munich congress on violence against women put it, "We believe that our strategies and tactics should be consistent with our goals, and our goal is not violence, not domination and power, as presently understood and practiced."[60]

The projects were often idealized as a nonviolent but still revolutionary strategy that allowed feminists to work "for democracy and against domination."[61] The influential editor of *Courage*, Sybille Plogstedt, argued that women who entered the state's military services or took up violence in a revolutionary cause were alike in surrendering their autonomy for "a blind interpretation of the principle of equality" that "accepts still more conformity to men, sharing their obsession with destruction."[62]

Pacifism as a Feminist Principle

Because most feminists saw "obsession with destruction" as part of the state's male orientation, they called for women's resistance to remilitarization. Peace politics was framed as intrinsically feminist. Drawing on West German women's 1950s struggles against reintroduction of military service and joining NATO, they wanted West Germany to define itself as a pacifist state, repenting for its military sins. NATO's proposal to station midrange, tactical nuclear missiles in Europe in the early 1980s reawakened the dormant peace movement across Europe, especially in West Germany.[63] There were massive demonstrations in Bonn in 1981 and 1982. This popular mobilization engaged the women's public, which framed militarization as specifically male. The state set off a further uproar when it proposed in 1981 to include women in the West German Army (Bundeswehr).

On the other side of the Wall, the GDR response to NATO stationing rockets in the West was to propose more military training in the schools and mandatory service for women in its People's Army (Volksarmee). The smothering control the state exercised over civil society meant there were no large demonstrations in the East, but these proposals also stirred grassroots opposition. Peace mobilizations both East and West accelerated through the 1980s, and peace was a key mobilizing appeal to women in East Germany as well as to the movement-inspired women's public of the West all the way to 1989.

This engagement put German feminism on a different course from mainstream feminism in liberal countries. Internationally, debates had begun about whether women should be in the military as a matter of "equal rights and equal obligations."[64] If there were a real need for soldiering, most US feminists argued, both women and men could and should defend their country; moreover, if women served, the military would be less tempted to macho adventurism. West German feminists and East German women engaged in dissident politics saw possible military service in a much more negative light, since they read their history as one in which militarization was deeply problematic.

Neither gender equality nor the liberal idea that women might change the way the state and military functioned by entering these institutions resonated in West Germany. As Helke Sander memorably put it, this was "a strategy that presumes that one can come into a business as the cleaning lady and change it to produce something else."[65] Alice Schwarzer and *EMMA* took the "little difference" view that women should be subject to the draft as a matter of full citizenship. However, Schwarzer declared that she personally would be a conscientious objector and expected most women would also resist actual military service.[66] The pacifism of women—their *Friedfertigkeit*—and the strategic role women could or should play in political actions for demilitarization was debated, but the German feminist position, East and West, was consistently antimilitary.[67]

In the East, protests over the proposals to give military training to children and call up women to serve led to arrests and deportations. Alongside grassroots mixed-gender peace groups emerging in the 1980s, Women for Peace formed to speak as mothers to oppose military education in schools. Women for Peace viewed women as pacifist by nature, and organizing women was a political strategy to take advantage of this natural tendency.[68] As a dissident group, Women for Peace had to meet in secret; some of its activists were expelled to the West or imprisoned in the East, a reaction they interpreted as meaning that their resistance mattered.[69] This specific organizing of women by women built a network of resistance "around the kitchen table" that became one seed for the emergence of a more widespread feminist critique of GDR politics and the broader resistance to the state that brought it down in 1989.[70]

East German women dissidents experienced men and the churches as allies rather than opponents for meetings and demonstrations. As peace activists, they shared a negative view of state power. Since the GDR leadership fit the issue of military service into the framework of women's equality politics that characterized its education and employment policies (in theory, if not in practice), the split between this women's movement (for peace) and the official East German

women's equality movement (aligned with the state) undermined public identification with feminism. The churches did not claim to be for women's equality,
but they were perceived as standing for women's values of caregiving and nonviolence. Unlike the discursive framework of West Germany that made church
and state allies in oppressing women, the East German state and churches were
framed as opposed to each other. Either could be seen as supporting women,
depending on where women placed their emphasis: self-determination (speaking autonomously apart from the state) was politically dangerous, but being
for women's equality was not dissident.

In West Germany the rhetoric of the equality of women and men stirred
anxiety on both Left and Right. The value of women's supposed difference was
captured in the gendered militarism/pacifism divide. Even among feminists,
equality was explicitly disavowed as a goal that implied excessive sameness.
Whatever the projects revealed about the tensions of working with women
and through the state, they did not encourage feminists to claim to be citizens
like men, including a right and responsibility to bear arms. In confronting the
maleness of the state, women's practice of active citizenship was still imagined
as providing "sand rather than oil in the machinery" of the state itself.[71]

CONCLUSION: INSTITUTIONALIZING AUTONOMY?

The development of discursive resources and organizational practices went hand
in hand for German feminists, as is likely true of all social movements. Feminists needed not just resource mobilization to get their organizations up and
running but also discursive work to decide what these organizations were for
and what means were consistent with their ends. In this stage of mobilization,
when activists are new to the cause and strategies are emerging, the formulation
of principles and choices of particular practices to achieve them together will
define the movement and set a course for its later development.[72]

In this case, the movement-defining principle was autonomy. The abstract
idea needed to be translated into more concrete aims and ongoing practices.
This was the period in which this important work happened. Autonomy came
to include a set of organizational forms (autarky and local, grassroots groups)
and practices (choosing women's side and speaking from experience). The fact
that these organizations were stringently understood as only for women was

not the sole effect of these decisions. A relatively narrow definition of feminist (women who could meet the standards of autonomous politics by working in and for the projects) became the norm. The wider women's public the projects created—women put into movement by feminism—acted in some cases quite efficaciously to keep the work of the projects going, but most women moved by feminism had no opportunity to embrace the identity of feminist themselves since it was so narrowly defined.

The gradual institutionalization of the projects brought out serious contradictions in their guiding principles, making it clear that choosing women's side and speaking from experience were more contradictory than expected and needed organizational and discursive attention to keep the projects working. But the difficulties these strategies encountered did not make them failures, even though most feminists came to see them as fundamentally flawed. *Despite* the contradictions of project work, activists learned to run organizations, confront the state with their demands, and see the state at least sometimes meet them more than half way. This practice of empowerment was life-transforming for many women. *Because of* the contradictions in project work, activists began to see a more complex landscape in which women and the state were not inalterably opposed, and there was a need to represent women collectively, not just encourage each individual to speak from her own experience as the earliest c-r groups had done.

This desire to represent women sometimes moved the activists into intersectional conflict around ethnicity, sexuality, and nationality. It also led to effective mobilizations of the women's public around abortion rights, violence against women, and militarism, which became popularly understood as *"women's"* issues, with abortion rights framed most exclusively as women's concern and antimilitarism least so.

The idea that women could and should have a voice in representative democratic politics was a paradoxical outcome of the project movement. Even as the projects affirmed their outsiderness and oppositional stance to the state, they became entangled with it. Since they relied on the state's dough to continue to grow, feminists began to want a seat at the table when local, state, or national governments made funding decisions. Moreover, the projects were in practice representing women, calling on the women's public to demonstrate against the state or demand support for particular projects, but with no effective mechanisms to legitimate that representative role. Immigrant women and women of color were increasingly calling them to account for their misrepresentations.

The West German corporatist mode of governance allowed "women as a group" to be recognized by the state as having collective interests, but in practice the projects provided a quite restrictive space for the debates about what these were. In part because project work demanded a career level of time commitment, even if temporarily, and in part because being in a project implied standing outside the system, relatively few women "moved by the movement" could choose project-based activism as the way to be feminist. These *frauenbewegte Frauen* (women-moved-women) began in the late 1980s to look for organizational spaces that offered a wider variety of activism than found in the student milieu where the projects first emerged.

Overall, the project phase of feminism was successful if the criteria are discursive—naming problems, placing them on the public agenda, claiming resources to address them. In building their counterpublic, feminists defined what "violence against women" was and what could be done about it. In the words of Barbara Kavemann, an activist in the movement from its beginning, the projects against male violence collectively "changed public perceptions, showed that support was possible and that change could be made, and spread an innovative influence through the entire field of social work and related occupations."[73] But, as this quote also illustrates, the distinction between feminist projects and social work blurred over the course of the decade. Both the problems discovered and successes achieved pointed toward a need to change political strategy.

Before exploring where these changes took the movement, it is worth noting how the West German projects and women's public differed from the radical feminist collectives in the United States of this period. First, the "women's culture" of West Germany was self-defined not as a community but as projects and a public that supported them, that is, not as an end in itself, a source of feelings of identification and support, but actions oriented to a political agenda of mobilizing a broad constituency of women, theorizing a practice of autonomy as women, and engaging confrontationally with the state.[74]

Second, US projects, including shelters, were more readily taken over by liberal feminists with no ambivalence about professionalism, credentials, or organizational hierarchy. In West Germany, the project form was so important to the identity of autonomous feminists that the struggle to extend and improve it as a change strategy remained crucial throughout the 1980s.

Third, the women-and-lesbian identity of the movement helped keep both straight women and lesbians active in the projects and identified with the movement, but deferred explicit discussion of the relations between a politics of gender and of sexuality. In the United States, the "radical" feminism of local projects identified them with cultural nationalism and lesbians, who were imagined to have a natural affinity for women-only spaces.

Finally, the corporatist form of the state made the question of collective representation more central than that of individual achievement, not only for feminists but for the wider public they were attempting to mobilize. This not only allowed a women-only political practice to resonate more widely as a route to self-representation but also focused feminist attention on achieving a collective voice in the state, rather than ending stereotypes and decategorizing women as increasing the opportunities for individual women to advance, which is what many US feminists prioritized.

As the decade went on, West German feminists came to the conclusion that acting only as outsiders, as "sand rather than oil" in the machinery of the state, was not going to transform women's lives. They began to want their own machinery, so they could not just oppose what the state did wrong but also make the state do more of what they saw as right. Despite the projects' discursive successes in naming male violence as a problem and creating a public concerned with ending it, some feminists were coming to the conclusion that the *Frauenhaus* approach had failed as a way to put the state on "women's side" against violence.

As Barbara Kavemann summed up this case, the projects structurally could not act to reduce male violence, nor did they change the way the police or other institutions responded to it. She argued that "the assumption that supportive advocacy [for women] alone could change the gender relationship has not proven true," and that "the *Frauenhäuser* must fear that they serve as a social fig leaf and merely manage the consequences of violence. . . . The responsibility for men's violence just has been handed over to women in a new form."[75]

Although those who valued the grassroots model of the projects saw it as "spreading underground" and "hard to uproot," like grasses and weeds themselves, some project feminists began to see the institutionalization of the projects as outsiders more as an expression of anxiety about the power and maleness of the state than as an effective route to transforming it. Suggesting that at least some of those in the projects suffered from *Berührungsangst* (fear of contact), activists like Kavemann argued that feminists should enlist the state as an ally and work with it, not just against it.[76]

These concerns led West German feminists into their next stage of organizational development, moving inside state and party systems, even as the mobilization of East German women in dissenting peace groups began to create a space in which they could separate their own ideas of women's interests from the state's claim to have emancipated them. In both movements, working "for women" had triggered an ongoing rethinking of women's collective relationship to "father-state."

CHAPTER 5

WE WANT HALF
THE POWER
Feminists and Political Institutions,
1982–1990

As the meeting broke up, about six hundred women streamed out of the auditorium in small groups, actively debating what they had just experienced. The occasion was the founding congress of the Women's October 6 Initiative in Bonn in spring 1982, and it had been a contentious meeting. Women from the political parties had been invited to present policy ideas that would "take women's side," but they were met with catcalls from the audience. Some autonomous feminists angrily accused "party women" of being apologists for their parties, there merely as recruiters. Other "project feminists" argued that the new Green party (*Die GRÜNE*) was a potentially woman-friendly ally that could give them voice in the political system, even a chance to change the system itself.[1] Some were openly skeptical. They made a sharp distinction between autonomous feminists and "Green women." One woman near me turned to her friends, waved her arm in their faces, and declared angrily, "Just look at me, look at me! Does that arm look green to you? I am not a "green woman"! I am a feminist, and I will stay a feminist, no matter how often or how strongly I work for the Greens!"

This tension between project- and party-based ideas of feminist strategy grew throughout the 1980s. The day after the federal elections of October 5, 1980, some feminists decided something needed to be done nationally to advance a more woman-friendly agenda. Their October 6 Initiative was a controversial effort to break with the strategy of institutionalization through local, autonomous feminist projects. When it made its debut with the women's public at the meeting described above, the Initiative intended to provoke explicit discussion about the separation between party politics and feminism. It brought together "women from the women's movement, women from parties, unions and civic associations, women working on their own" to "look for a way to represent our interests ourselves, and better than has been happening until now."[2] An early member described the group as "seeing itself as an APO for women," a feminist grassroots political organization like the broad Extra-Parliamentary Opposition group in the 1960s.[3]

Trying to mix autonomy with party politics proved difficult. Most autonomous feminist groups responded critically to Sybille Plogstedt, founding editor of *Courage*, when she argued in 1983 that the projects and anti-218–Action Groups should come together into a nonhierarchical *Alternative Frauenrat* (Alternative Women's Council, a revived and redefined *Weiberrat*, the Revolutionary Women's Councils of the early 1970s).[4] Even such a weak network structure was strongly resisted by most autonomous feminists, who saw it as a dangerous retreat from their principles. US feminists, in contrast, had networks of interest groups increasingly concentrated in Washington and state capitals, where they could lobby on feminist issues. Australian *femocrats* leaped at the chance to enter government policy positions (coining the term to describe a feminist in a position to work on women's issues within the civil service).[5]

With a new, movement-centered political party seeking electoral support in the West, some feminists saw a window of opportunity for empowerment. Of course, the emergence of the Green party was not the only reason West German feminists reconsidered their role in formal politics. The internal contradictions of feminist practice in the projects, the problems in working both with and against the state, the struggle to connect project feminists and the women's public, and the desire for more radically transformative successes were also good reasons for autonomous feminists to rethink rejection of electoral politics. Even without the Green party, they had reason to think that inclusion need not mean tokenism and powerlessness—"coming in as the cleaning lady" as Helke Sander described it—but might be a claim for women's fair share of state power.[6] As half the population, why stop at less than half?

The Green party initially attracted feminists because it promised electoral politics done on antihierarchical principles: to spread positions around and avoid superstars, the party said that those who won seats in elections were not to be freed from other responsibilities and that no one could hold a high-ranking office in both party and parliament.[7] It was antimilitarist, proenvironment, and open to grassroots participation (one need not be a member to work in a policy group or even run for office). It even did not use the word "party" in its name.

Since feminists increasingly felt the project version of autonomy was too restrictive and unrealistic, they had real interest in an alternative organizational route. The struggle was whether self-determination could be stretched to include collaboration with other organizations, men, and the state without losing its core sense of empowering women as a collective political actor. It was not obvious on October 6 whether this effort would succeed. But the women's public was increasingly visible, making women-moved-women a target for political parties to recruit. The electoral effort threatened feminism's exclusive identity with and close ties to project-centered work, and many resisted this.[8] But with a feminist constituency for the Greens and feminist activists within it, Green strategies began to transform the party system, and changes in party agendas began to shift the goals and strategies of feminist work.

On the other side of the Wall, the East German dissident movement was growing in strength, also opening a window of opportunity for women to challenge the socialist state's claim to have liberated them. The universities, churches, and peace movement provided important openings for women to rethink their much vaunted emancipation, identify problematic political relations, and organize explicitly to make feminist change. Had East German women lacked these arenas for discursive work, even the opportunities presented by the emergence of organized political dissent and ultimate collapse of the state would not have led to feminist mobilization, as the absence of significant feminist voices in all other Eastern European transitions demonstrated.[9]

This chapter follows the opposite courses of feminist development East and West. Feminists in the East moved away from their state just as those in the West moved toward theirs, moderating their rejection and beginning to work in conventional party politics and in government policy machinery for women. By seeking political power through the electoral system and creating women-centered administrative offices in the state, West German feminists hoped to make politics responsive to women's collective interests. As women in the East emerged as feminist actors with new demands on the state, they had particular difficulty finding an organizational form that gave them sufficient distance from the state to avoid co-optation (the problem they saw in the DFD, the Communist Party-led women's association) but could still offer them a politically effective voice.

In more theoretical terms, I examine how states and parties collaboratively construct a web of meaning around the term "women" and institutionalize this meaning in the needs the state recognizes and the programs it establishes.[10] Despite this shared framework, particular frames remain contested within and across national lines.

PARTY POLITICS:
GREENING THE LEFT, CHALLENGING THE RIGHT

In the 1980s, West German feminists were not alone in their unhappiness with the two major parties, the Social Democrats (SPD) and Christian conservatives (CDU and CSU). In cities and student enclaves, discontent was rampant with both the SPD (popularly symbolized as red for socialism) and the CDU (black for clericalism, and tightly tied to its even more Catholic and conservative Bavarian sister party, the CSU). These parties both presented an economic-growth program focusing on construction and manufacturing jobs and reliance on nuclear energy. Both supported NATO-led militarization and male-breadwinner families, making them unlikely allies for feminists. In young, urban milieus, the alternative, as in the United States, was found in movement politics: environmental consciousness, antiwar sentiment, and feminism intertwined with "60s radical" values that questioned economic and political hierarchies and rejected economic success as a measure of personal worth.[11]

But unlike the United States, where winner-take-all elections make smaller parties merely spoilers, the FRG mix of individual seats and proportional representation meant that discontented voters only had to win 5 percent of the total vote to get party representation in parliament. The small, liberal Free Democrats (FDP, symbolized as yellow or gold, for its free market stance) had already demonstrated how to exercise influence with small numbers of voters. By exceeding the 5 percent hurdle and forming a coalition with a larger party, the employer-friendly FDP shaped the space for considering feminist claims—opening it wider, as it had done with the SPD in 1969 to reintroduce the abortion question, and tightening it in the early 1980s as it allied with the CDU and CSU against further expansion of the welfare state.

The FDP in the early 1970s appealed to some feminists because the party advocated reproductive rights and affirmed individualism in general and women's rights, personal freedoms, and economic opportunities in particular.[12] The SPD focus on protective legislation and a family-first definition of working-class interests made it a more problematic ally. The 1982 FDP coalition with the socially conservative and business-friendly CDU/CSU traded its support for individual-liberal principles for neoliberal economic ones. Disillusionment drove some women leaders out of the party and hardened opposition to electoral strategies among some project feminists. But it also pointed to the gap in the political spectrum for a classic liberalism that would prioritize personal freedom, self-expression, individual rights, and participatory democracy while rejecting neoliberal, free market ideology.

Such values reflected the individualist emphasis of liberalism and were essential parts of the student milieu's "new," postmaterialist orientation. The mix of antimodern, antigrowth, antitechnology, and anticapitalist rhetoric made these activists difficult to place on the familiar spectrum from Left to Right.[13] Those who called these mobilizations "new" social movements emphasized the rejection of the "old" politics of Left and Right and the postmaterialist values of their generally young supporters, and deemphasized the continuity of their values with classical liberal claims. In the United States, claiming personal freedoms focused on sexuality, with highly contentious mobilizations over abortion and sex education; in Germany, liberalism posed more sweeping challenges. Liberalism's marginal position in Germany had affected women differently from men, as state policy positioned them as objects of protection rather than supporting their personal autonomy. So while feminists shared the personal politics of the "new social movements," they were also trying to reshape the long historical legacy of patriarchal family protectionism on both Left and Right.[14]

As the new social movements sought ways to exercise influence—protest demonstrations were impressively large but ineffective in changing policy—their eyes turned toward elections. In the 1970s a coalition emerged from a set of local citizen groups (*Bürgerinitiativen*) pushing for more participatory democracy; it crystallized into a formal electoral alliance of Green and Alternative List candidates in 1980.[15] Environmental politics notably separated this new Green party from the SPD, which was seen as representing the pork-barrel interests of conventionally employed male workers in the partnership of unions, big business, and the state. Greens saw this corporatist alliance as literally paving the countryside in the name of building the road to prosperity, and wanted it to stop.

But Greens also wanted a new, more participatory kind of politics. Their base of support was infused with antiwar, anticapitalist, antitechnocratic ideas that feminist projects shared. Although always a minority, feminists were a large enough group to have leverage in the coalition, just as the Greens had leverage on government policy, once they came into the Bundestag in 1983 and into governing coalitions in five states by the end of the decade. The Green party emphasized its commitment to women's self-determination, as with the campaign advertisement shown in Figure 4, from a mid-1980s state election depicting a vote for the Greens as how the fairy-tale princess Rapunzel would free herself. The poster also emphasizes the party as one of (social) movement, an opportunity for women moved by feminism to act on their own behalf.

The addition of the Greens to the electoral equation thus shifted the political calculus in a woman-friendlier direction. Participatory democracy, valuing nonmarket work, and women's empowerment in society were the three issues the Greens addressed in feminist-friendly terms. These issues show how interaction among feminist frames and party platforms worked, as all the parties were increasingly challenged to reconfigure their framing of women's interests to speak to the new women's public feminists had called into being.

Participatory Democracy: Representing Women and Changing Politics

Both men and women to whom the Greens appealed were concerned with widening the parameters of politics and challenging the state to be more just and democratic. Embracing nonhierarchical collective structures of local, grassroots participatory democracy was how they framed themselves as at odds with the "old" parties and the interests they represented. For the Green party to claim successfully to represent this constituency, it could not do politics-as-usual. The Greens wrote party rules to institutionalize a minimal division of labor and power. All elected offices were to rotate, and rather than committees or shadow ministries, the party developed its bills in "working groups" (AKs)

FIGURE 4 This election cartoon changes the fairy tale of Rapunzel being rescued by a prince to one of her self-liberation by voting "Green women into the state parliament." It is a poster for the Green party in the state-level election in North Rhine Westphalia, and its caption reads: on top, "BREAK OUT: *for the self realization of women*"; and by the flower, "Politics requires movement(s)!"
Source: NRW Green Party State Office (Landeszentral, GRÜNE/Bündnis '90).

with membership open to nonparty members. Even candidates for office did not need to join the party.[16] A feminist could be a Green party activist without becoming a "Green woman" in any formal sense.

But institutionalizing participatory and nonhierarchical politics proved no less tricky for the Green party than for feminist projects. Once the party won 5 percent of the popular vote in 1983, the reality of managing the work, money, and publicity involved in being represented in the Bundestag began to undermine participatory ideals. How the party should adjust to these pressures divided *Realos* (realists) from *Fundis* (fundamentalists).[17] The realists wanted to get the work done—including winning elections—to get the power to change broader social relations; the *Fundis* believed that compromising principles to win elections meant giving up the chance actually to transform the political system. Project feminists entered on the *Fundi* side, but some became deeply involved in the *Realo* work of day-to-day party maintenance, winning campaigns and raising the percentage of women in office.[18]

Feminists gained political presence through the Greens. Women were ten of the twenty-eight representatives when the Green and Alternative List entered the Bundestag for the first time, and Green electoral success handed feminists a media microphone. Alternative List Representative and autonomous feminist Waltraud Schoppe made an unprecedented speech about sexism on the floor of the Bundestag, and Green women made a public scandal out of sexual harassment by focusing on the behavior of one male Green representative.[19] Green politics made history in 1984 when all three official speakers in its parliamentary delegation (*Fraktion*) were women, as were all three executives running its daily business.[20] This so-called *Feminat* was subjected to intense media scrutiny which highlighted the otherwise unspoken normality of male dominance.

Although the *Feminat* made women's political leadership credible, their exercise of authority occasioned much discussion of whether women in power positions were really so different from men. Some feminists saw this as meaning that women who were not willing to conform to male norms were not selected for leadership roles. They framed it as a variation on the problem of excluding mothers from power that Helke Sander named on the occasion of the famous tomato toss.[21] For such *Fundis*, the party had to model an alternative way of doing politics to remain credible. *Realos*—both men and women—thought including women, the symbolic outsiders, in roles of authority was enough in itself to demonstrate the party's transformative potential.

Navigating these tensions, the party decided in 1986 to establish a 50 percent women's quota with a "zipper principle." This "zipper list" placed men and women candidates alternately on the electoral list, ensuring that women and men would be equally represented among those taking office, regardless how few or many votes the party drew. The zipper list was effective because it not only increased the number of women making policy among the Greens, but also it offered a competitive advantage in attracting the votes of the feminist-inspired (*frauenbewegte*) women's public by positioning the party as woman-friendly.

This move empowered the women's caucuses of the other parties, which became worried they might lose women voters. The SPD feminist-influenced caucus, the AsF (Arbeitsgemeinschaft socialdemocratischer Frauen) had existed since 1973 but only began to see its influence rise in the 1980s, and the CDU created the Frauenunion in 1988.[22] Before the Green zipper list, women in these parties had met little success in bringing more women into elective office and decision-making roles, but this changed almost immediately afterward. In 1988 the SPD endorsed a principle affirming that at least 25 percent of the places on party electoral lists and in leadership positions would be reserved for women, a goal for which the AsF had pushed in vain since the 1970s.

Quotierung—pledging to achieve some stated proportion of women by adopting a quota—did not say how the goal would be achieved or impose penalties for failure. The quota was self-imposed, by party vote, and applied only to the party's own offices and candidate lists. But Green quotas shifted the norms of the whole party system, as Figure 5 shows. The women's share of SPD seats more than tripled from 10 percent (or less) through 1986 to 34 percent (or more) from 1994 on. CDU/CSU seats "only" doubled from 7 to 14 percent in the same period (see Figure 5).[23] Because the women's public was apparently paying attention to gender representation, women's mobilization inside the parties for such quotas paid off.[24] Quotas in countries with proportional representation have proven successful around the world for increasing women's representation and feminist advocacy in national legislatures. West Germany was no exception.[25]

Policies explicitly aimed at women's interests also increased dramatically. Framing these policy goals fractured along party lines, although the Greens' working groups provided a stimulus to both revaluation of motherhood on the

Women's Share of Parliamentary Seats by Political Party

Bundestag	CDU/CSU	SPD	FDP	Greens	PDS/ Linke Partei
8th WP 1976–80	7.5	6.7	10.0	-	-
9th WP 1980–83	7.6	8.3	13.3	-	-
10th WP 1983–87	6.7	10.4	8.6	35.7	-
11th WP 1987–90	7.7	16.1	12.5	56.8	-
12th WP 1990–94	13.8	27.2	20.3	37.5*	47.1
13th WP 1994–98	13.9	33.7	17.0	59.2	43.3
14th WP 1998–2002	18.3	35.2	20.9	57.5	58.3
15th WP 2002–5	23.0	37.8	25.5	58.1	100.0**
16th WP 2005–9	20.4	35.6	24.6	56.9	46.3
17th WP 2009–	20.6	38.5	24.7	54.4	52.6

* The Greens had no list-based representation in the 12th Bundestag, the first in which both East and West parties participated, only those individuals who won local seats.
** Because the PDS did not cross the 5 percent hurdle in the 2002 elections, it was represented only by two women who had won local district elections and did not function as a party.

FIGURE 5 Women's Share of German Parliamentary Seats by Political Party for Electoral Periods (WP) 1987–2010 at the Start of Each Session (in percent)

Source: Data from Beate Hoecker, „50 Jahre Frauen in der Politik: späte Erfolge, aber nicht am Ziel." In *Aus Politik und Zeitgeschichte,* Beilage zur Wochenzeitschrift *DAS PARLAMENT,* Heft 24–25/2008, S. 10–18, and http://www.bundestag.de/ blickpunkt/104_Spezial/0402020.html.

Right and affirmative action for women state employees on the Left. The discourse of feminism became a policy discourse, political in the classic sense: it engaged participants outside the project milieu, tied goals to party preferences, and identified specific women's interests with public policy choices.

The Value of Nonmarket Work: Supporting Motherhood

Asserting the significance of placing value on things the market does not regard as important (be these environmental costs, community engagement, or household labor) tended to bring Greens together with portions of the CDU and CSU. These conservative parties had historically framed women in family terms, for example, defining the 1949 constitutional paragraph guaranteeing women equal rights as valid only within the limits of "functional differences" in the family.[26] The CDU and CSU now picked up feminist-created interest in improving the status of women and revaluing the tasks associated with motherhood. Policy proposals still emphasized the role of women in the family and the importance of the family to society, but they now were targeted to win support from younger women voters.

In 1985 the CDU National Party Congress in Essen endorsed "Guidelines for a New Partnership Between Husband and Wife."[27] This model was particularly advocated by CDU family ministers Heiner Geissler (in 1983–86) and Rita Süssmuth (in 1986–90). Support for mothers was offered not just rhetorically but also financially. The CDU and CSU government built on the SPD-led family support policy of 1979, a maternity-leave provision that gave employed women six months of paid leave and prohibited employers from firing them. The CDU and CSU extended this to a longer-term child-rearing subsidy (up to two years) independent of prior employment status.

This "new partnership" rhetoric shared several frames with autonomous feminist discourse: that women's distance from the capitalist market was a virtue, and that full-time mothering was valuable work for which the state should pay. Süssmuth's rationale for including mothers not previously employed in the new "leave" payments was that the money should compensate women for the valuable time they were devoting to child care. The CDU rhetoric of "reconciliation of work and family" framed the issue as helping women juggle their responsibilities, not seeing that men had any part in the problem.[28] But by mixing appeals to making the "personal choice" to stay home available to all mothers with the "recognition of reproductive labor as work," the rhetoric echoed popular feminist "pay for housework" proposals.

However, the actual subsidy was also contingent on staying out of the paid labor force (with the exception of very part-time jobs that carried no benefits) and was not enough to live on, keeping it fully compatible with the male-bread-winner policy system. Further encouragement for women to leave the labor force was offered by securing a mother's right to return to her firm, though not to her same job, for three years. This made the policy a target of criticism from those in the movement concerned with women's labor force position, which it significantly compromised.[29]

Whether this was a "feminist policy" became the subject of debate both in and out of the movement. Before becoming CDU/CSU minister for Family, Women's, Senior and Youth Affairs, Rita Süssmuth had been the initiator and first director of the Institute for Research on Women and Society, an autonomous feminist project. When she was appointed minister of Family and Youth in 1986, she insisted that the mandate be extended to women. She became a popular and prominent CDU/CSU member, without ceasing to consider herself a feminist. Her frequent use of the word "feminist" to describe herself in public in the late 1980s was widely regarded as broadening the meaning of the term and making it more socially acceptable. Even the Left-leaning autonomous feminists who thought Süssmuth did not deserve the label thought this did feminism a service.[30]

The CDU also adapted the feminist idea of recognizing women's reproductive labor as work by calculating a year out of the labor force raising children as contributing to a woman's pension entitlement. Although reckoned as low-wage work, not on the basis of the individual's own foregone earnings, this economic entitlement was a small step toward officially counting women's work as a social contribution.[31] Adopting this policy demonstrated how resonant the feminist framing of women's reproductive work as valuable and underrewarded was. Even conservatives refused to rely on markets alone to define the value of labor.

The attraction of these CDU policies to some feminists was evidenced in the debate unleashed by the *Mother's Manifesto* produced by a group of autonomous feminists who met under the auspices of the Green party in 1986.[32] These mothers had been organizing for a few years in autonomous "mothers' centers."[33] The centers defined "mothers" as women engaged in intensive full-time child care; the language of the *Manifesto* followed this narrow definition by dividing women into "career women" and "mothers." The former, even if raising children, were lumped with "nonmothers" as enemies of an empowering politics by and for (nonemployed) "mothers."[34]

The *Mother's Manifesto* demanded a more mother- and child-friendly society. It argued against measuring a "politics for mothers solely on the basis of overcoming the division of labor by gender," and proposed beginning "with support for mothers in their initial position" as (nonemployed) mothers. While praising the Green party for its support, it insisted that women's politics be done without "any effort to force or maneuver it into a pre-existing party line or party structure." These "mothers" defined themselves as progressive, and their goal was to "develop a model of emancipation that took account of the value of the traditional content of women's work, that is, giving care to people, perceiving social relatedness, questioning so-called 'objective pressures,' and offering [mothers] appropriate social, political and financial recognition."[35]

While the *Manifesto* authors insisted that their Green politics was "as fundamental as it was absolutely realistic," a substantial number of prominent "Green women" repudiated it. Their counterstatement agreed that "the 'typically feminine' tasks in the home and in the paid economy were undervalued" and that "the entire public sphere is so structured to make it only barely possible to participate in it when also caring for children, the elderly or the sick."[36] But they saw the policy direction of the *Manifesto* as dangerously aligned with the CDU platform. The signers of the counterstatement emphasized that the Greens "in distinction to other parties" had not accepted "the family as the only legitimate and right form of life and as therefore worthy of support, but had tried to create acceptance and space for other ways of living." They insisted that overcoming the gender division of labor was an essential goal for feminists, and no less achievable than the "real support" for mothers the *Manifesto* demanded.

There are two ways to interpret this public debate about supporting mother-work. On the one hand, it responded to a political opportunity in which the CDU and CSU sought to modernize their approach to families without weakening support for the conventional policy model. By embracing the feminist rhetoric of a mother-friendly society while keeping women defined nearly exclusively by their position as reproducers, and offering carrots rather than sticks as the policy tool to keep women out of the paid labor force (or from advancing in its better-paid sectors), conservative policymakers convinced even some autonomous feminists that they were women-friendly and established their credibility in the women's public.

On the other hand, the debates over the "new partnership" and *Mothers' Manifesto* can also be seen as West German manifestations of a transnational feminist debate about equality and difference that reached its peak in the 1980s.[37] American books like Carol Gilligan's *In a Different Voice* and European ones like the *Milan Women's Bookstore Collective* volume were translated into German and embraced enthusiastically by advocates of seeing women as having very different needs and values from men.[38] As public policy around the world was shifting toward framing equal citizenship for women as a norm, policies to achieve it in practice varied. American public policy affirmed equal treatment norms, with sometimes exaggerated disregard for actual differences in social positions; West German policy extended and reaffirmed state interest in protecting mothers and children, with sometimes exaggerated disregard for the inequality in gender relations that put them at risk. As party-based opportunities increased for a policy discourse centered on difference, so did opportunities for claiming a right finally to realize equal rights and economic justice. But this claim also took a different form than it did in liberal political contexts.

Affirmative Action Before Equal Treatment

The politics of motherhood was in tension with the demand for women's advancement (*Frauenförderung*) that also emerged in the mid-1980s. Its advocates were found in the Green party, in the SPD, and in labor unions. Alice Schwarzer also weighed in on the women's advancement side.[39] But it would be a mistake to see this argument in West Germany as a claim for equality instead of "difference." It did not emphasize equal treatment of women and men as individuals, as classic liberal antidiscrimination policy would; rather, it called for active state engagement to shift the structural gender arrangements that disadvantaged women socially, economically, and politically. The ideal was women's advancement, and the policy goal was to take "women's side," choosing to advance women even if it cost men something.

Despite the enduring sense that men and women had conflicting interests, changing men was no longer seen as hopeless. At a personal level, of course, women had all along been struggling against men as "pashas," the term popularized as a critical description of male entitlement, like "macho" in the United States.[40] But some began to think that changing men collectively as husbands and fathers might be a legitimate political ambition. For example, the Munich feminist project housed in the city hall used the image of a man pushing a baby carriage to illustrate its commitment to equality (see Figure 6).

Even though men were no longer irrelevant, the policy goal was not to treat women and men "as if" equal in the hopes of making them so, as liberal nondiscrimination laws might, but to address both genders in their distinctiveness and bring them into a less hierarchical relationship. Both *Quotierung* and *Frauenförderung* were described as "affirmative action" or "positive discrimination." Although the term "affirmative action" was borrowed from the United States, its German meaning differed.[41]

In West Germany, the claim that the state should take an active role to advance the position of groups with special needs is a well-institutionalized part of the discursive framework, especially with regard to class membership and

FIGURE 6   Carrying season's greetings from the Frauenakademie München (FAM), an autonomous group of feminist academics, this card celebrates five years of existence of the women's equality office in the Munich city government by depicting a man pushing a baby carriage as their "best wishes."
Source: FAM, reprinted with permission of the artist, Root Leeb.

inequalities. Feminist framing emphasized state action for women as something the state owed women citizens collectively. Parties on both Left and Right found the claim resonant. The Right used the state to act on behalf of "mothers" (as economically dependent full-time child-rearers); the Left wanted to use the state to meet women's special needs (as victims of violence or mothers who wanted more economic opportunity).

The Green version of affirmative action for women called for *Quotierung* (quota rules) for public and private employers, not only the political parties. The Greens proposed a gender-equity bill that was not an antidiscrimination law in the American sense but a requirement that "women with adequate qualifications be hired preferentially for any position in which they were underrepresented until a level of at least 50% was reached in all areas and at all levels." The Greens called for reducing work hours to six per day for both women and men to both redistribute unemployment (already increasing, especially among younger people) and to allow both genders to be involved parents, not "placing the first-line responsibility for child rearing only on women."[42]

The idea of quotas in employment, supported by both project feminists and Green women, began to make inroads among the SPD and unions in the 1980s. Heide Pfarr, an early and strong SPD advocate of a quota strategy, argued that the alternative was to continue discriminatory "male quotas." She cited a 1981 railroad policy in Lower Saxony that explicitly limited women to 10 percent of the assistant station manager jobs.[43] She envisioned quotas as a short-term strategy to open access to male-dominated positions until there was a critical mass of women, and as negotiated by union-management contracts rather than demanded by law. This reflected the labor history of West Germany, where union strength in collective bargaining meant relying on bargaining agreements to secure fairness.

This push for preferential quotas came without significant prior legal basis for equal treatment. The first law governing "equal treatment of women and men in employment," passed in 1981, was known as the European Community Conformity Law because it was adopted under pressure from what would become the EU. In order to coordinate national laws to equalize conditions of economic competition between member-states, the European Community demanded that member-states prohibit direct discrimination against women (or men). The West German law complied, but barely, requiring explicit evidence of discriminatory intent and lacking redress. For example, the law required only compensation for the actual cost of an application that was explicitly rejected on the basis of gender (paying a successful woman plaintiff only for the envelope and stamp her application cost her, not lost wages). Such tiny sanctions posed no deterrent to even blatant discrimination.

The weakness of antidiscrimination law was largely due to the absence of a party with a strong interest in advancing it. The SPD was reluctant to support anything that might undercut protective legislation. Maximum age rules for promotions had a disparate impact on women, but rather than eliminating the rules, the SPD favored exceptions for mothers based on their number of children. "Special help" and gender-specific protection offered a resonant approach to remedying women's difficulties in the workforce, and the proposed quota model was consistent with union and party style of addressing women as a special-needs group.

This approach reflected Left skepticism about equal rights (*Gleichberechtigung*), framing it as a "merely liberal" (thus nonprogressive) political value. Feminists engaging within the SPD to move the party in a more prowoman direction did not try to overcome its disinterest in antidiscrimination law, but instead sought to reshape its tradition of protection for women. They adopted a new advocacy role, taking the idea of women working for women into both party and state. This was more consistent with the classic Left emphasis on collective representation. In this way feminists used their alliances in the Greens and SPD to open an alternative, nonelectoral route to political power, where women could represent women in the policy machinery of government.

WOMEN IN THE STATE: INSTITUTIONALIZING POLITICAL ADVOCACY

State advocacy for women as a distinctive political constituency took the form of formal offices inside the government to "create equality" (*Gleichstellung*) from the top down as an explicit policy goal. The women's offices resonated with the project model of "women helping women" and with the popular understanding of the state having an active strategy to provide for the welfare of its citizens. But for feminists to enter the state as advocates, and work with and on men to change male-dominated institutions, implied a shift just as radical—and initially controversial—as alliances with political parties.

The groundwork already existed. In 1974, the SPD government had established a staff office for women in the Federal Ministry for Youth, Family, and Health, which tried to improve reentry prospects for women who had left the labor force, offered training programs to enter male-dominated trades, and built relations with select feminists in the projects.[44] This office funded the first Berlin *Frauenhaus* and negotiated the first affirmative action plan in a private company. This kind of advocacy from within the state was seen as offering real bargaining power for advancing gender politics, as unions did for class.[45]

Representing Women in State and Local Government

This institutional advocate for women was a *Frauenbeauftragte*—a person, grammatically female, responsible for representing women. I translate it as "women's affairs officer," though this understates its assertively female gendering (a woman given responsibility for women). Those appointed to a state *Gleichstellungsstelle* (*GSS*, a newly created position for actively making equality) were called *Frauenbeauftragten*.[46] The tension between advancing women as a group, which resonated in the West German Left, and advancing gender equality through nondiscriminatory practices, which did not, is captured nicely in the policies and politics of these offices.

The first state-level offices for women's affairs were set up in Hamburg and Hessen in 1979, and the first city-level position in the mayor's office in Cologne in 1982.[47] The Cologne women's affairs officer had been in the women's project movement and saw her goals as working especially on funding women's projects and examining city planning for its impacts on women.[48] Both Hamburg and Hessen emphasized developing career options for women, especially in city government. A mix of advocacy for women as citizens and as civil service employees became characteristic of such offices as they spread.[49]

The *GSS* strategy took off like wildfire. Already in 1984, North-Rhine Westphalia, a strongly SPD state, mandated that every town of more than ten thousand have a women's affairs officer. To coordinate local efforts across party lines, a National Network of Local Women's Affairs Officers was founded in 1985, an organizational innovation autonomous feminists would have fought just a few years previously.[50] The concept of women's offices proved so popular that by 1987 the number of city offices had grown to two hundred fifty, and many state-level agencies and universities had their own. By 1990, the eleven hundred *GSS* at all levels of government included four hundred immediately established in the East when the GDR collapsed.[51] In short, this particular state machinery for advancing women's position was institutionalized quickly and enthusiastically, growing from nonexistent to normal in a decade. Unlike anti-discrimination law, it was not controversial in principle. Criticisms centered on its ineffectiveness, reflecting its broad mandate and relative lack of resources, resembling the *Frauenhäuser* in these respects.

Resources and authority did begin to expand. The first Action Program for Women was negotiated by the Green party in its coalition with the SPD in Hessen in 1984. The first women's affairs officer with state secretary rank, Marita Haibach (an Alternative List feminist rather than Green party member), was appointed the following year with control over a multimillion-dollar budget. In 1988, the SPD-Green government in Schleswig-Holstein elevated its women's equality of-fice to ministerial rank, and other states soon followed. Such a ministry would be headed by a prominent woman politician, have a civil service staff doing policy research, allocate and oversee grants to state and local women's groups, and have a formal mandate to develop legislative proposals. At first, pressure from outside feminist groups was critical for establishing such positions.[52] But the innovation was quickly normalized and became widespread even in CDU/CSU governments.

The first women in these positions saw themselves primarily as autono-mous feminists.[53] As the offices became more institutionalized in government, incumbents also varied more, with some appointed from the ranks of state or city administrators, some party loyalists, and some from feminist projects.[54] Budgets and access to formal decision-making roles varied, with Green and SPD appointees typically having more authority and resources. Women's affairs officers differed in program preferences, but they all saw the position as having three essential tasks: extending the reach of the women's public, meeting women citizens' special needs, and representing women employees in civil service.

Extending the Women's Public

To make the women's public effective, women's affairs officers tried to build bridges between autonomous feminists and women in mixed-gender organiza-tions who had been "moved by the movement." An engaged women's public provided the women's affairs officer her leverage, and the more organizational power in this public, the more effective she could be. By overcoming both

autonomous feminists' suspicions about the state and traditional women's organizations' suspicions of feminists, the women's affairs officer could develop
women's collective voice to advance feminist goals with, rather than against,
the state. Criticized by some as turning the movement into an NGO or interest group/lobby, this strategy provided new tools to activists, notably expertise
and insider influence.[55]

At least some autonomous feminists responded to bridge-building from
these new "state feminists" with organizational outreach back. In 1987, Halina
Bendkowski and other autonomous feminists started FrauenfrAktion as an
autonomous umbrella organization in Berlin to link women in state and local
governments (regardless of party) with autonomous feminists. The national
Green party formed the FrauenAnStiftung to use the tax money allocated to
it on the basis of its electoral success to fund autonomous women's projects.[56]
The strategy of working in and outside the state, in cross-party coalitions, as
representatives of all women, developed feminist legitimacy.

By 1990, the idea of a "women's coalition" (*Frauenbündnis '90*) was taken up
by prominent women politicians at the national level (among them Süssmuth
of the CDU and Schoppe of the Greens). Even though the coalition did not
survive beyond a few meetings, it expressed the desire for unity among women
that had become a dominant motif.[57] The new sense that women's political
power rested on a unifying peak organization that could speak for them reflected a model that had been successful for labor unions.[58] Like unions before
them, the organizers found it easier to focus on the goals of particular subsets
of members than to sustain broad participation.

Meeting Women's Special Needs

Meeting women citizen's special needs often was translated into advancing
feminist projects. Well-institutionalized projects like the local *Frauenhaus* or a
women's center demanded funds, which the women's affairs officers were expected to secure. Women's affairs officers also supported new project-like initiatives. Depending on their own politics, mentoring projects for women going
into business (CDU), training women with computers (SPD), or "women's
night-taxis" to supplement public transportation for women after dark (Green)
might be especially favored. Choosing among projects was tricky, and some
tried to avoid this aspect of the role as much as possible.

Their reluctance reflected a new organizational dilemma. If the office tried to increase its budget (a sign of power in a bureaucracy) by funding projects, it would become the target of the furious disappointment of those who were not funded, as many inevitably would not be. If it left the funding of feminist projects to other relevant departments, the mere existence of a women's office would be an excuse for these agencies to cut women's funds. Thinking of women as a separate group with special needs collided institutionally with defining women as citizens with interests that spanned the full spectrum of government activity.

The idea of identifying women's needs as special led many women's affairs offices to focus on policy interventions in areas with few institutional competitors for funding. These areas included addressing violence against women (such as the *Frauenhäuser*, antirape programs, or projects counseling incest survivors) and women's sexuality (reproductive health care and prostitutes' rights). Especially at the local level, feminists engaged with city planners to sponsor curb cuts and kneeling buses (for strollers) as an uncontroversial form of affirmative action for mothers. Unlike the Americans with Disabilities Act, which produced similar physical changes in the US urban landscape, these accommodations were negotiated rather than legally mandated. The focus on women as a special needs group and on violence against women as an issue produced policy interventions like "designated parking places" for women (see next page, Figure 7). These places were located in a supposedly safer place (under a street light or near a cashier) to protect women from sexual assault. This reservation of special space for woman in a parking place both symbolically recognized women's presence and framed them as a special-needs group.

Enhancing Women's Opportunities in Employment

The equality offices' third goal was to advance the position of women within the civil service itself. The lack of effective laws against discrimination made it difficult to pressure private employers to hire or promote women. The women's affairs officer took on the job of developing procedures for hiring and promoting women by making state or city government a test site and moral model for affirmative action hiring policies.[59]

The test revealed considerable tensions. The unions' legal role as worker representatives collided with the equality officers' claim to speak for women, since women employees were both women and workers. Some women's af-

FIGURE 7   My photograph of a "women's parking place" could have been taken in
nearly any large German city, as women's equality offices lobbied for special protections
for women. In addition to parking by the lights or cashier, a subsidized taxi ride at night
also associated sexual assault with strangers, from whom the state would take action to
protect women.
Source: Photo by author.

fairs officers were elected by women employees alone, underlining that women
were a group entitled to collective representation. Conflicts emerged when a
women's affairs officer wanted to modify seniority rules to make more allowances for mothers or sought penalties for sexual harassment, since mostly male
unions had opposing interests.[60] The conflict between women's and union
representatives indicated that autonomous feminism was no longer able to
avoid confrontation with the "old Left" by focusing just on issues of violence
and sexuality.

Still, as unions and feminists competed to represent women as workers, the
women's public inside the unions and SPD found this a new source of leverage. Feminist-inspired activists in the unions and women's affairs offices drew
on networks with feminists in projects and academia that mutually strengthened them by exchanging expertise and practical information. This advocacy
work shifted labor politics in more feminist-friendly directions. In 1988, for

example, the union-friendly, SPD-led state of North Rhine Westphalia passed a law mandating women's advancement through affirmative action hiring in state and city government (*Frauenförderungsgesetz*).

Important as these union and party women were becoming to the movement, they were still not feminists in the narrow West German sense. An economist who had worked with unions and the SPD for at least this entire decade on making policy more woman-friendly surprised me, for example, when I asked in 1991 if she considered herself a feminist by saying, "Oh, no, I have always worked with men!" The idea of autonomy as mandating a gender politics separate from class politics remained powerful. Even though feminists had given up their reluctance to enter the state, feminist identity still carried a connotation of separateness. West German women's gender interests were conceptualized as represented by collective organizations run by and for women alone.

This institutional division between class and gender politics is evident in the ill-fated West Berlin kindergarten strike of 1989.[61] State-funded kindergartens were still overcrowded and underfunded (as in the days of the *Kinderläden*), and the all-female, unionized workforce wanted limits on class sizes and better pay. While their union (ÖTV) supported the wage demand, the largely male leadership did not accept the teachers' analogy between rising class sizes and production speedups. As representatives of all city workers, they were more concerned about the pressure size limits would put on the overall city budget. When the union finally did authorize a strike, it did not call for job actions by the city workers in other, male-dominated jobs, as it otherwise would. Such union politics left the daycare workers vulnerable.

But so did gender politics. Women in the SPD and Greens, some of whom called themselves feminists, had—amazingly—won half the seats in Berlin's governing senate. But they saw the daycare strike as a labor issue and themselves as acting for the employer, the city, and interpreted closing kindergartens as a cost-saving measure rather than as a loss of essential services for women. Only after the strike had gone on for eleven weeks were local autonomous feminist groups able to mobilize support. By then the strike was lost. Women in a female-dominated field, doing reproductive work, fell into the conceptual crack between "women's issues" and "labor issues." Being "for all women" ran a real risk of not being for working women, just as being "for all workers" had allowed unions to minimize their commitment to women.

It is striking that West German women entered the state not only through electoral offices but simultaneously through new policy machinery for women in its administrative arm. These official women's advocates shared the goal of representing and advancing women as women, but their route to access also divided them by party, obscured intersectional concerns women shared with men of their race or class, and gave more voice to affluent and socially integrated citizens. Their effectiveness was hampered not only by their low level of funding but by the enduring myth of a unitary women's interest. The actual intersectionality of women's interests with their multiple identities and loyalties made a single "women's party" a chimera, but one that framing women as a collective political actor encouraged West German feminists to chase. For example, there were two failed attempts to form a separate "women's party" in the 1980s and early 1990s.[62]

The separatist legacy of autonomous feminist projects continued to echo in the institutional politics of the women's affairs offices. When I asked a West Berlin women's affairs officer in 1990 if she would support a program to train men for conventionally female jobs like kindergarten teacher or nurse, she exclaimed, "Of course not!" As I explored her emphatic and unwavering opposition, she denounced American programs to do this as "silly." Rather than helping women, which is how she understood her job, she thought such a program would take jobs from women to give to men.[63] Being a "women's affairs officer" did not make it her job to think holistically about gender relations or changing men. Even "inside" the state, feminists who defined autonomy as their goal imagined a politics for women alone.

The overall direction of feminist change in West Germany was toward the state. Political parties, electoral offices, and state and local governments presented different types of obstacles and opportunities, and by the end of the 1980s feminists had gained a foothold in them all. The West German era of autonomy was over, but not without leaving marks on the way issues were framed and organizations structured. These marks became most evident when West and East German feminists found themselves sharing a single political space, since in the 1980s, as West German feminists were moving from an outsider stance into the state, East German women were moving from accepting the state as representative of their interests into more dissident, outsider roles. This development posed challenges in the GDR with which Western feminists were not familiar.

IS THE TIME OF RENEWAL PASSING US BY?
MOBILIZING EAST GERMAN WOMEN

The House of Democracy on Friedrichstrasse in Berlin was a ramshackle but lively place in early 1990. In the middle of downtown East Berlin, now newly open to the West, and only a few blocks from where the once-massive Berlin Wall was being chiseled into souvenir chips of concrete, the House of Democracy had been taken over from its previous owners, the SED. Vivid social-movement posters hung on the walls and hand-lettered signs directed the visitor to the offices of movements such as New Forum, Democracy Now, and the Independent Women's Association (Unabhängiger Frauenverein, UFV). This visible location in the center of political action symbolized the UFV role as representing "the" East German women's movement to the emergent GDR government and the rest of the world. It was the UFV whose members were appointed to the cabinet of the transitional East German government to represent women's issues. Organizationally, it stood for East German women's distinctively feminist aspirations in the midst of the *Wende* (transition).

This position was temporary and precarious. Less than a month after the Wall fell, on December 3, 1989, about three hundred women who had been active in one or another of these contexts had come together in a Berlin theater to formally establish the UFV, an umbrella organization with the purpose of playing a role in the remaking of the East German state and society. The DFD, the "old" GDR women's movement organization, was a discredited tool of the SED. There was a felt need for some sort of political representation—as one group of academic feminists asked, "Is the renewal of society passing us by?"[64] The UFV, woven from diverse strands of feminism that had developed over the 1980s, was a way for women to step into the historic moment of transformation as movers and shakers, not merely observers or victims.

The UFV presented an apparently single organizational face of a new autonomous feminism and was often mistaken for its only voice. The reality was more complicated. Feminist mobilization arose in many contexts in the GDR and became even more diverse in the new political landscape. Three strands of feminist organizing came together in the UFV for a little while: political dissidents and peace activists who were very critical of the state; local lesbian and mothers' groups that were not political in any conventional sense;

academics and others sympathetic to the GDR's achievements who wanted
to reform socialism from the inside out.

Politics Means Resistance to the State

The most obviously political actors among the feminists gathered in the Berlin
theater were the peace activists. They typically engaged in local protest activities against the GDR and were the smallest group present, not because they
were less feminist, but because their energies were already absorbed in mixed-
gender political groups such as the Initiative for Peace and Human Rights or
New Forum. Their self-conscious activism as women could be traced back to
mobilizations in the early 1980s as part of the East German peace movement.
Stationing short-range tactical nuclear missiles in Europe had not only stirred
West German protest but also spurred oppositional mobilization and built dissident identities in the GDR.

The leading group, Women for Peace, had formed in 1982 "around the
kitchen table" of Bärbel Bohley, the "mother of the revolution" who was ar-
rested and deported for her activities.[65] The organization grew as other women
reacted to state crackdowns against these protestors. Ingrid Miethe's extensive
interviews with these activists (who merged later with New Forum, a mixed-
gender group) reveal how the women recognized themselves as effective political actors through the state's efforts to suppress them. Being against the state
and prodemocracy was as important to them as being against the military, but
gender separateness was not their self-concept; they mobilized as women for
peace and against the state, but not for any distinctive "women's agenda." These
dissidents led peace marches with one eye out for the state's tanks, but paradoxically were also GDR loyalists who did not take advantage of the cracks in the
GDR's border defense to rush for the exits in late summer 1989, instead taking
to the streets to assert "We are the people" and "we're staying here."

The Politics of the Personal

A second, far larger group of UFV founders were women who, through various
local activities, had gradually come together to address contradictions in their
personal lives as woman. Since the GDR banned organizing outside officially
recognized groups, even discussions of "private" issues of sexuality and domestic
labor went underground. However, the GDR allowed churches to hold meet-

ings, so an astonishing array of local women's groups formed under the shelter of the Lutheran Church. Among the earliest were women theologians who had access to meetings with their West German counterparts since the mid-1970s and now shared feminist perspectives with them.[66] Feminist theologians in the East were active in their churches, and theological topics such as male hierarchies in the church often spilled over into wider political discussions. They became institutional allies for the other groups who began to meet in the 1980s.

One type of group formed among mothers home full-time on their paid maternity leave. They gathered in church spaces (without necessarily being members of the church or sympathetic to Christianity) to counteract the social isolation that resulted from their loss of work-based networks. Their discussions of their social marginalization as women and mothers had an increasingly feminist edge.[67]

More surprisingly, perhaps, the church offered space to groups of homosexuals to address issues of identity and sexuality in relation to the relentlessly antigay rhetoric and laws of the GDR. These groups soon split along gender lines.[68] Lesbian groups were the most active in doing public outreach in a climate in which this was incredibly difficult. Not only was organizing illegal, but also there was no access to resources such as photocopiers or mimeographs; announcements of meetings were hand-copied and distributed personally. By 1986 large numbers were turning out at local activities and cross-city organizing had even begun, with the first of three annual lesbian conferences held in Dresden. A national women's festival in Jena in May 1989 drew two hundred women, a miracle of word-of-mouth organizing.

The first feminist newspaper in the East, *Frau Anders* (A Different Woman), began in Jena even before the Berlin Wall came down. Begun by and for lesbians, these groups increasingly involved heterosexual women, especially academics, artists, writers, and musicians who were drawn to their mélange of cultural politics, civic activism, and feminist knowledge work. Such groups rarely defined themselves as "political." Although creating a more democratic public space and finding a distinctively women's voice made them politically suspect, they rarely experienced the direct repression that defined being "dissident."

By 1989 members of these diverse local groups began to define themselves as a "women's movement." The groups were most developed and dense in the southern part of the GDR (Leipzig, Jena, Erfurt, Dresden). Had the UFV founding meeting been held in one of these cities rather than Berlin, local groups rather than academics would probably have dominated it.[69] These local groups were primed to act. For example, in December 1989, as state power collapsed, several local women's movement groups jumped in to seize the buildings housing their towns' secret police (Stasi) and convert them into women's centers or shelters for battered women.[70]

Politics as Working from the Inside Out

The Berlin location for the founding meeting was advantageous for the attendance and influence of academic women, who were relatively privileged by ties to the SED, but also critical of the party. Especially in the social sciences, some Berlin-based scholars had been involved officially and unofficially in research on women that had proved consciousness-raising.[71] The GDR-sponsored official research group on the status of women at the Academy of Sciences in Berlin, established in 1981, did several studies that showed state policies toward women were not offering the liberation the government proclaimed. Not wanting to hear this critique, the state refused to publish their findings. The studies circulated surreptitiously and other research was done without state authorization or resources.[72] By spring 1989, planning was already underway for a Center for Interdisciplinary Research on Women at Humboldt University in Berlin. The researchers involved opened the center as soon as the state collapsed in December.

Some of these academic women were committed socialists and party members. As such, they had privileged access to international conferences and feminist scholarship published in the West. For example, Hannah Behrend, a longtime party member who had come to the GDR from England with her ideologically committed parents after World War II, taught American and British Black feminist writers' works in her university English classes.[73] Others took advantage of their new ability to go across the border to buy books and copy articles that had previously been forbidden.[74] For all activist scholars, the ability to turn a feminist lens on GDR gender relations was an inspiring opportunity. Academics already had a political analysis, so they were as quick to seize the discursive resources of the party as grassroots activists had been with the physical Stasi headquarters.

Academic feminists tended to see the SED not as evil but as failing, despite good intentions, to advance the cause of women's emancipation. Present in significant numbers for the UFV founding meeting, they wanted to reform but retain the basic parameters of the East German state. They hoped to keep policies that in their view had worked well, while modifying the state to make its political processes more democratic and its substantive gender politics more effective. They published their critique of GDR policy toward women in the national women's magazine, *Für Dich*, in early November. One of the more junior scholars, Ina Merkel, a historian, drafted the UFV statement of principles. She also served as its representative in the newly restructured but still SED-led transitional government formed in the immediate aftermath of the Wall's collapse.

The UFV statement especially critiqued the state for its patronizing treatment of mothers, the "mommy politics" that defined women alone as responsible for children and reproductive work, by giving women (not men) a day off per month to do "their" housework, and the long child-care leaves that left them isolated and high-risk employees for training or promotion.[75] The statement idealized the option of part-time work—for both women and men with children—as allowing parents to stay connected to their workplaces, argued for policies that would not define only women as likely to take paid time off, and strongly critiqued the narrowly production-centered ideology of the GDR. The UFV program envisioned a nonpatriarchal family in which men had a more active role, more opportunities for women in the workplace, and a democratic grassroots voice in politics. These demands resonated with the entire assembly.[76]

Participatory Democratic Politics in the "Time of Chaos"

The UFV window of opportunity was open for a remarkably short time. In the immediate chaos of the collapsing GDR, the UFV was quite successful in providing women a voice. In December it elected two members to the national Round Table, and in January a representative joined the GDR's final national cabinet. In February the UFV was represented in many local Round Tables that took over city and town government functions. In March the GDR national assembly (Volkskammer) endorsed the "social charter" the UFV had played a major role in writing, which was imagined as a basis from which the GDR would negotiate with the FRG to preserve social entitlements. All this political activism was perceived as extremely energizing and empowering. As one activist reflected ruefully afterward, "the time of chaos was the best."[77]

That vision ended with the March 1990 national elections that swept from power all the oppositional groups native to the GDR, including the

UFV. The resounding victory of the large West-affiliated parties, especially the CDU, which was most actively promoting unification, made the social charter irrelevant. The goal of institutional politics in the East was now to join the West. The transitional government set up a ministry for women's affairs, as was common in the West.[78] The first draft of the unification treaty mentioned women only once, with the handicapped, as groups whose "special needs should be respected." The East German state was not being reformed from the bottom up, as the UFV had expected and desired, but replaced from the top down.

The UFV, like other oppositional groups, campaigned strongly against unification and lost. Activist women ("mothers of the revolution," in Ingrid Miethe's phrase) dropped out of sight as the men doing party-centered politics took over.[79] West German Chancellor Helmut Kohl promised no one would lose through unification and offered an apparently advantageous currency conversion.[80] He emphasized the commonality of the German nation ("what belongs together now grows together"). The new political playing field was a unified Germany, created officially October 3, 1990.

Virtually no one in the UFV knew how to do politics in this new situation. Rather than trying to connect with the women's public of the West, their concern remained what they saw as the distinctive interests of East German women. They did not allow West German women to join the organization or to set up chapters in the "old federal states" (the West). As Round Tables lost influence, the UFV lost its access to decision-making structures. Its ability to present itself as "the" representative of women's aspirations faded, dismissed by media claims that the UFV's defeat at the polls (along with all the other social movement parties) meant East German women had "repudiated feminism."[81] The hope of reforming socialism to make it better for women was over.

Diversity in the UFV itself now made it difficult to formulate new organizational goals. After its rousing initial call for women's participation in politics, a serious antidiscrimination policy in the workplace, and the transformation of men and families though gender equality in the division of reproductive work, it had not found an organizational form to translate these broad concerns into specific policy. It was divided between those who wanted a weak umbrella over strong local groups and those who wanted to turn it into a registered political party or a unified national lobbying group.[82]

Although their diversity had captured the variety of currents that contributed to bringing down the GDR government, members now struggled among themselves over what the UFV should become. Those with a more general oppositional stance were strongly opposed to working with reformers who had been part of the communist state and whose SED membership—or Stasi informant role—now labeled them as dangerously antidemocratic. These one-time insiders often affiliated with the Party of Democratic Socialism, PDS, the successor to the SED that controlled its substantial assets.

The PDS assertively used feminist rhetoric (for example, critiquing patriarchy) to profile itself as modern, antihierarchical, and different from the SED, while arguing that GDR policy toward women represented accomplishments that should not be lost.[83] It adopted women-friendly positions the Greens had initiated, such as the zipper list, and defended abortion rights and kindergartens. But it was not in the least attractive to feminists who had fought the SED, who saw any successor party as inherently undemocratic.

Even in the chaos of transition, the specific routes feminists had taken to their positions continued to shape not only their perceptions of what would be good for women but also what organizations and political strategies could realize their goals. In the "time of chaos," participatory democracy was widespread—from official Round Tables at all levels of government to burgeoning participatory protest groups—and experienced as exhilarating and life-changing.

The empowerment proved short-lived. Rather than remaking East Germany, feminists joined other activists in disappointment with the rush to unification. The political terrain on which East German feminists found themselves was new and difficult to navigate. But they came to this new citizenship with formative experiences of repression, empowerment, and loss that continued to be important to them, no less than the struggle to achieve autonomy and then to enter the state continued to be for West German feminists.

CONCLUSION: THE CHALLENGES OF REPRESENTING WOMEN

Although the courses of women's activism in this decade varied strikingly between East and West, it is important to note how much variation emerged within each state. Differences that had always existed among feminists emerged as strategically significant as more women were empowered to act on "women's interests" in both the FRG and the collapsing GDR. Differences in relating to the parties were rooted in political socialization on each side of the now fallen Wall, and these were certainly not homogeneous in either state. Still, the willingness to work with and in the state that autonomous feminists in the West discovered during this decade contrasted with the taken-for-granted attitude among many East German feminists that the state was the focus of politics, whether one worked to reform it or to overthrow it.

The UFV slogan was, "You can't make a state without women."[84] The 1980s had made women's role in state-making more significant to both West and East. But remaking the West German state posed different challenges from building a new one. Before addressing the challenge of making the unified Federal Republic include women as full citizens, the varied meanings of "women" would have to be addressed. The histories of the two states and movements created an important division that would have to be dealt with for women to decide how they would relate to this newly unified state.[85] The windows of opportunity that opened in each separate state in the 1980s were replaced by a single window. But how to take advantage of it looked different to the women on each side of the "wall in our heads" that still separated the nominally unified country.

The complexity of finding a common definition of what it would mean to "choose women's side" and work politically for women was increased by the very different experiences of the state each side had. A woman in the GDR had been defined as a "worker-mother" who was a full-time employee as well as responsible for children and housework.[86] The state helped support women and children, whether they were married or not, and made them more autonomous of husbands in forming households, but assumed housework and children were women's responsibility alone. This ascription of domesticity to women, and the double day of labor it created, was a major target of East German feminist critique of the state as a public patriarchy.

FRG policy and practice instead made the "wife-mother" the object of its protective policies. By making paid employment counternormative for mothers and expecting men to be breadwinners and heads of households in which women remained economically and socially subordinate, the state enshrined the patriarchal relations of private families in public policy. This was the chief target of West German feminist critique. Since it was so difficult to form a self-supporting household or raise children without a better-paid partner, feminist definitions of women's interests focused on empowering women as mothers and freeing them from their dependence on men, which were not pressing issues for East German feminists.

These state constructions of the meaning of women and their interests were discursively institutionalized, that is, anchored in the language of both countries' laws. These frameworks pointed East and West German feminists in different directions and added to the complications created by their differing organizational histories. A third source of division was to be found in the power relations between the "newcomers" and the already institutionalized West German movement. How important this fact was only became apparent after unification. But as different as these two German states had been, the GDR and the FRG had both appropriated the role of deciding what was good for women and paternalistically providing it. Virtually invisible as decision-makers, women had been defined by the social politics of their state, rather than by their own political actions. Hannah Arendt would call this state of affairs one in which "the political" had been squeezed out by "the social."[87]

But now, women's alienation from their own agency in politics was no longer so prevalent. Whether through the long road autonomous feminists had followed into electoral and administrative roles in the state, or through the chaotically empowering movement politics of the collapsing GDR, women had emerged as collective political actors who wanted to define their own needs for themselves. "Women," however, have repeatedly proven resistant to being confined in a single definition. The differences of personal and political experience between women in the West and in the East produced sparks of both heat and light when the two women's movements collided in the process of German unification, each with its own vision of making a new, more feminist state.

CHAPTER 6

YOU CAN'T MAKE A STATE WITHOUT WOMEN
German Unification, 1990–1995

THE WOMAN I WAS INTERVIEWING sputtered with anger. An academic sociologist, Birgit had taught introductory courses at the University of Leipzig and done research on families, but her real passion for the past few years had been feminism. She helped develop an interdisciplinary study group at the university and a local women's newspaper. She had been eager to see the GDR opened to criticism over its treatment of women and was not sorry to see the total collapse of the country after the Berlin Wall fell. Birgit had gone into the West as soon as she could to gather feminist materials and visit a mother's center. She saw the possibility of teaching about gender and women's movements in the Eastern part of newly unified Germany as the opportunity of a lifetime.

And it was not going to happen. The all-male committee of social scientists who came on behalf of the Federal Republic to review her credentials cleared her of the taint of Marxism attached to anyone teaching the required courses on Marxist-Leninist social theory. They applauded the quality of her research on families and youth. But they looked baffled at her request to teach women's studies. "Can you believe it! They told me that this is not a recognized field of study in the West!" she exclaimed. Though she and I both knew this was not true, she had no way to resist. She hoped to continue with her feminist research anyhow, but as a "hobby," since as a single parent what she needed now was a stable income.

All around her, both women and men were losing what they thought were tenured positions, factories and stores were closing, and unemployment skyrocketing. Meanwhile, new institutions in both the public and private sectors were opening up, with unfamiliar bureaucratic procedures and surprising rules. Women whose jobs or companies disappeared found themselves in a quandary: if they took their children out of public child care because they were now home to take care of them, the child-care center might close overnight for lack of demand. And the unemployment office informed them that they did not qualify as available for work unless they could show that their children were already in child care. But how were they to pay the no-longer token fees from their unemployment benefits? And why should they have to?

When the Berlin Wall fell on November 9, 1989, it turned out not to be the beginning of an era of reform for an independent German Democratic Republic (GDR), but the start of a process of German unification. In less than a year, on October 3, 1990, formal unification was completed, and the GDR was absorbed as five new states for the Federal Republic of Germany (FRG). This new, unified Federal Republic was structured along the same lines as the old one. This was a tremendous shock for everyone, but most especially for women and men in the "new federal states." Overnight, as "immigrants in our own country," they faced the hurdles of adjusting to different laws and different ways of doing things in everyday life. With the notable exception of abortion law, unification meant coming under West German laws and procedures.

The GDR women's movement was a small boat caught in this maelstrom. The East felt the brunt of social change, but patterns institutionalized for feminism in the old Federal states of the West were also rearranged, for both good and ill. The slogan of the East German women's movement organization, the UFV, that "you can't make a state without women" was put to the test in a way no one had anticipated.

East Germans did successfully put one issue on the FRG political agenda: the classic struggle over women's self-determination in abortion. That this was such a key part of the unification process was a surprise to some, but vividly illustrates the significance of cultural frames for political decision making.

The story of unification is not only one of the struggles ex-GDR women faced trying to get a foothold in the FRG, though the challenges in employment and changes in family relations were massively dislocating for women's daily lives. The feminist projects and equality offices built in the former GDR illustrate the dual challenges of adaptation and resistance for women also trying to do feminist politics. These were compounded in the tensions and misunderstandings arising from the different positions of women "from the East" and "from the West," despite efforts made by feminists on both sides to work through them. Overall, the story of unification is one of disunity, and it theoretically leads to reflections on what this brief period reveals about the bigger picture of struggles over differences among women in Germany and globally.

REPRODUCTIVE RIGHTS ON THE POLITICAL AGENDA

As the GDR was collapsing and its population rushing to embrace the opportunities for travel, freedom of political expression, and consumer goods offered in the West, one issue caused some to hesitate. Legal abortion in the first trimester had been a fact of life for people in the GDR since 1972. Skeptics about the merits of unification—feminists, dissident movements in general, and the PDS—pointed to the criminalization of abortion in West Germany to stir popular doubts. In the end, abortion law was the only aspect of the FRG system that was not immediately applied to the East, but set aside in legal limbo to be decided two years after unification by the new parliament.

The meaning of this pending decision and the political resources deployed to influence it could hardly have been more different in the ex-GDR and FRG. Although appearing even-handed, even the language of the treaty tilted the playing field westward. By defining the issue as a legal resolution that "better guaranteed the protection of unborn life and a constitutionally correct management of a conflict situation for pregnant women than is the case in either part of Germany at this time," the high-court judges appointed in the West became arbiters of constitutional correctness under the FRG Basic Law.[1] Exempting the decision from the initial imposition of FRG laws over the entire country was a victory, but only a partial one. Whether the glass was now half-full or half-empty depended on which side of the Wall you had lived.

For feminists from the West, deferral provided an opportunity to revisit and revise their existing abortion law, which made abortions criminal unless a woman could win approval for legally accepted "justifications" of fetal deformity, threat to the mother's health, rape, or "social necessity" (*soziale Not*). For feminists in the former GDR, already confronted with loss of political power and often facing unemployment or poverty for the first time in their lives, the possibility that the law would also take away their right to make their own decision about having a child was an appalling threat. The distinct discursive legacies of each state also colored the ways the movements responded to this volatile situation.

Feminist Opportunity in the West

For years, autonomous feminists had been unwilling to accept the 1974 "social necessity" exception as a victory, since it meant that women were not making their own decisions by right, but rather asking for "charity" from doctors in a "situation of need." Most women simply sighed with relief that they now had such a legal loophole, but feminists were outraged that women needed a doctor to certify a situation of need—the exception under which more than 80 percent of all legal abortions were carried out. Throughout the 1980s, demonstrations against §218 were the most frequent occasion to call the women's public onto the streets, with, at best, modest success.

Mobilizing the other side, the Catholic Church and the more conservative Catholic-dominated states, Bavaria and Baden-Wurttemberg, tried to end what they saw as the abuse of the social need exception, to prevent health insurance payments for abortions, and to limit the number of providers.[2] When a CDU-led government came to power in 1982, women politicians of all parties worked behind the scenes to ensure that it did not introduce legislation that would tighten the need exception or otherwise limit women's access.[3] The issue continued to boil beneath the surface, but no party wanted to raise it in the Bundestag, and unlike the United States, parties in West Germany tightly control the legislative agenda.

The subterranean pressures for limiting or expanding women's abortion rights exploded in 1988, in what came to be known as the Memmingen case. In the Bavarian town of Memmingen, local authorities brought charges against hundreds of women and their gynecologist, Horst Thiessen, for engaging in illegal abortion. The prosecutor argued that the grounds offered by these women failed to meet the definition of social need, so the social necessity exception was being abused. In the end, 174 women were fined, more than 100 others investigated but not convicted, and Dr. Thiessen sentenced to two and a half years in jail.

The case was a media sensation and an occasion for massive protests. The major newsmagazine, *Der Spiegel,* ran a lurid red-and-black cover screaming "witchcraft trial" (*Hexenprozeß*) in bold letters against flames. The idea that these were the modern equivalent of the witchcraft trials of the seventeenth century was expressed frequently in the mainstream press.[4] Of course, the many local feminist newspapers and the national magazine *EMMA* also took up the theme of witch hunts and church-state attacks on women.[5] Unlike the mainstream press, they provided details of the situations that were defined as not "real" emergencies, for example, a woman whose pregnancy meant she would lose her apprenticeship, whose boyfriend beat her, or whose husband had deserted her. Many were outraged that individual women's circumstances became the objects of public discussion and their decisions were being second-guessed by a (male) judge.

The attention given to this case brought to the surface, belatedly, what had been happening for years without media coverage. Between 1983 and 1988, an average of more than 170 prosecutions of women for illegal abortion occurred annually, resulting in about ten convictions each year, a steady campaign of intimidation.[6] The media now estimated that about two-thirds of all abortions the previous decade had been done illegally. Audits showed that many more doctors were putting in insurance claims for reimbursement of abortion services than were reporting the abortions, which criminal law demanded. Such arbitrary enforcement underlined the hypocrisy of the law.[7]

Thousands of women took the streets again, as had not happened since the early 1970s. More than seven thousand women came to Memmingen for a demonstration in February 1989, shortly before some decisions were to be announced. After Dr. Thiessen was sentenced in May, most cities saw demonstrations.

The media directed attention to the differences in practical rights for women in different parts of the country. With similar populations, in 1989 Stuttgart in the conservative south registered only 18 legal abortions, while northern Dortmund recorded 4,124. This massive media coverage and its wider implications faded only after the protests on the streets of Leipzig, the exodus of citizens from the GDR, and the fall of the Wall became more compelling stories. No one expected the FRG government also to collapse, but it could hardly preach democracy and ignore the aroused constituency for changing the law. The coincidence of Memmingen and the collapse of the GDR finally offered Western feminists a good opportunity to win a better law.

A Threat to Women in the East

Since East German women had lived under a regime that allowed first-trimester abortions without regard to reasons, hearing the Memmingen story gave them pause in the rush to unification. The government intervention into private choices shown by this story suggested, disturbingly, that West Germans were not as free as they claimed and that GDR gender achievements were now at risk.

The 1972 GDR abortion law was part of the same international reform movement that led to the 1974–76 reforms in West Germany (and the 1973 *Roe v. Wade* decision in the United States), and reflected similarly unsatisfactory experiences with criminalizing abortion.[8] But the lack of public discussion left the stigma associated with abortion untouched, so the debate about abortion law that began at the time of unification was a new experience for East Germans.[9] Unlike West Germans (or Americans), the GDR population had not formed political positions through decades of struggle.

The self-determination for women in matters of reproduction institutionalized since the 1970s in East Germany included not only a legal right to abortion in the first trimester but also free contraceptives and generous support for childbearing. Married or not (about one-third of all GDR women who gave birth were not married), mothers received state-provided paid leave (the "baby year" feminists in the West had envied, twelve to eighteen months in the final years of the GDR), subsidies for basic necessities like rent, food, and transportation, and state child care.[10]

Women and men in the East whom Elizabeth Rudd interviewed a few years after unification were quick to point out that the GDR had been "family friendly": it offered a slower pace and no incentives for devoting extra time to your job, so the competitive "elbow society" was newly experienced as incompatible with family time.[11] Both women and men found it outrageous that women would lose the opportunity to make their own decisions about having a child, in unsettled times, when the risks of choosing a child were so much higher. As soon as the idea surfaced that East Germans would be placed under the West German §218 criminalizing abortions, many protested that a right that women "had exercised responsibly" was being taken away for no good reason.[12]

Their sense of outrage was very different from that expressed in the West, being filtered through their distinctive experiences with dictatorship and democratization, and a political landscape in which church and state were opponents, not allies. For ex-GDR feminists, self-determination of abortion had a significant parallel in self-determination of democracy and was perceived as a fundamental political right of the free individual.[13]

Those close to the Lutheran Church, where much of the movement for democracy had been nurtured, saw abortion in terms of democracy. One writer in a church-related newspaper argued that a primary Christian value was "respect and tolerance for the decisions of conscience of those who think otherwise (*Andersdenkende*)," a clear allusion to the *Andersdenkende* the GDR had imprisoned and exiled. Another wrote that "the equality of women and men in creation is reason for Christian Democrats particularly to advocate the equality and value of women! We Christian Democrats should separate ourselves from undemocratic traditions in this regard." Another asked why a real democracy would undermine "the centrality of the individual person, in this case the individual woman."[14] Abortion as a test of women's citizenship in a true democracy was a feminist position that resonated with religious speakers in the East.

For reformers who had not given up on the principles of socialism, the threat to abortion rights symbolized a threat to the legacy of the GDR and their reform aspirations for it. They framed the 1972 law as an "accomplishment" and restrictions as "backward," and they called for combining democratic rights with continued social benefits from the state. These reformers related the absence of abortion rights for women in the FRG to the absence of political rights in the GDR. The moral "utopia" (an intentionally built, good society) behind the abuses of the past was used to suggest that good intentions of those criminalizing abortions cannot prevent such laws from becoming abusive. A letter to the editor said, "A humane purpose sanctifies no inhumane means. That too is a bitter lesson from the GDR past."[15]

Even East Germans who had not been politicized before the *Wende* often saw the West's model of counseling and state permissions as "a demeaning judgment about women in the former GDR. It suggests that they acted without a conscience for the past twenty years when, as the law allowed, they made their own decisions for or against the birth of a child."[16] For both women and men in the East, abortion decisions were framed as about democracy, freedom, rights, and the moral status of women and of all East Germans as political actors. It was "not just a women's issue," since it touched on core feelings evoked by the democratic movements of the transition, reflected the political inequalities already being felt in the unification process, and threatened families' and individuals' fragile sense of control over their lives, destabilized already by rapidly rising unemployment. As a matter of practical import and symbolic significance, abortion rights jumped to the top of the agenda for the people of the former GDR, but as a threat to be resisted rather than an opportunity to be seized.

The Politics of Reform in Unified Germany

The unification treaty gave the new German parliament two years to devise a law that would respond to these concerns and withstand an inevitable constitutional challenge. The leadership for this struggle was very different from that of the 1970s. Rather than a massive popular mobilization confronting relatively unwilling parties, with the government taking charge of the reform, protest on the streets now was muted and the debate in parliament was directed primarily by a cross-party coalition of women officeholders. This echoed their role behind the scenes in the 1980s. Women parlimentarians now stepped forward as the legitimate representatives of women's interests in abortion and were deferred to as such by both the male party leadership and the autonomous women's movement.[17]

Women representatives were a clear majority of members of parliament speaking on the bills being introduced (about 75 percent of those who spoke).[18] The broad coalition of women legislators drafted their own bill, separate from those of their parties, and it was this bill that was—with some modifications—enacted. The revised law removed the power of doctors or judges to evaluate women's reasons and to decide that they were insufficient, thus addressing concerns the Memmingen trials raised in the West. But in addition to a waiting period, the law imposed mandatory counseling on women. This was to be "pro-life oriented but outcome open," that is, explicitly designed to manipulate rather than coerce women into having the child.

The law struck many women in the East as inherently disrespectful, as if they had suddenly stopped being the moral and responsible actors they had been. Yet it was experienced by many women in the West as a gain for self-determination. Even West feminists who felt it did not go far enough in respecting women's right to make the decision—including *EMMA*'s publisher Alice Schwarzer—saw it as "better than nothing." Considerable pressure was brought to bear on party-based feminists to accept the compromise. Unwilling to risk the gains it offered, few FRG feminists were willing to take to the streets to push for a more radical reform.[19]

Framing Changes and Conflicts

Not only did FRG feminists think it hopeless to get a better law past the scrutiny of the constitutional court, but over the course of the 1980s many of them had backed away gradually from a position of pure self-determination in matters of reproduction. While women's self-determination mattered, many feminists now gave it a more maternalist spin: abortion should be a woman's choice because of her special connection to the fetus and moral role as its guardian.[20]

This heightened maternalism was especially evident in parliament. For example, women representatives routinely described the fetus as a "developing child" (the court's language), and the pregnant woman as a "mother to be" (*werdende Mutter*). Unlike liberal arguments that frame the fetus as the property of the woman or an issue of privacy of medical choices, this maternalist discourse positioned the fetus as so much part of a woman's "self" that abortion was equivalent to "partial suicide." Since "all women would be mothers if they could," speakers claimed it was unimaginable that women/mothers would "choose" abortion unless they saw no other viable option. Given the special association of mothers with their children, "it would be ridiculous for doctors or judges—who after all only know what the woman tells them" to be thought more morally capable than the woman of making the correct choice.[21]

Women in parliament who embraced the language of women as inherently inclined to be mothers accepted the state's paternalistic role in helping them realize their natural choice. The economic power of the state would "help not punish" women in need (the SPD slogan) and combine with its moral role in counseling to lead women to "say yes to the child" (the CDU slogan). The cross-party women's bill included state gestures of future support for child care as well as mandatory counseling to help women deal with a "crisis pregnancy."

In parliament, the only resistance to the "helping" view of the state came from a handful of women representatives from the East and formerly autonomous Western feminists, who argued that ending a pregnancy need not involve a psychic crisis. To them, counseling was an insult, since "apparently no other country sees women in pregnancy conflicts as such morally and ethically weak persons."[22]

The shift toward maternalism and state protection was evident outside parliament as well. Even the few autonomous feminists who took to the streets no longer chanted, "My body, my right."[23] The 1970s idea that women's bodies were their own, to do with as they pleased, had faded in the 1980s, as most autonomous feminists in the FRG took a critical stance toward surrogate mothering and new reproductive technologies. They opposed treating women's organs or babies as their "property," their bodies as private (and thus "rentable") space, and legally unconstrained ("free") choice as an individual right, arguments that carried the day in liberal policy frameworks such as the United States. The demand of the 1960s and 1970s for the absolute right to self-determination for women was seen as a "ghost" haunting the movement more interested in an actively regulatory and protective state.[24]

Skepticism toward "unnatural" foods and genetic manipulations, widespread among the Greens, joined with long-standing feminist concerns about the power of doctors over women's bodies now to define in vitro fertilization (IVF), embryo transfer, and other reproductive technologies as dangerous assaults on women.[25] The identification of women as mothers, and motherhood as a crucial aspect of women's power, made the potential of such technological interventions not only a threat to women's health but also to their unique social value. New reproductive and genetic technologies were challenged internationally by feminist groups such as FINNRAGE in the 1980s, but this oppositional stance resonated particularly strongly in Germany.[26]

The discursive opportunities of the FRG favored this framing. West German feminist involvement with the Green party and the alternative milieu offered a supportive context for shifting the balance of argument away from individual rights toward collective opposition to technology, including calling on state authority to block hi-tech medicine.[27] In Germany, stem-cell research and IVF, for example, continue to be opposed by the Greens, not just by conservative Christians, as they are in the United States. Historically grounded opposition to anything with eugenic implications also mattered. Later-term abortions were typically for eugenic reasons, and disability rights advocates in the 1980s focused on eliminating eugenic grounds for abortion. This overall context made feminists' earlier demand for complete abolition of §218 through the whole course of pregnancy problematic for them. A first-trimester window in which women needed to provide no specific reason seemed more acceptable. These obstacles to continuing their own past abortion politics encouraged autonomous feminists simply to allow women in parliament to control the issue.

In this two-year period after unification, the mobilization in the former East Germany also subsided, not because of approval for the law—the vocal dissidence of the few East German women in parliament confirmed this—but because the problems confronting ex-GDR citizens multiplied exponentially. Loss of jobs and housing, debates over who had been involved with the Stasi (political police), and unfamiliarity with the bureaucracies of their new state overwhelmed concerns about abortion law.

The Half-full, Half-empty Glass

The abortion law passed by the Bundestag in 1994, after small modifications by the FRG constitutional court, gave a woman the limited right to make the decision herself in the first trimester. It continued to define abortion as a criminal act but promised never to punish it if the woman went through "pro-life oriented but outcome open" counseling. It imposed a waiting period after this counseling. It withdrew coverage by health insurance, but allowed women without means to seek state funding to make sure they had access to the same rights as anyone else.

Though the law attempted to eradicate regional differences by mandating that counseling be widely offered in every federal state, implementation still varied. In 1996, Bavaria passed a restrictive law that forbade outpatient abortions and allowed doctors' homes and offices to be searched for evidence of breaking this law.[28] In states formerly part of the GDR, such as Brandenburg, abortions continued to be performed by most doctors, and financial aid was facilitated as much as the law permitted, reflecting the climate of respect for women's decisions institutionalized there.

Even if they were disappointed, women in the West gained legal protection from "another Memmingen," and this offset their concern with the loss of rights the law imposed on women in the East. The new law, along with most changes sweeping through the new federal states, was seen as simply one more way women in the East were "the victims of unification." While this framing overlooks the opportunities as well as costs in the change, the struggles facing feminists in East were indeed massive.

THE POLITICS OF SURVIVAL: REBUILDING FROM A POLITICAL TSUNAMI

The UFV had been one of a number of democratizing organizations that had a seat at the Central Round Table governing the last days of the GDR. In the brief and chaotic period of the peaceful revolution, the UFV had made feminism visible and given women activists real hope. Its slogan, "You can't make a state without women" (*ohne Frauen ist kein Staat zu machen*), resonated with feminists in both the East and West. But for all the activists in the House of Democracy, feminist and nonfeminist alike, the promise of making a new state out of the ruins of the old was quickly overtaken by the reality of being incorporated in a triumphalist Federal Republic.

Because dissidents had embraced a vision of freedom and self-determination, not of an individual in a free-market free-for-all, they experienced the incorporation of the GDR into the FRG as a moral defeat. It became a practical defeat when the movement-based parties (where skepticism about unification was most vocal) received an electoral drubbing from the strongly prounification CDU led by Chancellor Helmut Kohl. It was even more of a defeat for the UFV, which saw itself as cheated out of its one seat in parliament by the movement coalition it had entered. Voters represented by the Greens in the West also were punished for their skepticism about unification, with the Green party falling below the 5 percent qualification for entering parliament at all. The remaking of the state was going to be led not by movement parties, but by the CDU and CSU, bolstered by an influx of voters from the East.

These new CDU voters saw the party as speaking to and for them: it was the most promarket/anticommunist party, allied with the church (which had supported democratic dissent), and vehemently in favor of unification. Angela Merkel, a pastor's daughter who had not been much engaged in the earlier protest movements, presented a typical case of how the CDU recruited educated women with self-determined lives (a physicist, divorced and remarried, maintaining her birth name) who might in other circumstances have been feminists. Like many women in the GDR, Merkel benefited from the state's educational policies, but also faced discrimination, more as a Christian than as a woman. The SED government, not a domestic regime of male authority, shaped her oppositional priorities. Her autonomy as a woman was anchored in GDR social policies; her autonomy as a citizen had been restricted but was now opening in the West. Shortly after unification, Chancellor Kohl appointed her to the Ministry of Women's Affairs, where she was to be (in his words) his "Mädchen" (girl).[29]

Kohl's government drove unification forward full steam. It pushed through massive transfer payments to the East (including a consumer-friendly high exchange rate for East to West currency that wrecked the already shaky companies of the GDR) and rapid privatization of the economy. The dissidents who had envisioned freedom as a mix of state-secured social benefits, participatory democratic citizenship, and civil society's openness to a variety of lifestyle choices now felt betrayed by the voters. Feminists felt among the most betrayed, since women voters did not embrace them as their representatives.[30] As the UFV struggled to compete in state and local elections and participate in a proliferating landscape of new feminist projects, many receiving funds from the state, it burned out some activists and repelled others by internal conflict (especially over past closeness to the SED). By 1995 the UFV was for all practical purposes inactive and irrelevant, although it did not dissolve itself formally until 1998.[31]

The failure to "make a state with women" through the UFV did not imply that women lacked feminist concerns, but showed how hard it would be to stand up politically for women's empowerment.[32] One difficulty was the number of possible parties—not only the UFV, but also the movement alliance (Bündnis '90) and even the SED successor party, the PDS—that claimed to represent the women's public. Another was the way the GDR had co-opted the term "women's emancipation" and demonized "feminism" as bourgeois and man-hating.[33] A general skepticism about all "-isms" also made explicit appeals to feminism difficult. Finally, women simply found it hard to cope with all the changes, since women's paid work, roles as mothers, and opportunities to engage in politics were all restructured simultaneously.

Exclusion from the Workplace in a Context of Mass Unemployment

The book of statistical data about women in the GDR that was publicly released for the first time in 1990 (*Frauenreport '90*) pointed out that 90 percent of all women had been employed (including women on full-time paid maternity leave of twelve–eighteen months) and most worked full time (unlike the typically part-time jobs of West German women). The average employed GDR wife contributed 40 percent of the family income, compared to 18 percent in the West. So the wave of unemployment that swept over the former GDR—a loss of 40 percent of all jobs in just three years—was as traumatic for women as for men. Its gendered aspects meant women faced blatant discrimination on top of structural disadvantages.[34]

The story that opened this chapter was one of many I heard about the androcentric attitudes and exclusionary practices decision-makers of the Federal Republic brought to the restructuring process. For men in powerful positions, having no idea that women's studies existed was only one of myriad ways ex-GDR women's experiences were made invisible. One young East Berlin woman recounted how she had gone to the unemployment office to register for a job as a carpenter, her trade, only to be told that women were not allowed to be carpenters in the FRG and she had better retrain as a secretary.[35] Although women had been concentrated in the banking industry in the GDR, where financial service jobs were not highly regarded or well-paid, FRG takeover of the banks included massive replacement of women workers with men from the West.[36] As Heike Trappe shows statistically, women in the former GDR were much better represented in male-dominant occupations than women in the West, but their percentage was rapidly moving downward toward the FRG's idea of normal.[37]

The absence of laws effectively barring discrimination in the FRG allowed government unemployment offices to accept employers' stated gender and age preferences. In 1992, employer preferences dictated that 40 percent of job openings in the new federal states were listed for men, 11 percent for women, and only 49 percent open to either. This was an even worse ratio than in the "old states," where 25 percent of the jobs explicitly called for men, 12 percent for women, and two-thirds (65 percent) were gender-neutral.[38] Collective-bargaining agreements also set wage rates that paid "East Germans" less than "West Germans" for the same jobs in the same workplaces, reflecting a common belief that "they" didn't know how to work as hard as "we" did.[39]

Such perfectly legal preferences for West-raised workers and men contributed to gender differences in the official unemployment figures (20 percent for women, 11 percent for men in 1992). Actual job losses were two to three times as great, since many workers left the labor force entirely or ended up in special make-work programs (ABM).[40] Women were pushed out especially at the top—of the roughly 100,000 women who held upper management positions in the GDR, there were too few to count reliably by 1992.[41] Of the 20,800 vocational training positions created in existing GDR firms privatized during 1990–92, only 3,400 went to women.[42]

But women also faced more unemployment at the bottom, where the gender segregation and discrimination of the GDR's own practices had consigned them. Textile factories and food-processing plants were among those that simply disappeared, and with them the jobs of their mostly female workforces. In jobs opening up—for example, in retail sales—employers were allowed to use age as a criterion, so older women were particularly hard hit. Already by March 1991, 45 percent of women aged fifty to sixty had left the labor force, and among the half that stubbornly remained, more than 30 percent were unemployed.[43] Many former East Germans wondered at the fact that half the population was now working sixty hours a week and the other half had no work at all.

The restructuring of the universities provides another example of how women were clobbered by the combination of prior structural disadvantages with new forms of discrimination. Women faculty in the GDR had been disproportionately in the humanities and social sciences and in lower-level teaching rather than research director positions. Two Western biases, against teaching and in favor of the hard sciences (as ideologically untainted), hit women harder than men when the universities ended tenure and abolished approximately 60 percent of all academic positions.[44] Underemployed West German academic men found openings in ex-GDR universities, while older East-trained women in these academic jobs were typically pushed out. One older (midfifties) woman academic literally cried as she explained to me how her hopes for freedom of research (access to international journals and photocopying machines especially) were dashed by her unemployability in the university system in West Germany (where anyone who did not hold a professorship by age fifty was ineligible for appointment). The overall losses of women faculty might have been even more disproportionate if the new women's affairs offices in the Eastern universities had not aggressively defended their jobs.[45]

This tidal wave of economic dislocation hit women accustomed to significant roles as cobreadwinners, so its impact was cultural as well as material. The drive to push women out of the labor force to mitigate the unemployment of men was overt in West German media initially. Newspapers and magazines trumpeted, in a satisfied tone, that ex-GDR women had rejected feminism (by not voting for the UFV) and now were eager to quit their jobs and become housewives. However, as soon as survey data were released, the numbers decisively contradicted this picture.[46] Based on representative samples, comparisons of women in the old and new states showed a much higher commitment to paid work among East German women. Against all odds, and sometimes at tremendous personal cost, ex-GDR women struggled to maintain their status as wage earners, not only for the money but because it was part of their identity.[47] The illustration in Figure 8 is of the widely circulated cartoon by an East German woman artist, Anke Feuchtenberger, where the image of strength is the working mother, who is not confined by domesticity but carries it forward into the public sphere. This image offered, along with the witch (symbolizing beauty) and (the brave) princess kissing a frog, a post-fairy-tale view of themselves that ex-GDR feminists embraced. Unlike the Green image of Rapunzel escaping without a prince (Figure 4, in Chapter 5), bravery as East German feminists understood it demanded hoping against hope for transformation (first panel of Figure 8).

Motherhood Amid the Maelstrom

The extent of East German women's "stubbornness" in clinging to a mother-worker identity is most apparent when looking at women's family and fertility behavior a decade after unification.[48] As they confronted the unfamiliar and uncongenial policy conditions of the FRG, women continued to try to realize their ambitions.

The policy framework of the FRG was, as noted before, oriented around a male-breadwinner and wife-mother, with strongly institutionalized patterns of support for women being full-time homemakers when they had children. The wage, tax, and school systems all presumed married women would depend on husbands for financial support and devote themselves fully to child care.

Alle Frauen sind mutig! stark! schön!

Unabhängiger Frauenverband - Auch für Frauen und Kinder eine sorgenfreie Zukunft in dem Europäischen Haus

FIGURE 8   This cartoon by East German artist Anke Feuchtenberger depicts a princess kissing a frog as the image of bravery, a working mother as the image of strength, and a witch as representing beauty. The German caption asks for a vote for "Independent Women's Association—for a future without worries for women and children as well—in the European Parliament."
Source: Anke Feuchtenberger.

Even though West German feminists critiqued this dependence, they had not found a route out of it, other than choosing to forgo children and marriage. The question was whether East German women would now have to assimilate to FRG norms.

In 1989, the last year of two separate states, there was still the clear demarcation between "mothers" and "working women" in the Federal Republic that the Mother's Manifesto had expressed. The double-day pattern, typical of East German (and American) women, where most mothers had full-time jobs was still rare. Of West German women, 85 percent were mothers and only 40 percent of married women with a child under six were employed at all. Their nonemployment was not just a brief period out of the labor force. Only half of all West German married women with a child over age fifteen still living at home held a paid job, and half these jobs were part-time.[49] Despite some feminist success in instituting affirmative action for mothers, most still faced tremendous problems reentering the labor market. When they managed to do so, it was typically well below their formal training and education level.[50]

This was a dramatically different pattern from the integration of motherhood and paid work that was the standard biography of East German women— 91 percent of GDR women in 1989 had children, yet only 20 percent of women aged twenty to thirty and 7 percent of women aged thirty to thirty-four were on maternity leave or otherwise out of work.[51] The East German state encouraged early childbearing, even building "mother-and-child dorms" to facilitate combining children with higher education (one-third of women graduating university already had at least one child), and made marriage normative but economically optional for women by subsidizing basic goods and reducing the income gap between women and men. Full-time working women earned 76 percent of what men did, compared to only 68 percent among the much smaller, more select group of full-time working women in the FRG.[52] In 1989, the modal age for GDR women to give birth was twenty-four, compared to twenty-eight in the West, and the percentage of births occurring outside marriage considerably higher (34 versus 10 percent). Divorce was more common— and less consequential—in the East.[53] Most women were mothers as well as workers, but wifehood was not critical to being a mother.

Unification thus created a massive "natural experiment" in the rapid change in policy framework East German women faced, while still armed with the framing resources they had developed in their personal and political socialization in the GDR. The first result of this experiment was a massive, historically unprecedented drop in births. The number of children born in the former GDR declined by 60 percent in just five years. Media in the West politicized this drop as a deliberate act of defiance, a "birth strike" by East German women, a claim rebutted first by Irene Dölling's interviews and then by demographic evidence over the next decade.[54] But while not a gesture of protest, it did reflect women's commitment to remain employable in the face of active job discrimination and disappearing state support for child care.[55]

The demographic shock of the drop in births prompted Western analysts to argue that ex-GDR women were just deferring childbearing while they assimilated West German marital norms.[56] While data suggest that deferring births is an area where women in the new states did come to resemble those in the old ones (with age at first birth and age at first marriage both rising), other evidence points to a "stubborn" attachment to worker-mother rather than wife-mother identities.[57] For example, by 2000 an absolute majority of births in the former GDR occurred outside marriage (52 versus 19 percent in the West) and 15 percent of women aged twenty-five to twenty-nine lived in nonmarital unions with children (versus 3 percent in the West). The reasons women in the former GDR gave for putting off children remained notably different from those in the West—the former emphasizing the difficulty of achieving financial security and finding a husband who would participate in child rearing and the latter naming a desire for travel, fun, and self-realization.[58] Women in the former GDR continued to prioritize a job and supporting themselves over being married, and they made decisions—like deferring births—that helped fit children into that model.

From the start, polls indicated that the East had a much higher level of support for a two-earner family, greater awareness of discrimination against women, and less support for the idea that a stay-at-home mother has a warmer relationship with her child, and these differences with the West proved remarkably resilient.[59] Behavior reflected this: after a decade, there were still higher proportions of four to six year olds in full-time daycare (56 versus 20 percent), infants in any out-of-home child care (34 versus 7 percent), and higher levels of husbands' participation in housework (sixteen hours versus twelve weekly) and in child care (10.5 hours versus 8.5) in the new states than in the old FRG.[60] This way of life, while different from that of the FRG, is not so unusual internationally. Even back in 1990, ex-GDR women were closer to European and American norms than women raised under the wife-mother system of West Germany.[61]

This meant that the struggle for autonomy among women in the East could not long focus on abortion, since sustaining their worker-mother identity in a suddenly unsupportive political and cultural framework was a more pressing challenge. While not taking to the streets in large numbers—to the disappointment of some West German feminists—ex-GDR women were indeed fighting for their autonomy. In the immediate aftermath of unification, this struggle often seemed individual. Yet a decade later, a distinctively Eastern set of gender norms had created new facts on the ground for policymakers. The addition of East-raised women had added new force to feminist demands for women's access to jobs and child care, and feminist activism was not subsiding.

Collective Forms of Gender Political Action

Overtly political feminist work in the former GDR relied on a mix of gender-inclusive and women-centered political actions. This more collaborative stance of ex-GDR women with men had roots in their common experiences before the transition, as well as in their shared experiences of dislocation, exclusion, and insecurity in the FRG.

In the GDR, women and men shared experiences at work, and most women and men alike were excluded from significant participation in public life. The idea of a profound difference between genders (one being private and the other public) was less inherently plausible. Since the 1970s, women authors in the GDR had implicitly critiqued its "mommy politics" as failing to adequately involve men in families or take on the desegregation of conventionally women's jobs. The founding statements of the UFV and a wide range of local women's groups now were explicit in demanding change in men, as well as empowerment for women, as a strategy to advance women's liberation.[62] Ex-GDR feminists engaged from the start in political actions with men. With unification, two feminist strategies migrated from West to East and were changed in the process: autonomous women's projects, and gender-equality offices in government.

The project focus grew from combining local UFV work, begun before the transition, with an influx of money from the FRG for employment projects. The latter, known as ABM jobs, were to provide temporary work in community service groups; feminist projects were just the sort of nonprofits at which unemployed women could now get a job. Hundreds of new projects, focused on everything from computer skills to counseling, began between 1990 and 1992. Unlike the projects in the West, which were chronically understaffed and short of funds—and even more so with the shift in federal financing to the East—these ABM-funded projects were a coveted employment opportunity and were relatively well-funded and staffed in comparison to the former GDR's otherwise devastated economy.

Keeping to a strict definition of "feminist" was impossible. Women setting up these "women's projects" competed with other project entrepreneurs for funding, and job applicants were motivated by financial need, not just feminist commitment.[63] Many projects, including feminist ones, mixed interpersonal support, practical advice on how to navigate the bureaucracies of the FRG, and encouragement to set up small businesses. Many relied on experienced project feminists from the West to teach them how to write grants, do evaluations, and publicize their services. These ex-GDR projects also did not necessarily embrace the antihierarchical culture of feminist projects (but were not authoritarian, either).

Many of the most recognizably feminist projects in the East, such as EVA in Berlin and the feminist magazines *Zaunreiterin* in Leipzig and *weibblick* and *Ypsilon* in Berlin, were sites of extensive cultural experimentation, networking, and political consciousness-raising. Questioning what the FRG had to offer ("Test the West," a cigarette slogan in the FRG, was repurposed as a political one in the East) and exploring the limits of creative freedom went hand in hand. These cultural projects drew on grants from Western media foundations and produced exhilarating displays of creativity.[64]

After the stinging defeats of unification, the UFV decided not to try to be a political party and became a civic association instead. Now its members were engaged in a massive number of time-consuming local projects, sometimes in competition with the restructured remnant of the GDR's women's movement association, the DFD. Such overburdened projects could hardly even try to speak for women or build a politicized women's public. Before long, the money began to run out—ABM funds began being phased out as early as 1992. Local communities faced huge demands on their budgets, difficult to meet even with federal subvention (a special unification tax had been levied in the West to pay for the costs in the East). Women's projects needed insider allies simply to survive.

They found such allies first in the Women's Roundtables. Echoing the roundtable form invented as part of the transition, these were local forums for women to define and act on common interests across partisan lines, whether in or outside government, the universities, the new women's projects, churches, or the DFD. Women's Roundtables at the local level took the lead in defending child-care centers, and succeeded to a surprising extent, laying the groundwork for efforts to extend child care in the West.[65] The Roundtables also pushed to support women's ambitions institutionally, trying to get gender-equality offices better resourced and respected.

Establishing gender-equality offices (*Gleichstellungsstellen, GSS*) had been among the last acts of the GDR, when the Central Roundtable mandated a *GSS* in every town of over ten thousand. This formal institutionalization in the East helped to make equality offices seem essential in the West as well, even if staffed with a volunteer and given minimal resources, as was often the case with local offices in CDU-dominated governments. By 1991, these offices were essentially universal across Germany and remained so for the next decade.[66]

Introducing a *GSS* in the East was a different experience from what it had been in the West. First, it did not face resistance from either the state or a women's movement. It was part of a general overhaul of administrative structure, not a novelty introduced into it, and was taken up enthusiastically by the Women's Roundtables, including CDU women who had come out of the dissident movements. The GDR tradition of commitment to gender equality, however poorly fulfilled, was still valued. Second, the *GSS* in the former GDR struggled against a massive flood of new problems facing women and the false sense that there were more than ample resources in the West to deal with them. This misperception raised expectations in the East and provoked jealousy in the West.

Most important, the *GSS* in the new states differed from those in the old FRG in defining their mission as one of fostering gender equality rather than advancing women. The latter concept was contaminated by the GDR history of "mommy politics" (*Muttipolitik*) institutionalizing special treatment for mothers. The housework day and baby year were targets of feminist critique during the transition for how they locked women (not men) in domestic roles, producing both economic disadvantage and a double day for women. Ex-GDR feminists preferred not to target mothers—or women—but to see both women and men treated equally in and through supportive social measures. This focus on being for both women and men, along with early incorporation in the routine administrative structure of the new states, broadly legitimized the work of the *GSS*.

The East German insistence on running their equality offices with "equality officers" (of either gender) (*Gleichstellungsbeauftragten*) rather than "women's affairs officers" (*Frauenbeauftragten*) began to challenge the model of "advancing women." State help and protection for women or mothers alone was seen as problematic, and feminists articulated their concerns in a critique of *instrumentalism*. "Instrumentalizing" women meant that the GDR offered benefits to women not because women wanted them, but rather to make women more useful to the state, whether or not the benefits were incidentally good for women. Concerns about the birthrate and levels of economic production shaped GDR policy "for women." This instrumental approach was emerging in global development policy at this time, too; by 2000, as more countries began to embrace "prowoman" policies, this ex-GDR concern seemed prescient.

Because the German term *Frauenpolitik* includes both politics actively by and for women (only) and policies about women as (passive) objects of state concern, ex-GDR feminists were not attracted to it as an approach. They instead wanted an equality politics (*Gleichstellungspolitik*) that would transform unequal gender relations, not just support women alone. They pressed for *GSS* offices—in the West as well as in their home states—to target men as well as women, and ultimately, their view prevailed. The label at least changed even in most of the Western offices.

This shift from women to gender in the old states was controversial among feminists and diluted by concomitant pressure by the CDU and other conservative forces to "depoliticize" the offices. Nonetheless, the idea of gender transformation as centrally involving men—the ex-GDR view—began the reconsideration of the FRG feminist strategy of excluding men and empowering women. In this first period, its most obvious effect was to strain the relationship between feminists East and West.

THE STRUGGLE FOR SISTERHOOD: EAST-WEST DEBATES

Comparing notes in 1990 with a longtime feminist friend from Frankfurt am Main, I was surprised by the disappointment she expressed about her recent journey East. "It's an underdeveloped country for feminism," she asserted. Moreover, she worried that unification would "put West Germany back twenty years." Since this contradicted my own experiences with active, progressive, if often exhausted and confused women struggling to get a foothold on a slippery and constantly moving political terrain, I was curious about what she interpreted as backward and threatening.

Two main themes emerged. First, in her eyes, ex-GDR women "had no feminist identity" and demonstrated "masculine identification" in the language they used to describe themselves. A woman would stand up in a meeting and use the male form *Professor* or *Elektriker* to identify her occupation, rather than adding the "-in" grammatical ending. Having long struggled to achieve visibility for women through feminizing language, feminists in the West felt their gains at risk if women from the East considered such issues trivial, as men in the West had. West German feminists employed language change to proclaim a self-conscious identification with women as a group. They worried that focusing on the economic situation for women as workers (rather than as women) meant returning to a "production-centered" view of politics, in which women's problems would be only "secondary contradictions." This posed a real threat to what feminists had accomplished in twenty years of struggle with the Left.

But ex-GDR feminists struggling against economic displacement from their jobs and homes were baffled by the Western feminists' emphasis on the language used for jobs rather than on jobs themselves. As several East German interviewees pointed out, the women of the old states were themselves drastically underemployed (both in numbers and quality of jobs) and more segregated in conventionally female occupations than they had been, so who were they to talk about "backwardness"?

The second theme my Western friend raised highlighted the different priorities of the two movements. "They invite men to their meetings," she fumed. "They have no idea of what it is to be feminist because they are afraid to do anything without their men." Indeed, East German feminists did welcome men. One argued, "It's good for them to come and listen to and learn from us for a change. We had to sit and listen to them for too long."[67] East German feminists saw West German women as the ones who were afraid, and considered themselves powerful and self-conscious political actors who were not about to allow themselves to be silenced. Their solidarity with men also rested on shared experiences of losing their livelihoods, being thrown into the frantic rat-race for scarce jobs, and feeling far more performance pressure on the job, if they had one.[68] Rather than the experience of men in the public domain and women locked into the private that had been formative for West German feminists twenty years previously, East German feminists shared with men many of their most painful and rewarding social and political experiences, from the exhilaration of the marches and movements that had brought down the GDR to their experiences with the often baffling FRG.

For example, an East Berlin couple whom I had first met when doing snowball interviews about UFV events told me a story they found hilarious about the husband's first foray West in the days immediately after the Wall fell. One of his missions was to go to the feminist bookstore on Savigny Place and buy books from a list his wife had given him. The bookstore clerk glared at him and informed him she was only willing to sell him the books because he was so obviously an (ignorant) East German and a "*Softi*" (nice guy). Both were proud that his being a *Softi* was so apparent, outraged by the condescension, and amused by the self-defeating nature of a store that offended and rejected willing customers.

Although West German feminists often found it hard to believe, giving priority to common struggle did not mean that East German women were deferring to men or lacking feminist imagination. Based on their experiences with "socialism as it existed," they rejected all ideology (including feminist) as out of touch with everyday life. Separatism seemed ideological and thus silly. So did the cultural politics of language. To an East German feminist, the West German feminist looked like an *Emanze*, the early twentieth-century cross-dressing gender rebel, in her concern with external appearances.[69] Moreover, the old FRG emphasis on state policy to defend and advance women and support motherhood seemed both limited and naïve. GDR policies were not so much rejected as seen as halfway measures—they had not gone far enough to recognize male violence against women or direct men into sharing work at home or entering "women's" occupations. Their idea now was not merely to share their struggle with men, but to use the state to change gender relations; if the state was going to help women achieve that goal, men would need to be involved.

In the eyes of the feminists from the old states, it was these ex-GDR women whose perspectives were too limited and naive. Dismissively called *Muttis* (mommies) because nearly all had children, they seemed simply to take motherhood for granted, bringing their children to meetings and assuming child care would be provided. In fact, child care was not a norm at FRG feminist events. Having long been structurally compelled to choose between a mother-life and a worker-life, more had chosen not to have children and engaged in polarized debates about alternatives (for example, around the *Mother's Manifesto*).

From the perspective of practical theory, both arguments were limited by the experiences participants took to be true of all women, but which actually reflected the material and discursive structures of the systems in which women had formed their feminism. Their naiveté lay in failing to recognize how strongly rooted in these social structures both perspectives were. In an important way, this confrontation was the first serious struggle over diversity that feminists on either side of the Wall had faced. By articulating structurally grounded differences in perspectives, the clash between East and West feminists in unified Germany in the 1990s resembles some of the confrontations between White and Black feminists in the United States in the 1980s. Both unsettled a hegemonic view of feminism based in the experiences of the more powerful and privileged group.

The power differences between East and West were apparent to both sides, not merely among feminists. In fact, in popular discourse gender was often employed to symbolize political power and powerlessness in the unification process as a whole. In one cartoon a yawning man wearing pajamas in the colors of the FRG flag swings his feet out of bed to step on a throw-rug in the shape of a woman wearing the GDR emblem; in another it is the political parties of the FRG courting a GDR girl. Most common were the depictions of unification as a marriage in which the wife/GDR loses her identity/name and becomes subordinated to the husband/FRG.[70] Symbolically, the GDR was inevitably female: tricky or dependent, coy or complaining; the FRG was always in charge.

The structural power of the West in unification made the experiences and perspectives of Western feminists dominant over those of the ex-GDR women, and they defined the East as "an underdeveloped country for feminism." But the structures of social policy and legacies of women's struggles on the two sides of the Wall had instead produced two different feminisms in a single political space. Despite the *Mutti* and *Emanze* stereotypes, however, feminists actively began to work out their differences.

Building an East-West Relationship

One FRG feminist who was commuting between Munich and Leipzig as a consultant on feminist projects explained that when she was in Leipzig she was overwhelmed by the enormous challenges, but when she went home they receded into "newspaper stories" and "memories" remote from her day-to-day life. In Leipzig, acknowledging her childlessness made her feel defensive; in Munich, she "couldn't imagine my life with a child."[71] The sporadic and voluntary nature of her engagement, her defensiveness about difference, and her formal role as a consultant teaching new project directors the ropes of the FRG bureaucracy were fairly typical of the initial contacts West feminists had with their counterparts in the former GDR.

A feminist in the new federal states had a very different experience. She might often be invited to visit projects in the West to see how they were run, to workshops where West German experts advised her on constitutional law or how social benefits were organized, or to conferences at which West German feminists tried to get to know their "sisters" from *drüben* (the other side of the Wall). But West Germans were in charge of all these encounters, and differences in power, privilege, and perspectives surfaced quickly and painfully.[72]

As several books that tried to work out the mutual animosities pointed out, from the perspective of the East-based feminist, her "half-sister" in the West enjoyed fabulous privileges of wealth and security, while she as Cinderella was struggling to get by. The Western "sister" also saw herself as a struggling outsider and competing with the "new girls" for resources and recognition.[73] For example, West German feminists saw the explosive growth of feminist projects in the East as draining away hard-fought resources as budget cuts were imposed in the West to cover the expenses of unification. At some level, not only disappointment that ex-GDR women failed to rush to join "their" movement, but psychological investment in seeing their long struggle in the West as a necessary stage of development probably made it hard to see the projects and equality offices developing so quickly in the East as their peers.

Strategies could be shared if they were transformed to fit political circumstances, as with women's projects and gender-equality offices. There were ongoing efforts to network across difference and actively work together. The originally East Berlin-based feminist magazine *weibblick* reached westward in 1992 and dedicated itself to "helping with the coming together of East and West and putting the realities of life, the everyday life of women in the center of this process."[74] Some Western groups were active in and with ex-GDR feminist politics. FrauenAnStiftung, the foundation for women's issues funded by the Green party, played an active role in supporting UFV activities, and a socialist women's group (associated with the journal *Das Argument*) was credited with convincing the PDS to accept the zipper principle in elections.[75] Trade union and SPD women supported efforts to fight discrimination in the distribution of ABM jobs and to count women losing jobs as unemployed.

Despite different perspectives and needs, common space was created for some East-West collaboration. Feminists in both East and West mounted a "Women's Strike Day" on March 8, 1994, which put on the largest feminist street demonstrations most West cities had seen since the anti-218 initiatives of the early 1970s and affirmed the symbolic value put on International Women's

Day especially in the East. The Weiberwirtschaft (Women's Economy) began in 1987 as a West German project, mixing profit and nonprofit work with feminist outreach. By 1992 it had acquired the building of a bankrupt factory in East Berlin and enlisted a group of about fifteen hundred largely Western feminist donors to redevelop the space. As a mixed-use development, Women's Economy offered low-cost office and workshop space to women's start-ups, subsidized housing for single mothers, a child-care center, and a canteen. East German women were in need of the housing and start-up space, and West German women were drawn to the women's community aspect. After massive reconstruction, the complex of buildings began to rent out space in 1995, meeting women's needs for economic, practical, and socioemotional support through a mix of state politics and entrepreneurship.[76] But even a successful collaboration like this hardly erased the suspicion that inequalities of status and differences in perspective created on both sides.

However strained the relationship, unification was fruitful for feminism in Germany. East Germans' stronger desire to see gender equality recognized as a valid goal, even if not an actual accomplishment, helped create a constituency to effectively support SPD- and Green-initiated efforts to amend the FRG constitution to take a more affirmative stance. The clause that said "women and men have equal rights," which Elisabeth Selbert and other SPD women had successfully struggled to insert in 1949, now was seen as inadequate. Women's affairs officers and Left-leaning politicians were joined even by CDU-affiliated voices from the East arguing for more commitment to women's equality as an active state goal. Under this cross-party, cross-gender pressure, the constitutional clause was modified in 1994 to say, "The state shall promote the realization of equal rights for women and men and strive to abolish existing disadvantages."[77] This was a significant shift, overruling the high court's previous position that male advantages were natural and functional for society.

The constitution was not the only signal of change. In 1993, the reform of FRG naming law allowed women to retain their birth names, unhyphenated (though only with the husband's consent). In 1997, after ten years of struggle and considerably later than in the United States, the law was changed to recognize the possibility of rape within marriage. Overall, the definition of women as wives and mothers subjected to the authority of the husband as patriarch weakened in the West, while women in the East went into business on their own and continued their "stubborn" independence in family formation. With more "masculine" technical and managerial interests and training than West German women, ex-GDR women challenged the FRG feminist understanding of women as having a deeply socialized different relation to the labor market than men did.

It would be wrong to think of these changes in political culture as "coming from" the East in some simple way, since literal movements of populations blurred the boundaries. Many of those raised in the East went westward to pursue economic opportunities, and some of those raised in the West began to see the whole world from a more "Eastern" perspective. By 1995, diversity was inside as well as between the old and new states, and many forces to press gender politics forward were from outside Germany. The earthquake of unification had produced new openings of opportunity into which some of these forces could flow.

CONCLUSION: POWER, PRIVILEGE, AND POLITICS

Despite the individual and collective losses women in the former GDR experienced, it is a mistake to view this period as one of failure. Frequent references to "women as the losers of unification" reflected an awareness of the real costs women in the East suffered and the challenges to feminist organizing across Germany presented by the new diversity among women. Yet feminists in the East pointed to their experiences of repression in the GDR, where an autonomous women's movement had been forbidden, to emphasize the value of their freedom in the FRG to create conditions under which women could come together, outside the family and autonomously from the state, to formulate and express their interests. For many, the economic losses they suffered are still considerably offset by such political gains.

As a general insight for a practical theory of feminist politics, this case suggests that feminists in democratic countries should be cautious of taking the right to organize autonomously, a significant aspect of feminist mobilization in all countries, so much for granted that it is undervalued and undertheorized. Although in purely economic terms, this period of unification was a sheer catastrophe for women in the former GDR, these women also experienced it as an important opportunity to resist instrumentalization by the state and formulate their own interests as women, individually and collectively. The critique of instrumentalization they formulated, no less than the demand for more egalitarian families they raised, point toward developments that only came later to the FRG. In the 1990s, making men targets of efforts to change gender relations and increasing instrumental state attention to securing women's rights posed challenges to the specific kind of feminism West German women had institutionalized. East German women's experiences gave them a theoretical perspective attuned to these challenges.

Despite the obstacles facing them on the new terrain of the unified Federal Republic, ex-GDR women proved to be "decisive and determined agents" in more than their own abortion decisions. In the arena of conventional politics, where the battle over abortion was fought, in their "stubborn" individual struggles over jobs and family, and in the collective mobilizations in projects, equality offices, movement conferences, and demonstrations where East met West, ex-GDR women were not passive victims but active agents giving shape to the emerging new Germany. At least some of the changes in postunification Germany were precipitated by the voice brought into the system by women and men raised in the GDR. In their lives the transition was an earthquake, even if for many in the West it felt like a distant tremor.

Another implication for the feminist politics globally is found in considering how the interplay between feminist achievements and party politics, as detailed in the previous chapter, was transformed by the unification process, and in turn offered new opportunities. The deep red PDS (successor to the SED), and its explicit claim to represent a distinctively Eastern, gender-emancipatory perspective, vied with the democratic movement-based parties (Bündnis '90/ Green, a merged party created in 1993) for the role of challenging the taken-for-granted assumptions of the West's major parties. Since the PDS continued to draw votes in the East, it broadened the spectrum of critique in parliament and offered support for specific feminist reforms, even though it was still seen as an illegitimately antidemocratic party by many in the West. In 1998, the left-wing of the SPD bolted, rejecting the party's restructuring of the health, welfare, and employment systems (the "Hartz reforms"), and by 2005 it had worked out an alliance with the PDS to construct a new party, Die LINKE (The Left). Since the PDS, like the Green party, put not only a zipper list but gender-equality measures in its platform, the newer Left being constructed across Germany had a more explicitly supportive relation to feminist goals than either the New Left of the 1970s or the old-guard unions and SPD. Along with the continuing gains in women's representation, these party shifts made it harder for feminists simply to reject the "male Left" as an insensitive, patriarchal enemy.

Perhaps most importantly, questions of diversity were raised in a painful but ultimately productive way in the unification process. As a decentralized movement that relied on a discursive community to support feminist identity, the Western movement had used the concept of autonomy to bind their multiple agendas together. Diverse as these meanings seemed, and despite the conflicts they had generated over the years, they did not stretch to include the ways women from the GDR experienced autonomy.

The problem facing feminists on this new political landscape was not dealing with diversity but acknowledging real differences of power and privilege. The ongoing dialogues between East and West opened up important discussions in Germany about how to "feel feminist" without being self-righteous and dogmatic about how feminism is supposed to feel, what particular strategies are correct, and with whom alliances can be made. These are in many regards the kinds of intersectional questions that challenges from women of color raised for White feminists in the United States and Great Britain in the 1980s.

The German case is particularly informative because these differences cannot be culturally essentialized as due to "race" or reduced to mere economic differences of class. Gender itself was the structural principle in the two competing German states that significantly shaped the differences among women, and it was not identical or unchanging. Gender systems worked together with the political processes of unification that empowered the West and disempowered the East. Essentializing differences among women as characteristics that can be listed (race, class, age, sexuality), or displacing them onto the structural arrangements of racial or class inequalities, can miss the ways gender itself variably structures state practices, cultural norms, citizen's experiences, movement strategies, and political expectations. These structures of gender—and the political structures that allow more or less autonomy of different kinds for citizens in general—can lead to important national differences in women's visions of feminism, even in a globalizing world.

It may be particularly hard to see how autonomy varies in kind as well as extent if the political and economic definitions of liberalism are confounded.

The political definition of liberalism (democratic self-determination, free speech, individual self-development, civic openness to a variety of life arrangements) is certainly not the same as the economic definition of liberalism (usually called neoliberalism) as the more or less absolute priority of markets, property relations, and unfettered capitalism. Confusing the two may encourage those who seek the former to embrace the latter too uncritically, as seems to have been the case in much of the postsocialist world, not only in the former GDR.

But concern about combating neoliberalism can allow economic progressives to fall prey to the abuses of protectionism, instrumentalism, and authoritarianism in some socialist traditions, and to look the other way when political freedoms are suppressed if the state is "taking care of" women, children, and the poor. The East German experience offers important lessons about turning to the state, no less than the West German experience does about the problems of trying to remain apart from it.

For all German feminists, dealing with difference became especially urgent in the second half of the 1990s. From coping with the challenges of unification, the center of gravity for feminist activities shifted toward transnational bodies like the UN and the European Union. Moreover, a second and third generation of children of immigrants now called Germany home. The challenge of productively dealing with diversity continued to grow in the decades that followed unification.

CHAPTER 7

KISSING THE FROG?
Butler, Beijing, and Brussels
Remake Gender Relations, 1995–2005

WHEN THE WELL-KNOWN feminist philosopher Judith Butler came to Berlin in 1997, I went to hear her lecture. Waiting for the bus, I became aware that all the other women at the bus stop were going to the same event. Arriving at the city library where she would speak, I realized I had stumbled into an event more like a rock concert than an academic lecture. The hall held around five hundred people, but huge speakers were set up on the lawn for the overflow, and at least a hundred people were already encamped there. I managed to squeeze into the hall both to hear Butler speak and to observe the mostly young, almost all female, crowd. Butler's lecture was a dense, subtle argument, delivered in English, about gender and resistance, drawing on the figure of Antigone.[1] The audience clearly valued her talk even if they did not understand every nuance. The text was summarized the next day, along with a Q&A with Butler, in a several page story in *taz*, the Berlin-based national newspaper most movement activists read. Yet just as the Berlin performance was only one stop on Butler's triumphant German lecture tour, Butler herself was just part of a sweeping change in approach to gender politics.[2] The "Butler boom" particularly swept up younger German feminists. Understanding gender as performance arrived in Germany with a bang.

But along with the rethinking of gender theories that Butler set in motion, ideas about gender in Germany were being transformed from the top down by Brussels (seat of the European Union) and Beijing (site of the Fourth UN World Conference on Women). International policy-making initiatives were shaping the political opportunities for feminists to a greater extent than ever before. Much of this policy followed the trajectory of attention away from "women" to "gender," as Butler's analysis did, and increasingly focused on changes at the individual and institutional level rather than collective mobilizations as such. While the grassroots enthusiasm for Butler among young women was unequivocal, older-generation feminists who had worked their way into positions of political influence were more divided in their views about the choice of gender rather than women as the object of feminist politics, whether from Butler, Brussels, or Beijing.

Should women embrace transforming men or the male-defined state? The image of women's bravery East German artist Vera Wollenberger had made familiar—the princess kissing the frog who might become a prince (the first panel of Figure 8 in Chapter 6)—was a performance some were not sure was worth the cost. Could the embrace of any number of brave women really be that transformative? Decisions in Beijing and Brussels heightened tensions around the meaning of gender and the relative weight of performance and agency, on the one hand, and enduring structures of inequality, on the other.

The metaphor of kissing the frog thus has a dual resonance for thinking about relations of power. While it implied that German feminists should re-evaluate their collective anxieties about getting too close to men or father-state organizationally, and engage more in changing men and masculinity, the image also suggests a daring and transformative performance of sexuality, as Butler emphasized. Although often skeptical, German feminist projects increasingly included attention to men and masculinity. Awareness of how gender intersected with sexuality, race, age, and other inequalities also opened space for gay men to ally with lesbian and feminist activists and highlighted the marginality of racial/ethnic and immigrant women in European feminisms.

This chapter explores the tensions in feminist politics between the individualizing strategies of gender performance and gender mainstreaming, both of which became more popular in many countries in different mixes in this period. I first look at the Butler boom and how there came to be such enormous receptivity to this poststructural approach, especially, but hardly exclusively, in Germany. The controversy highlights the generational divide as feminism was changing and as past struggles made it harder simply to take women's side.

The turn toward a different way of doing feminist politics in Germany was driven not only by feminist theory but by global practice, particularly transnational influences from Brussels and Beijing. Transnational influences came through interventions of women of the global South in the UN and networks of feminists in the EU. Both provided discursive legitimacy and material resources to feminist work.[3] Both interventions triggered a major struggle in German feminist practice between politics for women and gender policy reform. Both the mainstreaming model advanced by the UN in the Beijing Platform for Action and the antidiscrimination policies made in Brussels by the EU added force to the gender politics side.

All of these new forces lead to a reconsideration of intersectionality as a transnational feminist theory, particularly the challenges to feminist practice this approach poses in Germany and Europe. The reemergence of a discourse of race in Europe has made rethinking gender, class, and race relations more important but added a source of new struggles. The conflict in Germany about "diversity" politics highlights European feminist concerns about losing a commitment to gender justice if intersectional approaches replace the more institutionalized class-based model of feminist politics.

WHY BUTLER AND WHY NOW?

Judith Butler's best-known book, *Gender Trouble*, was translated into German in 1991 as *Das Unbehagen der Geschlechter*, echoing Freud's *Das Unbehagen in der Kultur* (*Civilization and its Discontents*). This translation emphasized deep structural unease rather than the difficulty or provocation in the English meaning of "trouble."[4] The title resonated with those who felt feminists were facing a society in which gender relations were already unsettled. Without abandoning a feminist challenge to the constraints of gender, Butler offered a more interactive and malleable sense of how gender was done in discourse and action than the structural critique of women's exclusion built into the patriarchially defined state. Butler's "poststructural" approach harked back to earlier feminist struggles over gender-marked language and self-determined sexuality, but

without the emphasis on reproduction (either biological or social) or the an-
tagonism between women and men that characterized these earlier struggles in
West Germany. Her social constructionist view of individual agency as the root
of all social structures was also more optimistic about change than the view of
institutionalized constraints expressed in the German theory of *Zweigeschlecht-
lichkeit* (the binary gender system).[5]

The strength of German feminist theory lay in analyzing the ways gender
relations were intertwined with emergence of modernity as an era characterized
also by the formation of nation-states, the emergence of capitalism, and the
shift from religion to science as a legitimating principle for social arrangements.[6]
This historical-structural model accounted for power arrangements in terms
of centuries of slow change, deeply institutionalized patterns, and collective
identities anchored in material positions. The weakness of such macrostructural
approaches for capturing women's political agency—their diversity of aims,
the vitality of their decisions, and their ongoing and creative interpretation of
feedback from their actions and alliances—was precisely what poststructuralist
theories targeted. The subjectivity and strategy emphasized in Butler's conception of gender as performance provided feminists more opportunities to think
about choice and change in women's and men's lives.

Making a women's public and doing women's politics—*Frauenöffentlichkeit*
and *Frauenpolitik*—based on women's shared structural position in universal
relations of reproduction had long given West German women a sense of collective purpose. Yet many of the developments of the past decades—the difficulty
of "choosing women's side" in the projects, the partisan framing of women's
interests in electoral terms, the conflicting views of women and society East and
West German feminists brought to the table—sowed increasingly widespread
doubt about the unity of interests among women. Some found Judith Butler's
emphasis on multiplicity and performance within genders a hopeful feminist
alternative to a dualistic view of men and women, particularly opening up visions
of how men and women could really both be expected to change.[7] Especially
for younger women and lesbians, acknowledgment of multiple and contested
identities among both women and men more accurately described their reality.[8]

The meeting of queer and feminist politics that Butler inspired especially
posed issues for those lesbian feminists who wanted to rethink the separatist
agenda of the 1970s but still embrace cultural rather than formally institutional

forms of political activism.[9] They wanted to revive the creative freedom of the
early mobilization in both East and West without the problematic project form
of organization. Rather than laws and economic relations, they looked again
to identity, discourse, and interpersonal relations as opportunities to challenge
the taken-for-granted nature of gender, undermining the structures of men's
and women's daily lives with non-state-based tools.[10]

There was also a generational difference at work. Younger feminists in particular took up Butler's "undoing" gender analysis as a way out of the quanda-
ries in which the older autonomous women's movement seemed to be stuck.
In their eyes, the structural theories of Left-based politics that had so strongly
shaped earlier feminism were unable to account for the changes in gender relations evident around the world.[11] For them, Butler's poststructural gender
theory implied successful engagement by both women and men in performances
that undid constraints on individual choice. Older feminists drew a different conclusion from the changes they observed. They stressed opportunities
for accelerating change in a feminist direction through further integration of
women's hard-won expertise into the policy system and mainstream institutions, now with the force of women's organizational lobbying and party positions to back them up.[12]

Others saw the poststructural focus on power as fluid, contested, and multiple, the view with which Butler was identified, as a dangerous distraction from
the struggle against the multifaceted and deeply embedded hierarchical social
relationship between women and men. One such skeptic, Mechtild Janssen,
scoffed that it was as if "the magic words social construction would dissolve the
hierarchical structures and categorical position of women."[13] They insisted on
giving priority to gender as the most fundamental social principle of inequality, with other interests added to and modifying the subjection of women, but
in no way as significant historically or structurally. Among the skeptics, all
poststructural analyses posed a threat to feminist politics, which they thought
should understand women as distinctive, singular, and central.

German debates over structuralism and poststructuralism resonated widely
through the movement because they were seen as not merely theoretical but
having real implications for feminist practices. Moreover, to critics, poststructuralism seemed dangerously individualistic, even *neoliberal.* Neoliberalism,
used as a derogatory term meaning placing capitalist values over social solidar-

ity, was a common critique against the market-based restructuring of welfare states that began to accelerate worldwide after the collapse of the socialist regimes of Europe.

Class, Gender, and Neoliberalism

The poststructural alternative highlighted the extent to which feminist structural theories were built on socialist-inspired, historical-materialist roots that offered a weak sense of individual agency and emphasized a unitary collective actor, whether women or the working class. Not only had such theories been struggling with the legacies of authoritarian socialism in the East, but *Autonomen*, Greens, and feminists in the West had also found them inadequate to address their aspirations for individual self-determination. The so-called new social movements had been the result. Classical political liberalism put more store in freedom, choice, and individual development, radical ideas in German political culture, and ones most German feminists, both East and West, embraced. In this context, political liberalism, which valued empowered individuals freely participating in democratic decision making, was a transformative claim for women's self-determination.

Yet the liberal framing of equal rights—affirming democratic representation and entitlement to personal autonomy for women as well as men—still evoked considerable ambivalence. Although critical of the rigidities of the West German institutionalized male-breadwinner system and patriarchal corporatist bargains among unions, management, and the state, and of East German authoritarian, instrumental decisions about what was good for women, few if any German feminists considered neoliberalism or its fundamentalist belief in markets a better alternative. With both poststructuralism and neoliberalism coming from the United States, it was easy to assume that the language of choice they shared made them cousins, if not twins.

Discourse that blurred the line between liberal human rights (individual autonomy and democratic political freedom) and neoliberal market rights (deregulation, privatization, and enhanced competition) made poststructural arguments seem particularly radical, even threatening. The critical edge in the feminist corporatist politics "for women" framed the fight for gender equality as a challenge to the individualist, competitive, privatizing tendencies of markets. Although the label socialist feminist is inappropriately narrow, the typical practices of German feminist politics were structural in representing women as a unitary collective actor, and poststructural theory fundamentally challenged this approach.

Structural analysis, which privileged women's autonomy not as an individual achievement but as a collective good, to be achieved by women consciously becoming "a gender for themselves," was also destabilized by the growing diversity among feminists. One legacy of unification was the incorporation of women with very different life experiences into a politically unified FRG. But this moment was also the end of the cold war, which drew attention to the failures of socialism across Eastern Europe and began a gradual process of rapprochement between Eastern and Western European nations. The practical need for a theory to replace gender dichotomy and structural opposition with individual multiplicity and performance was most acutely felt in Germany, positioned squarely on the fault line of these dying dichotomies.

Thinking about gender and its discontents posed concrete problems for feminist politics in Germany, organizationally as well as theoretically, in addressing the ongoing changes in class-based politics. Butler appeared at a propitious moment to crystallize these concerns rather than resolve them. The struggle over the appropriate target for feminist politics was not unique to Germany, but its effects were felt more intensely there because German feminists had so strongly institutionalized their commitment to the political representation of women (like workers) to confront a system of structural oppressions. Resistance to neoliberalism intensified their struggles over the future direction of organizational development. But around the globe and in Europe, despite shared fears about neoliberalism, feminists increasingly focused on forms of gender politics that took diversity among women into account, developed transnational coalitions, and worked closely with the state and supranational institutions of governance.

THE UN AND THE EU: GLOBALIZATION
MEETS EUROPEANIZATION IN GERMANY

At the Heinrich Böll Foundation in Berlin in 2001, about sixty women gathered from around the country for a workshop on introducing *gender budgeting* into city and town governments as a means of achieving gender democracy. Many presenters were drawn from municipal gender-equality offices where they had been experimenting with implementing such programs. The idea of gender budgets, a breakdown of where government expenditures had different impacts on women and men, had come originally from feminist political economists such as Marilyn Waring, a New Zealander whose influential 1989 book, *If Women Counted*, emphasized how much women contributed to national economies and how little they got from their governments in return.[14] The idea traveled from academic policy studies into international development circles, being explicitly recommended as a political strategy in the context of the 2000 follow-up meeting to the Beijing conference. Now it was being brought home by German feminists, especially those with experience with gender and development projects around the world. In this 2001 meeting, they deployed a new transnational frame to shape the spending priorities of their own cities and towns.

The idea was not totally new. Without invoking the term gender budgeting, Title IX in the United States had institutionalized comparative analysis of spending and participation in women's and men's sports. In Münster, Germany in 1993, the city budget was challenged by a feminist research group as spending too little on "women's needs," and the city government responded by more than doubling this (tiny) amount.[15] In the UK since 1999, a Women's Budget Group of feminist economists and policy activists had offered annual gender budget analyses of national spending.[16] By 2000, gender budgeting was part of a transnationally recognizable discursive framework, part of a general governmental strategy called *gender mainstreaming*, and an increasingly regular part of the policy process. Gender-equality officers invited to this Berlin meeting wondered whether such gender budgets would offer an effective new way of doing politics for women at the local level or throttle women's advocacy with neoliberal cost-effectiveness criteria, using the language of gender to legitimize the cuts.

As this case shows, the strategies, organizations, alliances, and concerns of German feminism in the late 1990s and early 2000s were being enriched not only by a flow of ideas expressed by non-German authors such as Judith Butler and Marilyn Waring, as they always had been, but also by being drawn into organizational engagement with global institutions. This growing transnational strategic effort was evident not only in formal organizations, networks, and alliances, but in policy discourses, strategies, and tools. The UN and the EU in particular provided new frameworks of discursive opportunity and key material resources for this work in Germany. Women's transnational organizing everywhere in the world owes much to the UN, its affiliated institutions, and the feminist supranational networks and NGOs revolving around it.[17]

But in Germany, as in other European countries, women's political mobilizations reflect an additional dimension provided by the growing importance of the EU as both lawgiver and administrative regulator. The activities of feminists at the EU level changed how its *acquis communitaire* (body of legal decisions and precedents) developed, and these successes changed feminist opportunities in Germany, as in all member-states.[18] Strategies from these sources now informed the practices of feminists in Germany and in the European networks in which they were increasingly embedded.

An Unlikely Godmother: UN Discourses and Networks

Peg Snyder, the long-time director of UNIFEM, coined the phrase "unlikely godmother" to describe the formative role the UN played in the growth of transnational feminism. Among the gifts the UN offered this baby movement were treaty language (a discursive framework on which to build) and material opportunities to organize and press claims on national governments in all corners of the world.[19] The 1995 Beijing Conference on the Status of Women was the culmination of these organizing efforts. Its mix of government resolutions and nongovernmental organizing for their implementation had unsurpassed effects on spreading global feminism. From Mexico City (1975), to Copenhagen (1980), Nairobi (1985), and Beijing (1990) each successive UN conference mobilized more local and regional groups in preparatory conferences, gave women from less developed regions more practical voice and political influence, drew more participants to the Non-Governmental Forums that accompanied the formal meeting of governments, and spawned more transnational feminist networks and non-governmental organizations (NGOs).

The organizing around the 1995 Fourth World Conference on Women made "gender" the key word expressing a broad agenda of empowerment and social equality for both women and men. Although there was considerable controversy in Beijing over adopting the language of gender (with the Vatican among the most vocal opponents of what it saw as an attack on the natural duality of persons), feminists there created a solid and successful front in favor of recognizing both the multiplicity and fluidity of gender, on the one hand,

and the necessary engagement of both women and men in challenging gender inequalities, on the other.[20] The gender approach of the UN framework prioritized integration of feminist aspirations with the "general" goals of social change, such as economic development.[21]

At the Beijing Conference, the governmental delegates adopted a Platform for Action (PfA) that defined gender as the target of equality policy and proposed a number of specific steps that governments should take to bring their laws and policies into accord with international principles of promoting gender equality and protecting women's human rights. After the conference, most delegates went home to put pressure on their governments not merely to endorse but also to implement the PfA.[22]

In the Platform for Action, gender mainstreaming emerged as the central strategic idea. As the UN's Division on the Advancement of Women explained:

Mainstreaming a gender perspective is the process of assessing the implications for women and men of any planned action, including legislation, policies or programmes, in all areas and at all levels. It is a strategy for making women's as well as men's concerns and experiences an integral dimension of the design, implementation, monitoring and evaluation of policies and programmes in all political, economic and societal spheres so that women and men benefit equally and inequality is not perpetuated. The ultimate goal is to achieve gender equality.[23]

Worldwide, the mainstreaming mandate became one of the most crucial aspects of governmental and NGO activities in the post-Beijing era, and its usefulness is already the subject of a vast literature.[24] In Europe, its principles and strategies have been significantly intertwined with the development of another transnational force, the EU, which quickly picked up the mainstreaming mandate from Beijing and made it its own.

EU Gender-equality Policies

The increasing reach and power of the EU became significant for gender politics as part of a multilevel strategy by feminists across both member and nonmember countries to use every tool it offered for moving national policy. Founded in the 1957 Treaty of Rome, the EU endorsed gender equality as a goal in the Maastricht Treaty of 1993.[25] The 1997 Treaty of Amsterdam formally mandated positive action toward gender equality via gender mainstreaming.[26] The EU made explicit reference to Beijing to legitimate this position, but other events of 1995 also shaped the treaty's mandates.

First, Sweden and Finland joined the EU. Their accession offered opportunities for wary Scandinavian feminists to negotiate an explicit EU commitment to active policy work for gender equality to protect their progressive policies from erosion to a lowest common denominator.[27] Second, the European Court of Justice, which interprets EU law, struck down a German law mandating affirmative action for women in civil service hiring. This case, *Kalanke v. Bremen*, led European feminists to push EU treaty-writers for explicit reaffirmation of affirmative action principles in the new treaty. The gender-equality framework established by the Treaty of Amsterdam was no gift, but like progress at and through the UN, won by feminist mobilization at multiple scales and sites.[28]

Europeanizing the Political Opportunity Structure

The EU embrace of gender mainstreaming in all policy domains was consequential to Germany, not only because the European Commission (the EU executive body) in Brussels distributed significant funding to countries and regional organizations as "carrots" but because the European Court of Justice brandished the "stick" of judging national policies to be out of compliance. EU agencies and observatories compiled statistics on member-states across various dimensions, identified best practices that could be more widely adopted, and "named and shamed" particular states for falling behind in achieving EU goals.[29] The European Commission drew up formal Roadmaps for Gender Equality that provided five-year plans. Setting such goals and timetables ("soft law" in EU parlance) gave new resources to feminist researchers and policy scholars, who could now contribute their expertise to define standards of female-friendliness. The EU directly funded European-level networks of experts (observatories) to compare policy outcomes on gender issues such as inclusion of women in science or in political and corporate leadership, and created European-level umbrella organizations, not only of trade unions and employer groups (the traditional "social partners") but also of women's associations, disability rights groups, and migrant organizations.

One of the first of these newly recognized civil society actors with voice in policy making at the EU level (the flourishing of which Sabine Lang has called "democratic participation by proxy") was the European Women's Lobby (EWL), established in 1991. It is an umbrella organization of national-level women's groups in the member-states and draws 85 percent of its funding from the EU.[30] Because the EWL formally links only national-level groups, its German participants are the women's organizations that work with governments (like the association of women jurists or women's affairs officers) and the Frauenrat (the Women's Council, against which the 1970s feminists had rebelled).[31]

With the EWL, as with its topic-specific observatories, the EU created more openings for influence above the nation-state. This formalization transformed the political opportunity structure so that feminists could use the EU to pressure national governments to meet what could now be called European standards.

Feminists' desire to influence such standards and press national governments for their enforcement encouraged the formation of supranational groups (for example, Women Against Violence in Europe, WAVE). Although the EU was mandated to concern itself only with economic issues and to leave social policy to its member-states, cross-EU feminist organizing was notably successful at defining violence against women as an issue with significant economic implications and drawing EU support for programs to combat it.[32] Sexual assault, domestic violence, and sexual-harassment policy mobilized networks of feminist advocates across Europe, and these EU transnational advocacy networks defined national best practices and shared strategies for changing gender relations.

As Keck and Sikkink define them, transnational advocacy networks (TANs) are loosely organized associations of political actors who share common values, mobilize expertise rather than large numbers to exert influence on decision-makers, and operate across national borders toward specific, limited goals.[33] TANs are not social movements, though they may include social-movement organizations or individual activists in them. Feminist TANs created sufficient pressure to change policy in areas where there was consensus (such as increasing affirmative action policies and funding for research on and services to victims of domestic violence) but also unleashed debates about appropriate feminist policies for issues such as prostitution and trafficking.[34]

European organizations and networks also opened up opportunities at the national level, especially by bringing EU resources to bear when domestic opportunities were blocked.[35] The observatories of experts assessing the success of governments in meeting EU directives provided regular opportunities for feminists in the slow-moving states to chastise the national parties in power for their failures. Germany, a relative laggard on women's representation in higher education and management careers, public child-care support, and maternal employment and work opportunities, provided a target-rich environment for such pressure tactics. Feminists in academia, government, foundations, and other policy institutions who had expertise in gender research now had good reason to network, research, evaluate, and publish cross-national assessments.[36]

The European feminist TANs sometimes found allies in the networks of gender-equality offices institutionalized across Germany, but the transnational emphasis on gender policy making also sometimes collided with the German emphasis on taking women's side. Moreover, the EU-driven expansion of feminist NGOs working closely with the state, particularly in encouraging mainstreaming and antidiscrimination policies, still worries those who suspect that the state is basically unreformable: that kissing the frog will be more likely to kill the princess than make the frog a prince. Critics argue that the "NGO-ization" of the women's movement risks cutting off feminists from the grass roots that nurtured them, shifting policy attention to gains for elite women, and making feminism more accountable to its experts than to its constituency.[37]

As gender mainstreaming traveled from Beijing to Brussels to Berlin, feminists everywhere debated whether the mandate was a technocratic fix, a displacement of women from the center of politics, or a tool with unrealized transformative potential for gender relations.[38] For unified Germany, the EU agenda-setting process pushed gender mainstreaming, antidiscrimination law, and work-family reconciliation policy into the center of debate.[39] Antidiscrimination law, easily adopted in many other European countries, proved especially controversial in Germany because its liberal premise of individual protection by law is at odds with structural understandings of women's position institutionalized by both Left and Right across Germany. These tensions grew along with EU and UN influences.

Gender Mainstreaming

Article 2 of the Amsterdam Treaty provided that promotion of equality between men and women is a task of the EU as a whole, to which member-states must be committed. The treaty provides that the EU should aim to eliminate inequalities and promote equality between men and women in all its activities, naming gender mainstreaming its "primary strategy."[40] The document implies that policy elites (rather than movements or women) will now bring "the gender perspective" into governance, "creating space" for "articulating a shared vision" among women and men.[41] This EU mandate put the onus on member-states to train administrators and monitor actual implementation of mainstreaming measures. Although some states took more participatory approaches (Ireland, for one), German gender mainstreaming was clearly a "Top-Down-Strategie."[42]

In 1998, the SPD and the Bündnis '90/Greens took the reins of government (the first national Red-Green coalition) just in time to respond to the gender-mainstreaming mandate of the Treaty of Amsterdam. It was not surprising that the (SPD-appointed) national minister for women's affairs introduced gender mainstreaming as a government priority. Reelected in 2002, the coalition again committed itself to the strategy, which the parties affirmed "shall be established on a sustained basis" for implementing the constitutional mandate for equality of men and women, and mandated training experts and collecting data across all agencies.[43]

The results of this new type of institutionalized feminist politics were mixed. On the one hand, feminist training for bureaucrats blossomed. From 2003 to 2010, the feminist-led and federally funded Gender Expertise Center at the Humboldt University in Berlin offered free training to civil servants across all agencies.[44] From 2000, gender training was also offered by the Green party's Heinrich Böll Foundation, whose teams, typically a man and woman, were castigated by some feminists as being more likely to reify gender difference in the minds of those they trained than to deconstruct it.[45] But across Europe, independent trainers and consultants proliferated, and some German feminists turned their academic expertise and experience into viable small businesses.[46]

States did more to train bureaucrats than to restructure actual organizational practices. Seeing gender at work did not translate easily into effective programs to de-gender administrative actions. Although the mainstreaming model called for a commitment from the entire organization, not just a poorly funded women's affairs office on the margins, it rarely received sufficient support from the top to reform the system. Administration pressure for gender-equality measures rarely went beyond funding a few model projects. As one critic put it, "Gender Mainstreaming, presented as a real call to revolution, is still the big 'black box' that is always beckoning us to see what is inside, even when everything suggests that it is empty."[47]

However, gender mainstreaming made it not only acceptable but necessary to talk about gender equality in German policy circles. Was this progress? Critics noted the state's tendency to substitute gender-mainstreaming projects for *Frauenpolitik* (women's policy/women's politics). Although feminist supporters argued that the two were complementary and equally essential strategies,[48] some states clearly used gender mainstreaming as a fig leaf to reduce the number, capacity, or resources of their women's equality offices.[49] For example, after CDU electoral gains, Brandenburg and Hessen abolished their women's ministries and eliminated the women's affairs office in their social ministries, using "mainstreaming gender" as the justification. Yet, at the local and county level Germany still had one of the largest women's policy machineries in Europe, with close to two thousand local gender-equality offices, coordinated by a national association.[50] Small-scale gender-training enterprises replaced the 1980s projects as a niche in which women's studies graduates could get state funds to do practical gender-equality work. As a "Top-Down-Strategie," gender mainstreaming engaged feminist energies, but no longer offered incentives to mobilize a women's public at the grass roots.

Antidiscrimination Law

The most radically different and most politically resisted EU policy innovation for Germany was the introduction of laws against discrimination on the basis of gender and other group membership. The core of German law stressed collective rights and state responsibilities to make policy for vulnerable groups, relying on the class-based model of state protections negotiated with its "social partners" (labor and management), and leading to collective-bargaining agreements between them. As late as 2000, there was no minimum-wage law, since organized labor was considered capable of collectively bargaining with management for fair wages and working conditions.

In the 1980s, West Germany's acceptance of the EU mandate to adopt laws barring discrimination against women in employment had been minimal and grudging. The European Court of Justice (ECJ) found its "EU Conformity Law" out of compliance with EU standards because it offered no meaningful penalties for violations.[51] Successful appeals by individual women plaintiffs showed that the ECJ could be used to pressure national governments for more viable antidiscrimination measures, but also that the court applied a more narrowly individualist definition of gender equality than German feminists held. The decisions it reached in the 1990s underlined this discrepancy.

Antidiscrimination, a liberal principle of equal treatment, is quite another matter than positive action on behalf of women, as the 1995 ECJ decision in *Kalanke v. Bremen* revealed.[52] The ECJ accepted a male plaintiff's claim that a mandate to hire a woman found "equally qualified" in a position in which women were underrepresented was a violation of the EU Equal Treatment Directive. It held that this directive prohibited "quotas," since any broad state mandate for when to prefer a woman paid insufficient attention to personal circumstances and other factors of individual difference.[53] After major European outcry, the ECJ partially retreated in the 1997 *Marschall* case, which allowed "softer" quotas (providing exceptions for individual cases). But the Treaty of Amsterdam overturned *Kalanke* by reaffirming the legitimacy of positive action for women, while also demanding that member-states pass broad antidiscrimination measures. Germany needed a new legal approach to ending gender discrimination.

Positive action for women is where German feminists had made progress. The so-called antidiscrimination bills the Greens (unsuccessfully) introduced in the 1980s all put more emphasis on active state actions to advance women than on equal treatment. In 1994, the postunification German constitution was amended to mandate the state to "promote the actual implementation of equal rights for women and men and take steps to eliminate disadvantages that now exist" (Article 3.2).[54] The German constitutional court previously had interpreted equal rights as allowing functional differentiation to override equal treatment in practice, for example, when the state formally recognized men as family breadwinners and offered them special benefits in this role and provided special protections for mothers. The amendment meant the constitution now demanded that justices reframe such differences as "disadvantages" rather than "functional."

Joining its amended constitution with the Treaty of Amsterdam, the German state now had two discursively legitimated objectives: to make policy for women that would structurally overcome their collective disadvantage in the labor market and to provide equal treatment to individual men and women. Some feminists saw this equal treatment directive from the EU level as a lever for progress, but others were deeply skeptical. German courts were already more likely to frame men as victims of "reverse discrimination" than to offer women tools to contest employers' institutionalized preferences for men, which were often still not recognized as inherently discriminatory.[55] As German feminists saw it, policy action advancing women (*Frauenförderung*) could address structural obstacles, but barring discrimination by gender accepted embedded inequalities in the name of a purely hypothetical even-handedness. But the Treaty of Amsterdam now emboldened some German feminists to demand both equal treatment *and* expanded, targeted opportunities.

As the Red-Green coalition came into office, feminists campaigned vigorously for a law that would combine nondiscrimination provisions with positive action and apply both to private sector employment. Until this point, advancing women as policy had been limited to the state as employer, with the belief that a change in civil service practices would echo through the economy. The first draft proposal submitted by the federal ministry responsible for women's affairs called for annual affirmative action reports from private industry and measures punishing noncompliance (introducing the potential for class-action suits in support of a plaintiff, which unions or other civil associations could file).

This proposal was summarily rejected by the chancellor and probusiness parts of the government, such as the minister of economics. What finally passed in 2001 was a legally nonbinding agreement between the government and business associations in which business promised to take "all necessary steps" to foster gender equality in hiring and promotion. It ignored the EU mandate for penalties for discrimination, provided women no representation or support in pressing claims, and only "encouraged" companies to adopt some sort of positive action plan.

German feminists saw this as a resounding defeat, particularly surprising since they had supposed the new Red-Green coalition government would be sympathetic to their concerns. But however outraged the activists in the unions and women's affairs offices were, they failed to frame the nondiscrimination issue for the broader women's public or mobilize visible protest activity for positive action in the private sector. Still, feminist discouragement and disappointment with the Red-Green coalition was widespread by 2005.

Overall, the EU emphases on gender mainstreaming and antidiscrimination law mobilized European feminist networks but in Germany were met with less than real enthusiasm. Some blamed formalization in NGO structures and top-down strategies for the lack of grassroots mobilization in Germany and around the world. Optimists saw the incorporation of gender in political discourse and policy making in Europe as potentially transformative, especially in laggard states such as Germany. On the ground, however, the EU push for making gender the target of transnational policy work had complicated effects on practical theories of what feminism was supposed to do.

WOMEN'S POLITICS OR GENDER POLITICS?

The worldwide tension can be somewhat simplistically presented as pitting "gender" against "women" as the object of feminist politics. It reflected a sense that transnational feminist politics to this point had been caught up in either tinkering with the rules to allow more women to compete with men (particularly in liberal states like the United States and Great Britain) or tailoring policy for women as they now were (particularly institutionalizing supports for motherhood and for women victims of violence, as in Germany), in both cases leaving feminists without resources to transform the system as a whole.[56] If the former was too neoliberal, the latter was too structural to encompass women's own agency and offer much hope of desirable transformations in the short-term.

For those who saw gender relations as the target of feminist politics, transforming the whole system meant moving away from policies by/for women (*Frauenpolitik*). Complex systems of power affecting both women and men needed to change, and women could not do this without men as allies.[57] A zero-sum struggle with men over power and resources was judged not only futile but misguided, since policy experience had brought many feminists to see the interrelatedness of gender relations with other inequalities.[58] More powerful women could tinker with gender arrangements to benefit themselves, but such partial modifications would not help, and might even hurt, less advantaged women and men.

Feminists who had been engaged in global development issues were particularly active in making this critique. But in the eyes of feminists for whom "taking women's side" remained central, attention to gender was a distraction from priority to women, and they were skeptical of "equality politics" as a cross-cutting social transformation. In their view, serious transformation demanded a radical commitment to women alone. This might be inside state policy machinery—as in the institutionalized offices for women's affairs—or in women's projects and movements that remained autonomous of political parties, unions, or other mixed-gender mobilizations. There could be no more general politics than a politics "for women."[59]

In Germany, the tension between structural and poststructural analyses of gender had direct organizational ramifications. For example, since 1988 the Greens had underwritten an autonomous feminist foundation (FrauenAnStifting).[60] At the peak of its powers, in the early 1990s, it had almost fifty employees, sixteen foreign offices funding women's projects all over the world, an educational arm offering lectures and courses around Germany, and an annual budget in the millions. As part of the Green shift to gender politics, a restructuring in 1997 abolished it, and integrated *gender democracy* into the mission of the Böll Foundation, leaving only a tiny research appendage (Feministisches Institut) autonomously in women's control.

Feminists active in Green politics divided sharply over this move. Some applauded making gender democracy part of the mission for all members, as both a principle for how internal affairs should be handled and a goal for all the foundation's social change programs, and worked (with men) to steer the overall course of the Foundation's work.[61] Some were outraged, defining it as an affront to feminist autonomy as a principle and an illegitimate seizure of resources in practice. These defenders of autonomy were convinced that focusing on gender rather than women sent a dangerous signal that feminism was not a priority. They felt sure that men would provide only lip service to feminist objectives and that real decision making would not be on a gender-equal basis. They opted for the Feminist Institute and greatly reduced funding, or they walked away from the Greens entirely.[62]

What did *gender democracy* mean? The Böll Foundation used it to imply integrationist rather than purely autonomous feminism. The concept was for women to enter in and exercise half the power in society and politics, since anything less would fall short of achieving full citizenship of both women and men. The feminists who opposed it did so because gender democracy was a 180-degree turn away from autonomy as a political strategy. The conflict between these visions played out not only among the Greens but also in various institutional contexts.

First, in project-related feminist work, the decline of a strategic emphasis on autarky was unmistakable: feminist bookstores closed, while domestic violence projects expanded to also address changing men. Rather than looking for funding for more *Frauenhäuser* where women could reassemble their lives autonomously, antiviolence activists shifted their focus to society-wide transformations. For example, a Berlin group formed an intervention project to work with and on the state, and the city-state of Berlin and the federal government began funding the group in 1995.[63] This feminist initiative (BIG), like other intervention projects nationwide in the later 1990s, sought laws to expel batterers from their apartments, impel them into counseling or prison, and worked cooperatively with police and medical providers.[64] Feminists once active in combating violence only against women began to see domestic violence as encompassing victimization of the elderly and children, and even potentially men.[65]

Second, gender came to the fore in the academy. Humboldt University in (formerly East) Berlin established the first professorship called Gender Studies in 1997, a break with the conventional *Frauenforschung* label (meaning research both on and by women). Men began to be welcomed to feminist seminars that had originally been only by and for women, and German feminists counted among their prominent gender researchers Michael Meuser, whose 1998 book offered a constructionist-feminist analysis of gender and masculinity.[66] This new antistereotyping politics included the belated development of a "men's movement" supporting feminist-inspired transformations in men's personal lives.[67]

Third, making gender the target of politics forged a common bond among gay men and feminists in creating a poststructural politics of sexuality. As Robert Tobin's history of gay sexuality in Germany shows, the "queering" of gay politics came as an import from the United States in the 1990s. In the 1970s and 1980s, West German gay politics had been nearly exclusively male, and early efforts to mobilize lesbians and gay men together in the East had not borne fruit. Both East and West, lesbian organizing took place within feminism, offering a politicized all-woman alternative to the power struggles of heterosexuality, but did not suggest any reason to work with gay men. But by 1995, German discussions of sexuality became infused with American discussions of a "LGBT community," including semitranslated symbols and terms from US discourse, such as *Regenbogen* (rainbow) and *sich outen* (coming out).[68] New alliances emerged as the Butler boom transformed heterosexuality itself into an issue for feminists, and German feminist scholars such as Sabine Hark and Heike Raab joined in bringing queer theory to bear on explaining and contesting gender inequalities.[69]

All of these transnational influences, including the impulses from Butler, Beijing, and Brussels, led to a deeply controversial but strongly transformative shift in German feminist politics. The move away from the focus on women as the single, central constituency for whom feminists could speak and whose side they could take was controversial. The new politics of gender stirred fears that women themselves would be forgotten, but even more strongly reinforced new feminist interests in working in, with, and on the state and in developing alliances with men. The interest in poststructuralist theory made alliances with queer politics more likely, but the broader transnational shift toward a discourse of gender encouraged even structuralists to recognize multiple and cross-cutting interests, form pragmatic alliances, and work on combining demands for gender equality with resistance to neoliberalism. The EU as a policy partner for gender equality was therefore viewed with particular skepticism, since the same political liberal promises of equal treatment also accompanied its market-centered economic policies. But in Germany, EU and UN engagement precipitated radical changes in feminist frameworks for addressing gender.

CONCLUSION: CLASS, GENDER, AND DIVERSITY POLITICS

The radicalism of the move toward liberal principles in the hybrid policy regime negotiated between the EU and its member-states can most clearly be seen in the framing transition involved in antidiscrimination law. The Treaty of Amsterdam insisted that member-states make discrimination formally illegal, but in doing so, it did not merely demand states pass laws barring discrimination against women in education and state employment, but placed gender in a new list with sexuality, nationality/ethnic origin, age, disability, religion, and worldview as characteristics that received protection from discrimination. Such provisions were to apply not only to government actions but to private actions by employers, banks, landlords, and schools. This law seemed to many similar to US legislation as it had developed over the years, but that was often less reason to embrace it than to suspect it of being a neoliberal threat to European, especially German, gender-equality policy.

Understanding this ambivalence takes us back to the fundamental differences between the metaphors for gender that had proved useful for feminists in the United States and Germany. Unlike the United States, where policy development had moved steadily from race to gender, sexuality, disability, and other issues of difference and inequality, the addition of these other differences challenged German feminist thinking that had begun by seeing gender as like class rather than like "race" or nationality.

By taking what had been a feminist demand for gender equality anchored in an understanding of overcoming classlike institutional subordinations, and extending it to what were seen as individual differences, the EU version of feminist politics conflicted with long-standing German feminist ideas about social and political solidarity. It is important to notice that class itself does not appear on the EU list of special types of diversity, which reflects the very different theoretical standing of class inequality. Class alone has been institutionally the heart of how political inclusion and social justice in Europe is understood and addressed. Advocates of gender-equality measures had struggled for decades to win a level of regard for the structural inequities facing women that would at least begin to join class as a matter of state concern, and they did so by mobilizing women as a collective actor who could make demands on women's behalf, as unions and social democrats had done for class interests. Was this now at risk?

The embrace of gender politics as a major concern of international bodies such as the UN and EU, a German constitutional mandate for state action to address gender inequality, and a national mainstreaming law enacted in response to the Beijing Platform for Action, all offered good reasons to see feminist principles as entering the framework of politics. Perhaps incorporating gender justice as essential to social justice and gender democracy as part of democracy was finally beginning.

But at the same time, this newly legitimate politics of gender was colliding with an accelerating politics of race. Although the term "race" remains taboo in Germany, and in continental Europe generally only refers to persons of African origin, a growing process of racialization of Islam began to erase attention to the real differences in national origin and religious practice among European Muslims to define them as a uniformly unassimilable group. Pakistanis in Britain, Algerians in France, Indonesians in the Netherlands, and Turks in Germany began to be understood as "Muslims in Europe" (not as European Muslims) and (whether secular or observant) as challenging the Christian culture of Europe.[70] In the increasingly heated context of how to understand immigration, including the belated integration of the growing numbers of children born in Germany to immigrant parents but with no clear route to citizenship, concerns about internal "otherness" focused on discrimination law and gender norms.

The EU effort to make member-states forbid discrimination against individuals on the basis of "national origin/language" and "religion/worldview" was thus a way to address race without granting it structural status or even acknowledging the ongoing process of racializing religion that was making racism—and race—more visible and viciously contested in practice across Europe. Anchoring EU antidiscrimination directives to these grounds, along with others conceptualized as more individual (age, disability, sexuality), framed the inequalities facing immigrants from Muslim countries as the individual prejudices of others, a matter of employers and neighbors learning to recognize "diversity" as good. Borrowing from the American "business case for diversity" that human-relations management had constructed (at the cost of losing the emphasis on social justice with which the struggle began), the EU defined antidiscrimination measures as part of its mandate for increasing economic prosperity and business competitiveness.[71]

Controversially for feminists, gender was now included in this list of "differences" to be acknowledged and protected, while social class was not. Discursively, in the German and European context, that meant a demotion of significance for gender. If all these forms of discrimination were to be treated like gender, the logical conclusion would be that gender be seen as and treated as like them. Moreover, in a system of collective representation in claiming political voice, equating gender with ethnic and religious diversity among those who were socially denigrated and/or noncitizens would be a significant step backward for women's demand for political inclusion and empowerment.[72] Why should feminists align with antiracist politics, when any indication of collective empowerment for "Muslims in Europe" was defined as "institutionalizing Shari'a" law at women's collective cost?

A second obstacle was institutional. In the United States, using litigation to advance normative change arose as a strategy in the civil rights movement, but in Germany using antidiscrimination cases to advance class or gender equality earned no such legitimacy. Echoing the class-based development of the welfare state, state action was situated in the political parties and in administrative programs to advance women and mainstream gender, especially in and through the civil service.[73] With gender mainstreaming, EU directives, and party-based inclusion of women representatives, feminists had made significant gains. This corporatist approach resonated much more deeply with German understandings of politics than the discrimination assumption that group-based treatment interfered with individual women's and men's rights and freedoms.

The gender strategy of transnational politics, insofar as it accepted the comparability of gender and class and their joint special significance for social policy, began to seem like it could replace a politics directed by and for women alone in Germany, though not without conflict. But to define gender merely a "difference" rather than a structural inequality like class simply did not resonate politically. This context makes German feminist ambivalence toward the EU directive understandable, but the degree of German resistance to any form of antidiscrimination law is still striking.

While nearly all EU member-states had followed its directive to pass such laws by 2003, Germany had not. The Red-Green government in 2004 officially proposed such a bill, but some of its own ministers took the highly unusual step of publicly denouncing it as a "job-killer" that would set off an "avalanche of lawsuits" and interfere with private landlords' judgment about "appropriate tenants" in neighborhoods. Because the bill triggered opposition focused on its desegregating and antistereotyping implications for immigrants, the proposal became popularly defined as being about religion/nationality "rather than" gender or sexuality. Advocates for the disabled mobilized visibly in support of the law, but feminists were notably absent from the public debates.[74] The law failed to pass before the government fell.

While it might seem surprising that antidiscrimination measures would be so controversial, the level of resistance to this reframing can be explained by the new relation that the law would establish between gender and "race" and the loss of a connection between gender and class as grounds for positive state action. In the final chapter, I take up some further ramifications of the shifting context of race, class, and gender in the twenty-first century. The struggles over immigration split the interests of feminists and racialized minorities in Germany and Europe and exacerbated political tensions between them.

At the heart of these debates is the issue of what makes a good family. Feminist challenges to the patriarchal male-breadwinner model are treated, on the one hand, as opening the door to real but limited reform of the work-family system and, on the other hand, as if the change had already been fully accomplished and was now being threatened by immigrant families. To conclude the story, I explore the family policy and family debates that globalization and modernization unleashed in Germany, and in that way, I circle back to the issues of race, class, and gender intersectionality and practical feminist theory with which this book began.

CHAPTER 8

FEMINISM, FAMILIES, AND THE FUTURE
Practical Theory and Global Gender Politics in the Twenty-first Century

O N NOVEMBER 23, 2005, the news echoed around the world: Angela Merkel had become the first woman chancellor of Germany. One of a handful of women heading governments anywhere, running an economically powerful state with a major voice in transnational institutions such as the EU and World Bank, Merkel assumed a position of great global significance. Moreover, as the leader of a Grand Coalition between her own Christian-Democratic Union and its usual opposition, the Social Democrats, she had a commanding legislative majority and unusual power to set policy. Alice Schwarzer, longtime publisher of *EMMA* and media-anointed spokesperson for feminism, immediately proclaimed, "We have become chancellor." Most media outlets interviewed Schwarzer and chimed in to claim that Merkel's personal victory equaled that of women collectively. The newsmagazine *Spiegel* announced that this event "was not the election of a chancellor but the triumph of the German women's movement."[1]

But reality is always more complicated. As around the world, the numbers of women in higher political offices have grown remarkably, but few women in leadership roles identify with feminism. Angela Merkel, as head of the leading German conservative party, the CDU, explicitly avowed that she did not and would not represent feminism.[2] Not only in Germany, the access of women to leadership roles in politics and private industry is rising while rhetoric against this is fading. Women's public roles are not depicted as a threat to the family, as in the 1970s and even 1980s, which paradoxically opens space for conservative, even right-wing, women to take positions of power in transnational corporations and national governments. The picture of change in women's social status is also mixed. Transnational discourse affirms women's rights, but German policy and practice, as in most states, too often fail to uphold them.

This chapter considers where German feminism has come in these past forty years of struggle and how its particular history offers tools for understanding the possibilities and constraints of the present moment. While Merkel's individual victory neither translates into a triumph nor signals a defeat for feminists, her government moved in a markedly different and surprisingly more feminist direction in family and gender politics than the Red-Green coalition it replaced. Modernizing family policy was meant to respond to real family needs, not to offer a route to feminist utopia. But because this policy direction is one that many feminists are pursing globally, its implications reach well beyond Germany.

Beginning with the specifics of the transformation of family policy under Merkel, this chapter underlines the book's story of path dependency in feminist policy since the origins of these changes are found in earlier chapters. Long before 2005, German feminists had accepted the embrace of the state, and in the 1980s the CDU was already using family policy to modernize its appeal to its disproportionately female constituency. Across the EU, family support measures are part of the political definition of both modernity and feminism. Called "work-family reconciliation," these policies encourage mothers' (part-time) employment and financially reward (women's) family-based labor while alleviating the poverty women and children otherwise face.[3] Germany's social policies are aligned with the EU-driven policy ideal of shared responsibilities between women and men, rather than with either the male-breadwinner family of the FRG or the mommy politics of the GDR.

In Germany, as in much of the world, feminism brought once-radical claims about family equality and nondiscrimination into the mainstream of politics, but has become entangled in state-driven modernization projects and detached from its roots. Political liberalism, democratization movements, and desires for personal autonomy are often co-opted by neoliberals arguing that market fundamentalism will provide such freedoms, striking fear in the hearts of many concerned with social justice. Some argue that feminism itself has become part of a neoliberal project, in which the usefulness of a flexible, one-and-a-half-earner family model is appreciated for meeting the production and reproduction goals of the state.[4]

Family matters also for the interplay of class and racial-ethnic politics with contemporary gender politics. On the one hand, the rise of a modernizing family politics in Germany—as in much of the world—differs notably from the antimodern mobilization around "traditional family values" in the United States. This reality undermines any claims for American leadership in global feminist movements and makes US feminist efforts to use European models of family support to guide American policy unrealistically radical.[5] But, on the other hand, the individualistic, modern, egalitarian family ideal now embraced by even conservative German policymakers serves as a discursive bludgeon against the family relations of immigrant minorities within Europe, particularly those who came—or whose parents or grandparents came—from predominantly Islamic countries. As feminism gained social acceptability, German feminists gained cultural authority to speak to the "backwardness" of Islamic culture. Some embrace this as an opportunity to secure the state's commitment to gender equality by endorsing repressive measures directed at immigrant women.

Given the different opportunities offered and paths taken, it is not surprising to see that the current intersection of gender and race politics in Germany differs dramatically from the discourses of feminism and antifeminism in the United States. The US "culture war" affirms the patriarchal family as a bulwark of morality and responsibility by attacking the moral standing of single mothers, sexually active teenagers, and people in same-sex relationships. Indications of decline of patriarchy are racialized as African American threats and associated with gay rights and women's liberation.[6] In Europe, the patriarchal family is instead depicted as a import from backward Islamic cultures; European values are defined as gender egalitarian and sexually tolerant: liberal in the classic political sense.

In both contexts, gender politics is framed as about modernity and families, not just about women, in racially specific ways. Such discursive differences highlight the intersectionality of all practical theories of feminist politics. The meaning of gender politics especially differs with the social locations of the women and families targeted as problematic in specific settings around the world.

This chapter directs attention back to the practical theories of feminism to reconsider the relationship between feminism as a goal and a women's movement as a strategy, and it returns to questions of intersectionality, radicalism, and the varieties of discursive and material opportunities feminists face today.

ANGELA MERKEL AND GENDER POLITICS

Anne Phillips distinguishes representing women *descriptively* by making them visible as actors (as a voting constituency or officeholders) from representing them *substantively* by addressing interests defined somehow as women's.[7] Merkel descriptively represents the globally resonant idea of women as politically empowered citizens; she also has set a substantive policy direction for Germany many define as in women's interests.

Descriptive Representation

To be perceived as a capable political actor, Merkel built on the remarkable cultural transformations in women's status since the 1970s. In Germany, as Chapter 5 showed, the quota system for party lists brought women's representation in the Bundestag from 10 to 33 percent of the seats by 2005. The Green party, which introduced the zipper list in the 1980s, pointed out that "without the women's politics of the Greens over the past 25 years, a female Federal Chancellor would still remain unthinkable."[8] This is certainly true, regardless of whether women found a personal role model in "our Angie" (physicist, East German, childless). Her victory, which *Der Spiegel* ascribed to feminism, resonated with the appreciation of women's political agency the Greens brought into German politics from national and transnational feminist mobilizations.[9]

Although the patriarchal culture of politics did not vanish, real change in gender relations resulted from Merkel's election. At the turn of the previous century, John Stuart Mill dubbed this the fait accompli effect, predicting that arguments about women's natural incapacity for higher education would only disappear when women actually became well educated.[10] By the beginning of the twenty-first century, women's movements had made women's political citizenship such a fait accompli as women emerged as decision-makers in governments around the world. Michele Bachelet in Chile and Ellen Johnson Sirleaf in Liberia became heads of government along with Angela Merkel in 2005, and Madeleine Albright, Condoleeza Rice, and Hillary Clinton represented the United States diplomatically for successive, opposite-party administrations.

The legitimacy of framing women as unsuitable for politics eroded and the vision of political power as inherently masculine blurred. Merkel's own visibility contributed to this process. Even during the course of the 2005 campaign, German attitudes shifted. Early in the campaign, only 56 percent of women (and 37 percent of men) said in principle they approved of a woman being chancellor. By the end of the campaign 84 percent of women and 70 percent of men did.[11]

Her election was also reckoned as a victory for the East since she was the first *Ossi*, or person from the former GDR, to lead the now-united country. Her life-course was not typical for women in either the East (where having no children was rare) or the West (where being a scientist was rare). Perceptions of Merkel are intersectionally filtered through her gender and the different histories of gender policy in the FRG and GDR.[12] The continuing division in gender norms between Eastern and Western states makes even her individual self-presentation ambiguous. On the one hand, she represents an East German model of emancipation—in a male-dominated profession, with an unflattering haircut, in a nondependent relationship with a man—interpreted as having given up her "femininity" in Western terms. On the other hand, she is no advocate of any return to socialism and its approach to women's liberation, so those who saw women's lives and politics as offering an alternative to capitalist values, saw in her the opposite of women's emancipation.[13] Even her changing hairstyles were open to conflicting political interpretations as more Western/modern (powerful) or more feminine/soft (weak).

Despite such ambiguities, Merkel created a powerful fait accompli effect, and her election created an emotional response to this symbolic achievement. Alice Schwarzer described the "ambivalent excitement" on the part of German women who could not help but identify with her, regardless of her politics.[14] Even if not the beginning of the end of male-defined politics, her chancellorship meant Germany joined the ranks of countries in which women could be assumed to be able to lead, and where women's insider roles in formal political institutions would shape future state policy. Women had indisputably become actors in, not only victims of, the state.

Substantive Representation

Representing women's policy interests is a deeper challenge. Maxine Molyneux notably divided the multiplicity of women's articulated interests into those rooted in their material position in daily life and social structures ("practical interests") and those that expressed women's aspirations for social transformation, which she understood to be anchored in the political and social theories they espoused ("strategic interests").[15] But Molyneux assumed a bipolar world in which socialism offered the compelling strategic vision challenging global oppression, not a postsocialist world polity where liberal discourses dominated. An emancipatory gender policy after 1989 had to fit a framework in which global claims for individual human rights overturned dictatorships and investment in human capital justified wealth-redistributing state policies.

By 2005 the transnational context for gender politics was given not by the conflict between communism and capitalism, but by proliferating NGOs, global and regional governance structures such as UN agencies and EU treaties, neo-liberal economic policies, and conflicts with Islam exacerbated by the "War on Terror." Together they now defined a global policy agenda of modernization for welfare states that included more egalitarian gender relations. German policy reflected both the class and race dimensions of this shift.

REMAKING MODERNITY:
EU POLITICS IN MERKEL'S GERMANY

In 2006, Merkel's Grand Coalition finally succeeded in passing an antidiscrimination law, as the EU had demanded for a decade. It also reshaped family policy to provide shorter child-care leaves at higher wage replacement rates, arguably making them more gender-inclusive than mother-directed. Both policies affirmed women's citizenship as individuals (in the liberal sense of personal autonomy and market freedoms) and as a social group (by endorsing an active state extending economic and social rights to the more vulnerable). Each policy was strongly influenced both by the EU's market liberalism and by feminist advocacy networks throughout Europe. Like Merkel's hairstyles, each was open to multiple interpretations.

The gender agenda shaped in Brussels was itself ambiguous. While the European Commission empowered civil society organizations like the European Women's Lobby and embraced the structural language of feminist change through gender mainstreaming, many of its resources went into training individuals to "value diversity." In effect, if not in intent, this approach demoted gender to one difference among many, rather than an economic organizing principle as structurally significant as class. EU policy observatories and NGOs favored an interventionist state role in the economy directed toward increasing workforce participation and flexibility. Both family and work policy arenas became targets for these various interests especially as they addressed women's perceived needs as workers and mothers.

Rethinking the Male-Breadwinner Family

Recall that in previous decades the CDU had introduced a few years of pension credits for child rearing and up to three years of paid child-rearing leave. These were seen as encouraging mothers to stay out of the labor market and indeed made their reentry difficult.[16] Under Merkel, the conservative parties shifted course, acknowledging women's rights to compete in the labor market (through more attention to antidiscrimination measures), women's and men's joint contributions to family breadwinning (through a restructuring of child-care leaves), and married women's interests in more egalitarian men (though targeted support for engaged fatherhood). This shift toward a more gender-balanced model of paid and unpaid labor is less surprising than it might seem.

All over Europe, birthrates were falling, less in the Scandinavian countries, which provided extensive work-family supports, and more in less work-friendly policy environments such as Spain and Italy.[17] The 2006 EU Roadmap for Gender Equality urged national governments to reform family policy to grow their populations and economies.[18] Germany, buffeted by its extreme drop in Eastern births after unification, was particularly anxious about the pension crisis portended by a low birth rate and aging population.

In previous decades, West German feminists and nonfeminists had agreed on mothers' special social role in child rearing. Feminist theory and practice long declared caring labor a special female capacity the state should support and defend. Nonfeminists still described mothers in paid jobs as *Rabbenmütter*, mother ravens heartlessly leaving their chicks to be cared for in another nest.[19] The family leave the CDU introduced in the 1980s reflected this male-breadwinner bias. Unlike the GDR's baby year, it was so long and poorly paid that only mothers would take it, regardless of its ungendered designation as

a "parental vacation" (*Elternurlaub*). Families in the East were more likely to
have access to early child care and to keep both parents in paid employment,
but opportunities for both still lagged behind demand.[20]

The EU emphasis on economic competitiveness and growth implied "activation" of women into paid employment and "flexibilization" of jobs to include
more part-time and temporary contracts. This neoliberal pull complemented the
push from EU-wide feminist advocacy networks. The latter favored a Nordic
social democratic approach: extensive state support for early child care, a larger
and better-paid service sector, and expanded part-time opportunities encouraging women to reenter the labor market when their children were still young.[21]
The East German "birth strike" suggested strongly that young women would
rather renounce or limit childbearing than forsake employment.

Defining reproductive labor as women's special role thus became problematic
both for individual families and for the state's national interests in economic
competitiveness and biological reproduction. Disassociating women from intensive, long-term mother-work had once been too radical for most Germans,
even feminists; gender desegregation was now defined as in everyone's interest,
since the breadwinner/housewife marriage was successfully framed as inadequate
to meet postindustrial challenges. Among feminists as well as in popular culture, bringing women into demanding careers and men into engaged fathering
steadily gained support.[22]

The EU Parental Leave Directive of 1996 created a material and discursive
opportunity for the Red-Green coalition that it had failed to exploit. The Grand
Coalition now revisited work-family reconciliation policies in light of this directive. Negotiated with Europe-wide coalitions of employers and unions, it set
goals and timetables for member-states to extend to "men and women workers
an individual right to parental leave on the grounds of the birth or adoption
of a child to enable them to take care of that child, for at least three months,
until a given age up to 8 years."[23] Merkel's proposal followed the "daddy-leave"
models pioneered in Scandinavian countries, giving extra time to (married,
heterosexual) families in which men shared childrearing leave. Her government
invoked values of modernization and family friendliness rather than feminism
to legitimate this significant policy shift.[24]

The new policy, initially formulated by Merkel's close ally and minister for
Family, Women, Senior and Youth Affairs, Ursula von der Leyen, offers both

women and men a high level of replacement for actual wages for fourteen months (two designated solely for fathers) of child-care time, taken in large or small chunks anytime between birth and age eight.[25] It also expanded provision and funding of early child-care places nationwide, using the rhetoric of investing in future human capital to counter neoliberal pressures for reducing rather than increasing state spending. Limiting length while increasing the monthly benefits makes this more attractive for higher-earning women in particular, but also reduces all women's previous disconnection to the labor force. Some feminists viewed the policy as incentivizing childbirth and directed more at better-educated and more affluent sectors of the labor market, framing it unenthusiastically as neoliberal and offensively eugenic. However, like the earlier partial concession offered by abortion law reform, this measure drew much of the urgency out of popular discontent. As such, it was a canny concession from the leading conservative party to younger women voters they might otherwise lose to smaller parties, like the Greens, who embraced women's autonomy as a no-longer-radical value.[26]

For Germany, the new leave policy and child-care commitment was a profound change, even though it did not dismantle all state supports for male-breadwinner families that feminists found problematic (especially income-splitting between high and low earners in figuring income taxes).[27] The law acknowledged feminist criticism of framing the policy as a "parental vacation" by substituting a more active term, "child-rearing time." It also realized some of the intent of the 1980s feminist "pay for housework" demand, while defining those getting state support not as "housewives" but employees temporarily out of the labor force. The policy accepted the arguments that men needed incentives to change and that "helping women" with "their" work was not adequate state policy, as East German feminists had always said.

Why did this German policy window swing open at this specific moment? Some stress changes in the political field.[28] In addition to a long-term shift toward neoliberal views of activation and flexibility, short-term opportunities were afforded by the Grand Coalition, which gave modernizing factions of the SPD and CDU leverage over the propatriarchal politicians in both internally heterogeneous parties.[29] Others stress political agency, including Merkel's political skills, credibility as a woman leader, and inspired choice of Ursula von der Leyen as family minister (an aristocrat, career woman, and mother of seven) to manage the reform. Additionally, increased numbers of women in parliament (approximately one-third of all members) and steady criticism of Germany generated by comparative data from EU policy observatories helped open this policy window.

Another, demographic explanation emphasizes the transformation changing the face of Europe since the 1960s. The second demographic transition—delayed age of marriage, more education, fewer marriages and births—brought growing anxiety across the EU as states wondered how to finance their extensive public pensions.[30] Mitigating conflict between older and younger generations of workers and reducing the controversial flow of immigrants to enhance the shrinking labor supply were powerful short-term reasons to increase the numbers of tax-payers by keeping women in the labor force and supported the state's long-term interest in increasing birthrates. Both these demographic interests make modernizing family policy a state priority. Both also provoke feminist concern that women are (again) being instrumentalized to serve state needs rather than using the state for their own empowerment.[31] The question of what paid employment offers women, especially mothers, was again up for relationally realistic reconsideration.

Rethinking Women's Work and Achievement

The market-liberal EU approach to work-family policy implied gender desegregation in employment as well as in the family. Limitations on store opening hours were relaxed, and ECJ decisions against German law opened opportunities once totally closed to women, such as serving in the military.[32] Laws restricting women from night work and from "dangerous" occupations largely disappeared, replaced by rules that require part-time workers to get the same hourly wage as full-timers. The market-liberal EU defined states' economic role less as a protector of the weak than as a guarantor of fair competition, but their policies worked to increase women's opportunities and rewards in the labor market. By 2007, union women and Social Democrats had abandoned their long-standing defense of women-specific protections and joined the liberal-leaning Frauenrat (Women's Council) in protests for gender equality in pay and employment.[33]

The Frauenrat itself received feminist legitimacy and political influence from its role as the primary German representative to the European Women's Lobby. Scorned in the 1970s and viewed with suspicion in the 1980s, the Frauenrat benefited from the German unification and European integration processes of the 1990s. As a broker among state administrators doing gender mainstreaming, women politicians rising in the political parties and elected office, and diverse civil society groups receiving support from the European Commission, the EWL emboldened national member associations like the Frauenrat to embrace feminist causes from sexual harassment to domestic violence.

The EWL, its member associations, and the EU-funded network of expert observatories gave priority to bringing more women into gender-unconventional jobs, elite professions, and management positions in government and private industry.[34] Trans-European networks of women experts had credibility in pushing an equal rights agenda that German feminists had earlier resisted as too liberal, individualist, and competitive. Where German feminists in the 1970s had mocked the call for equality in management and science, many were now arguing for more opportunities to achieve, excel, and lead in male-defined fields.

During the previous decades many feminists' status had risen from student to professor, activist to politician, project entrepreneur to government administrator. Their interest in creating opportunities for other women had risen along with this. The discursive association of feminism and modernity encouraged popular representations of women and feminism that were less openly misogynist but provided a "market-friendly" view of femininity for the new generation. Organizations for women entrepreneurs and in business management sprouted across Germany.[35] The media ideal of *Alphamädchen* ("girls on top")—competitors unafraid of power and unworried about social decorum—still came in for feminist criticism, but networks for women entrepreneurs blossomed, echoing the state's growing emphasis on individual self-support.[36]

So, after decades of state resistance to EU antidiscrimination mandates, the Grand Coalition now brought Germany in line with this policy directive.[37] The law adopted in 2006, the Allgemeine Gleichstellungsgesetz (AGG, General Equality Law) was relatively weak, but a significant step toward institutionalizing equal treatment. Although no meaningful sanctions have yet been imposed on any German private employer for discriminating against women, the number of cases continues to rise. The national AGG office (which went online in 2009) increases popular awareness, too.[38] Whereas in 2005, a storefront in Berlin virtually at the doorstep of the Bundestag could display an explicitly gender-discriminatory help-wanted poster, the AGG began to make this publicly illegitimate.

As written, the AGG equally bars discrimination against gender, national origin, language, sexuality, worldview, religion, disability, and age. Like the failed Red-Green antidiscrimination bill, it blurs the differences among forms of social exclusion and carves out substantial exceptions. For example, housing discrimination is made illegal on all grounds equally, but only in buildings with more than fifty units, and not even then if even one is owner-occupied. What the AGG offered feminists was not enough to mobilize them as advocates for passing or enforcing this law. Instead, they framed it as "about immigrants" rather than about gender, apparently not noticing how immigrant women would particularly benefit, for example, when they sought independence by living away from their natal families or contested the rampant job discrimination that kept them dependent on male wages.[39]

Targeted legal strategies, such as the Norwegian model requiring that no more than 60 percent of the managing directors and corporate boards of directors be one gender, draw more interest than intersectional antidiscrimination law among European feminists.[40] By 2011, gender quotas for corporate directorships had become a hot topic in Germany, with the active support of "nonfeminist" women politicians like Ursula von der Leyen.[41] Unlike antidiscrimination law, such quotas appeal to corporatist thinking as forms of active state policy providing affirmative action for women as a group.

Despite this growing focus on opening opportunities at the top, social vulnerability at the bottom has been increasing too. Young women, like young men, even with a completed apprenticeship or higher education, find it ever more difficult to break into the stable and better-paid sectors of the labor market. The *Ich-AGs* (one-person corporations) introduced by the Red-Green coalition have not so much encouraged a boom in small business opportunities as a spread of unstable consulting jobs. The number of women employed is growing faster than their hours in paid work, which means short-hour, low-benefit jobs are increasing.[42]

Despite its privatization initiatives, Germany remains a "social market economy," not a market-fundamentalist one, in relation to class and gender intersections. In this regard, it is more European than neoliberal. Even with economic restructuring, EU measures for fair competition among member-states contribute to helping lower-waged women workers (for example, requiring paid maternity leaves and equal prorated wages for part-time workers). Even child-care benefits and leadership quotas offered to elite women are corporat-ist rather than individualizing.[43]

Expanding the care-providing sector under state auspices, as the EU strongly encourages, also helps women who would otherwise be providing care for children or the ill or elderly in private sector jobs, with fewer benefits and less employment security, and so subsidizes the wages of less educated women EU citizens. To the extent that state subsidies for citizens with care needs subsidize the wages of legal caregivers, the policy discourages employing third-country immigrants working off the books. Still, immigrant women domestic work-ers, documented and not, are a part of the labor force that continues growing.

The combination of new family leaves and the AGG do more to advance women's competitive position than to protect the workers and mothers with the most limited alternatives. Yet this market-friendliness is also a shift toward making state policy revolve around gender equality as a social value rather than around state protection of women as a classlike group of home-bound moth-ers. Supporting equal treatment of women and men as a principle is "radical" change for Germany, where the intersection of class and gender long legitimated group-based protection.

This radical shift reflects the intersection of actors with agendas (feminist lobbies at the EU level, institutionalized gender-equality offices at the national and local level, political parties competing for votes, and individual women's entrepreneurial projects) with the discursive and material opportunity struc-tures produced by German unification and EU market integration. In this new context, the interests of marginalized—often immigrant—women stir contro-versy in terms reflecting racialized rather than class-based definitions of needs.

INTERSECTIONAL FAMILY POLITICS:
RACE AND GENDER IN FEMINISM

The 2005 movie *Kebab Connection* provides an amusing but informative win-dow into the changing norms for gender and family in Germany. A Romeo-and-Juliet story about a Turkish-German young man and his pregnant German girlfriend, the movie uses pushing a baby carriage in public as a symbol of the purported unwillingness of "Turkish men" to be engaged fathers. This action becomes the site of extended conflict and fantasy between the young lovers, but it also offers ironic comment on the extent of change in West German men since the early 1990s, when a man with a pram could be an image of utopian feminist transformation (see Figure 6 in Chapter 5). Little more than a decade later, the movie suggested that it was now simply the hallmark of a modern German husband and the minimum expectation German women held for their partners. The movie thus played with the explosive tension in defining "Turks" (and other Muslim immigrants) as the source of resistance to modern gender and family norms.

Immigration from both EU and non-EU countries—along with the natural increase of population of second- and third-generation immigrant communities—makes racial and ethnic diversity more visible in Europe today than it was in the 1970s. The tendency for the new, religiously different immigrants to come from still-rural areas of Europe provokes distress at their style of life, as it did in the early twentieth century with Jewish immigration from the east, with such disastrous results. This immigrant visibility feeds anxiety about the implications of "diversity." The decrease of the ethnically German share of population to about 85 percent, less in major cities, is felt to endanger the reproduction of "the nation" as an imagined community.[44] As feminist theorists point out, concerns about national reproduction are good predictors of concern for gender and family policy.[45] German demographic change has not only legitimated supportive policies for "good" families but also created a context for racialized discourse about gender relations in "bad" families.

The primary targets in Europe are "Muslims," that is, immigrants from majority-Muslim countries, discursively figured as exemplars of patriarchal family relations. Europe's history of racializing religion as a major line of division, within and between countries, feeds into this process, since demands to renounce one's religion to be allowed inclusion in the nation have been used by Christians against Jews, and Protestants and Catholics against each other. Today Muslim is a similar category, one from which a person cannot escape merely by secularizing. Racialization (imputing of an unchangeable essence to ethnic groups) turns religion into a quasi-biological trait that legitimates exclusion and repression.

Beginning in the later 1990s, "feminism" became discursively mobilized on both Left and Right as a symbol of the threat Muslim immigrants posed to "European values." Fatal attacks on gay filmmaker Theo van Gogh in the

Netherlands and on young Muslim women who defied strictures against pre-marital sex and/or married without parental consent ("honor killings") received extensive media attention.[46] Feminists, including some with a secular immigrant background, such as Hirsi Ali, became media spokespersons for the perspective that a head scarf symbolized a fundamental conflict with gender equality, modernity, and democracy and thus should be repressed.

Significant numbers of European feminists defined veiling as a certain indicator of women's oppression by men in their communities and so wanted their states to "protect" women by outlawing their head covering. The cover of *EMMA* reproduced in Figure 9 below suggests how troubling feminist encounters with otherness could be. In this cartoon, a Muslim woman figures as the opposite of hip, enlightened European modernity. Not only were femi-

FIGURE 9   In this cartoon by Franziska Becker for *EMMA*, the hijab-wearing woman is disconcerting the German woman who is dressed somewhat provocatively, and there is no common ground on which they might meet. The equation of any kind of practice of covering with a hijab served to exacerbate the threat that even a simple scarf worn by Muslim women seemed to present to gender equality in Germany.
Source: Franziska Becker.

nists disconcerted by the emergence of any women who wore such a tentlike hijab, but this discomfort readily transferred to disapproval of any type of head covering worn by women on religious grounds. Turning to the state to stop it was a remarkable discursive shift from a gender politics centered on women's choice and autonomy.

In Germany, the federal government did not bar veils, but the constitutional court permitted individual states to do so, and about half did.[47] These anti-head-scarf laws exclude women wearing any head covering from jobs where women might represent the state (for example, as teachers and other civil servants) on the grounds that they thereby portray the state as backward and patriarchal.[48] Despite its gender-discriminatory effect, many feminists supported such exclusion of head-scarf-wearing women (but not religiously observant men) from state employment. Most German feminists framed the problems of Muslim/ Turkish/ immigrant women (terms largely used interchangeably) as due not to employment or housing difficulties but only to gender oppression within their natal communities.

For feminists who supported banning the head scarf, it exemplified gender oppression. Even wearing it by choice was seen as succumbing to sexist normative coercion (as could the choice to wear miniskirts, which no one proposed banning). They called on Germany to support "European values" of gender equality and personal freedom through state regulation, a sharp break from their earlier insistence on collective self-representation by the women affected (die Betroffenen).[49] Rather than framing Muslim/immigrant women as potentially self-representing political agents in their own right, as an intersectional analysis might, these feminists framed them as passive victims of an unchangeable Islamic culture and were willing to ally with the German state to rescue them.[50] Feminists who opposed legal bans on wearing a head scarf were more ambivalent about such use of state power. Most favored simply allowing the slow drip of acculturation to work across generations.[51]

Both advocates and opponents of a state ban on head-scarf-wearing were thus distracted into a debate about Islamic women's freedoms rather than their own. German feminists—overwhelmingly non-Muslim themselves—mixed together discussions of so-called forced marriages, veiling, and honor killings as all indicating a dangerously antiwoman culture coming into Europe from outside.[52] By framing hair covering, arranged marriages, and violence against women as a unified cultural "tradition" that made women victims of men's family power, both sides presumed a contrast between the hyperoppressed status of women in immigrant communities and the "lesser" problems facing German women in their own. This framing automatically congratulated the German state for its alignment with feminism (which might in other contexts be criticized as sorely lacking) and directed attention away from ongoing oppressions of immigrants by Germans themselves, including by women who relied on them for "affordable" domestic labor.[53]

The debate positioned all immigrants of Muslim background as having gender norms that contrasted sharply with "modern European values" of personal freedom, secularism, and sexual permissiveness.[54] The feminist movements in Islamic-majority countries were thus rendered invisible and unavailable for transnational alliances.[55] The modern European frame of mind was defined as including accepting topless and nude beaches, open displays of homosexual affection, drinking and smoking in public, sexually provocative dress and behavior—not all of which would be approved by majorities of non-Islamic German voters.

Moreover, the constructed "Europeanness" of these values deliberately framed Germany and Europe in contrast to the "Puritan" attitudes and weak welfare state of the United States, as signs that Americans also lacked "modernity." As Jessica Brown shows, being open about nonnormative forms of sexuality—redefining prostitution as sex work, offering public encouragement to teens to use contraception, accepting public and media nudity, and legalizing civil unions for same-sex couples—has become a test of Europeanness that Americans as well as Muslims fail.[56] In fact, the lighthearted and youth-friendly approach to contraception, with condom use illustrated with "gummy bears" and "little vegetables" in the German public health advertising shown in Figure 10 would provoke a strong reaction in the United States, which is anxious about teenage sexuality and out-of-wedlock births. In the United States, patriarchal families are more often framed as needing state protection than as being a threat to national values.

Racializing and problematizing the immigrant family is an intersectional gender-and-race-based discursive strategy that builds a transnational European identity, but at the expense of non-Europeans, especially immigrant women. The citizenship classes that the German state mandates to teach immigrants

FIGURE 10 These humorous depictions of condoms include the claim that condoms can be worn "even by little vegetables," as well as the punning request, "a rubber, my little bear!" illustrated by condoms arranged in the form of the familiar Gummy Bear candy (*Gummi* can mean either rubber or gumdrop). Each of the posters is part of a billboard campaign for AIDS prevention called "*Mach's mit!*" (Join in!).
Source: FRG Federal Center for Health Education, Cologne.

modern European culture show how same-sex relationships and gender equality are used for "teaching tolerance" to those who are framed as lacking it.[57]
The state-interventionist side of the head-scarf debate resonates with public
opinion, quite unlike the classic liberal United States, where veiling is self-
evidently a matter of individual religious choice.[58] Feminism is increasingly
domesticated as a value that all (native) Europeans share, and which sets them
apart as a group from citizens of other parts of the world, including the United
States, rather than as a transnational force struggling to confront varieties of
gender subordination.

The politicization of the head scarf now contributes to its embrace by second or third generation or only mildly religious immigrant women, who wear
it to display solidarity with a culture under attack.[59] Although some German
feminists, such as Helma Lutz and Ilse Lenz, argue for an intersectional feminist
politics that incorporates the perspectives of immigrant women in Germany,
their strategy of developing shared goals through inclusion of voices from the
communities most concerned has as yet found little practical resonance outside
the academy.[60] Instead, there is a mushrooming of women's projects aimed at
rescuing oppressed "other" women and mainstreaming projects teaching "diversity." Awareness of these problems of "race" means German academics are
increasingly turning to American texts on intersectionality that place gender in
a dynamic relationship with race, class, sexuality, and other inequalities.[61] However, American texts employ a model of "race" that is rarely useful in Germany,
being less engaged with the discourse of modernity and its contradictions than
European feminists need to be. Just as European child-care policies responded
to national challenges and opportunities, not just feminist pressures, American intersectionality theories have respond to nationally specific assumptions
of similarity between race and gender politics. With their scant recognition of
class inequality and class politics and focus on individual difference, they need
reconfiguration to address European challenges.

The American "Other"

To say that European feminists face distinctive challenges in dealing with the
gender-class intersections of work-family policies and the racialized politics
of modernity is not to suggest that Americans have been able to solve their
own continuing problems with race and class. The partial successes of the civil

rights and women's movements of the 1960s and 1970s gave rise to a powerful counter mobilization in the 1990s and 2000s. "Reverse discrimination" and the threatened demise of the "traditional family," framing strategies from this reactionary movement, focus discursive attention on race and gender equality as threats to (patriarchal, White) families and away from the neoliberal arrangements that have greatly increased economic inequality and insecurity in workplaces and families.

Where the EU and UN brought political legitimacy to German feminist claims and aligned German women's interests with state goals, even if in racially problematic ways, most US feminists have little awareness of UN mandates and lack an effective discourse of class politics to address gender and social exclusion. In the absence of a reliable safety net or effective class representation through unions or social democratic parties, families are losing their grip on wages that make it possible to preserve the illusion that they are getting by, falling into the kinds of "hard living" that stresses communities and breaks up families, and having their class anxieties exploited politically.[62]

In this highly volatile situation, "family values" and feminism have been pitted against each other. Allies for US feminists in the executive, legislative, and judicial arms of the state and in the Democratic Party have been weakened or withdrawn. The Clinton administration offered welfare "reform" that ended poor mothers' entitlement to state income support when raising children, which had existed since the 1930s. Resentment of welfare has been stoked ever since African American families, demonized as morally undeserving, became widely perceived to be its main beneficiaries.[63] The Supreme Court, under Chief Justice John Roberts since 2005, is more conservative than any since the 1930s. Rather than being an ally for women and minority groups, as it was with notable effect in the 1950s through 1970s, the Supreme Court is undermining antidiscrimination law.[64]

More than in the rest of the economically developed democracies, feminists in the United States are fighting a nearly entirely defensive battle to retain former gains (such as abortion rights and equal employment regulations) that have come under ever-more vehement attack since the 1980s. The defeat of the Equal Rights Amendment to the Constitution in 1982 marked the beginning of this separate course.[65] The ongoing antifeminist assault from the Right targets all women's economic and reproductive rights, including access to reliable contraception and prenatal care, and frames poor women and African Americans as sexually and economically unreliable, while undermining the basic structures of opportunity and support all children need.

The intersectionality of this attack encourages US feminists to engage in broad movement alliances and networks, since intersectional arguments gain force when state power is mobilized to support the "family values" constituencies that oppose equal rights. Feminists find it practical to point out that women's reproductive rights, minority civil and economic rights, and gay rights are all linked and all depend on both political rights and representation. But organized market-fundamentalist resistance to giving the US government an active role in assuring its citizens' well-being has blocked or diluted most economic interventions. The level of hardships imposed by the absence of a universal system of health care, child-care provision, or paid family care leave are among the baleful effects on women of the absence of a discourse of class interest. Rather than gaining access to the state, as German feminists did, feminists in the United States have become an integral part of a coalition of the excluded.

VARIETIES OF FEMINISM, WOMEN'S MOVEMENTS, AND THE PRACTICAL POLITICS OF GENDER

This book's overall story of institutionalization of gender politics in Germany has focused on the lines laid down by its history. In the long term, it indicates how the politics of state building is entwined simultaneously with gender, race, and class from the start. Gender as well as class and race politics informed national debates over individual rights, social equality, and state protection. For feminists, this intersectional history created material and discursive challenges that shaped later struggles. The model provided by successful forms of class mobilization in Germany and in Europe as a whole, and an influential legacy of contesting the racialization of the state created by Black emancipation and civil rights struggles in the United States, still influence strategic choices and discursive development. But neither variety of feminism has yet taken a truly inclusive and intersectional direction. In fact, race and class metaphors for thinking about gendered freedom and empowerment create strategic blockages, despite their real strengths.

In the United States, the focus on gender as "like race" certainly has had positive aspects by stimulating early, resonant critiques of both race and gender oppression from White and Black feminists. The shared emphasis on being a "minority community" opened fruitful opportunities to connect gender and sexuality politics, forging alliances among feminists and queer theorists and shaping the politics of LGBT groups. Perhaps most important, the "obvious" connection between gender and race empowered women of color to take a leading role in theorizing the intersections of gender with race, class, disability, age, and other inequalities and encouraged alliances among all these "minoritized" groups.

However, this alliance has mobilized a strong reactionary movement that defends its vision of "family values," often with corporate funding and market-fundamentalist discursive support. The class dimension of inequality remains "radical" in American politics, even as individual women and minority men enter national leadership roles. Both a structural analysis and collective strategy for social justice are missing. Union power is at an all-time low, and disenfranchisement strategies have made it more difficult to make socially marginalized groups electorally effective. This is not feminism's problem alone, as its position in the coalition of the excluded testifies.

The German focus on gender as "like class," following in the footsteps of class struggles, has prioritized women's unity (as a political choice rather than a natural attribute) and focused on structural forms of exclusion and disadvantage with notable policy results. Motherhood is supported, materially and discursively, without insisting on sexual repression outside of patriarchal marriage; both contraception and unmarried motherhood are treated as women's reproductive rights. Even conservative leaders like Merkel and von der Leyen have embraced this approach, and its potential is far from exhausted.

But like the class model itself, the priority given to gender politically has made other forms of inequality only visible as subordinate types. Lesbians were mobilized as part of feminism but not of any cross-gender community doing sexual politics; immigrant women and girls were framed as targets of feminist concern only in regard to gender oppression within their communities. While awareness of gender as a distinctive structural force is its strength, ranking multiple subordinations and devaluing diversity within groups is a serious weakness. The priority given to shared collective identity undermines feminist efforts to deal with intersectional structures of inequality.[66]

The discourses of motherhood and modernity have proved especially contentious and paradoxical. Women in the 1970s and 1980s were excluded for being too achievement-oriented and in the 1990s and 2000s for being too religious and insufficiently individualistic. Making women's rights an argument for stigmatizing immigrants, especially Muslims, reduced immigrant women's opportunities to leverage changes in their own communities on their own terms. Some women's adoption of veiling as an act of resistance to a society that rejects their inclusion has fragmented both Muslims and non-Muslims into more and less secular, nationalistic, and xenophobic camps. Because feminism stands in a different relation with "race" in Germany and the United States, each variety of feminism faces distinctive challenges in dealing with families and family change. In Germany, not only has the modernization of the family been embraced as a goal of state policy, but also its civic value has been amplified through contrasting Europe's supposed egalitarianism with "traditional" Islamic and American cultures. Such discursive "othering" allows religious and patriarchal traditions to remain invisible or be strategically discarded even by conservative parties like the CDU.

But the variety of feminism found in the United States, with its absence of a strong class-based tradition of organized resistance to hierarchical authorities, is now struggling against religious and patriarchal traditions celebrated as part of national identity. Against this background, political party competition has made gender relations central, whether in limiting women's reproductive rights, demeaning poor families, or insisting on the need for gender difference in marriage. "Defending the family" is the preferred euphemism for antifeminist politics, even when it accompanies deep cuts in financial support for actual families facing hard times.

The nationalism in US "family values" discourse is directed at native-born citizens, especially denigrating African Americans and LGBT families. Ambivalence surfaces in American attitudes toward immigrants, who are often portrayed as having exemplary family values, even as they are seen as threatening "American" jobs. Anti-Black racism and antifeminism are entwined in these discourses, where the loosening of patriarchal bonds is framed as "Black" and as a threat to the nation from within. But the morality ascribed in this discourse to immigrants (hard-working, family-centered) does not offset the hostility nationalists feel toward "outsiders." Anti-immigrant discourse is not unique to Europe but intersects differently there with gender, family, and race there than in the United States.

VARIETIES OF FEMINIST CHANGE

What does this long story of feminist developments in one particular country offer theoretically? I suggest three different general contributions. I start by considering what intersectionality as a popular transnational discourse has to offer practical feminist politics, then I look to the continuing radical potential in political liberalism, and I conclude by considering where the women's movement has gone.

Intersectionality as Discourse and Practice

Although intersectionality has become a "buzzword" for feminists, it remains uncertain what concrete practices it implies.[67] Such strategic choices are hard to generalize across contexts that vary, as Germany and the United States do, in the historically specific processes through which gender and other relations of inequality have been mutually constructed. An effective discursive politics will need to attend to different meanings of intersectionality in national, historically constructed political contexts. Powerful claims about national honor, modernization, human rights, and citizenship offer discursive opportunities to actors with many different agendas, only some of whom are feminist. Where and how resonance will be found depends both on the strategic acuity of movement actors and the particular frameworks they seek to challenge.

One important opening for feminists in Germany came as EU political discourse framed modernization as economic competitiveness: fostering productivity (by increasing overall labor force participation, especially among women) and increasing flexibility in the economy (with more part-time and temporary work, especially for women). The claims to national pride in being modern and achieving competitive material success reinforced these opportunities and feminists seized them. Even though the neoliberal elements of this approach worry feminists, the resonant oppositional discourses anchored in socialist principles available in Europe balance them.

In the United States, modernization is a threatening rather than encouraging force. The anxieties created by growing economic inequality and insecurity mobilize those who are determined to resist change in what are defined as "traditions." In this context, feminism finds resonance for its claims for individual freedom and autonomy on the Left. Despite the supposed centrality of political liberalism in American political discourse, racialization is also historically important as a framing tool to make women's autonomy appear to threaten community, family, and the survival of all nonmarket values. The United States not only has retreated from its earlier principles of support for gender equality but exports policies that limit rather than expand women's reproductive rights.[68]

Like modernization, a discourse of rights is open to abuse in practical political struggles depending on historical context. The variety of feminism developed in Germany long considered any focus on legal and political rights as an obstacle to state actions to support, advance, and empower women. By assuming that antidiscrimination laws and similar formal rights were inherently powerless to unsettle and undermine women's subordination, the West German women's movement tended to work for rather than against women's interests defined only as mothers and dependents.

This presumed unity of interests, institutionalized in the twentieth-century welfare state, is unraveling in the twenty-first. Differences among women, whether between "mothers" and "nonmothers" the 1980s, between women raised in the GDR or FRG the 1990s, or between ethnic German women and women of immigrant backgrounds the 2000s, produce controversies about substantive representation. Policies that support the "typical" woman are challenged as making it harder for women who are or want to be "atypical." Relational realism suggests that such debates are valuable, not distractions for feminist politics. Unlike Molyneux's confidence that a theory can reveal the "strategic interests" of all women, an intersectional politics of gender demands discussion among multiple voices.

Conversely, the US variety of feminism focused on rights, took up a strategy of legal change, and left "radical" and "socialist" feminists out of the mainstream. Feminist women's movements had neither the material nor discursive resources to conduct an intersectional struggle for greater economic equality, and they left the "typical" woman behind while opening doors for those who wished to defy gender stereotypes. Without embracing "socialism," a taboo concept in US political discourse, feminists have found themselves without a resonant critique to unsettle other hierarchies rather than merely desegregate them by gender. Becoming a mother in the precarious and highly competitive American economy is not an empowering experience now, and it is becoming ever less so. US feminist theory needs a class analysis to make it intersectional in practice.

Rethinking Radicalism

Feminist theories are still routinely classified as liberal, socialist, and radical, adding fractionalized categories (Black feminism, psychoanalytic feminist, career feminism, and the like) to cover the gaps in the typology.[69] By looking carefully at a political context that is not politically liberal, the German case illuminates the radical potential of so-called liberal feminist ideas of self-determination, individual freedom, social autonomy, and civic culture to challenge state-driven, protectionist varieties of feminism from the grassroots. Feminist participatory actions were productive in producing state transformations in Germany. Moreover, in political contexts where authoritarianism is not merely a legacy but a daily reality, like the GDR, the values of civic engagement, participatory democracy, individual autonomy, and political voice are truly radical claims. To equate the political aspirations of classical liberalism with the social depredations of neoliberal market fundamentalism overlooks a transformative power that feminism has always claimed.

The political liberalism on which US feminism rode into the mainstream allowed this dangerous equation to flourish unchallenged. The structural analysis German feminists offered still provides a useful corrective to thin and careerist versions of liberal feminism. By pulling apart the politically liberal and market fundamentalist strains in claims about human rights, freedom, autonomy, and choice, those who wish to make a more democratic and participatory socialism the basis for feminism have helped reveal what classic socialist theory lacks and what classic liberalism offers.

German feminism was never just "socialist feminism," however useful socialist theories were as models. The "mainstream" of German feminism was a blend of what in the United States was "radical feminism," challenging production-centered market values and supporting local, nonhierarchical mobilization strategies, and "socialist feminism" in its insistence that there are historical, material roots to women's oppression. Both analyses were too truly radical in the United States to gain a foothold in practical politics, but as autonomous feminism has been slowly absorbed into the mainstream of German politics it has sowed seeds of what may yet become a radical transformation of gendered family and employment relations.

Rather than distinguishing "radical" from other types of feminism and mistakenly equating "liberal" feminism with the tangled mix of civic engagement, racelike rights claims, and neoliberal careerism that often characterizes the US mainstream, it may be fruitful to consider how both structural and poststructural theories of gender have their uses and limitations for pragmatic, mainstream feminist politics. As German activists showed, to treat feminism as a political choice and "women" as a political group formed for a particular purpose can successfully construct a common project (as working-class politics did) rather than passively reflecting a common set of perspectives or interests.

However, as the German victim-perpetrator debate showed, there is no single binary between powerful men and powerless women; as intersectional theories elaborate, every group has some level of power, and intersections among structural forces create diversity in power and position within every category of inequality. This idea is less radical today in Germany than it once was, but it still challenges pragmatic feminists.

Self-determination and state protectionism are in tension in a way that classical liberal theory highlights and feminist strategic discussion must address. Instrumentalism and market fundamentalism are the Scylla and Charybdis between which a practical politics of feminism must navigate. Neither states nor markets free women. Instrumentalism was challenged by East German feminists, who were able to show how the state used women to accomplish other goals—raising the birth rate or increasing labor supply—without changing society's gender relations, even though it trumpeted its achievements as women's emancipation. Similar instrumentalism is now opening policy windows and encouraging gender-equality rhetoric in Germany and the EU, but also with the danger that the appearance of state support will diminish women's own mobilization and obscure the extent to which state rhetoric hides social reality.

The dangers of market fundamentalism are made evident in the US case, where the absence of basic support for human needs and social infrastructure endangers women's lives. Fighting the serious challenge posed by "family values" conservatism, however, may lead mainstream feminists to overlook the values of classic political liberalism, assuming that it only serves neoliberal agendas, and to seek state support as a panacea.

Here the East German variety of feminism also offers critical insight, since the support of the state for their daily lives was a prerequisite for valuing the virtues of women's autonomy and values of classic liberalism in addition, not as a replacement. For them, state protection and support of women (female-friendliness) were important preconditions for—not equivalent to—women's emancipation, and self-determination and individual freedom inherently valuable feminist objectives. The GDR's women's movement challenged the idea that states or any other authorities know women's best interests and showed that the "chaos" of activism and practical debate is a better route to "strategic" representation than any settled theory, but it also revealed the fragility of democratic feminist politics.

The Future of Feminism

Although not providing a single answer to the book's initial question of where feminism today can be found, this study has pointed to a number of indications of its continuing vitality. Rather than standing outside and "throwing stones," feminists have moved into insider roles in Germany and in many transnational contexts. In the United States, feminists are more likely to be found outside, but more often in multi-issue alliances for social justice than in stand-alone women's movement organizations. These are good reasons for the decline of autonomous feminist organizing as a political force in both countries but, while different, neither can be seen reflecting a feminist failure to have transformative social effects or continuing influence.

In Germany, the gradual integration of feminist objectives with the modernizing goals of the state and the effective use of transnational networks through the EU and UN have given birth to a far greater emphasis on making policy changes that, once radical, now appear as modest reforms. Success has moved radical ideas for making a society more politically friendly to women and supportive of mothers' work into the realm of the achievable. Feminist tactics have thus also shifted toward pragmatic efforts for piecemeal reforms. The older demands for women's autonomy have faded, both because the driving force of the demands for abortion rights and gender equality in marriage have been deflected by more modest concessions and because engagement with the state has drawn feminists into using its tools to secure and defend women's rights.

The successes German feminists have had in bringing women into positions of political power and influence mean that organizing women as women apart from the state would tie one hand behind feminists' backs. Today their insider-outsider strategy implies working with men and mixed-gender organizations as well as with nonfeminist women who can be converted into pragmatic supporters of specific feminist goals. Thus an old-style women's-movement-only strategy would be counterproductive. It is not surprising that the energy German feminists are willing to give to building an autonomous movement is limited, even among those whose goals remain radically transformative.

The decline in usefulness of a women's movement as a mobilization strategy for US feminism reflects a quite different process. Committed from the start to an insider-outsider strategy, US feminists combined service organizations like rape-crisis centers and shelters, campaigns for antidiscrimination measures, and class-action suits with consciousness-raising and cultural strategies. But beginning in the early 1980s, with the rightward shift of the Republican Party (which for the first time abandoned its classical political liberalism), feminist ability to work with and through the state was blocked. Intense mobilization by antifeminists, including a fierce movement against both reproductive rights and financial support for poor mothers, put the struggle for women's rights clearly on the defensive.

Success in spreading feminist consciousness combined with a failure to advance much beyond the gains of the 1970s, gave US feminists opportunity and motive to build alliances with other threatened groups. With international input from the UN conferences, intersectional definitions of poverty and social class as feminist issues rose. Internal critiques by women of color also spurred commitment to a more inclusive struggle for social justice, in which women's rights and antiracist organizing were integral. Always concerned about the potential for essentialism, US feminists turned away from trying to instill a collective gender identity or mobilize a movement of women for women. Whether self-defined as radical, liberal, or socialist, they found more reason to build a general movement for social justice than to fight exclusively around a banner of women's rights.

Thus, for very different reasons than in Germany, the value of autonomous women's movement organizations as a strategy for advancing feminist goals also declined in the United States. The energy of American feminism has spread into related movements, including the effort to reinvigorate the union movement, the antipoverty struggle in the cities, the battle for lesbian and gay rights, and the resistance to anti-immigrant and anti-Black mobilizations. The implications for intersectional feminist politics in Germany and the United States are diametrically opposite, but few forces exist to encourage feminists to make a separate women's movement for gender equality their priority in either country.

The question remains: What will happen to feminism without a discrete feminist women's movement to develop "radical" ideas and mobilize activists? If feminist women's movements are no longer active enough to provide an incubator for developing awareness of issues confronting women and building intense commitment to changing gender relations, where will the impetus for practical feminist politics come? Will radically transformative ideas be invented somewhere that, even if they appear to be pragmatically unrealizable in the short term, give new urgency to women's own mobilization? Will there be a place and time where the commitment to a group called women will become a powerfully persuasive political choice?

The answers to these questions depend on historically contingent decision making, emerging from national political contexts and met with feminist resources that global and local discourse and material conditions jointly provide. Feminists in many countries, with a variety of feminist traditions on which to call, are engaged in seeking these answers. While it is easy to see where feminism has gone, relational realism suggests the impossibility of predicting where it will go, since the strategic choices to be made when opportunity arises remain indeterminate.

While US feminists can no longer claim to be at the forefront of global feminism, there are ideas and activities stirring in many countries that they and others might borrow, transform to fit particular national or regional circumstances, and recirculate into transnational feminism. The transnational opportunity structure, including the EU and its new forms of governance and flows of comparative policy making, invites creative feminists—in all countries of the world—to find and share their most promising strategies for the future.

REFERENCE MATTER

GLOSSARY

Abwicklung   liquidation

acquis communitaire   body of EU legislation, legal decisions and precedents

Aktionsgruppe für die Befreiung der Frau   Action Group for the Liberation of Women

Alternative Frauenrat   alternative Women's Council

Andersdenkende   people with unusual ideas

Außerparlamentarische Opposition   Extra-Parliamentary Opposition

Basisdemokratie   grassroots democracy

Berührungsangst   fear of contact

Betroffenheit   being affected by a problem or concern

Bund deutscher Frauenvereine   Coalition of Women's Associations

Bund für Mütterschutz und Sexualreform   League for the Protection of Mothers and Sexual Reform

Bundestag   FRG Parliament

Bundeswehr   FRG Army

Bündnis '90   Alliance '90/Dissident movement party formed at end of GDR

Bürgerinitiativen   citizen's initiatives

Bürgerliches Gesetzbuch   German Civil Code

Demokratische Frauenbund Deutschlands   German Women's Council (GDR)

Deutscher Frauenrat   National Women's Council (FRG)

Deutsche Gewerkschaftsbund   main FRG trade union confederation

deutscher Volk   the German people or nation

drüben "over there"; slang term for "the other side of the Wall"

Eigensinn stubbornness

Einzelgängerin a woman who goes her own way; does not work for the collective good

Ellenbogengesellschaft "elbow society"; slang for "competitive culture"

Emanze derogatory slang term for feminist, implying cross-dressing gender rebel

EU-Konformitätsgesetz EU Conformity Law (FRG)

Familienvater pater familias, head of household

Fraktion a parliamentary delegation

"Frauen gemeinsam sind stark" "Women united are strong"; sisterhood is powerful

FrauenAnStiftung Green party-funded foundation for women's issues/feminist agitation

Frauenbeauftragte a women's affairs officer

frauenbewegte Frau feminist-inspired woman, woman-moved-woman

Frauenförderung advancement of women as public policy

Frauenförderungsgesetz Women's Advancement Act

Frauenforschung research both on and by women

FrauenfrAktion a women's group connecting parliamentary and movement feminists

Frauenhaus "women's house"/shelter for battered women

Frauenöffentlichkeit women's public

Frauenpolitik politics by and for women

Frauenrechtlerinnen "women's righters"/suffragists/liberal feminists

Frauenunion Women's Union, CDU women's association

Fristenlösung trimester rule for legal abortion

Für Dich (For You [familiar]), GDR national women's magazine

Fundis Green party hard-liners

Ganzheitlichkeit the wholeness of the system

Gegenöffentlichkeit "counterpublic," Habermas's term for political opposition in civil
  society

Geschlechter genders

Gleichberechtigung equal rights

Gleichstellungsbeauftragte equality officer

Gleichstellungspolitik equality politics

Gleichstellungsstelle gender-equality office

die GRÜNE the Green party

Grundgesetz Basic Law/FRG Constitution

Hexenfrühstück a "witches' breakfast"

Hexenprozeß a witchcraft trial

Indikationslösung justification rule for legal abortion

Junkertum Junkerdom/squirearchy

Juristinnenbund Association of Women Lawyers

Kaiserreich German Empire

Keimzelle the organic basis, the fundamental germ cell, nucleus

Kinderläden   storefront child-care center

Leistungsprinzip   competitive demands of the market

Mädchen   girl

Mitbestimmung   codetermination

Multi-Kulti   slang term for "multiculturalism"

Mündlichkeit   political independence/voice (individual adult citizenship)

Muttipolitik   "mommy politics," a critical term for GDR support for women workers

Obrigkeitsstaat   aristocratic, undemocratic state

"ohne Frauen ist kein Staat zu machen"   UFV slogan: "You can't make a state without women"

Ossi   slang term for people from the former GDR

Ostjuden   Jewish immigrants to Germany from Eastern Europe

Parteilichkeit   taking sides in the system, in this case "for women"

Quotierung   quota system/affirmative action plan

Rabbenmutter   "raven mother"; a derogatory slang term for a mother using child care

Realos   Green party pragmatists

"Recht der Mündlichkeit und Selbstständigkeit im Staat" (Louise Otto-Peters)   women's right to political and economic self-determination or independence

Regenbogen   rainbow

sich outen   coming out (of the closet)/to "out" oneself as lesbian/gay

soziale Not   "social necessity"/economic or social need for abortion

staatsbürgerliche Bildung   civic education

staatsbürgerliche Rechte   political and civil rights

Staatsknete   state's "rising dough"; slang term for state subvention

Standesstaat   socially hierarchical state

Stasi   State Security/GDR secret police

Unabhängiger Frauenverein   Independent Women's Association (UFV)

Parteifrauen   women with political party allegiances

unzumutbar   unconscionable, unacceptable

Vaterstaat   "father-state"

Vergangenheitsbewältigung   coming to terms with the past/confronting and overcoming the past

Volksarmee   GDR Army

Volkskammer   GDR Parliament

Weiberräte   Women's revolutionary councils

Wende   turn, transition (used in reference to German reunification)

werdende Mutter   developing mother, mother-to-be

Zweigeschlechtigkeit   binary gender system

NOTES

CHAPTER 1

1. The equal rights clause was part of the original 1949 constitution, but unfortunately the courts always interpreted it as allowing "functional differentiation" by family role, making it toothless, an issue explored in later chapters.

2. The 109th Congress (2005–7) had seventy-one women in the House and fourteen in the Senate; the 111th Congress (2005–7) had seventy-eight women in the House and eighteen in the Senate (17.7 and 18 percent, respectively). In contrast, 32.8 percent of the representatives in the 17th Bundestag (2009–) were women, 31.2–31.8 percent in the 16th Bundestag (2005–9), and 32.5 percent in the 15th Bundestag (2002–5) (US data from http://womenincongress.house.gov [accessed on June 28, 2011]; German data from http://www.deutschland-auf-einen-blick.de/politik/bundestag/statistik.php [accessed on June 28, 2011], and http://www.bundeswahlleiter.de [accessed on June 28, 2011]).

3. S. Roth 2008.

4. Hall and Soskice 2001.

5. This also suggests that thinking of politics on a single continuum from socialism and social democracy on the Left to liberalism or neoliberalism on the Right is a dangerous oversimplification of a world in which religion, authoritarianism, and patriarchy are still actively entangled politically and often in opposition to both. Triangular trade-offs, rather than dichotomous positions, complicate feminist strategic choices.

6. German scholars doing important work on theorizing gender intersectionally include Klinger and Knapp (2008). See also Walby 2009.

7. Glenn (1999, 9) and her process-tracing application of intersectionality in Glenn (2002).

8. Molyneux 1985. Also see my critique in Ferree and Tripp 2006.

9. Connell 2002, 1987.

10. Salzinger 2003.

11. The concreteness of such local situations is best shown in Guenther (2010) and Enke (2007).

12. Identifying the contradictions of capitalism is of course associated with Marx, the American dilemma with Myrdal, and the paradoxes of equality and difference with Wollstonecraft and Scott.

13. Connell 2002. A gender project captures—in a more theoretically coherent and dynamic form—the misbegotten idea of "gender role" as a way of talking about the combination of belief and practice in distinctive forms. See Ferree 1990, for discussion of the problems in gender-role terminology.

14. Martin 2003.

15. Cassell 1977; B. Roth 2004. See also Wendy Brown (1995) for discussions of identity and group-ness.

16. Hull, Scott, and Smith 1982. Also see Crenshaw 1991; McCall 2005.

17. Ferree and Mueller (2004) elaborate the distinction between feminisms and women's movements.

18. Glenn 1999; Hancock 2007; Choo and Ferree 2010.

19. Underlying this approach is Gidden's theory of structuration (1984) and the discussion of structure and agency by Sewell (1992).

20. McAdam, McCarthy, and Zald 1996; Kriesi 2004.

21. "In any particular case, the coherence of social policies within and between substantive areas, while unlikely, is an empirical question" (Brush 2003).

22. Ferree 2003; Ferree et al. 2002.

23. See Keck and Sikkink 1998; Dorothy McBride Stetson and Amy Mazur (1995) and their RNGS research group laid the groundwork for understanding how feminism enters state policy making. The institutionalization of gender policy machineries is a topic to which Chapter 7 returns.

24. Fraser highlighted the struggle over need definition as fundamental, underlying political allocation of resources to meeting already defined needs and solving already defined social problems. Her 1989 argument owes a considerable debt to Foucault's overall approach to unpacking the meaning of classifications and terms, also articulated in Fraser and Gordon (1994). But the tradition of social construction of social problems as shaping policy solutions is considerably longer. See the integration of research on problem definitions in sociology and agenda setting in political science by Bacchi (1999).

25. Critical frame analysis—as pioneered by Bacchi (1999) and extended by Mieke Verloo and her colleagues (see www.quing.eu)—looks at such frameworks as institutionalizing different meanings for "affirmative action" and "gender equality" in formal policy documents in different countries. In a more historical vein, Pedriana (2006) shows how the American legal framing of "discrimination" became transformed and institutionalized in a way that made protective legislation for women problematic and eventually archaic. These comparative and historical studies share a view of *frameworks* as themselves shifting as new frames enter a system of meaning, but also as providing a slope of differential advantage to the *active framing work* being done.

26. There has been a marked process of transnationalization of feminist causes as women have mobilized to bring specific issues of citizenship rights onto the world stage and taken advantage of (and contributed to) a wider diffusion of political liberalism. The emergence of a world polity in which women's individual citizenship becomes normalized and violence against women criminalized has been traced through women's suffrage (Ramirez, Soysal, and Shanahan 1997), women's employment rights (Berkovitch 1999), female genital cutting (Boyle

2002), and rape law (Frank, Hardinge, and Wosick-Correa 2009). Both Jenness (2004) and Keck and Sikkink (1998) lay out frameworks for understanding transnational advocacy networks in gender politics. Excellent studies of the processes making such networks effective include Zippel (2006) for the case of sexual harassment, and Alfredson (2008) for domestic violence as a basis for changing asylum laws. Hester Eisenstein (2009) offers a more critical view of the success of liberal feminist rights talk globally.

27. The original framing of sexual harassment as a violation of women's rights came from MacKinnon (1978).

28. On radical flank effects, see Katzenstein 1999; Haines 1988. Levitsky (2007) highlights this as a division of labor; Rupp (1997) emphasizes the emotion work needed to sustain a radical perspective that is not achieving resonance.

29. H. Eisenstein 1991, 1996. Key work on feminist engagement with the state has been produced by the members of the Research Network on Gender and the State (RNGS) (http://libarts.wsu.edu/polisci/rngs/ [accessed on June 28, 2011]) led by Dorothy McBride Stetson and Amy Mazur, including and Mazur (1995) and Mazur and McBride (2010). See also Weldon (2002) on comparative policy on violence against women, which (like the RNGS project) finds that the combination of femocratic institutionalization in the state *and* accountability to an external feminist mobilization makes early adoption of strong policies addressing violence against women likely.

30. For feminist perspectives on state capacity and challenges to it, see Fraser 1989; Brush 2003.

31. Esping-Andersen 1990; Lewis 1997; Sainsbury 1999; Walby 2009.

32. Marshall and Bottomore 1964.

33. The idea of a male-breadwinner family structure developed through feminist scholarship on the history of capitalist variations in organizing production through families, beginning with Tilly and Scott's pathbreaking book, *Women, Work and Family* (first edition, 1978 [1989]). Other historians, such as May (1982) specifically pointed to how such family organization became anchored in modern forms of industrial organization. This historical process was then used in a comparative cross-national way by Lewis (1992 and 1997) to challenge the Esping-Anderson typology. The specific justification of considering Germany as a male-breadwinner state is affirmed by Ostner (1994) although, as this book will show, this work-family regime has begun to unravel in recent years.

34. O'Connor, Orloff, and Shaver 1999; Brush 2002.

35. Tripp (2006) provides ample evidence against this.

36. Although the extent to which the 1950s were a dead zone for feminist development in the United States is debated (with Taylor and Rupp's portrait of a movement in abeyance at the organizational level complemented by Tarrant's examination of the ferment of feminist ideas among women intellectuals), it is indisputable that the late 1960s were a moment of awakening consciousness and activism (DuPlessis and Snitow 2007). Evans provides a good sense of the tenor of that period in the United States, while Ferree and Hess offer a chronology of the events from the 1960s to 1990s that revitalized both feminist organizations and theorizing. Roth shows how this awakening period unfolded differently for Black, Asian, White, and Hispanic women, but in all cases was shaped by the student movements where young women had become active. See Tarrant 2006; Ferree and Hess 2000; B. Roth 2004. See also S. Evans 2003; Taylor and Rupp 1990; and DuPlessis and Snitow 2007.

37. Ferree and Mueller 2004; Zerilli 2005.

38. Note that Banks (1981) instead called "radical" feminism "moral reform" feminism, and MacKinnon (1987) called it feminism "unmodified." Jaggar's *Feminist Politics*

and Human Nature (1983) is the classic work on this particular conceptual triumvirate. Offen (1988) had already begun to challenge this typology as unsuited for historical comparative analysis.

39. In some ways, both Ferree and Hess (2000) and the collected articles in Ferree and Martin (1994) can be read as the more detailed US comparative case study that informs this examination of German feminist politics.

CHAPTER 2

1. The issue of racialization, or the social construction of difference as representing "race," is explored by Omi and Winant (1994) and Bonilla-Silva (2006).

2. See Glenn (2002) on the regional specificity of racialized citizenship and labor practices. She looks particularly at the Anglo-Hispanic polarity in the Southwest, the Black-White dimension of the South and the Asian-Haole division created in Hawaii as examples of how racialization infused American gender relations and vice versa. Kessler-Harris (2003) presents the "raced" character of citizenship and labor in the United States also in terms of varied responses to immigrants now seen as "White."

3. See Balibar and Wallerstein (1991) and Hill Collins's application of their argument (1998).

4. Classic accounts of the interweaving of race and gender, as well as the role of racism and nativism in women's rights struggles include Flexner (1959), Rossi (1973), and Beisel and Kay (2004).

5. Hull, Scott, and Smith 1982. There are several reviews of the huge literature on intersectionality that discuss the important role women of color in the United States played. See particularly McCall 2005; Hancock 2007.

6. Pascale 2007. Crenshaw (2008) makes the point that the women who were strong Hillary Clinton campaigners in 2007 and 2008 often were White women who did not see their own whiteness as in any way relevant to their political project.

7. McCall (2005) is an important exception; Acker (2006) also has tried to turn attention to class dynamics that intersect gender.

8. Note key accounts provided by Omi and Winant (1994) and Glenn (2002). See also Quadagno 1994; Neubeck and Cazenave 2001; Roberts 1997; Flavin 2009; and V. Mayer 2007, for important examinations of the intersections of race, gender, legal rights, and political discourses.

9. Myrdal 1969.

10. Swidler (1986) offered a now-famous view of culture as a tool kit, discursive resources in daily life that buttress formal decisions and laws and explain how framing a person or action as outside the parameters of cultural acceptability ("radical") generates resistance.

11. Edelman, Fuller, and Mara-Drita 2001.

12. Steinmetz (2007) is the authoritative account of German colonial projects and ideologies.

13. American exceptionalism is a familiar concept in political science, considered sympathetically with regard to political culture in Lipset (1996), and with regard to gendered policy formation in Skocpol (1992).

14. In Germany, the FDP originally represented both strains of liberalism, but as it tilted more to emphasize neoliberalism in the 1980s, after it broke its coalition with the SPD, the Green party took up the political liberalism cause, often with explicit rejection of market-liberalism.

15. Joan Williams of the Hasting Institute calls the inability to talk about anyone other than the rich and the poor in realistic class terms "the missing middle."

16. Sklar, Schüler, and Strasser (1998) compare US and German feminist socialist-leaning politics, stressing the ongoing conversations among them. They argue that feminist organizing did the work of class in the US setting, a claim Skocpol (1992) shared and framed as

the "maternalist" roots of the US welfare state. Socialist feminism offered one element in US feminist organizing but remained out of the mainstream; see discussions in Ferree and Hess (2000), S. Evans (2003), and Rosen (1987). S. Roth (2003), Blum (1991), and Cobble (2004) also explore the ways that social justice concerns in even US union-based feminism become manifest as discussions of racial-ethnic inclusivity.

17. While Zippel (2006) discusses these differences regarding sexual harassment policies, and O'Connor, Orloff, and Shaver (1999) consider the distinctive configurations of welfare regimes in liberal states and put the underdevelopment of the US welfare state in context, it is far more typical to suggest that the United States could simply borrow ideas from Europe and implement them here (for example, Gornick and Meyers 2005). Europhilic feminism substitutes the wishes of academic elites for goals formed by engagement with American political culture and institutions in their own right. If child-care and leave policies rooted in social democratic politics are to make headway in the United States, a more intersectional shift to greater social inclusion will be needed, both discursively and materially.

18. Boxer 2010.

19. Oppression based on social class was the analogy used to call men into a common struggle with women. In 1849, for example, Otto-Peters published this appeal to working-class men ostensibly from Georgine, a woman laborer: "You are demanding workers organize, that is, free themselves from capital, but you nonetheless assume that the power that you take from capital goes to just to you, and use it oppress the weaker. This is nothing more than changing who rules us, and gaining nothing from the change. You speak of brotherhood, but think nothing of not only excluding your sisters from your associations but deliberately denying them their work and withholding their very means of existence" (qtd. in Gerhard, Hannover-Drück, and Schmitter 1979, 193).

20. Boxer 2010; Pinl 1977.

21. The earliest social democratic position (1869 in Eisenach) made this a program point. See also Eley 2002.

22. Quoted in Thönnessen 1973, 15–16.

23. Dohm 1902.

24. Hervé 1995; Thönnessen 1973, 39.

25. Left-liberals were particularly represented by Lily Braun, Minna Cauer, and their Berlin group, Frauenwohl (women's welfare), and Zetkin claimed that their "proclaimed goal of working for all women was illusory" (qtd. in Quataert 1979, 110). As Quataert shows, this socialist-led split established a rivalry between class ideologies among feminists that has yet to be fully resolved (see also Boxer 2010).

26. In the effort to weaken what was perceived to be a growing influence of left-liberal groups in the 1900s, the BDF brought in new members from the Right (especially the League of Protestant Evangelical Women and urban and rural Housewives' Associations), which embraced a self-conscious nationalism defined as serving the integration of family and state. They were profoundly suspicious of the SPD and actively embraced conservative nationalism. Their support for women's suffrage was late and limited, accepting the class-specific limitations on voting that applied to men as the model for women.

27. Lida Gustava Heymann (1868–1943) wanted cooperation with the SPD and thus was accused by fellow members of the BDF, the umbrella organization of bourgeois women's groups, of being a secret member of the SPD, in their eyes a disreputable organization. Lily Braun (1865–1916) did "defect" from the BDF to the SPD, after trying unsuccessfully to bring the BDF to accept the SPD women's organization as a member group in the early 1900s. Braun's efforts to organize women teachers and clerks were viewed with suspicion

by the SPD, and she was required to "prove her loyalty" to the party by breaking off all her contacts with middle-class women's organizations (Meyer 1985).

28. Schaeffer-Hegel 1990.

29. Once legalized in 1890, but before women's political participation was legally allowed in 1902, the SPD went to considerable lengths to mobilize working-class women as members of the party despite their political disabilities as women, but liberal parties did not. See Quataert 1979, 230.

30. The SPD believed that as wives and mothers women would vote in the interests of their families, and thus winning the vote for women would strengthen the influence of the working class as a whole. It was just this fear that kept middle-class women resistant to the idea of enfranchising women and led to their support of extending the vote to women only on the class-limited basis that men had.

31. The left-liberal feminists formed legal advisory centers to help individual women understand and challenge the Civil Code. Most of the BDF, however, found challenges to the Code "too radical." See Böttger 1990, 45; Gerhard 1999.

32. See more extensive discussion of its founding and principles in an international context in Allen (2005).

33. R. Evans 1976, 134.

34. Moeller 1993, 49.

35. Allen 1985; R. Evans 1976, 134.

36. Cited in Gerhard 1999, 113.

37. Women's limited civil citizenship made this even more galling to many liberal women. The "contradiction that women are treated by the law as if they were an impersonal thing (*eine Sache*) but held responsible and ultimately punished like an accountable person" was made all the worse by the fact that, unlike its mother, "the undeveloped human fetus, even before it has made its life known by movement in the mother's body, is afforded the protection due to a creature outfitted with all the rights of a person" (Gräfin Gisela von Streitberg 1904, cited in Gerhard 1999, 112).

38. Gerhard 1999, 117; see also this discussion in Jochimsen 1971.

39. Augstein 1983. Some of the impetus for protest grew from a rising tide of prosecutions (from 411 in 1902 to 1,884 in 1916, to 7,193 in 1924), some from the socialists publicizing the doctors' prosecutions, and some from the 1929 play *Cyanide* that effectively dramatized the situation of poor women. See also Rucht 1994.

40. Unable to form a coalition with its rivals on the Left, the Independent Social Democratic Party (USPD) failed to pass its bill for complete elimination of §218 in 1920, and a similar bill introduced by its rival, the Communist Party (KPD), died in 1922.

41. The reform permitted abortion only when there was a serious threat to maternal health certified by a hospital commission. Another bill, proposing both the elimination of §218 and the introduction of equal pay for men and women was introduced by the Communist Party in 1931 but failed to win support from their party rivals on the Left.

42. Koonz 1987.

43. T. H. Marshall (1950) offers the most widely used classification of rights: civil (for example, free speech, free association, owning property, education), political (for example, voting, holding office) and social or economic (meeting basic needs such as food and shelter).

44. Schenk 1983, 39–43.

45. In both the United States and Germany, social justice feminists of the time did see protective labor legislation rather than women's self-organization as the best protection of vulnerable women workers from the depredations of capitalism. See the exchange of letters

between Jane Addams and other American feminists with the left-liberal and socialist feminists of Germany (Sklar, Schüler, and Strasser 1998).

46. Rupp 1978; Koonz 1987.

47. Freeman (1975) particularly emphasizes what she calls the "woodwork" feminists in
the state; Cott (1997) emphasizes the dispersion of feminists into political parties and civic
associations after suffrage offering valuable political continuity to US feminists in the 1960s.

48. Schenk 1983, 57.

49. Socialist leaders Rosa Luxemburg and Clara Zetkin were thrown in jail, left-liberal
Lida Heymann was forbidden to speak in public, her letters were censored, and she was
eventually ordered into exile. Only after the war were Lida Heymann and Anita Augspurg
able to join the Women's International League for Peace and Freedom, formed in 1919 in
Switzerland, in which they later became leading figures. See also Rupp 1997.

50. Gerhard 1999, 50–56.

51. Schenk 1983, 62.

52. See Schenk 1983; also Gerhard 1999. Agnes von Zahn-Harnack was the last president
and presided over the self-dissolution of the BDF. She spent the war in exile and returned
to Berlin in 1945 to try to reestablish a bourgeois women's movement.

53. Since many, including Heyman and Salomon, died in exile or never returned to
Germany after the war, their physical absence accentuated the loss of a sense of having a
valued personal and organization legacy on which to build.

54. Ferree and Hess 2000.

55. The feminist debate about responsibility for state evil (the "victim-perpetrator debate") begun in the 1970s focused on whether women's exclusion from the state made them
powerless and therefore innocent of its wrongs. See Gravenhorst and Tatschmurat 1990.

56. Gal and Kligman (2000a) argue that gender is often at the heart of rebuilding states,
not only because of its symbolic qualities, but also because it is the lynchpin of cultural and
biological reproduction of a nation. See also Yuval-Davis 1997.

57. Self-understanding of the DFR as successor to the BDF is found in Gerhard (1999).

58. Gerhard 1999, 62–87. The "moderate bourgeois and conservative women's politics of
the Weimar period is all that was represented in the West, and now stood for the entirety
of the women's movement. An image of woman was thus adopted that expressed the traditional role of woman and aimed at a harmony and complementarity of the genders, including in politics" (72) compared to Progressive Era rhetoric in the United States.

59. Moeller 1993.

60. Despite extensive parliamentary discussion of rapes by the occupation forces, rape
was not accepted as creating an exception—see discussion in Moeller (1993), and also informative comparison with Bosnia by Bos (2006).

61. Gerhard 1999, 73.

62. And for that reason, the group was banned in the conservative, southern parts of
West Germany. See Bauer 1994.

63. This is in specific distinction to Weimar, where the equal rights clause limited its
application to formal political rights alone.

64. Moeller 1993.

65. Penrose 1993; Maier 1992a; Harsch 1997.

66. In practice, the policies, though mainly contrasting, were never completely so; for
example, women were employed at higher rates in the FRG than discourse acknowledged,
and both states were politically male dominated and pronatalist. See Harsch 1997.

67. For example, the social welfare bureaucracy remained obdurately academic and male, and even teaching remained much longer in male hands. See Michel 1999.

68. Contrary to the classic ideas of Engels and Bebel, neither the entry of women into waged industrial production relations nor the political dominance of a socialist party emancipated women as expected, though both provided economic and social resources for women to use in their own struggles. However, East German state authoritarianism also produced home and family as an apparently safe, highly valued, and symbolically female refuge from politics for both women and men.

69. Z. Eisenstein (1993) sets out a similar argument using the texts of classic liberalism as her material.

CHAPTER 3

1. Although the initials are the same, the US Students for a Democratic Society did not explicitly link the American student movement to socialism the way the Sozialistischer Deutscher Studentenbund, German Socialist Student Association, did. Despite many similarities of political program, and whether or not it was a conscious strategic choice, the US movement's self-labeling as democratic (rather than socialist) and vice versa in Germany expressed their national discursive frameworks.

2. Bendkowski 1999.

3. Particularly the shooting of Bennie Ohnesorg in a demonstration against the Shah of Iran in Berlin.

4. Koch 2003.

5. The speech is reprinted in the first self-reflection of the movement, the 1975 *Frauenjahrbuch*, as an orientation to its emergence; also in Anders (1988).

6. See Doorman 1988.

7. Sander 1998, 283–303.

8. One parent-run kindergarten dedicated to an antiauthoritarian mode of child rearing was also established in 1967 in Frankfurt. The nonfeminist antiauthoritarian thread contributed to the enthusiasm with which the *Kinderläden* were greeted. See Doorman 1988.

9. The leftist groups who created *Kinderläden* did not think of them as helping women enter the labor force, since public policy already cast state-run child-care institutions as support just for women "who had to work." They were to be antiauthoritarian "alternative" schools that parents (in practice, mothers) ran. See von Rahden 2008.

10. Sander 1998, 297. West German women could be university students and mothers because university studies were essentially cost-free for any citizen who graduated from an intensively academic high school (*Gymnasium*) with a qualifying degree (*Abitur*). While mothers could stay enrolled, it remained difficult for them to graduate, in part because of the absence of child care.

11. Köster 1988.

12. Sander's speech, reprinted in Anders (1988).

13. *Weiberrat* is awkward to translate, since "Weib" is an old-fashioned term for woman that took on a pejorative connotation (most parallel to "dame" in English) and "Rat" is the word for council that was taken up by revolutionary workers and sailors after World War I (the word in Russian is "soviet"). There were eight groups calling themselves *Weiberräte* already at the November 1968 SDS meeting. By March 1972, there were at least thirty-five similar groups that came together in a national congress in Frankfurt.

14. Sander 1988, 284.

15. Ibid., 284–85.

16. Ibid.

17. Statement of the Action Group, cited in Anders 1988, 11.

18. Sander 1988, 284.

19. Reprinted in Anders 1988, 12.

20. While this led in some cases to a "mother-mythology" glorifying pregnancy and childbirth as self-realization, this "mother principle" also had a strong element of politically organizing mothers as mothers; see Jaeckel 1988.

21. This provided the theoretical basis on which the "new femininity" later developed as well; see Rentmeister 1988, 443–60.

22. *Frauenjahrbuch '76*, 3 and 77.

23. Ibid., 76.

24. Ibid., 75–76.

25. Ibid., 77–78.

26. This was not only a practical issue (women resented cleaning up WG bathrooms) but a symbolic one, where the power of women to make men be more like women could be manifested concretely. Such decals became widely available and remain ubiquitous in feminist households today.

27. MacKinnon 1989, 3. "Implicit in feminist theory is a parallel argument: the molding, direction, and expression of sexuality organizes society into two sexes: women and men. . . . As work is to Marxism, sexuality is to feminism socially constructed yet constructing, universal as activity yet historically specific, jointly comprised of matter and mind. As the organized expropriation of the work of some for the benefit of others defines a class, workers, the organized expropriation of the sexuality of some for the use of others defines the sex, woman." Her analysis melds Marxism and feminism in a way that is defined as "radical" in the United States but that was the main current of thought for autonomous feminism in Germany, resonating there because socialist discourse was legitimate and familiar.

28. A major slogan of the time was "ob wir Kinder kriegen oder keine, entscheiden wir alleine" (we decide ourselves if we have children or not).

29. See discussion of abortion prosecutions in Rucht 1994.

30. See Krieger 1988, 31–38.

31. Ibid., 32.

32. Ferree et al. 2002 show how abortion in the United States was advocated as a "doctor's rights" law, in which central importance was given to the "between a woman and her physician" argument.

33. Some doctors did support the women's campaign (for example, 329 offered their own public confessions of having broken the abortion law in an article in the newsmagazine *Der Spiegel* in 1974, and a few faced disciplinary proceedings and lost their jobs as a result). See Ferree et al. 2002.

34. Krieger 1988, 38.

35. Ferree et al. 2002.

36. My review of local feminist newsletters from around the country shows it was a regular theme in both large cities and small towns in the later 1970s and 1980s.

37. However, it was the only case in which members of parliament were allowed to vote against the government's proposal, and some members of the usually cooperative church-centered party did so.

38. All GDR abortions were done as in-patient operations of dilation and curettage, D&C, rather than the physically easier vacuum-aspiration method that was becoming the

norm in the United States, and women having abortions remained silenced and stigmatized. See Maleck-Lewy and Ferree 2000.

39. Harsch 1997; Thietz 1992.

40. Both were distinct from the term "women's movement," which applied to the mainstream DFR in the West and officially sanctioned and controlled DFD in the East.

41. Wegehaupt-Schneider 1988.

42. Robin Morgan (1970) was only one of a spate of books that were transnationally influential. Many came from the United States, but Dalla Costa and James (1972) discussed below, was widely influential in Germany, and Meulenbelt (1978) was also well received.

43. Katsiaficas (1997, 182–84) deals with sexism in autonomous movements.

44. Strobl 1988, 135.

45. Ibid., 136.

46. Not only by making Frauenoffensive able to publish them but by demonstrating to mass publishers that there was a profit to be made with such books. A major German publisher, Rowohlt, was able to outbid the feminist presses for the right to publish the German translation of Rita Mae Brown's *Rubyfruit Jungle* (1973).

47. The type of analysis offered in Stefan's *Shedding* (1979) is similar to Robin Morgan's "goodbye to all that" (reprinted in Baxandall and Gordan 2000) and Marge Piercy's "Grand Coolie Damn" essay (1969, available at: http://www.uic.edu/orgs/cwluherstory/ CWLUArchive/damn.html [accessed on June 28, 2011]). These critiques of the interweaving of men's sexual and movement politics in the United States resonated in movement circles, but the wave of self-recognition unleashed by *Shedding* in West Germany can only be compared to that evoked by Friedan's *The Feminine Mystique* ten years earlier in the United States.

48. By Carol Downer and Lorraine Rothman in 1971. The first, and for a long time the largest, women's health center (FrauenGesundheitsZentrum) was established in Frankfurt in 1979.

49. Friedan dubbed lesbian critiques of heterosexism a "lavender herring" by which she meant that making lesbians visible in the movement would hurt the credibility of the movement as a whole. While this was an accurate strategic assessment, it was totally insensitive to the moral justice of the claim.

50. Amazonen (Amazons Press) was specifically founded in 1979 to publish lesbian literature. It brought out a translation of Johnston's *Lesbian Nation* (1973). But the lesbian separatism of American feminism had, as Johnston's title suggests, a rationale grounded in an analogy with Black nationalism.

51. In the United States, the early battles about lesbian presence in the movement being a "lavender herring" that would distract from the "real" goals of women were resolved by accepting that for any woman to separate herself from the label "lesbian" was to capitulate to the stigma associated with homosexuality in the culture at large. Theoretically, the idea that the "woman-identified woman" was the lesbian, and the lesbian in all women was the feminist became fashionable. Adrienne Rich's ideas of the woman-identified woman and the lesbian continuum were especially critical here. See Rich 1980.

52. Perhaps because the German focus was on the self-determination of all women's sexuality and on making lesbians visible as such, rather than on confronting heterosexism or mobilizing the solidarity of heterosexual women in opposing stigma and discrimination against lesbians and gay men.

53. The collected essays of Putsch (1990) give a good sense of what the linguistic arguments were on both sides.

54. See Putsch 1990. She questions the degree to which the neuter gender is particularly thinglike in German, and notes a shift to give "real" gender to the grammar (for example, moving *Fraulein* from a strictly correct neuter to meaningful feminine in ordinary speech) rather than taking advantage of the neuter to replace the default male.

55. Between the 1960s when I learned German in college and the 1980s, when I came to speak German as a feminist, a whole range of words had acquired female forms (for example, as a nonsmoker, I became a "*Nicht-Raucherin*" and would be corrected if I slipped into a "generic" male form).

56. The feminist presence in the Green party, discussed in the next chapter, influenced Greens and Green-friendly sources such as the Berlin Tageszeitung (*taz*) to adopt this innovative spelling.

57. Taylor and Rupp 1993. They also attribute the hostility directed at cultural strategies in the United States to antilesbian sentiment in the broader women's movement. Cultural strategies in Germany that were seen as goddess- and/or mother-worshipping forms of claiming power also increasingly came in for criticism in the 1980s (see, for example, Pasero and Pfäfflin 1986). The next chapter discusses this tension in more detail.

58. P. Clemens 1990.

59. Morgner 1974; Wander 1977; Wolf 1979; and also Nagelschmidt 1994, on this literature. In addition, Katja Guenther (personal communication) points out a lively subculture of women's visual art groups and performing art groups (especially in the Kabarett tradition) in many large and small cities across the country. She suggests that the difference between these art forms and the published literature is only that they were never successfully transmitted to West Germans.

60. Katzenstein (1999) found institutional opportunity structure makes a huge difference in promoting a choice of mainstream or radical strategies, the latter often being concentrated on changing language while the former address practical opportunities where they have means to have an impact.

61. Penrose 1990.

62. Nagelschmidt 1994.

63. Ibid.

64. Rather than merely idealizing the division of labor between a breadwinner husband and a wife who did the full-time housework and child care, the law explicitly said that a wife could only be employed "insofar as it was reconcilable with her duties in marriage and the family," which were, of course, housework and child care. See Moeller 1993; also Berghahn 1995.

65. There also was a significant struggle in the United States between the feminists who favored and opposed protective legislation in the period between the 1920s and the 1960s. But US proponents of women's self-determination did not interpret this as collective (and thus were not talking about women-only unions or women's quotas in union decision-making). They advocated a class-limited version of liberal politics that stressed only individual women's freedom, not their collective claims. By the early 1970s, the struggle within the US movement over the sacrifice of protective legislation in order to have gender-neutral rights as workers and citizens had been won by those who favored the later. See Vogel 1993; Pedriana 2004, 2006.

66. *EMMA* (http://www.emma.de/) is often compared to *Ms.* Magazine and Alice Schwarzer to Gloria Steinem. In their purposes and celebrity, the analogy is excellent. Schwarzer, however, took a more strongly personal role in making *EMMA* "her" magazine and using it to advance her individual vision of feminism, which was sometimes energetically in conflict

with that of many autonomous groups. *EMMA*, and thus Schwarzer, also succeeded more than *Ms.* in becoming identified as "the" voice of feminism to many Germans, however misleading that identification might be.

67. Thistle 2006.

68. Hagemann 2006.

69. Dobberthien 1988, 76.

70. Pinl 1977.

71. Ibid.

72. Union ambivalence about women's organizing persisted throughout the 1980s. Ferree and Roth (1998a) detail the politics of an unsuccessful strike by Berlin daycare workers that only received lukewarm union support in early 1989.

73. Dalla Costa and James (1972) offered this as an international strategy, but it never resonated in the United States as it did in West Germany, Italy, and other strong-breadwinner economies. See Ferree (1983) for discussion of the pay-for-housework debate internationally among socialist feminists in the 1970s.

74. Dalla Costa and James 1972.

75. Ferree 1984; although, oddly enough, embraced by "radical" feminists in the United States, such as MacKinnon.

76. For example, the editorial endorsement "Lohn für Hausarbeit," 1977; Bock 1976; Plogstedt 1981. See also the discussion in Lenz 2008, 158.

77. Berghahn 2004, 59–78.

78. Moeller 2003.

79. Interview with Marliese Dobberthien, Stuttgart, 1981.

80. Ryan 1992. I frequently asked German feminists whether they would consider such an organizational type as a means of bringing influence to bear on policymakers and was told in no uncertain terms how utterly contrary to feminist principles such an organization would be. This is a theme that the next chapter explores in more detail.

81. *Frauen-Zeitung* "Programm vom 4.April 1849," selection reprinted in Nave-Herz (1994, 12).

CHAPTER 4

1. The German idiom everyone uses to describe this period is that projects "sprouted like mushrooms" from the fertile ground.

2. See Katzenstein (1999) on the institutional inclusion model and its differences from the past; see Echols (1989) on the separatist path.

3. Ferree and Hess (2000) explain the career feminist option as one valuing market individualism rather than the classical liberal politics of citizenship rights.

4. E. Clemens 1997.

5. Schenk 1983, 115–74.

6. Dackweiler 1995; Lenz 2008.

7. Although I have found no material on this, personal accounts indicate that there was a shelter movement in the GDR, too, in which families took in other women who were being abused and in which women pooled resources to pay for alternate accommodations for battered women. Because radio and TV signals from West Germany traveled into much of East Germany, most East Germans were familiar with the issue of battering long before 1989. Guenther (2010) argues that this history of exposure to battering as a social problem from the West explains why the shelter movement took off so quickly and became the most stable sector of project culture in the former GDR after unification.

8. This produced a vigorous theoretical debate about just what was new about NSMs. Most German feminists rejected the claims that feminism belonged in this category by not only citing feminism's long history and materialist rather than postmaterialist concerns, but also its mainstream reach on the abortion issue and the sexism of the male-led NSMs themselves. See Calhoun (1993) on the contested theory of NSM; Kontos (1989) and Ferree and Roth (1998b, 80–91) on feminism and NSMs.

9. A view of US New Left organizing that highlights the role of race in feminist development can be found in S. Evans (2003) and B. Roth (2004).

10. *Frauenjahrbuch '76*, 79.

11. Schenk 1983.

12. The tensions conflating women's with feminist with lesbian in US discourse are analyzed in Taylor and Rupp (1993). The "Frauen und Lesben" framing and socialist visual language are evident in the CD of posters that is part of the collectively edited book, *hoch die Kampf dem. 20 Jahre Plakate autonomer Bewegungen* (1999).

13. Cott 1986.

14. Evans and Boyte 1992.

15. See Oliver and Johnston (2000) on movement ideological work.

16. Habermas 1962. Feminist theorists in the United States such as Nancy Fraser, Seyla Benhabib, and Iris Marion Young also worked with these ideas, but no US feminist groups (to my knowledge) made them principles of practice.

17. The US term "woman-identified woman" derived from Adrienne Rich (1980) and was part of her broader argument about women's loyalty to women being expressed as lesbianism, while expanding the meaning of "lesbian" to include nonsexual forms of loving women. See also Brush 2003.

18. The history of persecution and murders of witches in Europe was suggested as a possible analogy with the Holocaust, and a memorial for the victims of this persecution was even constructed ("Symbol der Frauenbewegung . . . " 1986).

19. In Wiccan practice, this eve of May Day holiday is symmetrical with Samhain (All Soul's Day, the eve we now know as Halloween), falling between the spring equinox and summer solstice as Samhain falls between the fall equinox and winter solstice.

20. Brückner 1996.

21. Moeller 1993.

22. Hall and Soskice (2001) outline the corporatist form that characterizes West Germany, and Young (1999) focuses on the corporatism of governance to explain the difficulties facing feminists in both German states. Corporatist politics is notably different in many regards from that of liberal interest-groups.

23. The extensive sociopolitical theoretical work of Regina Becker-Schmidt and Ilona Ostner in the late 1970s and early 1980s helped to lay the groundwork of explanation of *weibliche Arbeitsvermögen* (feminine work-capacity), but many other feminist social scientists have worked with it. Historian Ute Frevert is a key theorist of German militarism as a gendered institution.

24. Brückner (1996) develops this entire argument more extensively.

25. Stegman 2004, 10. Wanting the projects to offer personal "alternatives" to conforming to capitalist demands was sometimes experienced as anxiety about becoming too "rational" or "technocratic" a personality (Stahmer 1977) or as needing to reject the role of a profit-making entrepreneur as a "temptation" toward "male-identification" (Stahmer 1976). Even among socialist feminists the United States there was little sense that economic success was a "male" goal, but in Germany feminism sometimes included active resistance to taking the

capitalist entrepreneurial role. See Brückner and Holler 1990, 44–48. For US projects, see Echols 1989; Whittier 1995; Enke 2007.

26. In attempting to avoid the market, some knowledge projects turned to the state for support, with mixed results. For example, the women's communication center in Munich (KOFRA, www.kofra.de) was threatened with withdrawal of state funds for including a lesbian group working for changing laws to recognize lesbian partnerships and decided to expel the lesbian group in order to retain its funding.

27. There are extensive discussions of feminists and money in "Geld oder Leben" (1985), the newsletter *Blattgold*, founded in Berlin in 1985 (http://www.blattgold-berlin.de/index .htm [accessed on June 28, 2011]), "Feministische Oekonomie—was ist das?" (1989), and Brückner and Holler (1990, 37).

28. Helmer 1988.

29. Stegman 2004, 14.

30. Hagemann-White 1988.

31. Arnold 1995.

32. Hagemann-White 1988, 49.

33. Ibid., 48.

34. *Frauen helfen Frauen* e.V. Für ein Frauenhaus in Bonn (self-published pamphlet, 1978), 20.

35. Schenk 1980, 98.

36. Ibid., 99; "Unterstützt die Frauenhäuser!" 1985.

37. For example, in Berlin in 2005 there were six houses with a total of 326 beds, forty additional refuges of other kinds with space for 115 women, but in 2004 there were 12,800 cases of domestic abuse reported to the police and in the five-year period 2000–2005 more than 24,000 calls to the violence intervention hotline (Richter 2005, 19).

38. Much of the help provided by women to women was called (and funded as) "counseling." This is especially true of services like the reproductive health counseling provided by the Frankfurt Women's Health Center (http://www.paritaet.org/hessen/fgzn/abc/cms/ front_content.php [accessed on June 28, 2011]), which had explicitly political content.

39. Brückner and Holler 1990; also Brückner and Holler 1986.

40. Schenk 1980, 112.

41. US shelter developments and organizational challenges are discussed in Ferree and Martin (1994), as well as in numerous studies of "women's nonprofits" (for example, Bordt 1997). The relations among radical and liberal feminists often is a key issue in US women's organizations (cf. Ryan 1992; Rossi 1978; Echols 1989).

42. Brückner and Holler 1990, 28.

43. Differences among women tended to cement the distinctions between helpers and helped. Beginning with the formation of Wildwasser, a Berlin project for sexually abused girls in West Berlin in 1987, the shift toward more projects for sexually abused girls (including special refuges for them called girls' houses, *Mädchenhäuser*) reflected the developing international awareness of incest as a real problem, not a psychoanalytic fantasy (see Rush 1989).

44. Brückner and Holler 1990, 43.

45. Ayim 1997.

46. Schwenke 2000.

47. Tekin 1994, 104.

48. Tekin 1994; Lennox 1989; Schulz 1991; Oguntoye 2007.

49. Hebenstreit 1984.

50. Schenk 1983.

51. Dissertations by Suzanna Crage (2009) and Jessica Brown (2010) demonstrate the different pasts constructed in immigration debates today.

52. Thürmer-Rohr (1983) gave this debate its label; see also Hagemann (2006); Lenz (2008, 378–82); and Quataert (2001). American feminist historians, Leila Rupp and Claudia Koonz in particular, stood outside the personal family histories that complicated German feminists' own responses and broke new ground rethinking women's past under Hitler. See Rupp 1978; Koonz 1987.

53. See Hagemann 2006; Quataert 2001. Bock (for example, 2002) is one of the best-known historians associated with the victim frame, and Koonz is a controversial framer of German women as perpetrators (1987).

54. Mies 1986; Thürmer-Rohr 1988.

55. Melzer 2009.

56. Bendkowski 1999, intro.

57. Klaus 1988, 129–33; the issue of terrorism and feminists who were highly visible in the RAF continued through the 1970s and 1980s. For example, Ingrid Strobl, a well-known contributor to feminist publications including *EMMA,* was convicted of support for terrorist activities and sentenced to a five-year jail term in 1989.

58. Schenk 1983; also Lenz 2008, 267–82.

59. Schenk 1983, 170–71.

60. Ibid., 170 or 122.

61. Ibid., 122.

62. Plogstedt 1979, 58.

63. US pacifist feminists developed encampments in New York state, echoing the better-known one in Greenham Common (UK).

64. US feminists increasingly came down in favor of military service as part of their duty as citizens. The claim that men protected women and children "at home," they argued, offered women little more than a "protection racket." See Stiehm 1982; Katzenstein 1999.

65. In Sander (1980, 16) cited in Schenk (1983, 86), and several other places, including Schwarzer (1981).

66. Throughout the 1970s the peace movement led increasing numbers of men to resist service in West Germany military, by registering as conscientious objectors and doing two years alternative service (from three thousand men in the beginning of the 1960s to fifty-five thousand in 1981). See Schenk 1983. In 2010, Germany abolished conscription for men since by then too many were doing alternative service to make military training worthwhile.

67. Mitscherlich 1992.

68. Interviews with ex-GDR activists in 1990 and 1991 all emphasized the women's peace movement.

69. Miethe 1999a.

70. Miethe 1999a; and interview with Ina Merkel (February 2, 1993).

71. Schenk 1983, 171.

72. Calhoun 1993.

73. Kavemann 2004.

74. For US discussion of "cultural feminism," see Echols (1989) and Taylor and Rupp (1993).

75. Kavemann 2004.

76. Schenk 1983, 170–71.

CHAPTER 5

1. Die GRÜNE (literally The GREENS) used "screaming" all-capital-letters in part because they did not want to include "party" in their name and needed to distinguish the officially registered party name from a mere color noun. Although Green parties are now common in Western democracies and are understood as environmental, the Green platform is considerably more complex and a focus of scholarly debate. See, for example, Markovits and Gorski 1993.

2. Personal collection, one-page flyer for Fraueninitiative 6.Oktober.

3. Interview with Herrad Schenk, Bonn, 1981. Note how this analogy compares to the 1963 description of NOW as a "NAACP for women."

4. See Plogstedt 1983; "Frauenpolitik zwischen Traum und Trauma" (Berlin: Dokumentation der 7.Berliner Sommeruniversität für Frauen), 1984; "Weiberräte contra Feminismus" 1984; and "Rat-los" 1984, 30.

5. H. Eisenstein (1996) popularized the term outside Australia, but Sawer, herself a femocrat, coined the term. See Sawer 1990.

6. The *Frauenbereich* (women's policy area) of the Berlin Alternative List was a center of debates over forming a separate women's party, one side arguing that being a woman did not imply a political agenda ("Frausein ist kein politisches Programm"), and the other side claiming it would be a source of both consciousness-raising and competition with the other parties. See archival material on the AL (FFBIZ Accession Number 400/320).

7. At least until those rules were abolished, the party shared work and glory relatively equally, but even so the "Alternative List" (AL) was an even more non-party-like party. In most elections voters saw an electoral list that was a Green and AL coalition slate.

8. Interviews with Renate Sabrosinski and Christel Eckart, October 2, 1990.

9. Russia did have a feminist movement arising from precollapse women's mobilizations.

10. An Australian, Bacchi (1996) led the discursive turn in feminist policy studies. Critical frame analysis of gender policy in Europe has been produced by the multinational comparative researchers associated with the EU-funded MAGEEQ (www.mageeq.net) and QUING projects (www.quing.eu).

11. See the postmaterialist and "new" social movements debate in Inglehart (1981).

12. According to Ingrid Mattäus, "The active beginning of such a party perhaps could get the traditional parties moving, through their fear of competition." See *Berliner Frauenkonferenz der traditioneller Frauenverbände und der Autonomen Frauengruppen* von 16–18 September 1977, Dokumentation–FFBIZ 349/91), 79–80.

13. The romantic pronature, anticapitalist aspects of the Green critique also sounded to some outside the party disconcertingly "light brown" (mildly neofascist), since defense of "nature" suggested "blood and soil" nationalist rhetoric. The "*Bürger*" (citizens) of these initiatives seemed "*bürgerlich*" (bourgeois) in claiming individual liberties and nonsocialist identities, but also raised fears of populism.

14. Regine Dackweiler, Ilse Lenz, and Sylvia Kontos energetically denounced the theoretical claims of male political scientists and sociologists who called autonomous feminist mobilization a "new social movement." Although I share their skepticism, "newness" did imply a challenge to dominant frameworks: for Americans the "new" movements revived and reshaped the suppressed socialist tradition in a more participatory way; in Europe the autonomous movements, including feminism, reinvented political liberalism without the straitjacket of neoliberal economics.

15. Markovits and Gorski 1993.

16. In 1980 the registered membership of all political parties was overwhelmingly

male, and male dominance varied only slightly among them (75 percent in the FDP, 77 percent in the SPD, 79 percent in the CDU, 86 percent in the CSU). Even in 2006, men remained in the majority of formal membership of even the most gender integrated parties (56 percent in the PDS/Linke, 63 percent in the Greens, 69 percent in the SPD, 75 percent in the CDU, 82 percent in the CSU), so these parties deliberately overrepresented women among the leadership. Data from Hoecker (2008).

17. In addition, there were the "*Promis*" or prominent people in the party, such as Joshka Fischer and Petra Kelly, media darlings who drew attention and whose ideas thus got more weight.

18. Phillips 1998.

19. Roggenkamp 1983, 18.

20. Schoppe plus Antje Vollmer and Annemarie Borgmann; Christa Nickels, Erika Nickel, and Heidemarie Dann were the *Geschäftsführerinnen.*

21. Interview with Adrienne Goehler 1985.

22. The FrauenUnion traces its own origins back to the less independent women's caucus in the CDU in the 1950s and 1960s, but its renaming in 1988 went along with a more externally visible and internally empowered organizational structure. See Wiliarty (2010) and FrauenUnion website: http://www.fu-bayern.de/fulv/content/index.htm (accessed on June 28, 2011).

23. Data from http://www.bundestag.de/blickpunkt/104_Spezial/0402020.html (accessed on June 28, 2011). For further details of women's party representation and how it changed, see Figure 5.

24. A party profile that did not appeal to women was dangerous indeed, since the disproportionate loss of male population in World War II made women a majority of German voters.

25. Tripp and Kang 2008.

26. Moeller 1993. The SPD accepted emphasis on gender differences in the interest of protecting women, rejecting as "equality foolishness" (*Gleichmacherei*) any interpretation of the law that did not take women's responsibility for children into account. Thus the German constitutional court was not out of line in the 1950s when it interpreted the equal rights paragraph as not interfering with assigning women the "function" of child rearing.

27. Schwarzer 1985.

28. The EU also moved toward defining "reconciliation of work and family" as a policy to help women rather than a strategy to change the gender division of labor. See Stratigaki 2004.

29. Although from 1986 it was available to fathers as well as mothers, the structure of the leave made it unattractive to anyone with a reasonable salary and desire to be employed on a lifetime basis.

30. In the late 1980s, Süssmuth often topped the polls as the most popularly admired politician of either gender.

31. From 1986, when the policy began, with calculating one year per child at the rate of 75 percent of the average wage, this benefit gradually increased; the time rose to three years per child in 1992 and the amount to 100 percent in 1996. See Berghahn 2004.

32. "Müttermanifest: Leben mit Kindern, Frauen werden laut." Dokumentation des Kongresses 12.–23. November 1986. Flyer produced by the Green party in 1987. Reprinted in *Frankfurter Rundschau*, March 27, 1987, and in Lenz (2008, 623–29).

33. Their advocates, such as Gisela Erler and Monika Jaeckel, presented these as successors to women's centers—a place for women to gather to overcome their isolation—but now with the assumption that they would bring their children.

34. Pinl 1987, 9.

35. Feminists in sympathy with the *Mother's Manifesto* and mother's centers (at least fifty of these were in operation in 1988 with another seventy planned) were often seen as advocating a "new femininity," embraced by some feminists with a general enthusiasm for applauding gender difference and viewed by others with concern. Lenz 2008; see also Beck-Gernsheim 1984.

36. Stellungnahme grüner Frauen zum Müttermanifest, Flyer 1987, reprinted in Lenz (2008, 637–40).

37. Pinl 1977; also Beck-Gernsheim 1984.

38. Gilligan 1993; Milan Women's Bookstore Collective 1990.

39. For example, the *EMMA* version sarcastically proclaimed, "It is time to understand that fathers want to be present outside their four walls. . . . To demand space for fathers and their children is not to weaken or divide the left." See "Vätermanifest: Leben mit Kindern—Väter warden laut" (1987, 26).

40. It is telling that both terms were borrowed from "Othered" languages, suggesting male behavior was seen as more extreme or more recognizably offensive there.

41. von Wahl 1999, 2008.

42. Stellungnahme, Section II. "Müttermanifest: Leben mit Kindern, Frauen werden laut," reprinted in Lenz (2008).

43. Pfarr 1985, 86.

44. Marlese Kutsch, the first director of this office, was a longtime activist in the male-dominated Mining and Energy Union. Reflecting the government's concern with looking good at the Mexico City conference on International Women's Year, her mandate was broadly to develop policies to promote gender equality.

45. Sollwedel 1982.

46. After German unification, East Germans pressed to gender neutrally rename these positions in gender-neutral language, calling them *Gleichstellungsbeauftragten* (people responsible for making equality).

47. In Hamburg: Leitstelle Gleichstellung der Frau, Senatskanzlei; in Hessen: Zentralstelle für Frauenfragen, Staatskanzlei.

48. Interview with Lie Selter, Cologne, September 26, 1990, the first *Frauenbeauftragte* in Germany at the local level. A student of Maria Mies, she saw connections between policy making for women in developing countries and at home.

49. I conducted twenty-eight interviews with such equality officers in the late 1980s; see discussion of similarities and differences in their mandates, resources, and power in Ferree (1995b).

50. Richelmann 1991; Wilken 1992.

51. Wilken 1992.

52. In 1987, three-quarters of local women's affairs officers said that women's groups, especially those associated with the SPD and unions (and in one-quarter of the communities, autonomous feminist groups), were instrumental in creating their positions (Goericke 1989, 71).

53. Interviews with Marita Haibach, Barbara Loer, and Lie Selter, pioneers of this approach.

54. Ferree 1995b. Reliance on insider tactics gave more voice to already privileged women. This tendency arose in other parts of the world, too, as women began to build expertise-centered advocacy networks around multiple issues. Alvarez (1999) is credited with identifying these issues in her work on "NGOization" of feminism in Latin America, but as this case shows, the process could also begin within governments.

55. Lang 1997.

56. Both *FrauenfrAKtion* and *FrauenAnStiftung* incorporate word plays: *Fraktion* is the parliamentary group of a party; an AK is the abbreviation for an *Aktionskreis*, or working group; and *Aktion* is the term for an autonomous political action like a demonstration. Thus the term melds women's intra- and extraparliamentary tactics. Similarly, *Stiftung* is a foundation, and *Anstiften* means inciting to action, so the *FrauenAnStiftung* is a women's foundation inciting women's mobilization.

57. However, in the same year, the minister for women's affairs who had succeeded Süssmuth (Ursula Lehr, CDU) called a "First National Equal Rights Conference" that excluded the autonomous groups.

58. Peak organization is the British term, now widely used throughout Europe, for the national umbrella group that encompasses the groups working on this issue or constituency, such as labor unions forming a Trades Union Council.

59. In 1984, the Hamburg *GSS* produced the first affirmative action plan for women in government employment. The guidelines said that "equally qualified" women candidates "should" be preferred, without defining how equal qualification should be measured or offering sanctions if women were not preferred. The model was much imitated in other states and cities and the affirmative action officer role eagerly embraced.

60. Zippel 2006.

61. Ferree and Roth 1998a.

62. One outgrowth of Women's Strike Day in 1993 was the effort of about three hundred autonomous feminists to found "The Feminist Party: Die FRAUEN (the WOMEN)," modeled on both the Green party and the UFV; although formally registered as a party, it had no electoral success.

63. Interview with Dagmar König, Wilmersdorf, July 23, 1991.

64. In an open letter to the Central Committee of the Communist Party of the GDR published in the women's magazine *Für Dich*, on November 1, 1989, and written in the previous months, as perestroika was shaking all the Eastern European countries.

65. Bohley was allowed to return in 1988. In many newspapers of the time she was referred to as "the mother of the revolution." See also Miethe 1999b.

66. West German feminist theologians, such as Sölle, had tremendous impact worldwide, and the feminist presence in theological discussion in Germany was impressive. East German women's fiction and West German women's theological writing reached many audiences that would not otherwise have considered feminist ideas.

67. For more detail on the politics of these and other emergent groups and how they contributed to the forming of the UFV, see Ferree (1994) and Ulrich (2000).

68. Ulrich 2000; Sillge 1991.

69. Indeed, before the Berlin meeting, an informal "national" meeting of the "illegal women's movement" already occurred in Erfurt on October 30 ("Frauen für Veränderung"), October 11 marked the founding of the autonomous group "lila offensive" in Berlin, and "Fraueninitiativ Leipzig" wrote its first platform on October 18.

70. Erfurt and Leipzig were among the first.

71. This had a parallel in the Soviet Union, where the demographic institute proved to be a seedbed for feminism nurtured by statistical studies of women's status (Sperling 1999). In the United States, President Kennedy's Committee on the Status of Women in 1963 similarly raised consciousness through statistics.

72. The special issue of *Feministische Studien* 1990 published some of this previously suppressed research, including Dölling (1990) and Nickel (1990).

73. Interview with Hannah Behrend, July 29, 1991.

74. Sadly, even as they were finally able to do their jobs as they had wished, they saw these jobs disappear. One tenured researcher who lost her job for being both too old (at fifty) and too "red" (for having taught introduction to Marxism) was in tears as she told me she had collected once-forbidden material from the now-open West but would never have a chance to teach it.

75. The child-care leave of eighteen months was only opened up to fathers and only in "exceptional circumstances" in 1986. Acquaintances of mine in Leipzig, parents of triplets, had fought for the father's right to leave to help his wife, a student at the time, with the child care this entailed. The line they thought had finally won them approval was his declaration that "even the best mother only has two breasts!"

76. Ulrich 2000.

77. Ferree 1994.

78. This last GDR women's office was below the state secretary level and only had five members, headed by Marina Beyer.

79. Miethe 1999b.

80. The two East Marks for one West Mark rate was very advantageous for savers, since the real rate was closer to ten to one. Many individuals in the GDR had saved cash, since there were shortages of goods to buy. However, trading East German for West German Marks at two-for-one converted the amount owed by East German firms for machinery or raw materials at the previous international rate into a large, unsecured debt, since the value of the goods they held no longer matched the redenominated debt. Whole industries collapsed when the payments could not be managed.

81. "Die sind tierisch hinterm Mond," 1990.

82. Ulrich 2000.

83. Spernbauer 2008; Maleck-Lewy and Ferree 2000.

84. "Ohne Frauen ist kein Staat zu machen" was the title given by the UFV to its statement of principles.

85. The "Mauer im Kopf" was a common phrase in public discourse to describe the mutual misunderstanding in the period of unification.

86. Ferree 1995c.

87. See Zerilli 2005.

CHAPTER 6

1. Quotes from the Treaty of Unification; see discussion in Ferree et al. 2002.

2. For statistics, see Ferree et al. 2002.

3. Interview with Carol Hagemann-White, September 20, 1990.

4. For example, Kühnert 1989.

5. "Hexenjagd," 1988.

6. Vultejus 1990.

7. See the more extensive coverage of media content and framing in Ferree et al. 2002.

8. The same law made contraception in the form of the birth control pill available at no cost. Second-trimester abortions were permitted only with the consent of a hospital committee when the health risks of a late abortion were outweighed by the medical condition of either the mother or the fetus. Beginning in the early 1970s and intensifying for the next decade, the GDR also adopted extensive social supports to encourage motherhood—extensive paid childbirth leave, virtually free public child care for nearly all children, hot lunches at schools, paid time off to care for sick children. In the 1980s, the GDR abortion rate was about one of every four pregnancies—about the same as in the FRG. See Ferree 1993.

9. See Harsch 1997; Maleck-Lewy 1995.

10. Ferree 1993.

11. Rudd (2000) and also Gal and Kligman (2000b) on family networks and postsocialism.

12. See Maleck-Lewy and Ferree 2000.

13. Wuerth 1999.

14. Maleck-Lewy and Ferree 2000.

15. Ibid.

16. From *Neues Deutschland*, cited in Maleck-Lewy and Ferree 2000.

17. Wuerth 1999.

18. Ferree et al. 2002.

19. Wuerth 1999.

20. Ferree et al. 2002; Ferree 2003.

21. Ibid.

22. Ibid.

23. Ullrich 1998; Wuerth 1999.

24. Ullrich 1998.

25. Gerhards and Schäfer 2006.

26. See, for example, German feminist activist Renate Klein's discussion at *http://www .wloe.org/WLOE-en/information/globalization/16oktberlin.html* (accessed on June 28, 2011).

27. Ullrich's content analysis of feminist journals documents this shift in detail (1998).

28. "Abtreibung: Klage in Karlsruhe," 1996; "Abtreibung: Bonus für Katholiken," 1996; "Abtreibung: 'Wirklich behertz,'" 1996. Bavaria also tried to define abortion as illegal if the woman fails to give a reason (thus putting the law in direct contradiction to the federal one), if the abortion is unreported, or if the doctor derives more than 25 percent of his or her income from abortion. This outraged doctors and was rejected as a violation of constitutional data protection, not women's rights. In the later 1990s, the federal government affirmed the legality of lay-run Catholic-leaning counseling centers as certifiers. These number in the dozens in Bavaria but are rare in the northeast (Berlin and Brandenburg together had only three).

29. This description later sounded ironic, when Merkel displaced Kohl as CDU party leader in 1998, then became the first woman chancellor of Germany in 2005, heading a new "Grand Coalition" government.

30. Sänger 2005.

31. Fuller accounts of the end of the UFV can be found in Ferree (1994), Ulrich (2000), and Sänger (2005).

32. Ferree 1994.

33. Penrose 1993. Ulrike Baureithel (1993) presents the typical "failure" framing. See also more general discussions of the devaluation of feminism in the immediate postsocialist period across Eastern Europe in Einhorn (1993).

34. There were 9.7 million jobs in East Germany in 1989 and only 5.8 million in December 1992 (Bialas and Ettl 1993).

35. My own fieldwork in Berlin in 1990 offered ample confirmation, particularly an interview (July 3, 1991) with two women in the Arbeitslosenverband, a mixed-gender association of the unemployed, who recounted their own experiences as well as those of their clients.

36. Maier 1992b; see also Maier 1992a.

37. See Trappe and Rosenfeld (2004) on the different segregation levels in the East and West, and change over time.

38. Roloff 1990; Maier 1993; Maier 1992a.

39. GDR unions were abolished and East Germans were a small, easily outvoted mi-

nority in the FRG unions. The "missing work ethic" was a common media theme in the immediate postunification period; years later Heiner Meulemann (2002) still considers a difference in approach to work one of many enduring differences attributable to GDR socialization.

40. ABM stands for *Arbeitsbeschäftigungsmassnahmen* (employment creation programs). Men were overrepresented in such government work as well. Bialas and Ettl 1993; Maier 1993.

41. In comparison, men experienced a 60 percent drop from 200,000 in 1990 to 80,000 in 1992. For highly qualified white-collar jobs, men's numbers dropped from 850,000 to 660,000, or 20 percent, while women fell from 600,000 to 420,000, or 30 percent just in the one year, 1990–91 (Maier 1993).

42. Ostner 1993.

43. Holst and Schupp, 1991. In addition to facing the perfectly legal age discrimination endemic in the FRG, because of the GDR's move away from affirmative action in the mid-1970s, older women were the ones more likely to be qualified in conventionally male fields, catching them in dual pincers of discrimination by age and gender.

44. Ferree and Young 1993.

45. Ibid.

46. See discussion in Ferree 1995a. For example, ex-GDR women in 1990 were less likely than women in the "old" Federal Republic (about 10 versus 25 percent) to say they would quit their paid jobs if they did not need the money. Only 8 percent of unemployed women (and 19 percent of women out of the labor force) in the East in 1991 said that they did not want to return to work.

47. Overt discrimination on the basis of "gender-plus" factors such as age and motherhood pushed some women into not only deferring children but seeking sterilization as part of the cost of remaining a desirable worker (Dölling, Hahn, and Scholz 2000). Nothing could be done to make a woman younger, and job ads explicitly noted their preference for women under forty-five. The majority of women over fifty who lost their jobs in the *Wende* never successfully reentered the primary job market.

48. *Eigensinn* (stubbornness) is a term popularized by Irene Dölling to describe East German women's adherence to GDR social norms in the face of countervailing pressure from FRG policy. See Dölling, Hahn, and Scholz 2000.

49. The emphasis on part-time employment in the FRG system distorts direct comparisons to the United States. Overall, 65 percent of German women aged 25–60 were in the labor force in 1991, compared to 75 percent of American women aged 25–54, but approximately two-thirds of the former and one-third of the latter worked part-time. Kirner 1993; US Dept of Labor 1992.

50. Schuldt 1993; Maier 1993.

51. Adler 2004; see also Kirner 1993; Roloff 1990.

52. Adler (2004) describes this as the GDR's efforts "to make motherhood and employment compatible so that the employed mother ideal could be realized, independent of marital status"; Conrad, Lechner, and Werner (1996) calls it "leading young adults step by step into the mainstream of socialist society." Neither description recognizes how these arrangements institutionalized the double day for women against which GDR feminists mobilized.

53. This drop was almost inconceivably large—greater than that produced by the Great Depression or two World Wars. See demographic analysis in Conrad, Lechner, and Werner 1996.

54. Dölling, Hahn, and Scholz 2000.

55. Adler 2004; Hank and Kreyenfeld 2003.

56. The drop was from approximately 11 per 1,000 women in 1990 to 5 per 1,000 in 1995.

57. Lee, Alwin, and Tufis (2007) demonstrates how little convergence there was. Indeed,women and men in the former East became more egalitarian at a faster rate than Western women did in the ensuing decade and a half.

58. Adler 2004. Lynn Cooke (2006) finds continuing differences in how much housework male partners contribute, with East German men more participatory.

59. Adler 2004; Cooke 2006; Lee, Alwin, and Tufis 2007; Beyer 1990.

60. Child-care statistics show regional differences in use, which reflect local availability as well individual decisions to enroll children; the domestic division of labor is calculated for married couples based on where the wife was educated. Both structural availability (311 public child-care places/1,000 children aged 0–3 in the East and 19/1,000 in the West) and individual choices reflect the persistence of a different gender culture in the former GDR. See Cooke 2007; Hank and Kreyenfeld 2003.

61. Lee, Alwin, and Tufis 2007.

62. Kahlau 1990; DiCaprio 1990; Dölling 199.

63. Even in EVA, a group I extensively observed in Berlin in 1991, there were sporadic debates about whether men could take part in some classes, primarily as to whether this would make the classes lose their distinctiveness from other projects serving unemployed men and women, reduce their competitive position in attracting women clients, or widen their market and allow them to be teachers to men as well as women.

64. The name *weibblick* associates *weiblich* (feminine) with *Weib* (archaic term for women reclaimed as radical in 1970s West Germany) and *Blick* (perspective). *Weibblick* survived to 2002 and EVA remains in existence in 2010, but most projects quickly died when subsidies were withdrawn. Mittman's discussion of these magazines (2007) is extremely thorough and insightful.

65. There is a need for more research on the direct effects of ex-GDR women's politics on transforming the political agenda of women in the former West.

66. Ferree 1995b.

67. Interview, Birgit Gabriel, July 18, 1991.

68. Rudd 2000.

69. George Sand (in France) and Luise Aston (in Germany) were the classic late nineteenth-century figures used to illustrate the idea of *Emanze*.

70. Morrison 1992; Carstens-Wickham 1998; Dueck 2001.

71. In the cohorts born in 1945–58, 8 percent of East German but 15–23 percent of West German women were childless, a percentage undoubtedly higher among academics and feminist activists such as the speaker. Kreyenfeld 2003.

72. For example, East-West Conference in 1990 organized by Ayla Neusel.

73. Helwerth and Schwarz 1995; Einhorn 1989.

74. Mittman 2007.

75. Spernbauer 2008.

76. For full details of the development, see http://www.weiberwirtschaft.de/informieren/genossenschaft/geschichte/chronologie/ (accessed on June 28, 2011).

77. "Der Staat fördert die tatsächliche Durchsetzung der Gleichberechtigung von Frauen und Männern und wirkt auf die Beseitigung bestehender Nachteile hin."

CHAPTER 7

1. Judith Butler's talk was part of what was later published as *Antigone's Claim: Kinship Between Life and Death* (2000). The Butler tour was described by Robert Tobin (1999) as "a triumphal march through a happily vanquished land. It was like the Beatles—14 year old girls fainting when they caught sight of her and so forth."

2. See Scott and Butler (1992) for the variety of poststructuralisms.

3. Alvarez (2009) analyzes the "NGOization" of feminist politics in Latin America. Lang (1997) applies this to Germany.

4. Butler 1990.

5. See Becker and Kortendiek 2004.

6. Knapp 2009.

7. See Hagemann-White 2000; Behnke and Meuser 1999.

8. Halina Bendkowski (1999) is often credited with coining the term "gender democracy."

9. Raab 2004.

10. A variety of programmatic readings given to Butler appear in Etgeton and Hark (1997). See also Becker and Kortendiek (2004) and Raab (2004) for discussions of these debates.

11. Interview with Sabine Hark, May 2005.

12. Interviews with Marianne Weg, Regina Becker-Schmidt, and Ute Gerhard, May 2005.

13. Jansen 2004.

14. Waring 1988.

15. Böker and Neugebauer 1994.

16. See the Women's Budget Group's website, http://www.wbg.org.uk (accessed on June 28, 2011).

17. Ferree and Tripp 2006.

18. Zippel 2007; Cichowski 2007.

19. See also Snyder 2006.

20. Buss and Herman 2003.

21. By 1995 addressing gender in relation to postcolonial or other political inequalities reflected the goals of many feminist organizations and women's NGOs around the world (see Ewig and Ferree forthcoming).

22. The United States is unusual in how little effect the PfA had on domestic policies and politics. Perhaps it is not surprising, given that it is one of a handful of countries that has still not ratified the Convention on the Elimination of All forms of Discrimination Against Women (CEDAW), the most basic UN treaty on women's equal rights.

23. "Gender Mainstreaming: Extract from the Report of the Economic and Social Council for 1997." Chapter IV, Coordination Segment (A/52/3, 18 September 1997), http://www.un.org/womenwatch/daw/csw/GMS.PDF (accessed on June 28, 2011).

24. *Institutionalizing Gender Equality* 2000; Budlender and Hewitt 2002. See also Transatlantic Applied Research in Gender Equity Training (TARGET). http://www.ssc.wisc.edu/TARGET/index.htm (accessed on June 28, 2011).

25. The Treaty of Rome already endorsed equal pay, a move in part inspired by fears of cross-national competition using women to depress men's wages (for equal pay provisions in the original treaty, see Article 119, 43, http://www.eurotreaties.com/rometreaty.pdf (accessed on June 28, 2011); for these provisions in the consolidated version, see Article 157 (ex-Article 141 TEC), http://eur-lex.europa.eu/LexUriServ/LexUriServ.do?uri=OJ:C:2010:083:FULL:EN:PDF.

26. As the successor to the Treaty of Rome, which established a basis for a European Community, and the Maastricht Treaty of 1993, which gave shape to the modern European Union, the Treaty of Amsterdam spelled out more clearly the rights and obligations of citizens of the EU. See the discussion of the implications of this process across different member-states in Wobbe and Biermann (2009).

27. There are three legal bases in the EC Treaty for EU legislation on equal treatment of men and women: Article 141(3) in employment and occupation; Article 3(2) outside the

employment field; and Article 137 in promotion of employment and improved living and working conditions. The Amsterdam Treaty continues to be followed by more treaties (for example, 2009 Treaty of Lisbon). Efforts toward greater unity (deepening) or including more members (widening) remain controversial, especially in the economic turmoil of global recession. Article 141 has been replaced by Article 157, Article 3 by Article 8, and Article 137 by Article 153 in the Treaty of Lisbon.

28. See Cichowski 2002. See also Keck and Sikkink 1998; Zippel 2004.

29. The effects of statistical comparisons, rankings, and league tables on changing organizational practices are well documented. See, particularly, Espeland and Sauder 2007; Lombardo, Meier, and Verloo 2009; Olds 2010.

30. For details on the European Women's Lobby (EWL), see www.womenlobby.org; Cichowski 2002.

31. Roth (2007) shows how in the new accession states of the EU, an alliance of women's organizations in postsocialist Eastern Europe founded in Beijing in 1995, KARAT, remains more significant to women although less powerful in relation to the EU. Ingrid Miethe and Silke Roth (2003) shows how KARAT has helped women of the former GDR move from being "backward" stepsisters of West German feminism to "elder sisters" with more experience dealing with "Western expectations" and EU norms than other Eastern European women.

32. See Sylvia Walby's analysis of this (http://www.equalities.gov.uk/pdf/Summ%20cost%20of %20domestic%20violence%20Sep%2004.pdf [accessed June 28, 2011]), and consider the DAPHNE programme (http://www.eurowrc.org/01.eurowrc/04.eurowrc_en/03.en_ewrc .htm [accessed on June 28, 2011] and http://ec.europa.eu/justice/funding/daphne3/funding _daphne3_en.htm [accessed June 28, 2011]) as an example of such success. Lise Agustín (2011) provides a useful analysis of the strengths and limitations of the EU Daphne approach.

33. See also Keck and Sikkink 1998.

34. Outshoorn and Kantola 2007; Agustín 2007.

35. Zippel (2006) demonstrates this with regard to sexual harassment law.

36. The *International Journal of Feminist Politics* (founded in 1999), *Social Politics* (founded in 1994), and *European Journal of Women's Studies* (founded in 1994) can be partly understood as transnational forums emerging to help meet the needs of these observatories, expert consultancies, and policy research institutes.

37. Alvarez 1999; Lang 1997; Lang 2009.

38. Lewis 2006.

39. The way the EU can exert any influence in this policy area is by making a "business case" for the harm interpersonal violence does to the economy (Walby 2004).

40. The official definition of gender mainstreaming offered by the EU is "the integration of the gender perspective into every stage of policy processes—design, implementation, monitoring and evaluation—with a view to promoting equality between women and men." For an extended definition and practical applications at the EU level, see http://ec.europa .eu/justice/gender-equality/tools/index_en.htm (accessed on June 28, 2011).

41. Woodward 2003.

42. Netzwerk Gender Training 2004.

43. See the *GenderKompetenzZentrum* website, available at http://www.genderkompe tenz.info/ (accessed on June 28, 2011).

44. See http://www.genderkompetenz.info/ (accessed on June 28, 2011).

45. For this critique see the Gender Manifesto of 2006, available in English and German at http://www.gender.de/mainstreaming/ (accessed June 28, 2011).

46. For examples, see the gender-mainstreaming page of the German Federal Min-

istry for Family, Senior Citizens, Women, and Youth: http://www.bmfsfj.de/BMFSFJ/
gleichstellung,did=67816.html (accessed on June 28, 2011).

47. Jansen 2004.

48. These concerns can be seen in assessments by the FrauenAkademie München, an
autonomous feminist research group (http://www.frauenakademie.de/projekt/main/main
.htm [accessed on June 28, 2011]), Barbara Stiegler of the Friedrich Ebert Foundation (2008)
and Barbara Unmüssig of the Heinrich Böll Foundation (2009).

49. Lang 1997; Lang 2007.

50. BAG, the Federal Association of Local-Government Women's Offices at http://www
.bag-frauen.de/ (accessed on June 28, 2011); Lang 2007.

51. Zippel 2006.

52. In Bremen, when a man and a woman gardener applied to be section chief and were
found equally qualified, the job was given to the woman. The man appealed; the ECJ held
that a mandate to hire women in jobs where they were underrepresented was not a legal
means for the state to help women overcome obstacles in the labor market.

53. The case *Kalanke v. Bremen* (ECJ Case C-450/93), as well as previous equal treatment
and non-discrimination cases, is covered in Hoskyns (1996) and in Emerton (2005). The European Court of Justice website provides the full citation to the Kalanke case and ECJ decision
(http://eur-lex.europa.eu/LexUriServ/LexUriServ.do?uri=CELEX:61993J0450:EN:HTML
[accessed on June 28, 2011]).

54. The original constitutional article just said "women and men have equal rights."
Although this original declaration alone would have been very significant in the United
States, where this sort of constitutional amendment failed in 1982, its history made it less
meaningful in Germany.

55. Zippel (2006) shows how German men used antidiscrimination measures to protect
themselves from charges of sexual harassment.

56. Rees 2002.

57. Connell 2005.

58. Hagemann-White (2000) captures this hope well: "It seems essential to me to say
farewell to the concept of *Frauenpolitik* with its constant confusion of women's interests and
gender democracy. All levels of government, federal, state or local, are responsible for con-
stituting a society with equal participation and rights for the genders, one with a sustainable
economy, healthful life conditions and peaceful conflict resolution. These goals are inseparable . . . [and] should emerge from civil society, which presumes local, open, tolerant dialogues. . . . Realizing this demands the participation of both genders." See also note 7, above.

59. Or as Sylvia Kontos (2004) said, criticizing Green politics at a GWI "Ladies Lunch":
"a bit of equality policy here and there just doesn't make it."

60. *Stiftung* is the noun for foundation; *anstiften* is the verb for "to incite": *AnStiftung*
creatively melds the two.

61. Along with gender democracy, the new foundation named combating discrimination against lesbians and gays and working for more inclusive immigration policies as its
organizational priorities.

62. In 2007, the Gunda Werner Institute for Feminism and Gender Democracy within
the Böll Foundation merged the Feminist Institute with the gender democracy staff office.
Named for a lesbian feminist activist who had been converted to the gender democracy side,
and endowed with significant internal resources, the GWI has become a locus for debates
on the future of feminism in Germany. See http://www.gwi-boell.de/web/institut.html (accessed on June 28, 2011).

63. BIG e.V. Co-ordination Team, 1998, 40, cited at the BIG Koordinerung website for the Berlin Intervention Project against Domestic Violence (BIG), http://www.big-interven tionszentrale.de/mitteilungen/0307_wave.htm (accessed on June 28, 2011).

64. See website for the Berlin Intervention Project against Domestic Violence (BIG), http://www.big-interventionszentrale.de/mitteilungen/0307_wave.htm (accessed on June 28, 2011).

65. For example, the EU-funded research project Coordination Action Against Human Rights Violations (CAHRV) headed by Carol Hagemann-White included taskforces on all these issues. See website http://www.cahrv.uni-osnabrueck.de/ (accessed on June 28, 2011).

66. Meuser 1998. In 2007, Michael Meuser became professor for gender studies at the University of Dortmund.

67. Hagemann-White points out (personal communication) that by defining gender equality as "women's business" feminists had, however inadvertently, silenced men; if they spoke out, they could be accused of taking over, and if they held a respectful silence, they were accused of disinterest. The same paradox in regard to the abortion issue pre-1994 is discussed in Ferree et al. 2002.

68. Robert Tobin (1999) provides a history of gay and lesbian politics and the ways language captured these nuances. The word "queer" in English first appears in German texts in 1992–93, begins to take off in 1994, and by the latter part of the 1990s is more typically "translated" as "quer" (on the diagonal). "Community" to describe nongeographical queer political alliances is literally untranslatable, since it implies a racial analogy that does not exist in Germany. Also, Tobin points out, German houses and apartments rarely have closets, so the metaphor of coming out (of the closet) was obviously carried over directly from the United States. The "rainbow" image in Germany had previously connoted not diverse sexualities but the variety of politics in the Green and Alternative List (hence their "Rainbow Associa-tion" of foundations renamed and replaced by the Heinrich Böll Foundation in 1996–97).

69. Hark 1999, 2005.

70. For racialization as a concept, see Brubaker 1992; Loveman 2001. For the German "transfer of resentments" from Jews to Turks who are, with women, now "outsiders within," see Weigel and Prigan 1992. For the consequences for Turkish men, see Ewing 2008.

71. Edelman, Fuller, and Mara-Drita 2001; Dobbin 2009; see also Woodward (2003), for the translation to EU politics.

72. Scott (2005) shows how in France, the demand for *parité* (gender-balanced repre-sentation) distinguished from any notion that "other groups" could claim rights to repre-sentation, with only gender seen as a "universal" quality of human difference.

73. In 2005, I photographed a window-sized advertisement for "male help wanted" in a drug store not half a mile from the federal parliament building, on a well-traveled route. The simple "normality" of thinking of jobs in sex-stereotyped terms had not changed enough to make this poster unacceptable, despite all the linguistic work to affirm women's presence.

74. For mixed feminist feelings and weak engagement of the EWL on mainstreaming policy, see Lang 2009.

CHAPTER 8

1. "Hier fand nicht die Kanzlerwahl statt, sondern der Triumph der deutschen Frauen-bewegung." See "Neues Deutschlandgefühl—Wir sind Kanzlerin," 2005. Schwarzer's phrase played on the screaming headline of the right-leaning tabloid newspaper, *Bild*, at the elec-tion of Benedict XVI that "we are pope."

2. Merkel in *EMMA* (rejecting Schwarzer's "feminism lite" label). See Schwarzer 2009.

3. Gornick and Meyers 2009.

4. Hester Eisenstein (2009) offers a polemic against this possibility, but Walby (2011) provides a counter argument.

5. Ibid.

6. The network of meaning in which "African American" sits at the center of all links about civil rights, (un)freedom and stigma also connects all rights-seeking, stigmatized groups to them and thus to ideas about race. Collins 2001.

7. Phillips 1987.

8. Cited in "Neues Deutschlandgefühl" 2005.

9. All above citations from "Neues Deutschlandgefühl" 2005.

10. Mill 1869.

11. von Ludwig and Meyer 2005.

12. As one supporter wrote ironically in *Die Zeit*: "If Angela Merkel had been a typical East German woman, she would have been a mother and already defeated by the shortage of kindergarten spots and lack of full-day schools in Bonn. Had she been a typical West German woman, she would have trumpeted her fury over these shortfalls and alienated everyone. Angela Merkel is a unified German model of childless success" (S. Mayer 2005).

13. Women were enlisted as spokespeople for the SPD and Greens to make just this argument through the media; see Ferree 2006.

14. Schwarzer 2000.

15. Molyneux 1985.

16. Zippel and Morgan 2003; Zippel 2009.

17. Cooke 2009; Lewis 2006.

18. These "Roadmaps" are issued every five years and are an important source of information about the opening and closing windows of EU opportunity structures for diverse feminist projects.

19. Adler 2004; Cooke 2007; Bennhold 2010, 2011.

20. Adler 1997, 2004.

21. K. Morgan 2009.

22. Beckmann 2008.

23. How this was to be paid for was left to member-states and/or management and labor negotiations. But a right to return to the same or comparable job was supposed to be guaranteed. See EU Directive 96/34/EC.

24. Although only circumstantial, Katja Guenther's work (2006) on the connections between Rostock (former East German) and Swedish feminists suggest that the UFV's critique of "mommy politics" in GDR may have influenced Swedish developments. Guenther shows clear evidence of consequential, strong networking in the Baltic region once the Wall came down.

25. See European Industrial Relations Observatory (EIRO) suggestions at http://www.eurofound.europa.eu/eiro/1998/01/study/tn9801201s.htm (accessed on June 28, 2011).

26. Wiliarty 2010.

27. von Wahl 2008; Wiliarty 2010.

28. Ibid.

29. von Wahl (2008) especially emphasizes this.

30. The term originates with Lesthaeghe (2003). The First Demographic Transition was the decline in mortality and family size associated with industrialization and modern medicine.

31. Jenson 2010, 2008.

32. Feminists were critical, but some women appreciated military service as a chance for good wages, adventure, and counterstereotypical activities. See Jeska 2010.

33. The website for the Working Group for Social Democratic Women (Arbeitsgemeinschaft Sozialdemokratischer Frauen (ASF) reports this engagement on "equal pay day": http://www.asf.spd.de/asf/aktuelles/2010/equalpayday/ankuendigung_equalpayday.html (accessed on June 28, 2011).

34. Rubery 2002; O'Connor 2005.

35. See partial list of such groups and networks at http://www.woman.de/katalog/wirtschaft/index.html (accessed on June 28, 2011), for example.

36. See Footage Galore/Alphamädchen website: http://www.germish.net/ (accessed on June 28, 2011).

37. Cooke 2011; Mandel and Semyonov 2005.

38. A Turkish-German mother, Sule Eisele-Gaffaroglu, for example, sued a bank for discrimination when it refused to let her return to her job after childbirth; she won her case, but the initially high penalty imposed by the court was then overturned as too punitive. See Preuß 2008; Hawley 2008.

39. Rottman and Ferree 2008.

40. Panel at Council for European Studies, Montreal 2010.

41. Kappert 2001; von der Leyen's proposal was for a more modest 70 percent cap on one gender. As Kappert points out, the CDU "had not lost its mind" but framed this as a means to improve economic decision-making.

42. Hohmann-Dennhardt, Körner, and Zimmer 2010.

43. Antidiscrimination policy and enforcement issues are covered also by the European Network of Legal Experts in the Non-Discrimination Field, which provides independent information and advice to the European Commission on how EU member-states are implementing antidiscrimination directives. This helps the European Commission to decide whether or not to take legal action against a member-state for failure to comply with the directives. The network of twenty-seven country experts—one for each member-state—is run by a management team led by MPG and the Human European Consultancy, with funding from the European Commission. See www.non-discrimination.net.

44. J. Brown 2010.

45. Yuval-Davis (1997) and Gal and Kligman (2000b) offer the most persuasive theoretical models for why this is so.

46. Korteweg and Yurdakul 2006.

47. Rottman and Ferree 2008.

48. Rottman and Ferree 2008. While exposing the state as patriarchal was precisely the point of earlier feminist criticisms, now the state was framed as an ally.

49. Consider earlier feminist claims that no matter how unappealing the choice of late abortion might be, it should be up to women themselves to make the decision, guided by their own consciences and sense of their options. Making it more possible for women to not choose abortion by providing better alternatives might have been carried over as trope for thinking about the choice of not wearing a headscarf, but was not.

50. Rottmann and Ferree 2008.

51. Ibid.

52. Different forms of the debate and interpretations of what veiling meant to women and for women's rights can be found all across Europe from 1990 on, reaching a crescendo around 2003. See comparative analysis in Koonz 2008; and Gresch et al. 2008.

53. See Song (2007) on the "diversionary effect" a focus on minority culture has on majority norms.

54. J. Brown 2010; Rottman and Ferree 2008; Ewing 2008.

55. See discussions of Turkish and Kurdish feminist movements in Al-Rebholz(2008).

56. J. Brown 2010.

57. Ibid.

58. Mushaben 2004.

59. Parvez forthcoming.

60. Lutz 2010, 2002; Lenz 2009.

61. See B. Roth 2004; McCall 2005; Hancock 2007. Kimberlé Crenshaw coined the term in 1991.

62. Kurz (1995) discusses the difference between the "stable working class" and the "hard living" (drinking, drug-using, violent, crime-dependent) section of the poor, and the ways in which hard-living results from economic distress and contributes to family breakups.

63. Quadagno 1994; Goldberg 2007.

64. Liptak 2010; the great "victory" of the Lily Ledbetter Equal Pay Act signed by President Obama as one of his first official acts was merely a restoration of the reach of a law that the Supreme Court had vitiated. The once-powerful tool of the class action suit against discrimination also has been largely lost, given the Supreme Courts' 2011 dismissal of women Walmart employees' standing as a class.

65. Ferree and Hess 2000.

66. Walby 2009.

67. Davis 2008.

68. Buss and Herman 2003.

69. For example, Judith Lorber 2005. See critique by Offen (1988) of rights based discourse as the only effective model of feminism.

REFERENCES

"Abtreibung: Bonus für Katholiken." 1996. *Der Spiegel* (December 16).

"Abtreibung: Klage in Karlsruhe." 1996. *Der Spiegel* (November 25).

"Abtreibung: 'Wirklich behertz.'" 1996. *Der Spiegel* (August 5).

Acker, Joan. 2006. "Inequality Regimes: Gender, Class, and Race in Organizations." *Gender & Society* 20, no. 4: 441–64.

Adler, Marina. 2004. "Child-Free and Unmarried: Changes in the Life Planning of Young East German Women." *Journal of Marriage and Family* 66, no. 5 (December): 1170–79.

———. 1997. "Social Change and Declines in Marriage and Fertility in Eastern Germany." *Journal of Marriage and Family* 59, no. 1 (February): 37–49.

Agustín, Laura María. 2007. *Sex at the Margins: Migration, Labour Markets and the Rescue Industry*. London and New York: Zed Books.

Agustín, Lise Rolandsen. 2011. "Gender Equality and Diversity at the Transnational Level: Challenges to European Union Policymaking and Women's Collective Mobilisation." PhD, Aalborg University, Denmark.

Alfredson, Lisa S. 2008. *Creating Human Rights: How Noncitizens Made Sex Persecution Matter to the World*. Philadelphia: University of Pennsylvania Press.

Allen, Ann Taylor. 1985. "Mothers of the New Generation: Adele Schreiber, Helene Stöcker, and the Evolution of a German Idea of Motherhood." *Signs* 10 (Spring): 418–38.

Al-Rebholz, Anil. 2008. "Zivilgesellschaft, NGOisierung und Frauenbewegungen in der Türkei der 2000er Jahre." In *Perspektiven auf die Türkei*, ed. Ilker Ataç, 321–41. Münster: Westfälisches Dampfboot Verlag.

Alvarez, Sonia E. 2009. "Beyond NGO-ization?: Reflections from Latin America." *Development* 52, no. 2: 175–84.

———. 1999. "Advocating Feminism: The Latin American Feminist NGO 'Boom.'" *International Feminist Journal of Politics* 1: 181–209.

Anders, Ann. 1988. *Autonome Frauen: Schlüsseltexte der neuen Frauenbewegung seit 1968.* Frankfurt: Athenäum Verlag.

Arbeitsgemeinschaft Sozialdemokratischer Frauen (ASF). 2010. "Equal Pay Day 26.März 2010." Accessed on June 28, 2011. http://www.asf.spd.de/asf/aktuelles/2010/equalpayday /ankuendigung_equalpayday.html.

Arnold, Gretchen. 1995. "Dilemmas of Feminist Coalitions: Collective Identity and Strategic Effectiveness in Battered Women's Movement." In *Feminist Organizations: Harvest of the New Women's Movement,* ed. Myra Marx Ferree and Patricia Y. Martin, 276–90. Philadelphia, PA: Temple University Press.

Augstein, Renate. 1983. "Abtreibung." In *Frauenlexikon. Stichworte zur Selbstbestimmung,* ed. Johanna Beyer, Franziska Lamott and Birgit Meyer, 9–13. München: C. H. Beck.

Ayim, May. 1997. *Grenzenlos und unverschämt* [mit Fotos und einem biographischen Essay von Silke Mertins]. Berlin: Orlanda Frauenverlag.

Bacchi, Carol. 1999. *Women, Policy, and Politics: The Construction of Policy Problems.* Thousand Oaks, CA: Sage Publishers.

Balibar, Etienne, and Immanuel Wallerstein. 1991. *Race, Nation, Class: Ambiguous Identities.* New York: Verso.

Banks, Olive. 1981. *Faces of Feminism: A Study of Feminism as a Social Movement.* New York: St. Martin's Press.

Bauer, Kattrin. 1994. "Der 8.März—Zur Geschichte des Internationalen Frauentags in Deutschland." *Beiträge zur feministischen Theorie und Praxis: FrauenStreik, Streitfragen* 17: 9–16.

Baureithel, Ulrike. 1993. "Wer setzt die Flötentöne in Europa? Deutsch-deutscher Einigungsprozeß und europäische Integration: Die Konsequenzen der gescheiterten Revolution der Frauen in Ostdeutschland." *Beiträge zur feministischen Theorie und Praxis* 34: 75–84.

Baxandall, Rosalyn, and Linda Gordan, eds. 2000. *Dear Sisters: Dispatches from the Women's Liberation Movement.* New York: Basic Books.

Beck-Gernsheim, Elisabeth. 1984. *Vom Geburtenrückgang zur neuen Mütterlichkeit: Über private und politische Interessen am Kind.* Frankfurt: Fischer Taschenbuch Verlag.

Becker, Ruth, and Beate Kortendiek, eds. 2004. *Handbuch Frauen- und Geschlechterforschung: Theorie, Methoden, Empirie.* Wiesbaden: VS–Verlag für Sozialwissenschaften.

Beckmann, Sabine. 2008. *Geteilte Arbeit? Männer und Care-Regime in Schweden, Frankreich und Deutschland.* Reihe: Arbeit—Demokratie—Geschlecht. Münster: Westfälisches Dampfboot.

Behnke, Cornelia, and Michael Meuser. 1999. *Geschlechterforschung und qualitative Methoden.* Opladen: Leske + Budrich.

Beisel, Nicola, and Tamara Kay. 2004. "Abortion, Race, and Gender in Nineteenth-Century America." *American Sociological Review* 69, no. 4: 498–518.

Bendkowski, Halina. 1999. *Wie weit flog die Tomate?: Eine 68erinnen Gala der Reflexion.* Berlin: Heinrich Böll Stiftung.

Berghahn, Sabine. 2004. "Der Ritt auf der Schnecke. Rechtliche Gleichstellung in der Bundesrepublik." In *Recht und Geschlecht. Zwischen Gleichberechtigung, Gleichstellung und Differenz,* ed. Mechthild Koreube, Ute Mager, 59–78. Baden-Baden: Nomos Verlag.

———. 1995. "Gender in the Legal Discourse of Post-unification Germany: Old and New Lines of Conflict." *Social Politics: International Studies in Gender, State & Society* 2, no. 1: 37–50.

Berkovitch, Nitza. 1999. *From Motherhood to Citizenship: Women's Rights and International Organizations.* Baltimore, MD: Johns Hopkins University Press.

Beyer, Marina. 1990. "Wer liegt unten?" *EMMA* 11: 46.

Bialas, Christiane, and Wilfried Ettl. 1993. "Wirtschaftliche Lage, soziale Differenzierung und Probleme der Interessenorganisation in den neuen Bundesländern." *Soziale Welt* 44, no. 1: 52–75.

BIG Koordinierung. 2011. "Berliner Interventionsprojekt gegen häusliche Gewalt - BIG." Accessed on June 28, 2011. http://www.big-koordinierung.de/mitteilungen/0307_wave.htm.

Blum, Linda. 1991. *Between Feminism and Labor: The Significance of the Comparable Worth Movement.* Berkeley and Los Angeles: University of California Press.

Bock, Gisela. 2002. *Women in European History.* Oxford: Blackwell.

———. 1976. "Lohn für Hausarbeit und die Macht der Frauen: oder Feminismus und Geld." *Courage: Berliner Frauenzeitung* 1: 27–28.

Böker, Marion, and Anne Neugebauer, eds. 1994. *Nichts ist unmöglich . . . Frauen fordern Geld in den Kommunen.* Münster: Unrast Verlag.

Bonilla-Silva, Eduardo. 2006. *Racism Without Racists: Color-Blind Racism and the Persistent Racial Inequality in the United States.* 2nd ed. Lanham, MD: Rowman and Littlefield Publishers.

Bordt, Rebecca. 1997. *The Structure of Women's Nonprofit Organizations.* Bloomington: Indiana University Press.

Bos, Pascale. 2006. "Feminists Interpreting the Politics of Wartime Rape: Berlin, 1945; Yugoslavia, 1992–1993." *Signs* 31, no. 4 (Summer): 995–1025.

Böttger, Barbara. 1990. *Das Recht auf Gleichheit und Differenz: Elisabeth Selbert und der Kampf der Frauen um Art. 3 II Grundgesetz.* Münster: Westfälishes Dampfboot Verlag.

Boxer, Marilyn J. 2010. "Rethinking the Socialist Construction and International Career of the Concept 'Bourgeois Feminism.'" In *Globalizing Feminisms, 1789–1945,* ed. Karen Offen. London and New York: Routledge.

Boyle, Elizabeth Heger. 2002. *Female Genital Cutting: Cultural Conflict in the Global Community.* Baltimore, MD: Johns Hopkins University Press.

Brown, Jessica A. 2010. "Citizenship of the Heart and Mind: Educating Germany's Immigrants in the Ideological, Emotional, and Practical Components of Belongingness." PhD, Sociology, University of Wisconsin, Madison.

Brown, Rita Mae. 1973. *Rubyfruit Jungle.* Plainfield, VT: Daughters Publishing Company.

Brown, Wendy. 1995. *States of Injury: Power and Freedom in Late Modernity.* Princeton, NJ: Princeton University Press.

Brubaker, Rogers. 1992. *Citizenship and Nationhood in France and Germany.* Cambridge, MA: Harvard University Press.

Brückner, Margit. 1996. *Frauen- und Mädchenprojekte: Von feministischen Gewissheiten zu neuen Suchbewegungen.* Opladen: Leske + Budrich.

Brückner, Margrit, and Simone Holler. 1990. *Frauenprojekte und soziale Arbeit, eine empirische Studie.* Frankfurt: Fachhochschulverlag.

———. 1986. *Frauenprojekte, Frauenmacht, Frauenland.* Paper presented at Bundesfrauenkongress zur autonomen Frauenpolitik, Essen, Germany.

Brush, Lisa. 2003. *Gender and Governance.* Walnut Creek, CA: AltaMira Press.

Budlender, Debbie, and Guy Hewitt. 2002. *Gender Budgets Make More Cents: Country Studies and Good Practice.* London: Gender Section, Commonwealth Secretariat.

Bundeswahlleiter. 2011. "Bundestagwahl 2009." Accessed on June 28, 2011. http://www.bundeswahlleiter.de/de/bundestagswahlen/BTW_BUND_09/.

Buss, Doris, and Didi Herman. 2003. *Globalizing Family Values: The Christian Right in International Politics.* Minneapolis: University of Minnesota Press.

Butler, Judith. 2000. *Antigone's Claim: Kinship Between Life and Death*. New York: Columbia University Press.

———. 1990. *Gender Trouble: Feminism and the Subversion of Identity*. New York: Routledge.

Calhoun, Craig. 1993. "'New Social Movements' of the Early 19th Century." *Social Science History* 17, no. 3: 385–427.

Carstens-Wickham, Belinda. 1998. "Gender in Cartoons of German Unification." *Journal of Women's History* 10, no. 1: 127–56.

Cassell, Joan. 1977. *A Group Called Women: Sisterhood and Symbolism in the Feminist Movement*. New York: McKay.

Chicago Women's Liberation Union (CWLU). 2011. "Classical Feminist Writings: The Grand Coolie Dam." Accessed on June 28, 2011. http://www.uic.edu/orgs/cwluherstory /CWLUArchive/damn.html.

Choo, Hae Yeon, and Myra Marx Ferree. 2010. "Practicing Intersectionality in Sociological Research: A Critical Analysis of Inclusions, Interactions and Institutions in the Study of Inequalities." *Sociological Theory* 28, no. 2 (June): 129–49.

Cichowski, Rachel. 2007. *The European Court and Civil Society: Litigation, Mobilization and Governance*. Cambridge: Cambridge University Press.

———. 2002. "'No Discrimination Whatsoever': Women's Transnational Activism and the Evolution of European Sex Equality Policy." In *Women's Community Activism and Globalization: Linking Local Struggles and Transnational Politics*, ed. Nancy Naples and Manisha Desai, 220–38. New York: Routledge.

Clemens, Elisabeth. 1997. *The People's Lobby: Organizational Innovation and the Rise of Interest Group Politics in the United States, 1890–1925*. Chicago: University of Chicago Press.

Clemens, Petra. 1990. "Die Kehrseite der Clara-Zetkin-Medaille. Die Betriebsfrauenausschüsse der 50er Jahre in lebensgeschichtlicher Sicht." *Feministische Studien* 8, no. 1: 20–34.

Cobble, Dorothy. 2004. *The Other Women's Movement: Workplace Justice and Social Rights in Modern America*. Princeton, NJ: Princeton University Press.

Collins, Patricia Hill. 2001. "Like One of the Family: Race, Ethnicity and the Paradox of US National Identity." *Ethnic and Racial Studies* 24, no. 1: 3–28.

———. 1998. "It's All in the Family: Intersections of Gender, Race, and Nation." *Hypatia* 13, no. 3: 62–82.

Connell, R. W.(Raewyn) 2005. "Change Among the Gatekeepers: Men, Masculinities, and Gender Equality in the Global Arena." *Signs: Journal of Women in Culture and Society* 30, no. 3: 1801–25.

———. 2002. *Gender*. Malden, MA: Polity Press.

———. 1987. *Gender and Power: Society, the Person, and Sexual Politics*. Stanford, CA: Stanford University Press.

Conrad, C., M. Lechner, and W. Werner. 1996. "East German Fertility After Unification: Crisis or Adaptation?" *Population and Development Review* 22, no. 2: 331–58.

Cooke, Lynn Prince. 2011. Gender-Class Equality in Political Economies. New York: Routledge.

———. 2009. "Gender Equity and Fertility in Italy and Spain." *Journal of Social Policy* 38, no. 1: 123–40.

———. 2007. "Persistent Policy Effects on Gender Equity in the Home: The Division of Domestic Tasks in Reunified Germany." *Journal of Marriage and Family* 69: 930–50.

———. 2006. "Policy, Preferences, and Patriarchy: The Division of Domestic Labor in East Germany, West Germany, and the United States." *Social Politics: International Studies in Gender, State & Society* 13, no. 1: 1–27.

Coordination Action on Human Rights Violations. 2011. Accessed on June 28, 2011. http://www.cahrv.uni-osnabrueck.de/.

Cott, Nancy. 1997. *The Bonds of Womanhood: "Woman's Sphere" in New England, 1780–1835.* New Haven, CT: Yale University Press.

———. 1986. "Feminism and social control: the case of child abuse and neglect." In *What Is Feminism?* ed. Ann Oakley, Juliet Mitchell, and Nancy Cott. New York: Pantheon Books.

Crage, Suzanna. 2009. "The Development of Refugee Aid Policy in Berlin and Munich: Local Responses to a Global Process." PhD, Sociology, Indiana University.

Crenshaw, Kimberlé. 2008. "The New Rhetoric of Racism." Paper presented at Women's Worlds Conference, Madrid.

———. 1991. "Mapping the Margins: Intersectionality, Identity Politics, and Violence Against Women of Color." *Stanford Law Review* 43, no. 6: 1241–99.

Dackweiler, Regina. 1995. *Ausgegrenzt und eingemeindet: die neue Frauenbewegung im Blick der Sozialwissenschaften.* Münster: Westfälisches Dampfboot.

Dalla Costa, Mariarosa, and Selma James. 1972. *Women and the Subversion of the Community.* London: Butler and Tanner Ltd.

Davis, Kathy. 2008. "Intersectionality as Buzzword: A Sociology of Science Perspective on What Makes a Feminist Theory Successful." *Feminist Theory* 9: 67–85.

Deutschland auf einen Blick. 2011. "Politik in Deutschland: 16.Deutscher Bundestag (Statistik)." Accessed on June 28, 2011. http://www.deutschland-auf-einen-blick.de/politik/bundestag/statistik.php.

DiCaprio, Lisa. 1990. "East German feminists: The Lila manifesto." *Feminist Studies* 16: 621–34.

"Die sind tierisch hinterm Mond." 1990. *Der Spiegel* (May 14).

Dobberthien, Marliese. 1988. "Gewerkschaftsfrauen." In *Der grosse Unterschied: Die neue Frauenbewegung und die siebziger Jahre,* ed. Kristina von Soden, 76–79. Berlin: Elefanten Press.

Dobbin, Frank. 2009. *Inventing Equal Opportunity.* Princeton, NJ: Princeton University Press.

Dohm, Hedwig. 1902. *Die Antifeministen. Ein Buch der Verteidigung.* Berlin: F. Dümmler.

Dölling, Irene. 1990. "Frauen- und Männerbilder. Eine Analyse von Fotos in DDR-Zeitschriften." *Feministische Studien* 8, no. 1: 35–49.

Dölling, Irene, Daphne Hahn, and Sylke Scholz. 2000. "Birth Strike in the New Federal States: Is Sterilization an Act of Resistance?" In *Reproducing Gender: Politics, Publics and Everyday Life after Socialism,* ed. Susan Gal and Gail Kligman, 118–48. Princeton, NJ: Princeton University Press.

Doorman, Lottemi. 1988. "Aufbruch aus dem Mütterghetto." In *Der grosse Unterschied: Die neue Frauenbewegung und die siebziger Jahre,* ed. Kristina von Soden, 25–30. Berlin: Elefanten Press.

Dueck, Cheryl. 2001. "Gendered Germanies: The Fetters of a Metaphysical Marriage." *German Life and Letters* 54, no. 1: 366–76.

DuPlessis, Rachel Blau, and Ann Snitow. 2007. *The Feminist Memoir Project: Voices from Women's Liberation.* New Brunswick, NJ: Rutgers University Press.

Echols, Alice. 1989. *Daring to Be Bad: Radical Feminism in America 1967–1975.* Minneapolis: University of Minnesota Press.

Edelman, Lauren B., Sally Riggs Fuller, and Iona Mara-Drita. 2001. "Diversity Rhetoric and the Managerialization of Law." *American Journal of Sociology* 106, no. 6: 1589–641.

Einhorn, Barbara. 1993. *Cinderella Goes to Market: Citizenship, Gender and Women's Movements in East Central Europe.* London and New York: Verso.

———. 1989. "Socialist Emancipation: The Women's Movement in the GDR." In *Prom-*

issary Notes: Women in the Transition to Socialism, ed. Sonia Kruks, Rayna Rapp, and Marilyn Young, 282–305. New York: Monthly Review Press.

Eisenstein, Hester. 2009. *Feminism Seduced: How Global Elites Use Women's Labor and Ideas to Exploit the World.* Boulder, CO: Paradigm Publishers.

———. 1996. *Inside Agitators: Australian Femocrats and the State.* Philadephia, PA: Temple University Press.

———. 1991. *Gender Shock: Practicing Feminism on Two Continents.* Boston: Beacon Press.

Eisenstein, Zillah. 1993. *The Radical Future of Liberal Feminism.* Boston: Northeastern University Press.

Eley, Geoff. 2002. *Forging Democracy: The History of the Left in Europe, 1850–2000.* New York and Oxford: Oxford University Press.

Emerton, Robyn, ed. 2005. *Women's Human Rights: Leading International and National Cases.* London: Cavendish.

Enke, Anne. 2007. *Finding the Movement: Sexuality, Contested Space, and Feminist Activism.* Durham, NC: Duke University Press.

Espeland, Wendy, and Michael Sauder. 2007. "Rankings and Reactivity: How Public Measures Recreate Social Worlds." *American Journal of Sociology* 113, no. 1 (July): 1–40.

Esping-Andersen, Gøsta. 1990. *The Three Worlds of Welfare Capitalism.* Cambridge: Polity Press.

Etgeton, Stefan, and Sabine Hark. 1997. *Freundschaft unter Vorbehalt: Chancen und Grenzen lesbisch-schwuler Bündnisse.* Berlin: Querverlag.

European Commission, DG Justice. 2011. "Funding: Prevent and Combat Violence Against Children, Young People and Women and to Protect Victims and Groups at Risk." Accessed on June 28, 2011. http://ec.europa.eu/justice/funding/daphne3/funding_daphne3_en.htm.

European Commission, DG Justice. 2011. "Tools for Gender Equality." Accessed on June 28, 2011. http://ec.europa.eu/justice/gender-equality/tools/index_en.htm.

European Court of Justice. 1995. "Judgment of the Court of 17 October 1995. Eckhard Kalanke v Freie Hansestadt Bremen." Accessed on June 28, 2011. http://eur-lex.europa.eu/LexUriServ/LexUriServ.do?uri=CELEX:61993J0450:EN:HTML.

European Industrial Relations Observatory (EIRO). 2011. "The EU Parental Leave Agreement and Directive: Implications for National Law and Practice." Accessed on June 28, 2011. http://www.eurofound.europa.eu/eiro/1998/01/study/tn9801201s.htm.

European Union. 2010. "Consolidated versions of the Treaty on European Union and the Treaty on the Functioning of the European Union." Official Journal of the European Communities (OJ) C 83, March 30, 2010. Accessed on June 28, 2011. http://eur-lex.europa.eu/LexUriServ/LexUriServ.do?uri=OJ:C:2010:083:FULL:EN:PDF.

Eurotreaties. 2011. "Treaty of Rome [1957]." Accessed on June 28, 2011. http://www.eurotreaties.com/rometreaty.pdf.

Evans, Richard. 1976. *The Feminist Movement in Germany, 1894–1933.* Thousand Oaks, CA: Sage Publications.

Evans, Sara M. 2003. *Tidal Wave: How Women Changed America at Century's End.* New York: Free Press.

Evans, Sara, and Harry Boyte. 1992. *Free Spaces: The Sources of Democratic Change in America.* Chicago: University of Chicago Press.

Ewig, Christina, and Myra Marx Ferree. Forthcoming. "Feminist Organizing: What's Old, What's New? History, Trends and Issues." In *Oxford Handbook on Gender and Politics.* Oxford: Oxford University Press.

Ewing, Katherine Pratt. 2008. *Stolen Honor: Stigmatizing Muslim Men in Berlin.* Stanford, CA: Stanford University Press.

Federal Association of Local-Government Women's Offices. 2011. Accessed on June 28, 201. "Berufliche Perspektiven für Frauen e.V." http://www.bag-frauen.de/.

Federal Ministry for Family, Senior Citizens, Women, and Youth. 2011. Accessed on June 28, 2011. "Nationale Gleichstellungspolitik." http://www.bmfsfj.de/BMFSFJ/gleichstellung,did=67816.html.

"Feministische Ökonomie—was ist das?" 1989. *Die Tageszeitung (taz)* (February 27).

Ferree, Myra Marx. 2006. "Angela Merkel: What Does it Mean to Run as a Woman?" *German Politics and Society* 24: 93–107.

———. 2003. "Resonance and Radicalism: Feminist Abortion Discourses in Germany and the United States." *American Journal of Sociology* 109: 304–44.

———. 1995a. "After the Wall: Explaining the Status of Women in the Former GDR." *Sociological Focus* 28, no. 1: 7–22.

———. 1995b. "Making Equality: The Women's Affairs Officers of the Federal Republic of Germany." In *Comparative State Feminism*, ed. Dorothy Stetson and Amy Mazur, 95–113. Thousand Oaks, CA: Sage Publications.

———. 1995c. "Patriarchies and Feminisms: The Two Women's Movements of Unified Germany." *Social Politics: International Studies in Gender, State & Society* 2, no. 1: 10–24.

———. 1994. "'The Time of Chaos was the Best': The Mobilization and Demobilization of the Women's Movement in East Germany." *Gender & Society* 8, no. 4: 597–623.

———. 1993. "The Rise and Fall of 'Mommy Politics': Feminism and German Unification." *Feminist Studies* 19, no. 1: 89–115.

———. 1990. "Beyond Separate Spheres: Feminism and Family Research." *Journal of Marriage and Family* 52, no. 4: 866–84.

———. 1984. "Feminism and the New Right." *Contemporary Sociology* 13, no. 2: 133–37.

———. 1983. "Housework: Rethinking the Costs and Benefits." In *Families, Politics and Public Policy: A Feminist Dialogue on Women and the State*, ed. Irene Diamond. New York: Longman.

Ferree, Myra Marx, and Beth Hess. 2000. *Controversy and Coalition: The New Women's Movement.* 3d ed. New York: Routledge.

Ferree, Myra Marx, and Patricia Yancey Martin. 1994. "Doing the Work of the Movement: Feminist Organizations." In *Feminist Organizations: Harvest of the New Women's Movement*, ed. Myra Marx Ferree and Patricia Yancey Martin. Philadelphia, PA: Temple University Press.

Ferree, Myra Marx, and Carol Mueller. 2004. "Feminism and the Women's Movement: A Global Perspective." In *The Blackwell Companion to Social Movements*, ed. David Snow, H. Soule, and Hanspeter Kriesi, 576–607. New York: Blackwell Publishers.

Ferree, Myra Marx, and Silke Roth. 1998a. "Gender, Class and the Interaction Among Social Movements: A Strike of West Berlin Daycare Workers." *Gender & Society* 12, no. 6: 626–48.

———. 1998b. "Kollektive Identität und Organizationskulturen: Theorien neuer sozialer Bewegungen aus amerikanischer Perspektive." *Forschungsjournal Neue Soziale Bewegungen* 11, no. 1: 80–91.

Ferree, Myra Marx, Dieter Rucht, William Gamson, and Jürgen Gerhards. 2002. *Shaping Abortion Discourse: Democracy and the Public Sphere in Germany and the United States.* New York: Cambridge University Press.

Ferree, Myra Marx, and Aili Tripp. 2006. *Global Feminism: Transnational Women's Activism, Organizing, and Human Rights.* New York: New York University Press.

Ferree, Myra Marx, and Brigitte Young. 1993. "Three Steps Back for Women: Gender, German Unification and University 'Reform.'" *PS: Political Science and Politics* 26, no. 2: 199–205.

Flavin, Jeanne. 2009. *Our Bodies, Our Crimes.* New York: New York University Press.

Flexner, Eleanor. 1959. *Century of Struggle: The Woman's Rights Movement in the United States.* Cambridge, MA: Belknap Press of Harvard University Press.

Footage Galore (formerly Alphamädchen). 2011. Accessed on June 28, 2011. http://www .germish.net/.

Frank, David John, Tara Hardinge, and Kassia Wosick-Correa. 2009. "The Global Dimensions of Rape-Law Reform: A Cross-National Study of Policy Outcomes." *American Sociological Review* 74, no. 2: 272–90.

Frankfurt Women's Health Center. 2011. Accessed on June 28, 2011. http://www.paritaet.org/ hessen/fgzn/abc/cms/front_content.php.

Fraser, Nancy. 1989. *Unruly Practices: Power, Discourse, and Gender in Contemporary Social Theory.* Minneapolis: University of Minnesota Press.

Fraser, Nancy, and Linda Gordon. 1994. "A Genealogy of Dependency: Tracing a Keyword of the U.S. Welfare State." *Signs* 19, no. 2 (Winter): 309–36.

Frauenakademie München. 2011. "Netzwerke und Projekte: Gender Mainstreaming." Accessed on June 28, 2011. http://www.frauenakademie.de/projekt/main/main.htm.

Frauenjahrbuch '76. 1976. München: Verlag Frauenoffensive.

Frauenjahrbuch '75. 1975. Herausgegeben und hergestellt von Frankfurter Frauen. Frankfurt: Roter Stern.

"Frauenpolitik zwischen Traum und Trauma." 1984. Paper presented at 7. Berliner Sommeruniversität für Frauen. Berlin.

FrauenUnion CSU. 2011. Accessed on June 28, 2011. http://www.fu-bayern.de/fulv/content/ index.htm.

Freeman, Jo. 1975. *The Politics of Women's Liberation: A Case Study of an Emerging Social Movement and its Relation to the Policy Process.* New York: McKay.

Gal, Susan, and Gail Kligman. 2000a. *The Politics of Gender After Socialism: A Comparative-Historical Essay.* Princeton, NJ: Princeton University Press.

———, eds. 2000b. *Reproducing Gender: Politics, Publics and Everyday Life After Socialism.* Princeton, NJ: Princeton University Press.

"Geld oder Leben." 1985. *Beiträge zur feministischen Theorie und Praxis,* 15–16.

Genderbüro. 2006. "Gender Manifesto." Accessed June 28, 2011. http://www.gender.de/ mainstreaming/.

GenderKompetenzZentrum. 2011. Accessed June 28, 2011. http://www.genderkompetenz.info/.

Gender Manifesto. 2006. Accessed June 28, 2011. http://www.gender-mainstreaming.org/.

Gerhard, Ute. 1999. *Atempause: Feminismus als demokratisches Projekt.* Frankfurt: Fischer Taschenbuch Verlag.

Gerhard, Ute, Elisabeth Hannover-Drück, and Romina Schmitter. 1979. *Die Frauen-Zeitung von Louise Otto.* Frankfurt: Syndikat.

Gerhards, Jürgen, and Mike S. Schäfer. 2006. *Die Herstellung einer öffentlichen Hegemonie. Humangenomforschung in der deutschen und der US-amerikanischen Presse.* Wiesbaden: Verlag für Sozialwissenschaften.

Giddens, Anthony. 1984. *The Constitution of Society: Outline of the Theory of Structuration.* Berkeley: University of California Press.

Gilligan, Carol. 1993. *In a Different Voice: Psychological Theory and Women's Development.* Cambridge, MA: Harvard University Press.

Glenn, Evelyn Nakano. 2002. *Unequal Freedom: How Race and Gender Shaped American Citizenship and Labor.* Cambridge, MA: Harvard University Press.

———. 1999. "The Social Construction of Race and Gender." In *Revisioning Gender*, ed. Myra Marx Ferree, Judith Lorber, and Beth Hess, 9. Landham, MD: AltaMira Press.

Goericke, Lisa-Lene. 1989. *Kommunale Frauengleichstellungsstellen—der gebremste Fortschritt.* Oldenburg: Bibliotheks- und Informationssystem der Universität Oldenburg.

Goldberg, Chad. 2007. *Citizens and Paupers: Relief, Rights, and Race from the Freedmen's Bureau to Workfare.* Chicago: University of Chicago Press.

Goldblatt: das Kulturmagazin. 2011. Accessed June 28, 2011. http://www.blattgold-berlin.de/index.htm.

Gornick, Janet, and Marcia Meyers. 2009. *Gender Equality: Transforming Family Divisions of Labor.* Cambridge: Polity Press.

———. 2005. *Families that Work: Policies for Reconciling Parenthood and Employment.* New York: Russell Sage Foundation.

Gravenhorst, Lerke, and Carmen Tatschmurat, eds. 1990. *Töchter-Fragen: NS-Frauen-Geschichte.* Freiburg: Kore.

Gresch, Nora, Leila Hadj-Abdou, Sieglinde Rosenberger, and Birgit Sauer. 2008. "Tu felix Austria? The Headscarf and the Politics of 'Non-issues.'" *Social Politics: International Studies in Gender, State & Society* 15, no. 4: 411–32.

Guenther, Katja. 2010. *Making Their Place: Feminism After Socialism in East Germany.* Stanford, CA: Stanford University Press.

———. 2006. "A Bastion of Sanity in a Crazy World: A Local Feminist Movement and the Reconstitution of Scale, Space, and Place in an Eastern German City." *Social Politics: International Studies in Gender, State & Society* 13, no. 4: 551–75.

Gunda-Werner-Institut für Feminismus und Geschlechterdemokratie. 2001. Accessed on June 28, 2011. http://www.gwi-boell.de/web/institut.html.

Habermas, Jürgen. 1962. *Strukturwandel der Öffentlichkeit.* Neuwied and Berlin: Luchterhand.

Hagemann, Karin. 2006. "Between Ideology and Economy: The 'Time Politics' of Child Care and Public Education in the Two Germanys." *Social Politics: International Studies in Gender, State & Society* 13, no. 2: 217–60.

Hagemann-White, Carol. 2000. "Von der Gleichstellung zur Geschlechtergerechtigkeit: Das paradoxe Unterfangen, sozialen Wandel durch strategisches Handeln in der Verwaltung herbeizuführen." Paper presented at Gender Mainstreaming, BzgA Forum Sexualaufklärung und Familienplanung, Nr. 4, Bremen.

———. 1988. "Die Frauenhausbewegung." In *Der grosse Unterschied: Die neue Frauenbewegung und die siebziger Jahre*, ed. Kristina von Soden. Berlin: Elefanten Press.

Haines, Herbert H. 1988. *Black Radicals and the Civil Rights Mainstream, 1954–1970.* Knoxville: University of Tennessee Press.

Hall, Peter, and David Soskice. 2001. *Varieties of Capitalism: The Institutional Foundations of Comparative Advantage.* Oxford and New York: Oxford University Press.

Hancock, Ange-Marie. 2007. "When Multiplication Doesn't Equal Quick Addition: Examining Intersectionality as a Research Paradigm." *Perspectives on Politics* 5, no. 1: 63–79.

Hank, Karsten, and Michaela Kreyenfeld. 2003. "A Multilevel Analysis of Child Care and the Transition to Motherhood in Western Germany." *Journal of Marriage and Family* 65, no. 3 (August): 584–96.

Hark, Sabine. 2005. *Dissidente Partizipation: eine Diskursgeschichte des Feminismus.* Frankfurt: Suhrkamp.

———. 1999. *Deviante Subjekte: Die paradoxe Politik der Identität.* Opladen: Leske + Budrich.

Harsch, Donna. 1997. "Society, the State, and Abortion in East Germany, 1950–1972." *American Historical Review* 102, no. 1: 53–84.

"Hausfrauen auch in Frauengruppen unterdrückt." 1975. *Frauenjahrbuch '75,* 120–29. Frankfurt: Verlag Roter Stern.

Hawley, Charles. 2008. "Adding Teeth—German Case to Test Boundaries of Discrimination Law." *Spiegel International Online* (July 4).

Hebenstreit, Sabine. 1984. "Rückständig, isoliert und hilfsbedürftig: das Bild ausländischer Frauen in der Deutschen Literatur." *IFG: Zeitschrift für Frauenforschung und Geschlechtstudien* 2: 24–38.

Helmer, Ulrike. 1988. "Frauenbuchläden in Frankfurt und anderswo." In *Der grosse Unterschied: Die neue Frauenbewegung und die siebziger Jahre,* ed. Kristina von Soden, 153–56. Berlin: Elefanten Press.

Helwerth, Ulrike, and Gislinde Schwarz. 1995. *Von Muttis und Emanzen: Feministinnen in Ost- und Westdeutschland.* Frankfurt: Fischer Taschenbuch Verlag.

Hervé, Florence, ed. 1995. *Geschichte der deutschen Frauenbewegung* (Beiträge von Wiebke Buchholz-Will). Köln: PapyRossa.

"Hexenjagd. Mann bläst wieder zum Halali auf abtreibdende Frauen in Memmingen und anderso." 1988. *EMMA* 9: 6.

hoch die Kampf dem. 20 Jahre Plakate autonomer Bewegungen. 1999. Hamburg, Berlin, and Gottingen: Verlag Libertäre Assoziation.

Hoecker, Beate. 2008. "50 Jahre Frauen in der Politik: späte Erfolge, aber nicht am Ziel." In *Aus Politik und Zeitgeschichte,* Beilage zur Wochenzeitschrift, DAS PARLAMENT (24–25). Accessed on June 28, 2011. http://www.bundestag.de/blickpunkt/104_Spezial/0402020.html.

Hohmann-Dennhardt, Christine, Marita Körner, and Reingard Zimmer. 2010. *Geschlechtergerechtigkeit: Festschrift für Heide Pfarr.* Baden-Baden: Nomos Verlagsgesellschaft.

Holst, Elke, and Jürgen Schupp. 1991. "Frauenerwerbstätigkeit in den neuen und alten Bundesländern: Befunde des Sozio-ökonomischen Panels." Deutsches Institut für Wirtschaftsforschung (DIW) Discussion Paper, 37.

Hoskyns, Cathrine. 1996. *Integrating Gender: Women, Law and Politics in the European Union.* London and New York: Verso.

Hull, Gloria, Patricia Scott, and Barbara Smith. 1982. *All the Women Are White, and All the Blacks Are Men, but Some of Us Are Brave: Black Women's Studies.* Old Westbury, NY: Feminist Press.

Inglehart, Ronald. 1981. "Post-Materialism in an Environment of Insecurity." *American Political Science Review* 75, no. 4: 880–900.

Institutionalizing Gender Equality: Commitment, Policy and Practice: A Global Source Book. 2000. Amsterdam: KIT Publishers.

Jaeckel, Monika, ed. 1988. *Mütter im Zentrum, Mütterzentrum: wo Frauen mit ihren Kindern leben.* Weinheim and München: Juventa-Verlag.

Jaggar, Alison. 1983. *Feminist Politics and Human Nature.* Totowa, NJ: Rowman and Allanheld.

Jahrbuchgruppe des Münchener Frauenzentrums, ed. 1977. *Frauenjahrbuch '77.* München: Verlag Frauenoffensive.

Jansen, Metchtild. 2004. "Wandel in der Arbeitsmarkt- und Sozialpolitik: Profitieren Frauen von den Veränderungen?" Paper presented at Feministisches Institut, Berlin. 15th Green Ladies' Lunch.

Jenness, Valerie. 2004. "Explaining Criminalization: From Demography and Status Politics to Globalization and Modernization." *Annual Review of Sociology* 30: 147–71.

Jenson, Jane. 2010. "Lost in Translation: The Social Investment Perspective and Gender Equality." *Social Politics: International Studies in Gender, State & Society* 16, no. 4: 446–83.

———. 2008. "Writing Women Out, Folding Gender In: The European Union 'Modernizes.'" *Social Politics: International Studies in Gender, State & Society* 15, no. 2: 131–53.

Jeska, Andrea. 2010. *Wir sind kein Mädchenverein: Frauen in der Bundeswehr.* München: Heyne Verlag.

Jochimsen, Luc. 1971. *§218. Dokumentation eines 100jährigen Elend.* Hamburg: Konkret Verlag.

Johnston, Jill. 1973. *Lesbian Nation: The Feminist Solution.* New York: Simon and Schuster.

Kahlau, Cordula. 1990. *Aufbruch! Frauenbewegung in der DDR.* München: Frauenoffensive.

Kappert, Ines. 2011. "Kein Gedöns: Der Ruf nach einer Frauenquote ist ein ökonomischer Imperativ" *Die Tageszeitung (taz),* January 31. Accessed July 7, 2001. http://www.taz.de/1/debatte/kommentar/artikel/1/kein-gedoens-1/.

Katsiaficas, George. 1997. *The Subversion of Politics: European Autonomous Social Movements and the Decolonialization of Everyday Life.* Atlantic Highlands, NJ: Humanities Press; reprinted Oakland, CA: AK Press, 2006.

Katzenstein, Mary F. 1999. *Faithful and Fearless: Moving Feminist Protest Inside the Church and Military.* Princeton, NJ: Princeton University Press.

Kavemann, Barbara. 2004. "Kooperation zum Schutz vor Gewalt in Ehe und Beziehungen: neue Entwicklungen und Strategien gegen Gewalt im Geschlechterverhältnis." *Aus Politik und Zeitgeschichte* B 52–53 (December 20): 3–9.

Keck, Margaret, and Kathryn Sikkink. 1998. *Activists Beyond Borders: Advocacy Networks in International Politics.* Ithaca, NY: Cornell University Press.

Kessler-Harris, Alice. 2003. *Out to Work: A History of Wage-earning Women in the US.* 2d ed. Oxford and New York: Oxford University Press.

Kirner, Ellen. 1993. "Leitbilder auf der Kippe." *Die Mitbestimmung* 6: 16–20.

Klaus, Lissi. 1988. "Frauen in der RAF." In *Der grosse Unterschied: Die neue Frauenbewegung und die siebziger Jahre,* ed. Kristina von Soden, 129–33. Berlin: Elefanten Press.

Klinger, Cornelia, and Gudrun-Axeli Knapp. 2008. *ÜberKreuzungen: Fremdheit, Ungleichheit, Differenz. Forum Frauen- und Geschlechterforschung*; Bd. 23; München: Westfälisches Dampfboot.

Knapp, Gudrun-Alexi. 2009. "Traveling Theories-Situated Questions: Feminist Theory in the German Context." In *Global Gender Research: Transnational Perspectives,* ed. Christine E. Bose and Minjeong Kim, 261–77. New York: Routledge.

Koch, Angelika. 2003. "Equal Employment Policy in Germany: Limited Results and Prospects for Reform." *Review of Policy Research* 20, no. 3: 443–57.

Kontos, Sylvia. 2004. "Grüne Frauen- und Geschlechterpolitik in Regierung und Partei— Stand und Perspektiven." Paper presented at Feministisches Institut, Berlin. 15th Green Ladies' Lunch.

———. 1989. "'Von heute an gibt's mein Programm'—Zum Verhältnis von Partizipation und Autonomie in der Politik der neuen Frauenbewegung." *Forschungsjournal Neue Soziale Bewegungen* 2 (Sonderheft): 52–65.

Koonz, Claudia. 2008. "The Muslim Headscarf: Veiled Threat or Religious Freedom?" Talk presented at Center for German and European Studies, University of Wisconsin, Madison.

———. 1987. *Mothers in the Fatherland: Women, the Family, and Nazi Politics.* New York: St. Martin's Press.

Korteweg, Anna, and Goekce Yurdakul. 2006. "Islam, Gender, and Immigrant Integration: Boundary Drawing in Discourses on Honour Killing in the Netherlands and Germany." *Ethnic and Racial Studies* 32, no. 2: 218–38.

Köster, Barbara. 1988. "Feministischer Alltag." In *Der grosse Unterschied: Die neue Frauenbewegung und die siebziger Jahren,* ed. Kristina von Soden, 6–19. Berlin: Elefanten Press.

Kreyenfeld, Michaela. 2003. "Crisis or Adaptation—Reconsidered: A Comparison of East and West German Fertility Patterns." *European Journal of Population* 19, no. 3: 309–21.

Krieger, Verena. 1988. "'. . . und rühmen sich öffentlich ihrer Verbrechen': Vom Kampf der Frauenbewegung gegen den §218." In *Der grosse Unterschied: Die neue Frauenbewegung und die siebziger Jahren,* ed. Kristina von Soden, 31–38. Berlin: Elefanten Press.

Kriesi, Hanspeter. 2004. "Political Context and Opportunity." In *The Blackwell Handbook to Social Movements,* ed. David Snow, H. Soule, and Hanspeter Kriesi. Malden, MA, and Oxford: Blackwell Publishing.

Kühnert, Hanno. 1989. "Freispruch im Abtreibungsprozeß: Am Ende der Kraft; Eine Kammer des Landgerichts Memmingen erkennt erstmals die Notlage einer Frau an." *Die Zeit* (February 10).

Kurz, Demi. 1995. *For Richer, For Poorer: Mothers Confront Divorce.* New York: Routledge.

Lang, Sabine. 2009. "Assessing Advocacy: European Transnational Women's Networks and Gender Mainstreaming." *Social Politics: International Studies in Gender, State & Society* 16, no. 3: 327–57.

———. 2007. "Gender Governance in Post-Unification Germany: Between Institutionalization, Deregulation, and Privatisation." In *Changing State Feminism,* ed. Johanna Kantola and Joyce Outshoorn, 171–98. London: Palgrave Macmillan.

———. 1997. "The NGO-ization of Feminism." In *Transitions, Environments, Translations: Feminisms in International Politics,* ed. Joan Scott, 101–20. New York and London: Routledge.

Lee, Kristen S., Duane F. Alwin, and Paula A. Tufis. 2007. "Beliefs About Women's Labour in the Reunified Germany, 1991–2004." *European Sociological Review* 23, no. 4: 487–503.

Lennox, Sara. 1989. "Feminist Scholarship and Germanistik." *The German Quarterly,* (Theme: Germanistik as German Studies, Interdisciplinary Theories and Methods) 62, no. 2 (Spring): 158–70.

Lenz, Ilse. 2009. "Geschlecht, Klasse, Migration und soziale Ungleichheit." In *Gender-Mobil? Vervielfältigung und Enträumlichung von Lebensformen—Transnationale Räume, Migration und Geschlecht,* ed. Helma Lutz, 25–68. Münster: Westfälisches Dampfboot.

———. 2008. *Die neue Frauenbewegung in Deutschland: Abschied vom kleinen Unterschied: eine Quellensammlung.* Wiesbaden: VS Verlag für Sozialwissenschaften.

Lesthaeghe, Ron. 2003. "The Second Demographic Transition in Western Countries: An Interpretation." In *Gender and Family Change in Industrialized Countries,* ed. Karen Oppenheim Mason and Ann-Magritt Jensen, 17–62. New York: Oxford University Press.

Levitsky, Sandra. 2007. "Niche Activism: Constructing a Unified Movement Identity in a Heterogeneous Organizational Field." *Mobilization* 12, no. 3: 271–86.

Lewis, Jane. 2006. "Work/Family Reconciliation, Equal Opportunities and Social Policies: The Interpretation of Policy Trajectories at the EU Level and the Meaning of Gender Equality." *Journal of European Public Policy* 13, no. 3: 420–37.

———. 1997. "Gender and Welfare Regimes: Further Thoughts." *Social Politics: International Studies in Gender, State & Society* 4, no. 2: 160–77.

———. 1992. "Gender and the Development of Welfare Regimes." *Journal of European Social Policy* 3: 159–73.

Lipset, Seymour Martin. 1996. *American Exceptionalism: A Double-edged Sword.* New York: W. W. Norton.

Liptak, A. 2010. "Court Under Roberts Is Most Conservative in Decades." *New York Times* (July 24).

"Lohn für Hausarbeit: Offener Brief an Alice." 1977. *Courage: Berliner Frauenzeitung* 2, 8: 38–40.

Lombardo, Emanuela, Petra Meier, and Mieke Verloo. 2009. *The Discursive Politics of Gender Equality: Stretching, Bending and Policy-Making.* London: Routledge.

Lorber, Judith. 2005. *Gender Inequality: Feminist Theories and Politics.* Oxford: Oxford University Press.

Loveman, Mara. 2001. "Nation-state Building, 'Race,' and the Production of Official Statistics: Brazil in Comparative Perspective." PhD, University of California, Los Angeles.

Lutz, Helma. 2010. *Fokus Intersektionalität. Bewegungen und Verortungen eines vielschichtigen Konzeptes.* Wiesbaden: VS Verlag.

———. 2002. *Crossing Borders and Shifting Boundaries. Gender, Identities and Networks.* Opladen: Leske + Budrich.

MacKinnon, Catharine. 1989. *Toward a Feminist Theory of the State.* Cambridge, MA: Harvard University Press.

———. 1987. *Feminism Unmodified: Discourses on Life and Law.* Cambridge, MA: Harvard University Press.

———. 1978. *Sexual Harassment of Working Women: A Case of Sex Discrimination.* New Haven, CT: Yale University Press.

Maier, Friedrike. 1993. "The Labour Market for Women and Employment Perspectives in the Aftermath of German Unification." *Cambridge Journal of Economics* 17 (September): 267–80.

———. 1992a. "Frauenerwerbstätigkeit in der DDR und BRD: Gemeinsamkeiten und Unterschiede." In *Ein Deutschland—Zwei Patriarchate?* ed. Gudrun-Axeli Knapp and Ursula Müller, 23–35. Bielefeld: University of Bielefeld Press.

———. 1992b. "The Transformation of the Service Sector in East Germany: A Case Study of the Banking Sector." Paper presented at International Working Conference on Labor Market Segmentation, Cambridge, England.

Maleck-Lewy, Eva. 1995. "Between Self-Determination and State Supervision: Women and the Abortion Law in Post-unification Germany." *Social Politics: International Studies in Gender, State & Society* 2, no. 1: 62–75.

Maleck-Lewy, Eva, and Myra Marx Ferree. 2000. "Talking About Women and Wombs: Discourse About Abortion and Reproductive Rights in the GDR During and After the 'Wende.'" In *Reproducing Gender: Politics, Publics and Everyday Life after Socialism,* ed. Susan Gal and Gail Kligman, 92–117. Princeton, NJ: Princeton University Press.

Mandel, Hadas, and Moshe Semyonov. 2005. "Family Policies, Wage Structures, and Gender Gaps: Sources of Earnings Inequality in 20 Countries." *American Sociological Review* 70, no. 6: 949–67.

Markovits, A. S., and P. S. Gorski. 1993. *The German Left: Red, Green and Beyond.* Cambridge: Polity Press.

Marshall, T. H. 1950. *Citizenship and Social Class.* Cambridge: Cambridge University Press.

Marshall, T. H., and Thomas B. Bottomore. 1964. *Class, Citizenship, and Social Development: Essays,* with an introduction by Seymour Martin Lipset. Garden City, NY: Doubleday.

Martin, Patricia Yancey. 2003. "'Said and Done' vs. 'Saying and Doing': Gendering Practices, Practicing Gender at Work." *Gender & Society* 17: 342–66.

May, Martha. 1982. "The Historical Problem of the Family Wage: The Ford Motor Company and the Five Dollar Day." *Feminist Studies* 8, no. 2: 399–424.

Mayer, Susanne. 2005. "Weil sie eine Frau ist/PRO." *Die Zeit* (August 25).

Mayer, Victoria. 2007. "Contracting Citizenship: Shifting Public Boundaries in the Context of Welfare Reform." PhD, Sociology, University of Wisconsin.

McAdam, Doug, John McCarthy, and Mayer Zald. 1996. *Comparative Perspectives on Social Movements.* New York: Cambridge University Press.

McBride, Dorothy E., and Mazur, Amy eds. 2010. *The Politics of State Feminism: Innovation in Comparative Research.* Philadelphia, PA: Temple University Press.

McCall, Leslie. 2005. "The Complexity of Intersectionality." *Signs* 30, no. 3: 1771–800.

Melzer, Patricia. 2009. "'Death in the Shape of a Young Girl': Feminist Responses to Media Representations of Women Terrorists during the 'German Autumn' of 1977." *International Feminist Journal of Politics* 11, no. 1: 35–62.

Meulemann, Heiner. 2002. "Werte und Wertewandel in Vereinten Deutschland." *Bundeszentral für politische Bildung (bpb): Aus Politik und Zeitgeschichte,* B 37–38.

Meulenbelt, Anja. 1978. *Die Scham ist vorbei: eine persönliche Geschichte.* München: Verlag Frauenoffensive.

Meuser, Michael. 1998. *Geschlecht und Männlichkeit. Soziologische Theorie und kulturelle Deutungsmuster.* Opladen: Leske + Budrich.

Meyer, Alfred G. 1985. *The Feminism and Socialism of Lily Braun.* Bloomington: Indiana University Press.

Michel, Sonya. 1999. *Children's Interests/Mothers' Rights: The Shaping of America's Child Care Policy.* New Haven, CT: Yale University Press.

Mies, Maria. 1986. *Patriarchy and Accumulation on a World Scale.* London: Zed Books.

Miethe, Ingrid. 1999a. *Frauen in der DDR-Opposition: Lebens- und kollektivgeschichtliche Verläufe in einer Frauenfriedensgruppe.* Opladen: Leske + Budrich.

———. 1999b. "From 'Mother of the Revolution' to 'Fathers of Unification': Concepts of Politics Among Women Activists Following German Unification." *Social Politics: International Studies in Gender, State & Society* 6, no. 1: 1–22.

Miethe, Ingrid, and Silke Roth, eds. 2003. *Europas Töchter: Traditionen, Erwartungen und Strategien von Frauenbewegungen in Europa.* Opladen: Leske + Budrich.

Milan Women's Bookstore Collective. 1990. *Sexual Difference—A Theory of Social-Symbolic Practice.* Trans. Patricia Cicogna and Teresa De Lauretis. Bloomington: Indiana University Press.

Mill, John Stuart. 1869. *The Subjection of Women.* Critical edition by Edward Alexander, 2001. New Brunswick, NJ: Transaction.

Mitscherlich, Margarete. 1992. *Die friedfertige Frau: eine psychoanalytische Untersuchung zur Aggression der Geschlechter.* Frankfurt: Fischer-Taschenbuch-Verlag.

Mittman, Elizabeth. 2007. "Gender, Citizenship, and the Public Sphere in Postunification Germany: Experiments in Feminist Journalism." *Signs* 32, no. 2: 759–92.

Moeller, Robert. 1993. *Protecting Motherhood: Women and the Family in Postwar West Germany.* Berkeley: University of California Press.

Molyneux, Maxine. 1985. "Mobilization Without Emancipation? Women's Interests, the State, and Revolution in Nicaragua." *Feminist Studies* 11, no. 2: 227–54.

Morgan, Kimberly. 2009. "The Political Path to a Dual-Earner/Dual-Caregiver Society:

Pitfalls and Possibilities." In *Gender Equality: Transforming Family Divisions of Labor*, ed. Janet Gornick and Marcia Meyers. Cambridge: Polity Press.

Morgan, Robin. 1970. *Sisterhood Is Powerful*. New York: Random House.

Morgner, Irmtraud. 1974. *Leben und Abenteuer der Trobadora Beatriz nach Zeugnissen ihrer Spielfrau Laura: Roman in 13 Büchern und 7 Intermezzos* [The Life and Experiences of the Troubadour Beatrice]. Berlin and Weimar: Aufbau-Verlag.

Morrison, Susan S. 1992. "The Feminization of the German Democratic Republic in Political Cartoons, 1989–90." *Journal of Popular Culture* 25, no. 4: 35–51.

Mushaben, Joyce Marie. 2004. "'Die Freiheit, die ich meine . . .': An American View of the Kopftuch Debate." *femina politica: Zeitschrift für feministische Politikwissenschaft* 13, no. 1: 98–104.

Myrdal, Gunnar. 1969. *An American Dilemma: The Negro Problem and Modern Democracy*. New York: Harper and Row.

Nagelschmidt, Ilse. 1994. "Frauenliteratur der siebziger Jahre als ,Brennspiegel' der Widersprüche und Ambivalenzen weiblicher Emanzipation in der DDR." In *EigenArtige Ostfrauen: Frauenemanzipation in der DDR und den neuen Bundesländern*, ed. Birgit Bütow and Heidi Stecker, 63–74. Bielefeld: Kleine Verlag.

Nave-Herz, Rosemarie. 1994. "Frauen-Zeitung Programm von 4.April 1849." In *Die Geschichte der Frauenbewegung in Deutschland*, 12. Opladen: Leske + Budrich.

Netzwerk Gender Training, ed. 2004. *Geschlechtsverhältnisse bewegen Erfahrungen mit Gender Training*. Königstein/Taunus: Ulrike Helmer Verlag.

Neubeck, Kenneth, and Noel Cazenave. 2001. *Welfare Racism: Playing the Race Card Against America's Poor*. New York: Routledge.

"Neues Deutschlandgefühl—Wir sind Kanzlerin." 2005. *Der Spiegel* (November 23).

Nickel, Hildegard Maria. 1990. "Gleschlechtertrennung durch Arbeitsteilung:Berufs- und Familienarbeit in der DDR." *Feministische Studien* 8, no. 1: 10–19.

O'Connor, Julia. 2005. "Employment-Anchored Social Policy, Gender Mainstreaming and the Open Method of Policy Coordination in the European Union." *European Societies* 7, no. 1: 27–52.

O'Connor, Julia S., Ann Shola Orloff, and Sheila Shaver. 1999. *States, Markets, Families: Gender, Liberalism and Social Policy in Australia, Canada, Great Britain and the United States*. Cambridge: Cambridge University Press.

Offen, Karen 1988. "Defining Feminism: A Comparative Historical Approach." *Signs* 14, no. 1: 119–57.

Oguntoye, Katharina, ed. 2007. *Farbe bekennen: afro-deutsche Frauen auf den Spuren ihrer Geschichte*. Berlin: Orlanda.

Olds, Kris. 2010. *Bibliometrics, Global Rankings, and Transparency*. Accessed on June 28, 2011. http://globalhighered.wordpress.com/2010/06/23/bibliometrics-global-rankings-and-transparency/.

Oliver, Pamela, and Hank Johnston. 2000. "What a Good Idea! Frames and Ideologies in Social Movement Research." *Mobilization* 5, no. 1: 37–54.

Omi, Michael, and Howard Winant. 1994. *Racial Formation in the United States: From the 1960s to the 1990s*. 2d ed. New York: Routledge.

Ostner, Ilona. 1994. "Back to the Fifties: Gender and Welfare in Unified Germany." *Social Politics: International Studies in Gender, State & Society* 1: 32–59.

———. 1993. "Slow Motion: Women Work and Family in Germany." In *Women and Social Policies in Europe*, ed. Jane Lewis, 92–115. Aldershot: Elgar.

Outshoorn, Joyce, and Johanna Kantola. 2007. *Changing State Feminism*. London: Palgrave MacMillan.

Parvez, Fareen. Forthcoming. "Debating the Burqa in France: The Antipolitics of Islamic Revival." *Qualitative Sociology* 34, no. 2: 287–312.

Pascale, Celine-Marie. 2007. *Making Sense of Race, Class and Gender: Commonsense, Power and Privilege in the United States.* New York: Routledge.

Pasero, Ursula, and Ursula Pfäfflin, eds. 1986. *Neue Mütterlichkeit: Ortsbestimmungen.* Gütersloh: Verlagshaus Mohn.

Pedriana, Nicholas. 2006. "From Protective to Equal Treatment: Legal Framing Processes and Transformation of the Women's Movement in the 1960s." *American Journal of Sociology* III, no. 6 (May): 1718–61.

———. 2004. "Help Wanted NOW: Legal Resources, the Women's Movement, and the Battle Over Sex-Segregated Job Advertisements." *Social Problems* 51, no. 2: 182–201.

Penrose, Virginia. 1993. "The Political Participation of GDR Women During the Wende." *Studies in GDR Culture and Society* 11/12: 37–52.

———. 1990. "Vierzig Jahre SED-Frauenpolitik: Ziele, Strategien und Ergebnissen." *IFG: Frauenforschung* 8, no. 4: 60–77.

Pfarr, Heide. 1985. "Quotierung und Rechtswissenschaft." In *Mehr als nur gleicher Lohn: Handbuch zur beruflichen Förderung von Frauen,* ed. Herta Däubler-Gmelin, 86–97. Hamburg: VSA Verlag.

Phillips, Anne. 1998. "Democracy and Representation: Or, Why Should it Matter Who our Representatives Are?" In *Feminism and Politics,* ed. A. Phillips, 224–40. Oxford: Oxford University Press.

———. 1987. "Divided Loyalties: Dilemmas of Sex and Class." *Capital & Class* 11, no. 2: 182–85.

Pinl, Claudia. 1987. "Mütterfrust gegen Emanzen." *Die Tageszeitung (taz)* (March 23).

———. 1977. *Das Arbeitnehmerpatriarchat: Die Frauenpolitik der Gewerkschaften.* Köln: Kiepenheuer & Witsch.

Plogstedt, Sibylle. 1983. "Wenn Autonomie zum Dogma wird: alternativer Frauenrat." *Courage: Berliner Frauenzeitung* 8, 12: 54–60.

———. 1981. "Staatsgelder für Frauenprojekte: die kleine Lohn-für-Hausarbeits-Lösung." *Courage: Berliner Frauenzeitung* 6, no. 2: 20–22.

———. 1979. "Kongreßdokumentation: Einleitungsreferat zum Frauenkongreß gegen Atom und Militär am 15./16.9.1979 in Köln von Sibylle Plogstedt." *Courage: Berliner Frauenzeitung* 4, no. 11: 58.

Preuß, Roland. 2008. "Diskriminierung—Schwanger, türkisch, degradiert." *Süddeutsche Zeitung* (October 30).

Putsch, Luise. 1990. *Alle Menschen werden Schwester.* Frankfurt: Suhrkamp Verlag.

Quadagno, Jill. 1994. *The Color of Welfare.* Oxford: Oxford University Press.

Quataert, Jean. 2001. "Socialisms, Feminisms and Agency: A Long View." *Journal of Modern History* 73, 1 (Sept.): 603–16.

———. 1979. *Reluctant Feminists in German Social Democracy, 1885–1917.* Princeton, NJ: Princeton University Press.

Raab, Heike. 2004. "'Queer Meets Gender': Prekäre Beziehung oder gelungene Koalition? Zum Verhältnis von Queer Theory und Genderforschung." In *Geschlechterverhältnisse: Analysen aus Wissenschaft, Politik und Praxis,* ed. Hella Hertzfeldt, Katrin Schäfgen, and Silke Veth, 56–65. Berlin: Karl Dietz Verlag.

Ramirez, Francisco O., Yasemin Soysal, and Suzanne Shanahan. 1997. "The Changing Logic of Political Citizenship: Cross-National Acquisition of Women's Suffrage Rights, 1890 to 1990." *American Sociological Review* 62, no. 5: 735–45.

"Rat-los." 1984. *EMMA* 5: 30.

Rees, Teresa. 2002. "The Politics of 'Mainstreaming' Gender Equality." In *The Changing Politics of Gender Equality in Britain*, ed. E. Breitenbach, A. Brown, F. Mackay, and J. Webb, 45–69. Basingstoke, England: Palgrave.

Rentmeister, Cillie. 1988. "Frauenwelten—fern, vergangen, fremd? Die Matriarchatsdebatte und die neue Frauenbewegung." In *Kulturkontakt, Kulturkonflikt: zur Erfahrung des Fremden*, ed. Ina-Maria Greverus, Konrad Köstlin, and Heinz Schilling, 443–60. Frankfurt: Institut für Kulturanthropologie und Europäische Ethnologie, Universität Frankfurt am Main.

Research Network on Gender Politics and the State (RNGS). 2011. Accessed on June 28, 2011. http://libarts.wsu.edu/polisci/rngs/.

Rich, Adrienne. 1980. "Compulsory Heterosexuality and Lesbian Existence." *Signs* 5, no. 4: 631–60.

Richelmann, Doris. 1991. *Gleichstellungsstellen, Frauenförderung, Quotierung: Entwicklung und Diskurs aktueller frauenpolitischer Ansätze*. Hannover: Kleine Verlag.

Richter, Christine. 2005. "Frauen zeigen häusliche Gewalt öfter an." *Berliner Zeitung* (March 9): 19.

Roberts, Dorothy. 1997. *Killing the Black Body: Race, Reproduction and the Meaning of Liberty*. New York: Pantheon Books.

Roggenkamp, Viola. 1983. "Grüner Alltag." *EMMA* 6 (June): 18.

Roloff, Juliane. 1990. "Vereintes Deutschland, geteilte Frauengesellschaft?" *Deutsches Institut für Wirtschaftsforschung (DIW) Wochenbericht*, 40.

Rosen, Ellen Israel. 1987. *Bitter Choices: Blue-Collar Women in and out of Work*. Chicago: University of Chicago Press.

Rossi, Alice. 1982. *Feminists in Politics: A Panel Analysis of the First National Women's Conference*. New York: Academic Press.

———. 1973. *The Feminist Papers: From Adams to de Beauvoir*. New York: Columbia University Press.

Roth, Benita. 2004. *Separate Roads to Feminism: Black, Chicana, and White Feminist Movements in America's Second Wave*. New York: Cambridge University Press.

Roth, Silke. 2008. *Gender Politics in the Expanding European Union: Mobilization, Inclusion, Exclusion*. New York and Oxford: Berghahn Books.

———. 2007. "Sisterhood and Solidarity? Women's Organizations in the Expanded European Union." *Social Politics: International Studies in Gender, State & Society* 14, no. 4: 460–87.

———. 2003. *Building Movement Bridges: The Coalition of Labor Union Women*. Boulder, CO: Westview.

Rottmann, Susan, and Myra Marx Ferree. 2008. "Citizenship and Intersectionality: German Feminist Debates about Headscarf and Anti-discrimination Laws." *Social Politics: International Studies in Gender, State & Society* 15, no. 4: 481–513.

Rubery, Jill. 2002. "Gender Mainstreaming and Gender Equality in the EU Employment Strategy." *Industrial Relations Journal* 33, no. 5: 30–56.

Rucht, Dieter. 1994. *Modernisierung und neue soziale Bewegungen: Deutschland, Frankreich und USA im Vergleich*. Frankfurt: Campus Verlag.

Rudd, Elizabeth C. 2000. "Reconceptualizing Gender in Postsocialist Transformation." *Gender & Society* 14, no. 4: 517–39.

Rupp, Leila. 1997. *Worlds of Women: The Making of an International Women's Movement*. Princeton, NJ: Princeton University Press.

———. 1978. *Mobilizing Women for War: German and American Propaganda, 1939–1945*. Princeton, NJ: Princeton University Press.

Rush, Florence. 1989. *Das bestgehütete Geheimnis: Sexueller Kindesmißbrauch.* Trans. Alexandra Bartoszko. Berlin: Orlanda-Frauenverlag.

Ryan, Barbara. 1992. *Feminism and the Women's Movement: Dynamics of Change in a Social Movement.* London and New York: Routledge.

Sainsbury, Diane. 1999. *Gender and Welfare State Regimes.* Oxford and New York: Oxford University Press.

Salzinger, Leslie. 2003. *Genders in Production: Making Workers in Mexico's Global Factories.* Berkeley: University of California Press.

Sander, Helke. 1998. "Überlegung zur Bewegung." In *Was Frauen bewegt und Was sie bewegen,* ed. Ingeborg Mues, 283–303. Frankfurt: Fischer.

Sänger, Eva. 2005. *Begrenzte Teilhabe. Ostdeutsche Frauenbewegung und Zentraler Runder Tisch in der DDR. Politik der Geschlechterverhältnisse,* Bd. 29. Frankfurt and New York: Campus Verlag.

Sawer, Marian. 1990. *Sisters in Suits: Women and Public Policy in Australia.* Sydney: Allen & Unwin.

Schaeffer-Hegel, Barbara, ed. 1990. *Vater Staat und seine Frauen: Beiträge zur politischen Theorie.* Pfaffenweiler: Centaurus-Verlagsgesellschaft.

Schenk, Herrad. 1983. *Frauen kommen ohne Waffen.* München: Beck.

———. 1980. *Die feministische Herausforderung: 150 Jahre Frauenbewegung in Deutschland.* München: Beck.

Schuldt, K. 1993. "Die Spaltung des Arbeitmarktes in geschlechtsspezifische Berufe." *Die Mitbestimmung,* (June): 21–27.

Schulz, Dagmar. 1991. *Das Geschlecht läuft immer mit . . . Die Arbeitswelt von Professorinnen und Professoren* (mit Carol Hagemann-White). Pfaffenweiler: Centaurus-Verlagsgesellschaft.

Schwarzer, Alice. 2009. "Das Kanzlerinnen Interview." *EMMA* 5 (September/October): 20–26.

———. 2000. *Man wird nicht als Frau geboren.* Köln: Kiepenheuer & Witsch.

———. 1985. "CDU-Parteitag." *EMMA* 5 (May): 21–27.

———. 1981. *So fing es an! 10 Jahre Frauenbewegung.* Köln: EMMA-Frauenbuchverlags GmbH.

Schwenke, Helen. 2000. "Frauenbewegungen in der Migration: Zur Selbstorganisierung von Migrantinnen in der Bundesrepublik." In *Frauenbewegungen weltweit: Aufbrüche, Kontinuitäten, Veränderungen,* ed. Ilse Lenz, Michiko Mae, and Karin Klose, 133–66. Opladen: Leske + Budrich.

Scott, Joan Wallach. 2005. *Parité!: Sexual Equality and the Crisis of French Universalism.* Chicago: University of Chicago Press.

Scott, Joan Wallach, and Judith Butler. 1992. *Feminists Theorize the Political.* New York: Routledge.

Sewell, William H., Jr. 1992. "A Theory of Structure: Duality, Agency, and Transformation." *American Journal of Sociology* 98, no. 1 (July): 1–29.

Sillge, Ursula. 1991. *Un-Sichtbare Frauen: Lesben und ihre Emanzipation in der DDR.* Berlin: Links.

Sklar, Kathryn Kish, Anja Schüler, and Susan Strasser, eds. 1998. *Social Justice Feminists in the United States and Germany: A Dialogue in Documents, 1885–1933.* Ithaca, NY: Cornell University Press.

Skocpol, Theda. 1992. *Protecting Soldiers and Mothers: The Political Origins of Social Policy in the United States.* Cambridge, MA: Belknap Press of Harvard University Press.

Snyder, Margaret. 2006. "Unlikely Godmother: The UN and the Global Women's Movement." In *Global Feminism: Transnational Women's Activism, Organizing, and Human Rights,* ed. Myra Marx Ferree and Aili Mari Tripp, 24–50. New York: New York University Press.

Sollwedel, Inge. 1982. "Von einer, die auszog, das Fürchten zu lernen." *EMMA* 3: 32–37.

Song, Sarah, ed. 2007. *Justice, Gender, and the Politics of Multiculturalism.* Cambridge and New York: Cambridge University Press.

Sperling, Valerie. 1999. *Organizing Women in Contemporary Russia: Engendering Transition.* Cambridge: Cambridge University Press.

Spernbauer, Christian. 2008. *Parteien in Einzelportraits: Die Partei des Demokratischen Sozialismus (PDS).* Norderstedt: Grin Verlag.

Stahmer, Anne. 1977. "Frauenprojekte-Frauengeschäfte." In *Frauenjahrbuch '77*, 124–43. München: Verlag Frauenoffensive.

———. 1976. "Feministische Tendenzen." In *Frauenjahrbuch '76*, 63–79. München: Frauenoffensive.

Stefan, Verena. 1979. *Shedding.* Trans. Johanna Moore London: Women's Press.

Stegman, Christiane. 2004. *Interaktion und Dominanz: Konflikte in der Zusammenarbeit am Beispiel von Frauenprojekten.* Hamburg: Institut für angewandte Sozialforschung.

Steinmetz, George. 2007. *The Devil's Handwriting: Precoloniality and the German Colonial State in Qingdao, Samoa, and Southwest Africa.* Chicago: University of Chicago Press.

Stetson, Dorothy McBride, and Amy Mazur. 1995. *Comparative State Feminism.* Thousand Oaks, CA: Sage Publishers.

Stiehm, Judith. 1982. "The Protected, the Protector, the Defender." *Women's Studies International Forum* 5, nos. 3–4: 367–76.

Stratigaki, Maria. 2004. "The Cooptation of Gender Concepts in EU Policies: The Case of 'Reconciliation of Work and Family.'" *Social Politics* 11, no. 1 (Spring): 30–56.

Strobl, Ingrid. 1988. "Zwischen Kürbisbrüsten und Entmannung: Bücher von Frauen für Frauen." In *Der grosse Unterschied: Die neue Frauenbewegung und die siebziger Jahre*, ed. Kristina von Soden, 134–47. Berlin: Berlin: Elefanten Press.

Swidler, Ann. 1986. "Culture in Action: Symbols and Strategies." *American Sociological Review* 51, no. 2 (April): 273–86.

"Symbol der Frauenbewegung und Mahnmal für die Opfer." 1986. *Frankfurter Allgemeine Zeitung* (April 28).

Tarrant, Shira. 2006. *When Sex Became Gender.* New York: Routledge.

Taylor, Verta, and Leila J. Rupp. 1993. "Women's Culture and Lesbian Feminist Activism: A Reconsideration of Cultural Feminism." *Signs* 19, no. 1 (Autumn): 32–61.

———. 1990. *Survival in the Doldrums: The American Women's Rights Movement, 1945 to the 1960s.* Columbus: Ohio State University Press.

Tekin, Ayse. 1994. "Unterschiede wahren, Zusammenarbeit möglich machen." *Beiträge zur feministischen Theorie und Praxis (FrauenStreik, Streitfragen)* 17, no. 36: 103–10.

Thietz, Kristen. 1992. *Ende der Selbstverständlichkeit: Die Abschaffung des §218 in der DDR.* Berlin: BasisDruck.

Thistle, Susan. 2006. *From Marriage to Market: The Transformation of Women's Lives and Work.* Berkeley and Los Angeles: University of California Press.

Thönnessen, Werner. 1973. *The Emancipation of Women: The Rise and Decline of the Women's Movement in German Social Democracy, 1863–1933.* Trans. Joris de Bres. London: Pluto Press.

Thürmer-Rohr, Christina. 1988. *Vagabundinnen: feministische Essays.* Berlin: Orlanda Frauenverlag.

———. 1983. *Gegen welchen Krieg—für welchen Frieden?* Köln: Eigenverlag des Vereins Sozialwissenschaftliche Forschung und Praxis für Frauen.

Tilly, Louise, and Joan W. Scott. 1978. *Women, Work, and Family.* New York: Holt, Rinehart and Winston.

Tobin, Robert. 1999. "Queer in Germany: Sexual Culture and National Discourses." Paper presented at "50 Years of Germany Through a Gendered Lens," Chapel Hill, North Carolina.

Transatlantic Applied Research in Gender Equity Training (TARGET). Accessed on June 28, 2011. http://www.sscc.wisc .edu/TARGET/index.htm.

Trappe, Heike, and Rachel Rosenfeld. 2004. "Occupational Sex Segregation in the Former East and West Germanies." *Work and Occupations* 31, no. 2: 155–92.

Tripp, Aili Mari. 2006. "The Evolution of Transnational Feminisms: Consensus, Conflict, and New Dynamics." In *Global Feminism: Transnational Women's Activism, Organizing, and Human Rights,* ed. Aili Tripp and Myra Marx Ferree, 51–78. New York: New York University Press.

Tripp, Aili Mari, and Alice Kang. 2008. "The Global Impact of Quotas: On the Fast Track to Equal Legislative Representation." *Comparative Political Studies* 41, no. 3: 338–61.

Ullrich, Kerstin. 1998. "Soziale Bewegung und kollektive Identität: Der Diskurs über Abtreibung und Reproduktionstechnologien als Beispiel feministischer Identitätskonstruction." PhD, Political Science, European University Institute.

Ulrich, Anne Hampele. 2000. *Der Unabhangige Frauenverband: Ein frauenpolitisches Experiment im deutschen Vereinigungesprozeß.* Berlin: Berliner Debatte, Wissenschafts-Verlag.

United Nations. 1997. "Gender Mainstreaming: Extract from the Report of the Economic and Social Council for 1997." Chapter IV, Coordination Segment (A/52/3, 18 September 1997). Accessed on June 28, 2011. http://www.un.org/womenwatch/daw/csw/GMS.PDF.

"Unterstützt die Frauenhäuser!" 1985. *EMMA* 1: 22–23.

U.S. Department of Labor. 1992. *Employment in Perspective: Women in the Labor Force.* Washington, DC: Bureau of Labor Statistics, 834.

"Vätermanifest: Leben mit Kindern—Väter werden laut." 1987. *EMMA* 5: 26.

Vogel, Lise. 1993. *Mothers on the Job: Maternity Policy in the US Workplace.* New Brunswick, NJ: Rutgers University Press.

von Ludwig, Udo, and Cordula Meyer. 2005. "Weil sie kein Mädchen ist." *Der Spiegel* (September 26).

von Rahden, Till. 2008. "'Germ Cells'—The Private Realm as a Political Project in the Bonn Republic: On Some Similarities Between the Fifties and the late Sixties." Paper presented at Conference on Gender and the Long Postwar, the U.S. and the Two Germanys, 1945–89, German Historical Institute.

von Wahl, Angelika. 2008. "From Family to Reconciliation Policy: How the Grand Coalition Reforms the German Welfare State." *German Politics and Society* 26, no. 3: 25–49.

———. 1999. *Gleichstellungsregime: berufliche Gleichstellung von Frauen in den USA und in der Bundesrepublik Deutschland.* Opladen: Leske + Budrich.

Vultejus, Ulrich. 1990. "Das Urteil von Memmingen." In *Das Urteil von Memmingen: Vom Elend der Indikation,* ed. Ulrich Vultejus, 9–34. Köln: Volksblatt Verlag.

Walby, Sylvia. 2011. *The Future of Feminism.* New York: Wiley.

———. 2009. *Globalization and Inequalities: Complexity and Contested Modernities.* London: Sage Publications.

———. 2004. *The Cost of Domestic Violence.* London: Women and Equality Unit, Department of Trade and Industry. Accessed on July 5, 2011. http://www.devon.gov.uk/de/text/cost_of_dv_report_sept04.pdf. Or; Accessed on June 28, 2011. http://www.equalities .gov.uk/pdf/Summ%20cost%20of%20domestic%20violence%20Sep%2004.pdf.

Wander, Maxie. 1977. *Guten Morgen, du Schöne: Protokolle nach Tonband.* Berlin: Buchverlag Der Morgen.

Waring, Marilyn. 1988. *If Women Counted: A New Feminist Economics.* San Francisco: Harper and Row.

Wegehaupt-Schneider, Ingeborg. 1988. "Das Private ist politisch: Selbsterfahrungsgruppen." In *Der grosse Unterschied: Die neue Frauenbewegung und die siebziger Jahre,* ed. Kristina von Soden, 17–19. Berlin: Elefanten Press.

"Weiberräte contra Feminismus." 1984. *Die Tageszeitung (taz)* (October 17).

WeiberWirtschaft eG. 2011. "Informieren: Geschichte: Chronologie." Accessed June 28, 2011. http://www.weiberwirtschaft.de/informieren/genossenschaft/geschichte/chronologie/.

Weigel, Sigrid, and Carol Ludtke Prigan. 1992. "Notes on the Constellation of Gender and Cultural Identity in Contemporary Germany." *New German Critique* 55: 45–50.

Weldon, Laurel. 2002. *Protest, Policy, and the Problem of Violence Against Women: A Cross-national Comparison.* Pittsburgh, PA: University of Pittsburgh Press.

White Ribbon Campaign Europe. 2011. "Daphne Program from the European Commission." Accessed on June 28, 2011. http://www.eurowrc.org/01.eurowrc/04.eurowrc_en/03.en_ewrc.htm.

Whittier, Nancy. 1995. *Feminist Generations: The Persistence of the Radical Women's Movement.* Philadelphia, PA: Temple University Press.

Wiliarty, Sarah Elise. 2010. *The CDU and the Politics of Gender in Germany: Bringing Women to the Party.* Cambridge: Cambridge University Press.

Wilken, Linda. 1992. *Einmischung erlaubt? Kommunale Frauenbüros in der Bundesrepublik.* Hamburg: VSA-Verlag.

Wobbe, Teresa, and Ingrid Biermann. 2009. *Von Rom nach Amsterdam: Die Metamorphosen des Geschlechts in der Europäischen Union.* Wiesbaden: VS—Verlag der Sozialwissenschaften.

Wolf, Christa. 1979. *Kein Ort, Nirgends.* Berlin and Weimar: Aufbau-Verlag.

Women in Congress. 2011. "Historical Data: Women Representatives and Senators by Congress, 1917-Present." Accessed on June 28, 2011. http://womenincongress.house.gov/historical-data/.

Women: Frauenseiten im Internet. 2011. "Wirtschaft." Accessed on June 28, 2011. http://www.woman.de/katalog/wirtschaft/index.html.

Women and Life on Earth (WLOE). 2011. "Women and Globalization: 16 October 2003, 'World Food Day', Berlin." Accessed on June 28, 2011. http://www.wloe.org/WLOE-en/information/globalization/16oktberlin.html.

Women's Budget Group. 2011. Accessed on June 28, 2011. http://www.wbg.org.uk.

Woodward, Alison. 2003. "European Gender Mainstreaming: Promises and Pitfalls of Transformative Policy." *Review of Policy Research* 20, no. 1: 65–88.

Wuerth, Andrea. 1999. "National Politics/Local Identities: Abortion Rights Activism in Post-Wall Berlin." *Feminist Studies* 25, no. 3: 601–31.

Young, Brigitte. 1999. *Triumph of the Fatherland: German Unification and the Marginalization of Women.* Ann Arbor: University of Michigan Press.

Yuval-Davis, Nira. 1997. *Gender and Nation.* London and Thousand Oaks, CA: Sage Publications.

Zerilli, Linda. 2005. *Feminism and the Abyss of Freedom.* Chicago: University of Chicago Press.

Zippel, Kathrin. 2009. "The Missing Link for Promoting Gender Equality: Work-Family and Anti-discrimination Policies." In *Gender Equality: Transforming Family Divisions of Labor,* ed. Janet Gornick and Marcia Meyers. Cambridge: Polity Press.

————. 2007. "The European Union 2002 Directive on Sexual Harassment: A Feminist Success?" *Comparative Political Studies* 7, no. 1: 139–57.

————. 2006. *The Politics of Sexual Harassment: A Comparative Study of the United States, the European Union and Germany.* Cambridge and New York: Cambridge University Press.

————. 2004. "Transnational Advocacy Networks and Policy Cycles in the European Union: The Case of Sexual Harassment." *Social Politics: International Studies in Gender, State & Society* 11, no. 1: 57–85.

Zippel, Kathrin, and Kimberly Morgan. 2003. "Paid to Care: The Origins and Effects of Care Leave Policies in Western Europe." *Social Politics: International Studies in Gender, State & Society* 10 (Spring): 49–85.

INDEX

ABM (special make-work programs), 158, 163–64, 170. *See also* Unemployment; *Wende*

Abortion: methods, legalization, and limits on (§218), 45, 62–66, 145, 146–55, 162, 173, 242nn40, 41, 257n28; methods, legalization, and limits on in GDR, 65, 73, 245n38, 256n8; methods, legalization, and limits on in US, 64, 81, 245n32, 246n38; party positions on, 40, 62, 115, 141, 146, 147, 150, 152, 209, 242n40. *See also* Abortion rights activism; Bundestag; Constitutional Court (FRG), decisions; Self-determination

Abortion rights activism: in first-wave feminism, 22, 37–42, 242nn37, 39; in 1960s & 1970s, 54, 56, 62–65, 70, 89–90, 107, 245n36; in 1980s & 1990s, 115, 145, 146–54, 162, 173, 245n33; in the US, 115, 220–21. *See also* Schwarzer, Alice; *Wende*; Women's Health Center (Frankfurt)

Abortion tourism, 65, 89–90. *See also* Abortion rights activism, in 1960s & 1970s

Action Group for the Liberation of Women, 53–59. *See also* Berlin, protests and projects in; Feminist groups, autonomous; Frankfurt am Main, feminist projects and protests; Childcare, *Kinderläden*

Affirmative action, 28, 48, 121, 124–28, 131–34, 160, 186–88, 192–93, 212, 238n25, 255n59. *See also* Antidiscrimination politics; *Frauenförderung*; *Frauenpolitik*; Race

African American, 10, 84; models of discrimination, 27–28, 169, 221–23, 226, 229; theory, theorists, 27–28, 99–100, 264n6. *See also* Antidiscrimination politics; Diversity; Immigration; Race

Agendas, policy, 11–12, 14–16, 18, 22, 55–56, 70, 108, 112–13, 116, 121, 136, 145–47, 151, 184, 188, 206, 211, 224, 227, 238n24. *See also* Framing; Opportunity structures

Alternative List, 116–21, 129, 252nn6, 7. *See also* Alternative movements; Autonomy; Greens/Green party

Alternative movements, mixed gender: in FRG, 55, 58, 67, 86–96, 103–4, 111–21, 136, 179, 181–82, 195, 205; in GDR, 104–6, 135–40, 155–56. *See also* Dissidents (GDR)

Antidiscrimination politics: in EU, 178, 188–92, 198–99, 211–12, 265n43; in FRG, 3, 80, 124–31, 157, 161–62, 170, 190–92, 198–99, 202, 206–7, 211–12, 225; in GDR, 140, 157–62; reverse discrimination discourses, 28, 190–92, 220; in US, 1, 19, 28–29, 71, 76, 81, 196–98, 220, 229, 266n64. *See also* Affirmative action; Bundestag; Employment,